Arnulfo L. Oliveira Memorial Library

Alice in Jamesland

Alice in Jamesland

The Story of Alice Howe Gibbens James

SUSAN E. GUNTER

University of Nebraska Press
Lincoln and London

Library of Congress
Cataloging-in-Publication Data
Gunter, Susan E., 1947–
Alice in Jamesland: the story of
Alice Howe Gibbens James /
Susan E. Gunter.
    p.   cm.
Includes bibliographical references
and index.
ISBN 978-0-8032-1569-6 (cloth: alk. paper)
1. James, Alice Howe Gibbens.
2. James, Henry, 1843–1916—Family.
3. Sisters-in-law—United States—Biography.
4. James, William, 1842–1910—Marriage.
5. Spouses—United States—Biography.
6. James family. 7. James, Alice Howe
Gibbens—Family. 8. James, William,
1842–1910—Family. 9. Women—United
States—Biography. 10. United States—
History—1865–1921—Biography. I. Title.
CT275.J2915G86 2009
973.8092—dc22
[B] 2008037796

Set in Granjon by Bob Reitz.
Designed by A. Shahan.

Dedicated to the memory of
Alexander Robertson James
and Frederika James
and to Michael James

CONTENTS

ILLUSTRATIONS *following p. 192*

 Acknowledgments

FIRST, I THANK WESTMINSTER COLLEGE for a sabbatical leave and a Gore Summer Research Grant; I also thank the Houghton Library at Harvard University for awarding me the William Dean Howells Fellowship in American Literature in 2005 to complete archival work on this book. Bay James graciously granted me permission to use archival unpublished James family documents; she also organized the memorable visit to Chocorua, New Hampshire, in 2005, so that I could visit Alice's summer home. Alice H. G. James's grandson Michael James was an invaluable help; getting to know him was the best part of this project. Other James family members, including Henry James IV, Robertson James, Sara James-Rileau, and John Hunter Gray, generously shared their knowledge of family history. Roberta Sheehan kindly allowed me access to the Alice Howe Gibbens Collection of the late William James III of Santa Fe, documents that made the book possible.

Alfred Habegger encouraged me to pursue this project and helped me plan the book's organization, suggesting a chronological organization. He proffered excellent advice on writing biography based on his work on Henry James Sr. and Emily Dickinson. Conversations with Eugene Taylor, Randall Albright, and Roberta Sheehan gave me direction for my study of William James's work. Sheldon Novick generously shared his extensive knowledge of the James family as well as clear instructions for biographers gleaned from his award-winning biography of Oliver Wendell Holmes and his two-volume biography of Henry James. I am grateful for his invaluable advice on final drafts of this manuscript and for sending me a copy of the manuscript of his book *Henry James: The Mature Master*. I benefited from the work of previous William James biographers, particularly that of Linda Simon and Robert Richardson, and from the many published books on the James family that are cited in the notes.

I am grateful to Eliot House for allowing me to stay in the F. O. Matthiessen Room during my visits to the Houghton Library. I thank house master Lino Pertile, house manager Sue Weltman, and house superintendent Francisco Medieros for their wonderful hospitality. F. O. Matthiessen wrote the first book on the James family, and I am indebted to his groundbreaking scholarship on the family group.

I am indebted to historians Susan Cottler of Westminster College; Peter Drummey and staff at the Massachusetts Historical Society; Dr. Harold Worthley of the Congregational Library; Debra Sullivan, Phillip Lawson Smith, Bill Tormey, and members of the Weymouth Historical Society; Doris Baumgartner of the Aiken Historical Society; Dave Lambert at the Massachusetts Historical Genealogical Society; staff at the National Archives; staff at the Harvard Archive; staff at the American Jewish Archives; and Kelly Gingras at the Hill-Stead Museum.

I also thank Bill Stoneman, Leslie Morris, Susan Halpert, Denis Beach, Rachel Howarth, Thomas Ford, and other staff at the Houghton Library; David Hales, Diane Raines, Hildegarde Benham, Eric Inouye, and Jessica Whetman at Giovale Library, Westminster College; Richard Virr at Rare Books and Special Collections, McGill University, and Eric Savoy, who helped me search the Leon Edel Collection; staff at the Bancroft Library, University of California, Berkeley; Paul Walker, Liz Murphy, and Joanne Lamotte at Tufts Library, Weymouth, Massachusetts; staff at the LDS Genealogical Library; staff at the University of Utah Western Collection archives; and staff at the Boston Public Library.

Julie Jensen and Michael Dorrell of the Salt Lake Acting Company invited me to attend playwriting workshops, where I learned methods of character development. I thank writer Wayne Johnson for letting me audit his screenplay-writing class; his sound teaching helped me develop a sense of narrative.

I thank Jim McLeod, present owner of Alice's childhood home, who gave me extensive information about her Weymouth house; Sharon Wick for allowing me to see her home, once the Porter home, at 944 Chestnut Street, San Francisco, and for sharing historical information about that house; and Greta Peterson for information about living at 95 Irving Street in the 1970s.

I had more than competent help from my research assistants, who researched the historical background for Alice's life: Nathaniel Garrabrandt, Arien McOmber, and Jennifer McLing Ruff. Readers at various stages of the manuscript include Peter Walker, Roberta Sheehan, Michael James, Diane Lefer, Natasha Sajé, Jeannine Heil, Mary Jane Ongley, Phyllis Whitfield, Susan Jones, Barbara Martz, Jeff Nichols, Richard Badenhousen, Galena Eduardova, Teresa Knight, Deanne Ilg, Jeff Nichols, and Helen Hodgson's graduate students in Westminster's professional communications program. Historical and medical information came from Dr. Alan Davies, former *Weymouth News* editor Patsy Murray, and emergency medical technician Hutch Foster. Professor Michael Popich of Westminster College and Professor Mark Gonnerman of the Aurora Institute at Stanford University provided further enlightenment on philosophy.

A special thanks to my excellent editor, Ladette Randolph, and her very competent staff, including Kristen Elias Rowley, Joeth Zucco, and Kate Salem, at the University of Nebraska Press. I also thank copyeditor Mary M. Hill for her painstaking work. She made this a better book. Working with this group has been a joy.

Finally, I thank my partner, William Gunter, for his gentle suggestions and his willingness to listen, listen, listen.

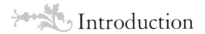 Introduction

I FIRST DISCOVERED ALICE HOWE GIBBENS JAMES, a vibrant woman who played a key role in the lives of two famous American geniuses,
psychologist and philosopher William James and his younger brother
writer Henry James, as a possible biographical subject when I transcribed
her unpublished letters for my first book, *Dear Munificent Friends: Henry
James's Letters to Four Women*. As I looked further into available archival sources, however, I discovered that while the remaining material was
provocative, Alice and her descendants had destroyed most of her letters
and diaries. In 1999 I abandoned the project.

During the course of my research for my two editions of Henry James's
letters, I met Roberta A. Sheehan, a William James scholar, and learned
that she had access to over three hundred letters written by Alice as well
as Alice's father's 1859 shipboard diary from the William James III of
Santa Fe Collection. When Dr. Sheehan learned of my interest in Alice,
she allowed me to read these valuable documents, which are deposited
at Harvard's Houghton Library. As I read over Alice's letters, I realized
that while gaps still existed in the record I had more than enough material to write her biography.

Understanding her life reveals new insights into the Jameses, a frequently analyzed family constellation. One way to understand an important historical figure (in this case, figures) is through the lens of a nearby observer. As Henry James claimed in his preface to *The Portrait of a Lady*, an intelligent observer, the *ficelle*, provides the best narrative point of view. Alice is that ficelle for the Jameses.

According to a recent biography of William James, his wife, Alice Howe Gibbens, was central to his work.[1] William James believed that one cannot understand a philosophy unless one understands the philosopher's temperament. In his case, knowing his wife allows further understanding of who he was. His philosophical theories postulate an overflow both of empirical evidence and in the way we conceptualize reality. Part of the overflow in his life was his close relationship with Alice, a relationship that has not yet been fully explored. The couple's extant letters to one another, her many letters to her children, and Henry James's and sister Alice James's letters to her all show her key role in her marriage and in the James family. She spent long evenings with her husband taking dictation and reading aloud, steadied him emotionally, provided a lively family life that became a rich source for his renowned text *The Principles of Psychology*, and encouraged him to investigate spirituality and religion. William sometimes referred to her maturing intellect: she was always abreast of his evolving projects and a valued fellow reader. Current attention to him reveals the richness of his ideas, which Alice called his "Truth." She believed his work would someday change intellectual history, and her relentless drive for his success helped make that event come true.

Not only does she cast light on William's daily life and his evolving work, Alice holds a mirror up to the complex, brilliant James family. She played a key role in facilitating the relationship between William and Henry, working steadily to keep them in touch with one another. The triangular relationship involving Henry, William, and Alice evades traditional binary oppositions, but it provides a rich vein for a biographer. After her husband's death she became an important friend for Henry. She had a loving, rewarding relationship with the aging Henry James Sr., a minor public figure in his day, and she supported the talented but troubled youngest James brother, Robertson. Moreover, the letters between her and her sister-in-law Alice, today a feminist icon, suggest that the two women became valued friends, together illuminating William's character. Alice

Howe Gibbens James was a steadfast center for this idiosyncratic family, although sometimes she was nearly overwhelmed by its demands.

Some earlier biographies of James family members, most notably those of Henry, Alice, Garth, and Robertson, are psychoanalytic in nature, revealing important insights. While it is true that James family members were frequently ill and depressed, not the least of them William, the group also had strengths, including humor and a great sensitivity to their cultural milieu. In Alice's case it is not possible to write another psychoanalytic biography, given the wanton destruction of her and William's letters to one another. However, conclusions are possible concerning her character and her positioning within the family. She was so fundamentally sound that she brought out the group's healthier qualities.

Who was Alice Howe Gibbens, the woman who married William James? An idealistic and fundamentally serious young woman, she was uniquely suited to join this clan, as she brought psychological soundness and unshakeable personal convictions to her union with the Jameses. A bright woman who lacked formal education beyond high school, she welcomed the opportunity to expand her education through her immersion in William's philosophy and Henry's fiction. She possessed a highly developed ethical sense, derived from religious teachings (Congregational and Swedenborgian) and from antebellum America's antinomian, perfectionist credos. All her life she followed the natural arc of nineteenth-century humanitarian movements, many of them in support of have-nots. By age ten she was a devoted abolitionist; at age twenty-five a member of Boston's Radical Club; in her thirties a supporter of the labor union strikers and anarchists involved in the Haymarket Square Riot; in her forties a fan of liberal British prime minister William Gladstone; and during her final years a committed supporter of Italian anarchists and accused murderers Nicola Sacco and Bartolomeo Vanzetti, even visiting them in prison. Though over time she occasionally manifested elitist attitudes, she never completely gave up her commitment to social reform or her drive to educate herself. A voracious reader all her life, when she was nearly seventy she enrolled in nursing classes to prepare herself as an international humanitarian aid worker, a role she longed to assume. Her letters vividly illustrate her ongoing personal development and growth. While Alice Howe Gibbens James followed nineteenth-century traditional paths of wife and mother, her story providing insights into what such roles entailed for upper-middle-class women, within those boundaries she kept her humanitarian beliefs, which evolved as she encountered experiences, finally acting upon them at the end of her life in pragmatic fashion.

This narrative focuses on Alice's daily life and her interactions with James family members, set against the backdrop of larger cultural and historical events: New England small-town life, the abolitionist movement, the Nicaragua passage, the California gold rush, Yankee occupation of the South during the Civil War and the subsequent cotton fraud scandal, expatriate life in Europe after the Civil War, the Haymarket Square Riot, the *Dreyfus* case, Queen Victoria's funeral, the San Francisco earthquake, World War I, the Sacco and Vanzetti trial, and other seminal events. This approach gives the James family and Alice greater historical resonance. At times the story Alice tells conflicts with other accounts of the Jameses, as for the most part I have presented events through her point of view. I mediate her view through other sources, however, including family correspondence and diaries, because many of her extant letters to her children present a generally optimistic view of events. Combining her insights with other sources and interpretations yields rich readings of Alice and this complex clan. Now that her letters are available to others, future scholars will be able to augment, verify, and further interpret these valuable primary documents.

Initially, I believed that Alice was victimized by the patriarchal values held by Henry James Sr. and by his eldest son, William. But as I learned more about her and the critical role she played within the family, I realized that she lost none of her own strength when she married. While a demanding husband and five children submerged her at times, she maintained her inner balance. By some lights she could be called an opportunist. She was relatively poor as a young woman, so marrying into an upper-middle-class family gave her greater opportunity. In addition, the marriage allowed her a wider scope for refining and developing her ethical understanding, because she knew that William was a man of principle. And her marriage, though often stormy, was fulfilling. William James loved her passionately.

Biographies, while factually based, are always stories, re-creations of what might have happened. There were stories all around Alice, stories of Jameses with blighted lives and Jameses whose genius revealed itself in varied ways. Her story is one of moral conviction, work, renunciation, and passion, the fascinating tale of a woman sometimes nearly eclipsed by those around her who retained enough of her own identity to script her tale in letters. In the autumn of 1907 William James gave a talk at the Harvard Annex, Radcliffe College. Alice was in the audience that day, and she wrote to Henry, by then her confidant, of her feelings.

> He [William] gave a most exquisite little address to the Association of College Alumnae at Radcliffe on the test of the higher education "The power to know a good man when you see him." It was wise, impressive and exquisitely formed.
>
> I thought as I listened to him that it was the only test which I have ever successfully passed—but perhaps I flatter myself and I was just born with a vocation for Jameses![2]

 Alice in Jamesland

I Stirrings

ALICE HOWE GIBBENS WAS BORN on 5 February 1849 in a beautifully proportioned Federalist Greek Revival home on King Oak Hill in Weymouth, Massachusetts. She was the first of Eliza Webb Gibbens and Dr. Daniel Lewis Gibbens's three daughters. Her mother came from a long, respectable line of Weymouth Whites and Webbs, her father from a Boston Irish Protestant family.

In 1849 Weymouth, formerly called Wessaguscus, was a patriarchal New England village thirteen miles southeast of Boston that was slowly being transformed by the shoe-manufacturing industry.[1] The community prided itself on having invented the town meeting, a particular form of New England local governance that has been viewed as the purest form of democracy. Alice's maternal ancestors played responsible roles in the town. One ancestor helped make the rules for managing swine running at large and for protecting the alewives, the small fish that swarmed the town's Back and Fore rivers, important matters in an economy based on farming and fishing. Her maternal grandfather, lawyer Christopher Webb, had been a fence viewer (making sure neighbors took care of their sides of a fence), a state senator, a representative to the Massachusetts General Court, and a selectman. Also, as overseer of the town almshouse he ensured that the poor had their daily ration of ale and cider.

Living and dying in the same Congregational parish, Alice's ancestors led narrow lives of service, piety, and rectitude. The faded tombstone in North Weymouth Cemetery to Alice's great-great-grandfather testifies to the beliefs that ruled the community:

In
Memory of
Capt. JAMES WHITE
Who departed this life
March the 1st 1793:
As corn maturely ripe is gather'd home
So his remains are brought into the tomb
To sleep in silence till that glorious day,
When Christ his light shall roll the front away.

Eliza Putnam Webb, Alice's mother, was a quiet, devout young woman who shunned public gatherings, attending only church functions and funerals. Somehow she met Bostonian Daniel Lewis Gibbens Jr., perhaps in neighboring Braintree, where Daniel's father had clerked in a retail store before moving to Boston to open his own establishment. Daniel Lewis Gibbens Sr. became a successful merchant, a pillar of Boston's First Congregational Church, a colonel in the Boston militia, and a member of the Massachusetts House of Representatives. His son Daniel Gibbens graduated from Harvard Medical School in 1847.

On 28 October of that same year Old North Congregational Church minister Joshua Emery married Daniel Gibbens and Eliza Putnam Webb. It was a union of polar opposites. A boisterous extrovert, Daniel was reputed to have been a wild, hard-drinking youth; he and his brothers caused their respectable parents considerable worry. Eliza, on the other hand, was grave and gentle, a woman ill suited to live with such a burly, excitable man. In 1848 Gibbens was admitted to the Massachusetts Medical Board. He became Weymouth's physician, and the couple established residence in North Weymouth in the home traditionally occupied by the town's doctor. The large, comfortable, post-and-beam house had an imposing front porch bordered by four two-story-high columns. It boasted many shuttered windows and four fireplaces, two up and two down. A white marble mantel decorated with an ornate bow topped the parlor fireplace, and a narrow, steep, curving staircase led from the parlor to the upstairs bedrooms. At an elevation of 163 feet the house commanded an impressive view of the Fore River and Boston Harbor. The King Oak and Queen Oak, both hundreds of years old, dominated the property.

The Weymouth of Alice's childhood was densely wooded with oak, red cedar, hemlock, beech, wild cherry, buttonwood, and tupelo. Berry bushes and vines grew everywhere, and flowers bloomed through the mild springs and summers: orchid, lady's slipper, violet, saxifrage, aster, arbutus, and hepatica. Even the rocky ledges were colorful, painted with spreading lichen.

When she was old enough, Alice rode with her father in the doctor's coupé, a horse-drawn buggy, when he called on his patients. Nineteenth-century small-town doctors were an integral part of the community: there were no medical specialists. Dr. Gibbens was a diagnostician, internist, surgeon, gynecologist, obstetrician, oncologist, psychiatrist—the list was nearly endless. Mid-nineteenth-century doctors often prescribed blood-letting, cupping, purging, and herbal remedies, depending in part on the community's beliefs. Gibbens's success in treating patients rested largely in his ability to inspire confidence, as many rural people preferred folk-based treatments that had no basis in scientific fact.[2] His medical degree from Harvard provided his formal credentials, but that was not enough. He had to convince his patients he could cure them. Perhaps it helped to bring his pretty little daughter along with him.

Alice loved her trips with her father, inventing an imaginary playmate, "Johnny Greene," an engaging boy who accompanied them. As the township was long and narrow, about nine miles long and two and a half miles wide, their trips took hours. Through her father's work Alice became acquainted with illness and death early in life. At age five she went to a playmate's funeral. Eliza Gibbens wanted her daughter to see "how completely my little friend had gone away."[3] Both parents encouraged her to view life realistically, a trait that would serve her well.

Alice's father settled into Weymouth quickly, promising to follow the path of his wife's proper ancestors. His marriage to the daughter of the Webbs and Whites allowed him an entrée into the community. In 1849 he was appointed to a committee formed to petition the legislature for a boundary division in the town. By 1850 he had taken a leading role in that civic group. In 1851 he was on the town school committee, chaired by Joshua Emery. Prominent community service could do nothing but help his medical practice. On 11 June of that same year Eliza Gibbens gave birth to a second daughter, Mary Sherwin. Gibbens seemed destined to a successful career and an agreeable small-town life. While the family attended Weymouth's Old North Congregational Church, Daniel Gibbens took both of his daughters to be baptized in his father's Boston church, Alice on 29 November 1849 and Mary on 19 April 1852, facilitating future ties for the girls with his own family.[4]

But despite her father's initial efforts to conform to Weymouth, Alice was not to have the predictable Yankee girlhood her mother had enjoyed. Not long after his arrival Dr. Gibbens resumed his former bad habits. Reportedly, he began to drink again. Although he was a sociable and intelligent man, his flaw was a damning one in antebellum America. Temperance was just one platform in the Evangelical United Front, but it sometimes aroused strong community feelings.[5] In 1826, at a meeting moderated by Alice's grandfather Christopher Webb, a strong advocate of the temperance movement, Weymouth passed an ordinance that the temperance committee should "admonish any persons in said town who are addicted to intemperance and endeavor to effect a reformation and if that shall prove ineffectual then to report such persons to the Selectmen that their names may be posted and all persons forbidden to sell them any spirituous liquors as the law directs."[6]

Evidently, Dr. Gibbens could not control his addiction, so in 1854 Eliza and Daniel Gibbens and their daughters were forced to leave King Oak Hill. Eliza and Daniel's marriage began to fall apart. Dr. Gibbens moved in with family members in Wrentham, Massachusetts, and left his wife and daughters behind in Weymouth with the Webbs and Whites.[7] Besides losing his wife's companionship, he lost two beautiful daughters. When Alice was five and Mary three and a half, Eliza took them to Wrentham to have a daguerreotype made. They held hands for their portrait, two little girls wearing calico dresses with pink fabric bows at the shoulders and red beaded necklaces.[8] Alice lost her rides in the doctor's coupé and her companionship with her father. Her only remaining intimate male companion was Johnny Greene.

In 1855 Alice's life changed dramatically again and, by her own account, for the better. The same bug—gold and the chance for a new life in the West—that had bitten so many New England men, including a Weymouth contingent, and lured them to California's gold fields bit Daniel Gibbens. Two of Eliza's brothers had already gone. The doctor decided to homestead in the Santa Clara Valley. Perhaps it was a way to reunite his family in a place where they could start over. He booked passage for all of them to California on a boat operated by Cornelius Vanderbilt's Accessory Transit Company from New York down the Atlantic Coast to San Juan del Sur, Nicaragua, and across Nicaragua, a twelve-mile stretch, in horse- or mule-drawn coaches. From there they traveled on another boat up the Pacific Coast to San Francisco Bay.

According to extant records, Alice may have sailed on the *Northern Light*.[9] The Vanderbilt ships, all large boats, were notorious for their deplorable conditions. Provisions were purchased in New York and packed in ice, so before long passengers were served spoiled meat. Ships frequently carried more passengers than were listed, so sometimes they slept on cabin floors or benches or on deck to escape the stench below. Passengers were advised to bring along six dozen cooked eggs, ten pounds of crackers, one pitcher, two tumblers, one chair or camp stool, one dozen towels, one or more cakes of soap, and one life preserver. A contemporary newspaper account described a similar Vanderbilt ship, the *Ariel*, as a "'filthy, nasty, pigstie.'"[10]

Despite the terrible physical conditions on the ship, Alice had the chance to see a tropical wilderness, a world very different from the world she had seen from the doctor's coupé. Large sea turtles swam along the coast, and during the passage across Nicaragua she could see trees and plants with bright green foliage, "oranges, lemons, limes, pineapples, cocoanuts, bananas, and bread fruit," big aquanno (iguana) lizards, snakes, brilliant butterflies, bright-plumed birds, river sharks, and, best of all, monkeys swinging in the trees.[11] The Nicaraguans with their dark skin and straight black hair were altogether different from Weymouth natives.

One day the Vanderbilt boat anchored near Nicaragua's swampy marshes, and Alice witnessed a battle between filibusterer William Walker, an American desperado and profiteer, and his soldiers and the country's Legitimist forces.[12] The rest of her life she remembered her fear at seeing dead bodies lying deserted in the heat. Soon after the Walker skirmish cholera broke out on the ship. Dr. Gibbens knew of the danger of cholera—it can lead quickly to severe dehydration and death. The doctor boiled his family's drinking water and kept them inside until after sundown. No one was allowed to go ashore. One night Eliza went on deck to converse with a fellow passenger, huddling under her cloak to keep warm. That same night the woman died of cholera, only four hours after contracting the disease, and her body was slipped overboard. A few days later Eliza contracted the disease, the last passenger afflicted. She nearly died, but although her recovery was slow, it was complete.

After crossing Nicaragua the family set sail again, this time most likely on either the *Brother Jonathan*, the *Nevada*, the SS *Cortes*, or the SS *Sierra*.[13] The family reached San Francisco Bay with all alive. The Valley, as Alice called it, held countless riches, though none of them could be measured in gold. She thought she had found the paradise she had studied in Old North Sabbath school. Daniel Gibbens claimed a ranch in the Santa Clara Valley, just across the Arroyo San Antonio from Rancho San Antonio, south of the small settlement of Mountain View. Their homestead lay in a vale covered with coastal live oaks and sycamores, willows marking the streambeds. Deer, elk, and bears roamed the area.

Sometimes Alice and her sister Mary attended a little school not far from their home where Eliza's sister, Nannie Webb, taught them briefly.[14] Often, though, her busy parents left Alice to her own devices. She made new friends, one of them Katharine "Kate" Putnam, who remained a friend all her life. The girls played about the huge coastal oaks, where they shared a playhouse furnished with wooden plates and toys. Some days Alice trapped western quail and tried to make them her pets. Crests with four distinct feathers adorned their heads, and their plumage sported a rich mix of color. Usually, they nested on the ground under bushes or trees. With as many as twenty-four babies hatched in one nest, the young birds made easy prey for a determined child.

Once Dr. A. Kellogg, who lived in San Francisco, took Alice up Telegraph Hill, a magical visit for her. He explained the sights and the names of the plants that grew there. Later he wrote her a long letter full of nature lore and "quite the kind of letter that a man who has time on his hands may write to a little girl of seven by whom he has been charmed and whom he knows to be quick-minded and engagingly curious about everything around her."[15] Alice's years in California increased her natural eagerness to understand the world.

The Santa Clara Valley did not always seem like paradise to Daniel and Eliza. The rattlesnake that Eliza killed on her front doorstep sickened her. Moreover, Dr. Gibbens's weakness overtook him, and he started drinking again. More than one night he came home drunk and depressed, and Eliza had to hide his pistol and razors from him. Some nights he did not come home at all. Another evening a gang of toughs and derelicts, driven from San Francisco by a vigilante committee, peered in her window. She ran for her errant husband's pistol and placed it on the table beside her. Too afraid to go to bed, all night long she sat and sewed in her chair, her lamp burning.

On 23 January 1857, about a year after arriving in California, Eliza gave birth to her third daughter, Margaret Merrill. Some women pioneers had the help of Spanish midwives, and Dr. Gibbens could have helped his wife if he had been sober that day, but no record remains concerning the circumstances of Eliza's delivery. Her second sister's birth was a joyous event to Alice: it was as if an angel had come during the night.

But, like his doctoring, Daniel Gibbens's ranching venture failed, and not only because of his personal weaknesses: western landownership proved more complicated than he had anticipated. Land litigation was common in the 1850s and 1860s, especially for the large Spanish land grants. Most of them had never been surveyed. Boulders, streams, and large trees designated the boundaries, but these features altered over the years. The original grantees' lax methods of recording, transferring title, and selling land added to the confusion. Dr. Gibbens's claim to the ranch proved useless. By 1860 a family named Murphy had acquired his land after the Gibbenses returned to New England.[16]

Before she left for Weymouth, Alice buried her little china dog beneath a live oak tree. Many years later the oak was felled in a storm, cracking and splintering to reveal a child's toy in its heart.[17] Alice's son Henry read her burial of the loved dog as emblematic of her "ever generous self-immolations," but it may be that she simply wanted to leave part of herself behind. Alice immortalized her experience in a poem written in a childish hand entitled "The Valley." Its last stanza frames her farewell:

And to the high mountains and the
Low green vallies I must bid a last
Fair well to the home I had loved so long fair well.

The next autumn Kate Putnam wrote to tell Alice that the only things left in their playhouse were their wooden plates.

While she must have felt the tension in her parents' relationship during her California years, Alice treasured her memories of Mountain View. Decades later, her daughter, her son-in-law, and her eldest son tried to find the Gibbens house but were unable to locate the site. Some of the great live oaks had been cleared, and the plain was dotted with orchards and market gardens. Nothing remained of Alice's heaven on earth.[18]

The return to Weymouth brought another breakup of Alice's family. The oppositions that had attracted Eliza Webb and Daniel Gibbens, her shy reserve and his uncontrollable conviviality, proved obstacles to marital compatibility. Not only was the marriage troubled, but the couple was nearly bankrupt after their California sojourn. Eliza and her daughters moved in with Eliza's mother, Susannah White Webb, in her one- and-a-half-story farmhouse near the Fore River, a house belonging to Great-grandmother Nancy White, who was still alive. It had a central chimney and brick ovens, and the railroad ran very close to their property.[19]

Temporarily, Daniel Gibbens went to Charlestown, the area near Boston where Bunker Hill is located. He wrote Alice letters about his neighbors, a goat, deer, a donkey, and a clever pony that would put its foot in a person's hand.[20] He urged his two older daughters to study botany and learn everything they could about plants by observing the shapes and textures of the leaves. While living in Charlestown he attended the Chauncey Street First Church with his mother, seeking solace from minister Rufus Ellis. Alice visited her father and her grandmother Mary Gibbens in Boston often during this separation. She remained deeply attached to her father despite his failings. During these separations Grandmother Gibbens adjured Alice and Mary to write to her son: "How often have you used your Pencils in notes to your Papa? I am certain, one hour once a fortnight devoted in writing to him would give your dear Father much pleasure, and like every other action of your lives, which affords another happiness, will also make you happy."[21] She also reminded her granddaughters to help their mother.

In Weymouth Alice returned to her former life, attending Old North Congregational Church and going to school. Evidently, she had lost nothing from her travels, because she was at the top of her class. Because of the family's difficult financial circumstances the Gibbens women had to make do for themselves most of the time with the help of one maid. Alice helped her mother with housework, sewing, and mending, as Mary Gibbens had advised. She kept happy memories of these times: one Christmas her uncle George Webb gave her a storybook entitled *Violet*, and she and Mary received dolls.

By age ten Alice had developed a social conscience and a sense of moral authority that remained with her all her life. Childrearing practices had changed during the shift from Puritan traditions to the reform period. Rather than punishing children to try to counteract their inherited depravity, evangelists encouraged parents to concentrate on their children's moral development. In some households this view persisted well into the 1850s, but only a few children became morally precocious.[22] Alice was one such child. Perhaps, too, her awareness of her father's weaknesses made her more sensitive to the plight of others.

Some of Alice's beliefs derived from her Congregationalist heritage. Congregationalists were descendents of the Separatists and Puritans who had settled the area. Each Congregational church governed itself, determining its affairs without interference from bishops or presbyteries. Congregations maintained a strong commitment to religious and civil liberties as well as to education. After the eighteenth century's Great Awakening, led by Jonathan Edwards, Congregational churches either kept to the Puritan tradition as Edwards had reenvisioned it or became Unitarian. Those congregations that remained within the Congregational wing became increasingly liberal as the nineteenth century unfolded, a number of them involved with abolitionist and antislavery movements.

After Alice read Harriet Beecher Stowe's 1852 best seller *Uncle Tom's Cabin*, the ten-year-old girl became an ardent abolitionist and was stunned at John Brown's execution in 1859.[23] His raid on the federal arsenal at Harper's Ferry and subsequent conviction and hanging made him a martyr for antislavery advocates.[24] Before and during Alice's childhood Weymouth was a hotbed of abolitionist activity. William Lloyd Garrison made several speeches there, as did Wendell Phillips, and town forums hosted a variety of meetings on the topic of slavery. Even Frederick Douglass made an appearance there not long after his escape to the North.[25] When the Civil War broke out in 1861, Alice empathized with the soldiers who fought for this great moral cause. She decided to sleep on the floor because they slept on bare ground. Sometimes she shredded lint for bandages. Just as she once admired John Brown, she and her sister Mary now adored President Lincoln.

Led by such diverse spiritual crusaders as Garrison, Theodore Lane, and Arthur and Lewis Tappan, the abolitionist movement exerted great moral suasion in New England in the years before the Civil War, its impact on culture and society at least as great as its political influence. The movement was an outgrowth of Protestant evangelicalism, Romantic beliefs in the perfectibility of human nature and the subsequent ability to transform character, the new nation's belief in fundamental republican principles, Transcendentalism, the voluntary associations, and other cultural movements. For a time leaders like Garrison concluded that all human institutions, not just slavery, were based on coercion and thus corrupt. Some of these nonresistants, as they were called, supported a sort of Christian anarchism or antinomianism and demanded the end of all human government, substituting in its place a biblical millennium.[26] Other reformers sought a solution in communitarian movements, small self-contained cells that could be governed by moral principles.[27] Many of the early female abolitionists later became leaders of the first feminist movements. The fervor that characterized Alice's interest in the abolitionist movement remained with her all her life. Though she never became a feminist, she had been imprinted with a perfectionist sensibility.

Alice's solace in knowing that her father was nearby, even though he no longer lived with her, ended in the fall of 1859, when Daniel Gibbens took passage as ship's doctor on the *Manhattan* for Liverpool, England. During his journey he wrote to his girls and to his Gibbens relations but not to Eliza. His shipboard journal entries reveal that while he missed his three daughters intensely, he never mentioned his wife. Wrestling with his soul all the way to England and back, he found a temporary peace at sea. Outwardly gregarious, inwardly Daniel was a solitary metaphysical searcher, relying on the works of Emanuel Swedenborg and Prentice Mulford to comfort him.

Swedenborg was an important eighteenth-century Swedish scientist who later became an influential religious writer and mystic. He had a strong following in the mid-nineteenth century, his American advocates including Ralph Waldo Emerson and Henry James Sr. In fact, in 1845 Emerson called the era "the Age of Swedenborg."[28] Swedenborg's gentler, more optimistic theology provided some New Englanders with a welcome corrective to their native Puritanism. The official arm of Swedenborgianism in America was the New Church, and it fit nicely with antebellum sectarian movements like perfectionism and millennialism. It had an influence out of proportion to its size, as other deviations from mainstream Protestant beliefs could be traced in part to Swedenborgian impulses.[29] Mulford, a humorist, telepathist, and inspirational spiritual teacher, wrote books on living and natural religion that had wide appeal.

A compassionate physician, Gibbens followed Swedenborg's precept, expressed in a passage copied at the end of his diary: "Charity itself consists in acting justly and faithfully in whatever office, business, and employment a person is engaged, and with whomsoever he has any connection."[30] Those who do their work excellently, no matter what that work is, fulfill their purpose on earth. Gibbens dressed wounds, administered rhubarb oil to the seasick, and ordered gruel for weak passengers. He learned to understand and sometimes respect people from different backgrounds. He pitied the "ignorant Irishman" returning with his three motherless children to the old country who wished himself and his children dead. His refusal to wash or feed his ailing child bothered Gibbens, who feared the child would soon be with its mother. He empathized, too, with one old man named Murty who refused to go below deck at night because he thought the other passengers would kill him. The next night Gibbens and one of the mates persuaded Murty to go to bed by taking him down themselves and charging the passengers *not* to kill him. Later they took away his pocketknives, made him a bed in the pump house, and locked him in.

Gibbens felt he understood himself better toward the voyage's conclusion, but in one of his most disturbing moments on the ship he dreamed that Alice was dead and in her casket. As he approached his destination his anxiety and discontent returned. On 6 January 1860 he mused that "the breaking asunder of the tenderest ties of life—might if anything could afford just pretext for melancholy reflection." And when on 7 February he wrote, "There be but little to hurry me anywhere," it would be impossible to think he believed Eliza Gibbens awaited him with open arms. Despite his anxiety at returning to an estranged spouse, he found an inner peace he had never experienced.

When Dr. Gibbens returned to Boston in 1860, he did not move back to Weymouth. Alice, her mother, and her sisters remained at the Webb house, while Daniel returned to his mother and again sought help from Rufus Ellis of First Church. The world around Alice and her father was changing: the country was on the brink of a long and bitter war. Two of her cousins enlisted in the Grand Army of the Republic, but her father remained in Boston, still wrestling with his demons despite the progress he had made at sea. Ellis felt Dr. Gibbens had improved. Gibbens gave him a sermon case as a New Year's gift, Ellis thanking him: "It is plain you have felt the Guiding hand of our loving & Almighty helper." The minister credited Gibbens's mother, Mary, with her son's spiritual transformation.[31]

But his transformation did not mean that Daniel and Eliza reunited. In 1862 Ellis recommended Dr. Gibbens for a civil post in Yankee-occupied New Orleans under Gen. George F. Shepley, then military governor in Louisiana. Gibbens accepted the post, and on 28 November he notified Alice and Mary of his safe arrival in the South. He had been wretchedly seasick during the voyage. While at sea he witnessed a Yankee vessel chasing a rebel steamer. He reported that upon reaching the city he found "a gloom about the streets that is very apparent."[32] Many of the inhabitants had fled, leaving the city to the Northerners.

Gibbens longed for worldly recognition that he could share with his girls. From his own accounting and letters written to him, he was a successful administrator. In 1864, two years after his arrival, he sent the family his picture. Holding a newspaper and sporting a full beard, he looked dignified, portly, and prosperous. That same year someone gave him a pair of handsome diamond cuff links and a set of shirt studs, perhaps a bribe of some sort, though at the same time General Shepley wrote a letter praising Daniel's judgment and integrity.[33] It seemed his fortunes finally had changed for the better.

During his absence an old man told Alice she looked exactly like her father had looked when he was fourteen.[34] She could take comfort in knowing that the Gibbens girls were not the only fatherless children in Weymouth. So many New England men had left their homes in 1861, nearly countless numbers wounded and dying on the battlefields serving their country, that fatherless families were the norm in some communities. On 11 May 1865 Alice received a loving letter from Gibbens. He expected to return to his family in the middle of June, later than anticipated. Though he complained of Louisiana's oppressive heat, he confessed he was sad to leave a city where he had made friends and at last found rewards at his work.[35] But eleven days later she learned he was not coming home in June: he was going to Mobile, Alabama. Her wait was not over.

In 1865 Mobile was at the center of the cotton fraud scandal that marked the Civil War's conclusion. Approximately 1.2 million bales of cotton that had been confiscated by the federal government remained in the South. The cotton represented a source of income needed to help defray the expenses of a costly war, but the Treasury Department agents responsible for overseeing the sales were not always honest.[36] By November 1865 $2 million of Alabama cotton money remained missing.[37]

Daniel Gibbens became an employee of the federal Ninth Agency, charged with gathering cotton from eleven Alabama counties. When he left New Orleans for Mobile, a city newspaper congratulated him "upon his prospects of improving his pecuniary resources."[38] He spent months in Alabama overseeing cotton sales.

The postwar South was now in ruins. Yankee army wagons traveled everywhere over the unpaved dusty streets, which were lined with oyster shops and coffee stores.[39] The women trimmed their clothes in the Confederate colors of red and white, sometimes sporting white marabou feathers with red edges on their hats, and talked about the Confederacy.[40] One day Gibbens passed two girls in the street. One remarked to the other in a nasty voice, "'Dear me, you don't meet anybody but Yankees and niggers.'"[41] Mobile observed a somber Fourth of July that year because its white citizens refused to celebrate this national holiday. After all, they had tried to secede from the nation. The military fired a thirteen-gun salute, and the blacks paraded with a troop escort, but otherwise the city was quiet.[42]

The sights along Mobile's wharves were a wonder to the doctor. One day he saw a flatboat that housed an entire family, a not uncommon sight in 1865. On one end of the boat there was a furnace on which food could be cooked, and in the middle of the boat a tentlike awning covered the family's beds. Next to the beds a cow was hemmed in by a rude slat enclosure. The far end had room for a large chicken coop. Discouraged by the war's vicissitudes, this Southerner had packed his family and all his worldly goods onboard and fled down the river to Mobile. Gibbens also saw a large steamboat that operated as a floating theater, with the performers living onboard; it was almost as large as the Boston Museum.[43]

The doctor did well financially in Mobile, sending Eliza a draft for $100 in July. He even speculated in chickens, providing the capital to buy fowl in Mobile and sell them in New Orleans.[44] Again in August he sent money to Weymouth. He promised to buy Alice a Steinway piano and a melodeon when he came home, and he asked Eliza to look for a house.[45] In her last letter to her husband she enclosed an advertisement for a house with a gas furnace, barn, and garden only three miles from Boston. Gibbens bought a ticket north on the Mobile & Ohio Railroad for 7 November 1865.[46] He would be with his family by Thanksgiving.

The Gibbens women managed reasonably well during Daniel's absence. A daguerreotype of the three Gibbens daughters taken during this time shows Alice as a pretty girl with classic features, her dark hair pulled tidily behind her head. She remained a talented student in both academic and musical studies. Now her mother could afford to give her extra singing and dancing lessons. Both Eliza and Daniel Gibbens were avid readers, so their daughters grew up valuing books. Alice read Chaucer, Milton, Washington Irving, and New England historian William Prescott. Her father sent her John Ruskin's *Modern Painters* and encouraged her interest in music.

Alice had a penchant for sobriety: she felt that she looked more natural when she assumed a grave expression. But despite her desire to appear a mature adult, she sometimes indulged in adolescent pranks with her sister Mary and her cousin Samuel Webb. Confessing her hilarity in a Sunday evening letter to her father, she added, "'It does not seem wrong to me to have a good laugh tonight—do you think so?'"[47] Daniel Gibbens encouraged her to always try to be cheerful, even if her thoughts felt like a cold nor'easter, as his did at times.[48] When her aunt Maria Gibbens taunted her with being "prim and old-fashioned," Alice tried waltzing with a young gentleman from Harvard, though she hated waltzing. She did not hate all dancing or parties or Harvard students, but she felt shy with the opposite sex, perhaps because she spent so much time in the company of women. While she liked dancing with her sister Mary, she wished for a wider social life.[49] "I dearly love to go where I can dance and hear music. In fact I think I should love to go into company and to parties, but I don't know as I never tried it."[50]

By the time Alice was sixteen she had become interested in specific young men, and they were interested in her. Despite her shyness and sobriety she had beaux. Perhaps that very shyness added to her charm. Her first boyfriend was her Boston cousin Frederick Hammond Gibbens, the son of Dr. Gibbens's half-brother Samuel Hammond Gibbens. In the summer of 1865 Fred kissed Alice. "But that young gentleman, having come at last to a just appreciation of my many and manifold excellences, moved also by my surpassing loveliness, He gave me a—kiss." At the end of the letter she wrote the word "cousin" over and over in a circle radiating around her name.[51]

It was not long before Alice's interest in young men and theirs in her began to disturb her mother. Another boyfriend was a Weymouth swain, John Lund, who courted Alice until the town gossips spread the rumor that they were engaged. When Alice went to visit Brookline friends, the talk ended, to her mother's relief. Proper Mrs. Gibbens also warned her daughter to stay away from Cambridge Class Day, part of graduation ceremonies at Harvard College.[52] Class Day had started as Valedictory Exercises, a student-run commencement ceremony attended by faculty and guests that was separate from the official graduation. By the mid-eighteenth century, however, these exercises had gained the reputation for being a drunken brawl; the Harvard Corporation had to hire a police guard by day and a watch at night for several days to control participants.[53] Around 1838 the event became Class Day and included afternoon dancing, at first square dancing and later waltzing and drinking.[54] A Winslow Homer drawing published in 1858 shows Harvard students dancing wildly on the green at this occasion.[55] Meeting a rioting student might pose a danger for Alice.

Despite her growing interest in boys, she continued her studies. The high school's demanding four-year curriculum included arithmetic, algebra, bookkeeping, geometry, rhetoric, astronomy, French, Latin, English grammar, chemistry, declamation, and composition. In 1863 and 1864 approximately forty students attended North Weymouth High School. Some of the young men had already graduated into the school of life; they were away fighting with the Union army. The principal, Mr. L. Z. Ferris, frequently provoked Alice with his fine rhetorical distinctions and his attitude toward young women: he thought female pupils should always smile. One day he tried to explain the difference between the words "surprise" and "wonder." "'Take this example now: If I see a girl never have a smile on her face, it would at first be surprising, but if it has continued for some time, the surprise would cease, though it would always be a wonder.'" Somber, independent Alice wanted to tell him she did not always feel like smiling. With her father, though, she revealed her quick wit and the fundamental optimism underlying her serious exterior.[56]

The end of the war and of her long separation from her father promised better times for Alice Howe Gibbens. Soon she would have a Steinway piano, a new home closer to Boston, and two reunited parents.

When the train pulled into the station from Mobile, Alabama, on 7 November, Daniel Gibbens was not onboard. On the eve of his departure he learned that he had been detained as a material witness in the trial of his boss, Bostonian T. C. A. Dexter. A military commission had charged Dexter with stealing 3,426 bales of cotton and with selling an appointment as special cotton agent in Choctaw County, Alabama, for $25,000.[57] Dexter tried to stall by appealing to have the trial moved to the U.S. District Court, but to no avail.[58] Forced to wait until December to testify before the tribunal, Dr. Gibbens returned to his old habits of substance abuse. This time he had been inhaling sulfuric ether or taking valerian or another narcotic.[59] He suffered delusions that the authorities were coming to arrest him, imagining he heard them coming in the house where he boarded. Three days before the trial he asked his friend J. F. Bailey to give his watch, diary, and ring to his mother.

On 2 December, two days before he was to testify, Gibbens spent the evening in his boardinghouse. At eleven o'clock he sat at a table, writing. When Bailey came in after a visit to Judge Andrews, Gibbens gave him a pencil to keep. Then he unlocked his trunk, peered inside, and remarked that none of them had ever expected to be away from home so long when they packed. The next morning, 3 December 1865, Daniel Lewis Gibbens was discovered in his room lying in a pool of blood, his throat slashed and his razor by his side. The surgeon called in could not save him. He asked for water and mumbled something about disposal of his possessions and about Uncle Joe. With his last breaths he said, "Lord, Lord." A telegram went to Eliza Gibbens in Weymouth, and two days later the *New Orleans Times* ran the headline "Melancholy Suicide at Mobile." A hasty autopsy showed he had taken ether before his death.[60]

Eliza Gibbens collapsed when she heard the news, forcing sixteen-year-old Alice to become the head of her small family. She nursed her devastated mother, cooked meals, and cared for her sisters.[61] Since Daniel Lewis Gibbens is not buried in North Weymouth Cemetery with the Whites and the Webbs, Rufus Ellis may have taken charge of his body and burial when his remains arrived in Boston.[62] On 12 December 1865 the *Boston Daily Advertiser* carried a small notice of his death: "Died: In Mobile, Ala., 3d inst., Dr. Daniel L. Gibbens, formerly of this city, 41." After his burial Alice decided to write to Mobile, seeking answers to her father's suicide.

On 27 December Bailey wrote to Alice of the circumstances surrounding her father's last days.

> I would that it had never devolved upon anyone much less myself to narrate to you the particulars of the sad and deplorable event. I would that your Father could have realized the wish dearest his heart to have come to you in all the vigor of his manhood, at this happy "Christmas tide" to have clasped you all to his noble heart in affectionate embrace, to have been made glad in your happy welcome & to have unfolded to you one by one his plans of future happiness; but even bright anticipations were not to be realized and alas how are our hopes withered by the rude blasts of affliction & our joy turned into sorrow.[63]

There exists no written record of Alice's feelings at the time of her father's death, but as an adult she almost never mentioned his name in her letters, and then only when a medium reported contact with a "Giblin" at a séance.

When Daniel Gibbens's estate was probated, it contained over $24,000, nearly the amount of the bribe involved in the cotton fraud case.[64] While Henry James II later claimed that Gibbens could have saved this large sum from his salary and from fees he earned notarizing documents, the claim seems implausible. He earned $4,800 a year at his job, an amount reported by a Gibbens relative.[65] From that sum he sent money home and paid his expenses. Assuming that he saved half that amount yearly, it seems unlikely that he could have earned the remaining $17,000, approximately $200,000 in today's currency, from legal fees.

The war over and her father gone, Alice returned to her previous life, at least overtly. She continued her visits to Boston to see her father's relations, and she followed her domestic pursuits: on 20 June 1867 the *Weymouth Gazette* reported that Alice Gibbens exhibited a hanging cushion at the Grand Fair, held that year at the town hall. Only her inner life had changed.

In 1867 Weymouth decided to erect a memorial to honor its Civil War dead.[66] The news became a steady drumbeat in the town, as subsequent issues of the paper made constant reference to the evolving plan. The memorial would draw the citizens of Weymouth together and provide an outward sign of the town's grief. By December 1867 an official committee had been formed. The *Gazette* carried a notice asking for the names of the deceased who had "lost their lives during the war of the Rebellion" so that they could be inscribed on the monument, which was to be erected in North Weymouth Cemetery.[67] The monument would feature a granite shaft and base, inscriptions, stone steps, and other embellishments. The names of the ninety-nine Civil War heroes would be recorded on tablets made from the finest white Italian marble.[68] For weeks the paper posted the names to make sure that no one would be forgotten. But for the Gibbenses, mourning remained a private affair. Daniel Gibbens was not one of the honored dead.

On the grand and glorious Fourth of July of 1868 all Weymouth gathered at Old North Church for the parade to North Weymouth Cemetery.

There were flowers, bands, dedicatory prayers, speeches by various officials, veterans, and a procession including "Widows and Children of Deceased Soldiers." Weymouth dedicated its monument in one of the most lavish ceremonies the town had ever seen.[69] That same month nineteen-year-old Alice Gibbens, her mother, her two sisters, and a Webb relation, Helen Merrill, sailed for Europe.

2 New Ventures

IN 1868, BEFORE LEAVING WEYMOUTH for Europe, Alice read an article in the *Boston Advertiser* describing the experiences of an American woman who had lived in Germany.[1] Alice invited the writer to lunch and gleaned the address of a pastor in the village of Leihgestern who boarded lodgers and gave German lessons. Through a combination of charm and appeal to charity, Alice persuaded the woman to write to the pastor and arrange accommodations for all five women.

Their trip was motivated in part by economic necessity. In 1868 the income from Dr. Gibbens's estate amounted to $1,800. The war had been colossally expensive for both the North and the South. From 1860 to 1879 the gross national product and per capita income declined. The boot and shoe industries were hit particularly hard, as these companies lost most of their Southern markets. Weymouth had many small shoe-manufacturing concerns at that time, so the local economy suffered.[2] Alice and her mother and sisters decided they could live better on their small income in Europe than they could in Weymouth, so they decided to go to Germany. Perhaps, too, they felt ashamed of the doctor's actions and were glad to leave their village, at least for a time.

Under Alice's leadership, in July 1868 the band set sail for the Continent on one of seven steamships that sailed from New York to Bremen that month: the *Union* on 2 July, the *Deutschland* on 9 July, the *Hansa* on 16 July, the *Bremen* on 23 July, the *Smidt* on 25 July, the *Circassian* on 25 July, and the *America* on 30 July.[3] With the exception of the smaller *Circassian*, whose 25 July voyage was her last, each ship weighed nearly three thousand tons and could carry close to nine hundred passengers while traveling at a speed of eleven knots per hour. These graceful long ships, with two or three masts, represented the latest in engineering know-how.

Conditions onboard were far better than those the family had endured on their Vanderbilt ship in 1856. The Gibbens group attracted the notice of a journalist onboard: "The most interesting passengers were a New England lady and her young daughters, all of an innocence and simplicity so superlative that one wondered how they could expect to survive a week on the Continent." Their cousin Helen Merrill accompanied them on the passage, though she returned to America after a few months. Alice, now a dark-eyed, smooth-complexioned beauty, and her two pretty sisters attracted the attention of other passengers in addition to the journalist who wrote about them.[4] As the group prepared to disembark, a rich, handsome Jewish man offered to escort them all the way to Leihgestern. Eliza Gibbens refused his offer on the grounds that she could not pay his expenses, but more likely it was because she feared the attentions of a Jew to her daughters. The ship's captain, Neineber, took pity on the women. He invited them to lunch in his Bremen home and then escorted them to their train.

From Bremen the Gibbenses traveled south nearly the length of Germany to the Hessen region. The bewildered, tired women disembarked from the train at Giessen, thirty-five miles north of Frankfurt. The Gibbenses were taken to a hotel and placed in an expensive suite. None could communicate well enough to ask for less extravagant arrangements. Alice spent the night on the floor beside Eliza's bed to calm her frightened parent. The next day she learned that their living arrangements had fallen through. The pastor with whom they had contracted, Pastor Eckstein, was ill, so he had assigned their contract to another Leihgestern pastor.[5] That day Alice and her band drove to the village in an open hack, past castles and Roman ruins.

Alice's strength was tested again when they reached the pastor's home. The toothless man with long curly hair fell on them like a wolf. His hard-looking wife, eager for their American currency, tried literally to pull them into her squalid house. Alice refused to let her group leave the hack. They immediately drove back to their hotel in Giessen. Guided once again by vague rumors, they left Giessen in the evening to avoid paying for another night in their hotel suite and headed south for Heidelberg. They stayed there for an undetermined time, first at a dreary suburban pension owned by a Professor Hoffmann and later with a Fräulein Theis, who regularly opened their mail. While in Heidelberg they walked on the two bridges across the Neckar River, Eliza Gibbens admiring the sunset while young German students admired her daughters. During their walks the women were often soaked by a downpour, and they became more and more depressed.

When Alice returned to Heidelberg in 1900 with her husband, she went up to the castle above the city. She wrote to her mother:

> The way used to seem so steep and long that I could hardly believe that I had reached it. I spent a couple of hours wandering about the quiet parts and sitting on the <u>Altan</u> with its beautiful view of the Neckar and the old bridge where I could see, as in a dream, you crossing with us three and so innocently admiring the sunset up the valley, while the passing student threw a kiss to Mary. How cheerful and patient and full of courage you were through that depressing year. The fragrance of your goodness seemed to float past me as I sat alone, a ghost of the past.[6]

Despite her responsibilities there was much for Alice to enjoy in this foreign city, so different from her native Weymouth. Mark Twain extolled Heidelberg's glories in *A Tramp Abroad*: "One thinks Heidelberg by day — with its surroundings — is the last possibility of the beautiful; but when he sees Heidelberg by night, a fallen Milky Way, with that glittering railway constellation pinned to the border, he requires time to consider upon the verdict."[7] Situated at the mouth of a narrow gorge, the city displayed Baroque buildings and cobblestone streets, and cafés lined the market squares.

Many days the women window-shopped along the Hauptstrasse. Often they lingered in front of their favorite shop, which displayed onyx pins and cuff buttons. Eliza longed to buy gifts for her daughters and loved ones in Weymouth. She finally dipped into her slender funds to buy Alice a coveted set. While she could buy little of the jewelry she saw, she remade dresses for her girls in the latest styles, copying the current German fashions.[8]

During the nineteenth century Heidelberg's university students were renowned for their lifestyles, which included dueling, singing, romance, and drinking. They strolled through the city wearing colored caps and escorted by bull terriers. It is surprising that Eliza Gibbens allowed her daughters to remain in this setting for any length of time, even though they lived at a distance from the town's center. However, Mrs. Gibbens only made decisions at Alice's prodding and then reluctantly. Whether there were students about or not, the Gibbens girls were courted by men everywhere they went.

During the summer of 1869 Alice went to Badenweiler, a health spa with mineral springs well over a hundred miles south of Heidelberg. The village possessed well-preserved Roman baths. She made friends there and liked the spot tremendously. Soon her youngest sister, Margaret, joined her, the two planning a stay of six months. Mary and Mrs. Gibbens then decided to go to Freiburg to be close to friends there and closer to Alice and Margaret.[9]

Finally, Alice quartered her family in Dresden as paying guests in the home of the cosmopolitan Adolph von Nostitz und Jänckendorf. The women toured other cities from there as their funds permitted. In July 1870 Germany became involved in the Franco-Prussian War, while the Gibbenses endured expatriation and relative poverty. Their move to Dresden may, in fact, have been due to that war. Part of the Prussian army's success came from its ability to mobilize quickly, and two army corps were headquartered at Mainz, quite close to Heidelberg, so that they could move quickly up and down the Rhine Valley. Key engagements, like that at Saarbrücken, were also fought near Heidelberg. The Gibbenses may have wished to be farther away from the escalating conflict.

Sometimes Alice feared that her mother, weary and anxious, would die as they sought suitable locations. Despite their difficult times she kept her good appearance. An image made in Dresden reveals Alice's serene beauty. She had small, perfectly shaped ears and a nearly straight nose, while her deep brown eyes looked like bottomless wells. Emblematic of her religious belief, her only jewelry was a white cross hanging from a black ribbon.

Later in life her excess weight would plague her, but images from this era do not suggest her size. In any case, nineteenth-century Western culture did not necessarily condemn women who were well proportioned.

Henry James II claimed that his mother studied singing with Clara Schumann during her stay in Germany, but Clara Schumann taught piano when she accepted pupils. Alice may have encountered the pianist in Berlin, where the women spent the last months of their German sojourn. Schumann accepted only the most talented pupils, so if Alice studied with her, she must have been an accomplished musician. While there, young Miss James appeared onstage at the Berlin opera house with another amateur, Clara Thies, who, as Alice would one day learn, also knew William James.[10] She did well enough with her music studies, or at least liked them well enough, to continue them when the Gibbens group moved one last time. Music was one of her passions, though she gave up any public performances after her marriage. Years later, although she was too shy to sing for guests, she sang German songs and English ballads like "The Three Ravens" and "The Earl of Moray" to her family. Her son recalled, "It seems to me that I have never listened to singing that was sweeter than hers used to sound. I'm confident that her voice was pure and warm, and I know that she had a very unusual gift of interpretation. . . . Grandmother would repeat that it was a great pity that Mother had never been willing to 'work' at her singing."[11]

For decades Dresden, Germany, was nicknamed "Florence on the Elbe." Perhaps because of this chance reference to Florence, Italy, or on the advice of other expatriates, the Gibbenses left Germany in 1872, spending most of their fifth and last year abroad in the Italian Florence. This ancient Tuscan, Medici-haunted city was a world comprised of stone: gray flagstone streets, narrow stone sidewalks, buildings made of piles of weathered somber stone that rose up and up, usually three or four stories. Omnibuses ran about the town from the center out to the various town gates and back.[12] The hills above the Arno were covered with silvery gray olive orchards. Old, thick vines clung to stucco walls, and daffodils bloomed everywhere in the spring. Dark green cypress, live oak, pomegranate, and fig trees bordered narrow, dusty roads. The houses in the near countryside appeared impregnable, fortresslike, secretive. Alice could stroll by the Duomo and by Santa Maria del Fiore, topped by Brunelleschi's cantilevered dome, where crowds had heard the fifteenth-century fanatical monk Savonarola preach. Its vast interior arched away toward heaven. Smaller Santa Croce may have been more to Alice's liking, that "great Florentine Valhalla," as Henry James dubbed it.[13] The bell tower of Giotto may have appealed to her more than the massive Duomo did.

To someone who had read Ruskin's *Modern Painters*, Florence's art treasures must have been enthralling. There was poignancy in Alice's interest in art, because it was Dr. Gibbens who had given her the copy of Ruskin. No matter how much she tried to block the memory of Daniel, it would have been impossible to forget him as she viewed the wonders of the Uffizi and the Academy. Perhaps she even saw the Bronzino portrait of Lucrezia Panciatichi, an oil painting of the glowing young woman with light red hair and white skin that plays a key role in Henry James's 1903 novel *The Wings of the Dove*.

This time Alice studied music with the charismatic Luigi Vannuccini, acclaimed Italian singing master. Vannuccini had been an opera conductor and later a concert pianist. He was also a minor composer. After settling in Florence, where he first had studied, he devoted himself to vocal training and became a noted singing master.[14] Alice's lessons allowed her to focus on something other than her responsibilities, indulging herself before she wended her way back across the Atlantic. Her return to America in 1873 brought her more bad news.

Eliza Gibbens's small capital lost value during the general economic downturn of 1873, though Alice did not know this as the women headed home. Later she deemed the timing of their return most fortunate, telling her youngest sister, "It came over me that if we had not gone home when we did, before we knew of the panic and Mother's diminished income, we too should have stayed on Heaven only knows how long—and Mother might have lost everything while doing so. How the past grows clear, now and then."[15] The two older daughters had to go to work to supplement the family's diminished income.[16] The four women went to Boston, where the job opportunities were better and where they could escape constant reminders of what their lives might have been had the head of their family been stronger. Alice and Mary found jobs in the Beacon Hill neighborhood at Miss Irene Sanger's private school for girls.

All four Gibbens women boarded on Tremont Street at the Hotel Van Rensselaer, where various spiritualist groups met. Tremont Temple Baptist Church was nearby, a venue for many important contemporary speakers: politicians, writers, ministers, spiritualists. Harriet Beecher Stowe gave a reading from *Uncle Tom's Cabin* there the year before the Gibbens moved to Boston. Alice could follow the fervid social movements that had attracted her during her childhood, as reformist causes still held sway in Boston and the rest of New England. Although the abolitionist movement was virtually concluded, now Alice developed a new interest, one she pursued until the end of her life. Her keen interest in mediums and psychics may have begun during her sojourn at the Van Rensselaer, if it had not started sooner.

Alice and her family's Swedenborgian beliefs were consistent with a strong interest in the spirit world. Swedenborg's cosmology, replete with spirits, visions, and angelic visitations, cast a long shadow over early American spiritualist cults. Although Swedenborgians and spiritualists were far from agreeing on everything, the Spiritualist movement owed a great deal to Swedenborg's conceptions of the physical, spiritual, and celestial worlds.[17] In the Swedenborgian theory of correspondences every natural manifestation has a counterpart in the spiritual world: every physical object represents a spiritual reality.[18] According to this theology, "there is but a short semiconscious interval between the death of the body and the commencement of the spiritual existence."[19] The dead, who are now spirits, will remember their loved ones when they join them in the spirit world. In his writings Swedenborg claimed to have extensive experience speaking to and associating with angels. These beings have substantial bodies with sensory perceptions and all the capabilities of humans.[20] If Swedenborg could converse with the dead, then it was possible the Gibbens women could reach their lost one. Eventually, William James would investigate spiritual phenomena that he could not research scientifically, spurred by his wife's interest in the other world.[21]

Every morning Alice and Mary walked from their hotel to their school, from Tremont Street across Boston Commons to Beacon Hill. Irene Sanger moved her school at least once while Alice and Mary Gibbens taught there. In 1876 Sanger kept a private school at 99 Charles Street, and in 1878 directories list a Miss Sanger at 76 Chestnut Street. There were a number of other private schools nearby. Beacon Hill had become an enclave of old Bostonian families, while the nouveau riche took up the Back Bay. There were a number of houses for rent or sale in Beacon Hill, providing space for the schools.[22] These schools were located in brick Federal-style row buildings, with shuttered windows and doors displaying brass door knockers. Boston grew rapidly, doubling its population every twenty years and requiring more schools for young women.[23] The schools vied with one another for students, much as Elizabeth Peabody and her sister Mary had competed for their students in the 1820s and 1830s.[24] Teaching in or running a private school was one of the few respectable ways that nineteenth-century women could earn money, so they fought hard to attract and keep pupils. By 1870, though the trend was deplored in some quarters, more than half the teachers in the United States were women. In the eyes of traditionalists years spent teaching constituted excellent preparation for women's most important role, motherhood.[25] No existing evidence suggests that Alice considered her teaching a career: it was a financial necessity, although she placed a premium value on education all her life.

Irene Sanger's school was most likely modeled on the female antebellum seminaries, more advanced schools than the eighteenth-century female academies, whose primary purpose had been to fit women for marriage. Many of these seminaries taught classics and sciences, with a curriculum resembling the era's male colleges. Early-nineteenth-century leaders like Emma Willard (the Troy Seminary, 1821) and Catharine Beecher (the Hartford Seminary, 1823) spearheaded this movement.[26] The seminaries operated on the premise that women could be intellectual equals to men, even if they assumed private lives rather than public ones after gradu-ation.[27] After the Civil War advertisements placed in newspapers and directories for these private schools boasted of their strengths in teaching languages and music in addition to other, more rigorous subjects. It was important for school principals and owners to find the best teachers, ones who could attract and keep students. Sometimes schools would note the credentials of a particularly strong teacher in their ads. Alice and her sister Mary were popular teachers and "beautiful girls," as one student noted, so they would have been assets to Sanger.[28]

Despite the long hours Alice spent teaching, she found time to pursue other activities. With her hard-won European sophistication and her dark beauty, her ability to speak German and her vocal talents, she made a positive impression before Boston society. Within two years of returning to New England Alice made friends with several Boston Brahmins. She knew the prominent Mary Bucklin Claflin, wife of the former governor of Massachusetts, William Claflin. One of five women serving on the board of trustees of Wellesley College, Mary Claflin maintained a salon in the best French tradition, entertaining intellectuals, academics, and political figures. She referred to Alice and her family as "'our lovely friends, the Gibbens.'"[29] The Claflins were part of a culture that embraced reformist causes and valued intellectual discourse, elements of Boston society that Henry James satirized in his 1884 novel, *The Bostonians*, through characters like Olive Chancellor and her cohorts, who are wedded to social reform movements. This culture suited Alice exactly.

In addition to the Claflins, Mary and John Sargent befriended Alice and her family. He was a Boston minister who founded the Radical Club, and his wife, Mary, was active in a number of causes. The Sargents had been committed abolitionists, and now, after the Civil War, they resumed their interest in perfectionist movements, though with a tempered realization that perhaps humanity could not perfect itself on its own. They invited their new friend to join the Radical Club. Alice's interest in social reform, an outgrowth of her childhood commitment to abolitionism, coupled with her intelligence and personal warmth, made her a logical choice for membership.

The Radical Club, later named the Chestnut Street Club, was founded in 1867; it lasted thirteen years.[30] Boston loved such clubs. This one grew steadily, from thirty members to nearly two hundred by 1880. Initial sessions focused on theological and religious questions, but ultimately scientific and educational issues claimed the group's attention. Members listened to papers and then argued their merits. The Radical Club was considered the most intellectual of Boston's discussion groups and was occasionally parodied in the press. Speakers included Ralph Waldo Emerson, Oliver Wendell Holmes, Julia Ward Howe, and John Greenleaf Whittier, and among the members were philosophers and thinkers Francis Ellingwood Abbot, Henry Pickering Bowditch, Thomas Davidson, and George Holmes Howison. Though the Radical Club was relatively short-lived compared to the longevity of many Boston clubs, its members debated topics considered to be the culturally pressing ones of their era. The group was dominated by the radical Free Religious Association, an ultraliberal faction of the Unitarian Church interested in scientific theism and the complete separation of church and state.[31]

The club met at 77 Chestnut Street at the Sargents' home, not far from Alice's first school.[32] The Sargents' parlor had a high ceiling with elaborate molding, a long rectangular mirror on one wall, a large painting of a woman on another wall, several marble busts, beautiful wooden and upholstered chairs, a rug with large medallions, curtains with swags, and elaborate chandeliers. It was an impressive and tasteful setting for the lofty subjects the club explored. The group had no formal constitution, and the only refreshments served were coffee and tea. Women could join, and one secret of the club's success, members thought, was the presence of both sexes, because the women encouraged the men to talk more civilly. Criticism of speakers could be severe. Julia Ward Howe compared club members' rebuttals to their invited speakers "to the ancient punishment whereby an offender was first smeared with honey and then hung up to be stung to death by wasps."[33]

Just as Alice had attracted men in Weymouth and in Europe despite her shy and serious demeanor, now she attracted men in Boston. Through her attendance at the Radical Club Alice gathered admirers, among them John Greenleaf Whittier and, later, Henry James Sr. Whittier was one of the famous "Fireside" or "Household Poets." He was poet laureate of New England, a journalist, a reformer, and a devout Quaker who had risked his life for the abolitionist cause. He celebrated rural New England life in poems such as "Snow-Bound" and "Maud Muller," constructing visions of a homely, nearly idyllic New England world that could have been Alice's Weymouth.

Aging poet Whittier quickly became Alice's devoted admirer. Their friendship was based on mutual political and religious convictions. He was also captivated by Alice's beauty and intelligence, finding her "an American girl unspoiled by years of sojourn in Europe." The difference in their ages (over forty years) did not prohibit them from developing a genuine liking for one another. Although he never married, Whittier was attracted to women throughout his life, and he in turn attracted them. Whittier railed against the asceticism of the early Christians; he did not believe in "putting the body into a cloister."[34] After his and Alice's initial meeting he visited the Gibbenses often, befriending her mother and sisters, too. He was one of the few male friends that Eliza Gibbens ever had.

In 1874, the first summer of their friendship, Alice visited Whittier at his home in Amesbury, Massachusetts, a small town bordering Maine, very close to the Atlantic. That fall she gave Whittier wine made by Benedictine monks at a Carthusian monastery south of Florence, an allusion to one of his poems in which he mentioned La Certosa, the name of the monastery.[35] He reciprocated her gift with his latest volume, *Hazel Blossoms*, hoping it would recall to her a day she spent with him the preceding summer. In the fall of 1875 he sent her colorful flowers from his meadow. He regretted that they had shriveled by the time they reached her, though their dried state made them more emblematic of him than her.[36] Later she sent him a piece of needlework.[37]

They also shared poems and books. Whittier sent Alice Prentice Mulford's pamphlet containing a sermon on the death of Sarah Walker and a volume by a Mr. Whitney on European travel.[38] He did not like one of Alice's favorite authors, Jane Austen, but Alice quoted Blake's poetry to him, which he did like.[39] In February 1875 Alice explained Swedenborg's allusions to the final extinction of evil. Their talk inspired him to write a poem entitled "The Two Angels," which he sent her as a token of his interest and affection. In his tribute to his young friend Whittier rejects the doctrine of eternal damnation and affirms God's love and forgiveness. In the poem two angels from heaven enter hell with the aim of redeeming damned souls. Through the power of God's love "hope entered into hell."[40] The verse affirms an optimistic theological stance, consistent with Alice's own religious optimism.

Alice's devoted friend realized how tired she was from her long days at Irene Sanger's school. He wished she could leave her weary school to hear the thrushes and song sparrows sing and see the woodland flowers: the delicate polygala, the yellow violet, and the purple rhodesia, memorialized in Emerson's sonnet: "If I had an Autocrat's power, I would cut short these merciless long terms & turn listless pupil & weary teacher into the sun & air."[41] After his seventieth birthday celebration he sent Alice some of the flowers he received. She kept those flowers all her life, preserving them inside the envelope in which he sent them. They are now in Harvard's Houghton Library, dry scarlet fragments testifying to his genuine affection for her.[42]

Alice's friendship with John Greenleaf Whittier was one of the brightest spots in her life during these trying years, but a passionate romance would have to wait.

3 He Loves Me, He Loves Me Not

WHITTIER WAS NOT ALICE'S ONLY admirer at the Radical Club. Family lore and various commentators claim that Henry James Sr. met Alice Howe Gibbens early in 1876 at a club meeting. Upon his return to 20 Quincy Street he announced to his wife, Mary, his son William, and his daughter, Alice, that he had met William's future wife. Henry Sr. became so convinced of the rightness of this match that he offered to augment William's salary if he married Alice Gibbens.[1]

At the same time that Henry James Sr. realized that she might make his son a suitable bride, Alice was choosing, too. This aging Swedenborgian's moral compulsion matched her own intense interest in ethical and educational issues. Though they had not conversed at length, Henry James Sr. had read several papers to the club, including one entitled "Nature and Person," extolling the evils of inescapable selfhood, and he attended other club meetings from time to time. His lecture, "Marriage," was well attended, probably because around 1850 he had agreed with the French Fourierists that marriage was outmoded and that individuals should be free to enact their own sexual desires. Backpedaling on that stance when he realized it might jeopardize his reputation, however, he voiced his support for marriage with the caveat that women were subservient to men. Marriage allowed them to rise in the social scale when they devoted themselves to their families.[2] Two decades later club members were curious to hear his current beliefs on the institution. The aging Henry Sr. claimed that through "woman's superior spiritual quality" men could be transformed from their animal state, their urge to procreate, to a better spiritual existence. Now men should voluntarily refuse to demean women. Although by the letter of marriage laws men held power over their wives, any man today who insisted on his wife's subjection "would be spiritually no man but an abject, imbecile cad, who ought to be denied a marriage certificate and relegated back to celibacy." He went on to assert, "Spiritual marriage consists in making woman henceforth the supreme object of the bond, and man its free, spontaneous, devoted, even adoring subject."[3] Without these conditions, marriage could only be a legal form of concubinage. Such a lofty conception would have appealed to Alice.

When Henry James Sr. met her at the Sargents' home, she was bright, calm, and attractive, with an unconventional beauty. Perhaps the James family patriarch recognized Alice's inner moral and spiritual convictions, viewing her as a principled woman who might not change the world alone but who could stabilize his brilliant son William. Alice's son Henry James II claims that it was burly, blue-eyed Thomas Davidson, Scottish-born writer and philosopher, who first met the Gibbens women and invited his friend William James to come to the Radical Club to meet Alice, "'the woman you ought to marry.'"[4] Perhaps it was both Davidson and Henry James Sr. who urged William to meet this remarkable woman. In any case, he attended the Radical Club that winter and met Alice.[5] Soon he was subjecting her to a courtship so bizarre, tormented, and tormenting that it is a wonder the two ever married.

Their first meeting was a success, at least by William's account. He wrote immediately to Mary Holton James, his brother Bob's wife, that he had met "'the future Mrs. W.J.'"[6] Nearly a decade earlier he had informed Bob that he would never marry. "For myself I have long since fully determined never to marry with anyone, were she as healthy as the Venus of Milo, for this dorsal trouble [his back pain] is evidently s'thing in the blood. I confess that the flesh is weak and passion will overthrow strong reasons, and I may fail in keeping such a resolve, but I mean not to fail."[7] He had changed his mind.

The Jameses were one of America's most notable nineteenth- and early-twentieth-century families, and they were financially secure. Henry James Sr. enjoyed a minor reputation as a writer, speaker, and Swedenborgian. His friends and acquaintances included Ralph Waldo Emerson, Margaret Fuller, Annie and James T. Fields, Thomas Carlyle, and William Makepeace Thackeray. Rough estimates suggest that Henry Sr. had an annual income between $3,000 and $5,000 from the estate of his father, William James of Albany, whose wealth was said to be second only to that of John Jacob Astor in New York State. This income put Henry Sr. and his family in the upper middle class.[8] Alice's future fiancé, William, born 11 January 1842 to Henry and Mary Robertson Walsh James, had more opportunity for education and fewer financial worries than Alice.

William, the eldest son, had three brothers and a sister. The second oldest James son, Henry James Jr., was a writer. At the relatively young age of thirty-three he had already received substantial recognition for his fiction and essays, publishing a collection of tales (*A Passionate Pilgrim*), a collection of travel essays (*Transatlantic Sketches*), and two novels (*Watch and Ward* and *Roderick Hudson*). He had taken up permanent residence in England, claiming that the cultural climate of Cambridge, Massachusetts, was ill suited to his needs as a writer. By the time Alice met William, the third James brother, Garth Wilkinson (known to the family as Wilkie), a Civil War veteran, was married and living in Milwaukee with his wife, Carrie. The youngest brother, Robertson (known as Bob) James, also a Civil War veteran, lived in Wisconsin with his wife, Mary. Wilkie and Bob, who never received some of the opportunities accorded to the two older sons, fell notably below the achievements of their brothers.[9] Bob, in fact, would become part of Alice's vocation. She must have met Wilkie at Mary James's funeral in 1882; however, he died in Milwaukee in 1883 before she had an opportunity to ever get to know him. The only female James sibling, Alice (hereafter called "sister Alice"), is today a major feminist icon. Her diary and letters were published posthumously and reveal her to be a brilliant observer of life. She conducted significant work in a women's correspondence school, found happiness with a lifelong partner, and maintained a keen interest in politics, all despite her bouts with depression and illness. When William first met his Alice, sister Alice lived at home with her parents.

William's early history was worlds removed from Alice's. He spent his childhood and youth traveling back and forth across the Atlantic, with repeated stops in New York, Newport, Boston, Germany, Italy, France, Switzerland, and England. His four siblings provided him with companionship when the family uprooted itself over and over in search of the ideal existence, the perfect sensuous education. While Henry James Sr. may have failed to become the preeminent thinker of his day, he was more stable than Alice's father. Mary James's role has never been adequately explained, but she loved her children and offered them a secure, though impermanent, household.

William was encouraged to pursue his own interests, though not necessarily a career, receiving an eclectic, if erratic, education. Discouraged from Civil War service by his father and by his poor health, in 1861 he enrolled in Cambridge's Lawrence Scientific School, where he studied chemistry, switching to Harvard Medical School in February 1864.[10] William did not graduate from medical school until 1869 because his health was not always good and because at times he interrupted his studies to pursue other opportunities. In 1865, in search of adventure and an alternative career as a scientist, he signed on with the expedition to South America led by naturalist Louis Agassiz. Agassiz was a determined opponent of Charles Darwin. By collecting specimens he wanted to prove the theory of evolution wrong. He expected to find signs of divine creation by cataloging the discrete geographic distribution of animals and plants and show that a divine being had planned that distribution. The same month that Alice took full responsibility for her small family, William sailed to South America and explored up the Amazon in Brazil. He discovered that a naturalist's calling was not for him, however. In a photograph taken during the time of his South American adventure he looks dashing and intriguing, a handsome young man with a slouch hat and dark glasses, moustache and beard, his hands stuck casually in his pockets. He resembles nothing so much as the hero—or maybe the dark villain—of one of the era's sentimental novels.

From 1866 to 1867 William's depression deepened; he even had thoughts of suicide. On Christmas Day, 1866, he confided to sister Alice, "I am drudging gloomily on at the medical school."[11] He suffered chronic back pain and intestinal ailments; his medical studies left him mentally exhausted.

In the winter of 1867 he contemplated ending his life. Finally, William and his parents agreed that a European trip might alleviate his distress. Less than a year before Alice took her family to Europe, in 1867 William took another leave from his studies and wandered through Germany, Switzerland, and France, seeking cures for his ailing back and spirits at his family's expense. It was not the only time their paths nearly intersected before Alice and William finally met one another.

On 16 April 1867 William sailed on the *Great Eastern* for Brest, France. From there he traveled to Dresden and then Teplitz. He went from restaurants to art museums to the opera to the theater to lectures. He tried the hot baths, the electric cure, the water cure, blistering, anything to relieve his painful back ailment. At times suicidal and at other times almost irrationally exuberant, he enjoyed the luxury, though perhaps at times it became the burden, of focusing on his own needs. While he floundered during his travels, he tried to learn from his experience. He wrote occasional essays for publication, including a review of Herman Grimm's novel *Unüberwindliche Mächte* (Invincible Powers). In Dresden he began keeping a diary of his reading and impressions, using that diary for several years to help conquer depression.[12] William survived his tendency to gloom by supposing that eventually he would make his mark in the world.[13]

During these uneasy years when he weighed his destiny, William was interested in women. He enjoyed their company and felt at ease with them, and they in turn fostered friendships with him. He flirted easily with young women, even his sister Alice.[14] Early in 1867 he asked her to find "some handsome, spirited & romantic creature whom I can fall in love with in a desperate fashion."[15] Sick and conflicted as he was, he was still charming. He had penetrating blue eyes, a thick, dark moustache, regular features, a firm chin, and almost hollow cheeks. He playfully described himself in the third person to his sister:

> He wore a handsome soft felt hat, now perhaps a little the worse for wear, but wh[ich]. slouched as it was picturesquely over his brow set off advantageously his handsome & expressive features, a neat blue american overcoat just bound with black tape by the most fashionable tailor of the fashionable town of Teplitz, and a chaste but rich scarf pin of plain gold protruded f[ro]m. the red scarf which encircled

his throat. In one hand he swung gracefully & carelessly an alpaca umbrella, and with the other, as he returned the glances of interest & curiosity with wh. the ladies greeted him he occasionally pulled his chin, on wh. a luxuriant beard of 2 weeks growth might be perceived to mantle.[16]

Throughout his European tour William explored his feelings toward women. He stared at a ravishing dark beauty in the window across from his in Dresden, he sent his photograph to a young Bohemian girl at Teplitz, and he nearly fell in love with a Miss Borneman, who wore a Swiss costume to a Berlin party. All of these were casual moments, expressions of his lively interest in the opposite sex. After taking the cold-water cure at Divonne-les-Bains in France, he sketched a detailed drawing of seven pretty young women in a semicircle watching a young man lounging in an outdoor cloth recliner. Only the top of the back of the young man's head and his gesturing arms are visible. He holds this bevy of beauties spellbound. Now blurred at the edges, the caption describes the cold-water cure as a remedy for melancholy. The image can be read as William's desire to mesmerize women with accounts of his ailments and cures, or perhaps it is a self-ironizing record of a real event.[17] When Henry found the drawing again decades later, he called it "the comic (so very charming) thing of the listening young ladies at the Divonne water cure."[18]

But up until 1868 William contented himself with merely looking. Gazing at women afforded him all the closeness he wanted. Although he looked at them all over Europe, he did little to develop a relationship with any of them. One woman he met abroad, New York musician and teacher Catherine Havens, attracted and held his interest, but they were perhaps too much alike: she also suffered from poor health.

In May 1868, when Alice was in Florence, William met Catherine, a fellow boarder at Madame Spangelberg's Dresden boardinghouse. She enchanted him with her talented piano performances.[19] On warm nights the two expatriates found themselves in intense discussions on the piazza, sharing intimate details of their respective problems. Catherine Havens was a childish-looking woman in her late twenties with a small face.[20] William found her highly intelligent but capricious. She suffered from "nerves," the nineteenth-century catchall phrase for any mental ailment not easily diagnosed. But this would have made her even more interesting to a latent psychologist who was later fascinated by insanity in all its forms. William told his friend Thomas Ward that she "has stirred chords in this dessicated heart wh. I long thought had turned to dust." Soon after their initial acquaintance Catherine invited him to go driving with her, an invitation he accepted even though he found her high-strung. He vowed to Tom that he would never give her up.[21]

When the next month Catherine went alone to Schwalbach for her health, William worried that she would succumb to ennui there. He complimented her clothing, and they shared an interest in books and political matters. Catherine declared that Henry James's short stories held her spellbound.[22] They copied out their favorite quotations from their reading and shared them with one another. While their relationship never seems to have progressed beyond the stage of friendship, William manifested the same sort of approach-avoidance behavior toward her that later characterized his courtship of Alice. Always acutely self-aware, he wrote to Catherine from Switzerland that he had written her a letter full of "a quantity of nonsense" that he decided not to mail. He had nearly told her all: his weakness, egotism, cowardice, emptiness, and fear that the good front he presented while trying to cheer her would mislead her. He decided they should wait for a face- to-face meeting, when they could wallow in revealing (and reviling) themselves to one another.[23] The friendship focused on weaknesses. Though their respective illnesses struck chords for one another, William James must have known that a pair of hypochondriacs would not pull well together.

Upon his return from his continental sojourn in November 1868, William resumed his medical studies and his correspondence with Catherine, though he was not sure whether she was in Scotland, England, or somewhere else. After 1869 there are no extant letters to her until September 1873. In one sense their friendship was a trial run for his relationship with Alice. He and Catherine became close friends, a friendship that allowed him to know a bright, musically gifted woman. When Catherine remembered William after his death, she recalled only his empathy with her poor health but nothing of romance.[24]

When William resumed his medical studies, he had cured neither his mental angst nor his physical maladies. In December he wrote in his diary,

"'Nature and life have unfitted me for any affectionate relations with other individuals.'"[25] He spent the winter of 1869 preparing his medical school thesis, choosing the stale topic of the body's reaction to cold.[26] On 21 June he passed the oral exams. He could now affix the letters M.D. after his name.

After his graduation William drifted, summering in Pomfret, Connecticut, where he rested and read Robert Browning's poems. He improved under his mother's watchful supervision, but by the winter of 1870 he had descended to the depths of darkest depression. There has been considerable speculation as to whether he became a patient at McLean Mental Hospital in Somerville, Massachusetts, that winter, but the evidence is inconclusive. However, there is no disputing the fact that he suffered overwhelming black spells during the winter of 1870 and again from December 1870 to April 1871. There are gaps in his correspondence during this period that could result either from a prolonged stay at McLean, from depression, or from both.[27] William toyed with the idea of taking refuge at McLean, once telling Henry Pickering Bowditch, a professor at the Harvard Medical School, that if he took charge of the lunatic asylum at Somerville, "I should feel assured of a refuge in my old and destitute days, for you certainly would not be treacherous enough to spurn me from the door when I presented myself—on the pretext that I was only shamming dementia."[28] William refused to accept his father's Swedenborgian God as an antidote to his spiritual malaise, and none of the available remedies for depression helped him.

William's younger brother Henry returned to Europe in February 1869, where he remained until May 1870, leaving William to cope with his depression without his companionship. Except for the months when William remained mute, the brothers wrote detailed letters to one another, exchanging advice on the treatment of back and bowels. William's to Henry were frequently very specific: diet, drops, length of walks—nothing escaped the new physician's desire to help his brother. Henry sometimes proffered advice on William's depression, though he had no specific remedies for that malady as William had for Henry's physical ailments. On 30 November 1869 he adjured William, "Your days are composed but of hours, by taking each hour 'empirically' & disposing of it as best you can, you can get thro' a month, & at the end of a month (probably) you find some appreciable result.—But I can't write to you about your back. The subject is to me too heavy—too sickening."[29] William confided a month later, "Meanwhile my stomach, bowels, brain, temper & spirits are all at a pretty low ebb, and I don't think I'm a very pleasing addition to the family circle."[30]

In January 1870 William experimented with chloral, which inflamed his eyelids.[31] After that episode he fell silent for three months. Chloral, introduced by O. Liebreich in 1869 as an anesthetic and hypnotic, can have serious side effects if the dose is even slightly larger than prescribed. The correct dose causes the patient to fall asleep for several hours and awake with no ill effects. Some patients, like the Jameses' cousin Minny Temple, who suffered from tuberculosis, took chloral to help them sleep.[32] But an overdose can depress the circulation and respiration, lowering the body temperature. This accidental overdose of chloral may have contributed to an episode that marked the beginning of William's long period of depression.

During these low winter months of 1870 William had a traumatic experience that he later recorded in *The Varieties of Religious Experience*, attributing the episode to a Frenchman. After his father's death Henry James II revealed that this experience was in fact autobiographical. The oft-cited passage reveals both William's despair and his vivid artistic imagination. In this passage he described his fear of his own existence and his vision of

> an epileptic patient whom I had seen in the asylum, a black-haired youth with greenish skin, entirely idiotic, who used to sit all day on one of the benches, or rather shelves against the wall, with his knees drawn up against his chin, and the coarse gray undershirt, which was his only garment, drawn over them inclosing his entire figure. He sat there like a sort of sculptured Egyptian cat or Peruvian mummy, moving nothing but his black eyes and looking absolutely non-human. This image and my fear entered into a species of combination with each other. <u>That shape am I</u>, I felt, potentially. . . . I awoke morning after morning with a horrible dread at the pit of my stomach, with a sense of the insecurity of life that I never knew before, and that I have never felt since.[33]

William ameliorated his depression through his study of French idealistic philosopher Charles-Bernard Renouvier. William began reading Renouvier while at Divonne-les-Bains, hoping to overcome the problem of evil in the universe by finding a moral attitude and a will. While he could not deny the existence of evil, he could decide to resist it.[34] His study of Renouvier's second volume of essays led him to believe that humans could sustain a particular thought through sheer willpower: it might be possible to resist evil through choosing to exert one's will against it. On 30 April 1870 he wrote in his notebook, "'My first act of free will shall be to believe in free will.'"[35]

With spring came relief from his depression and the return of his brother Henry and his Aunt Kate (Catharine Walsh, Mary James's sister, who lived with the James family for many years).[36] William spent the summer of 1870 at Pomfret again, but he made no progress with his health. He considered studying mathematics, but the scheme amounted to nothing. Aside from his continual reading, he did little the following winter. By the spring of 1871 his back had improved with the lifting cure, which involved exercises with weights. His eyes were not strong, though they slowly improved. He told Bob, who also suffered with eye problems and nervous depression, that his retinas were weak. He advised Bob to avoid using kerosene lamps, which were bad for the eyes.[37] Determined to keep up his studies, for a time William had someone read to him.

That spring William resumed his interest in medicine, buying a ticket for a lecture series on the eye.[38] He attended Henry Bowditch's lectures at Harvard Medical School in the morning and stayed to try his own experiments in Bowditch's newly created laboratory on Boston's Grove Street. William's classmate at Harvard Medical School, Bowditch had just been appointed a university medical faculty member. Through his intervention and that of newly appointed Harvard president Charles William Eliot, William's former chemistry teacher and neighbor, William began a new career. Despite the fact that the Harvard community knew of his various health crises, William was asked to teach physiology, an elective course, at the college during the winter term of 1873. Eliot sought talented young teachers, and he knew William had taken up his work again.[39] William called the appointment "a perfect godsend," and hoped that regular employment would focus him.[40] Just months before Alice began her short-lived teaching career, William began the work that would engage him for thirty-five years.

William was among the first of many talented faculty that Eliot would appoint during his forty-year tenure as Harvard's president. Under his strong leadership the curriculum broadened to give students more choices in selecting their courses, an elective system. Greek was no longer an entrance requirement, and compulsory Greek and Latin for freshman were abandoned.[41] Eliot founded the graduate school in arts and sciences, reorganized the law and medical schools, and eventually brought the various graduate programs together under a common governance system, molding Harvard into a more cohesive university rather than a group of loosely allied schools.[42]

While the first course that Eliot hired William to teach concerned the physical body, at the same time he began to expand his philosophical interests. In the early 1870s, along with Charles Sanders Peirce and Chauncey Wright, he helped establish the Metaphysical Club, which became an important influence on his evolving thought.[43] The club, whose members included Oliver Wendell Holmes Jr., Francis Ellingwood Abbot, Joseph B. Warner, Nicholas St. John Green, and John Fiske, rebelled against the post-Kantian idealism that held sway on Beacon Hill and at Harvard. Members met to explore all kinds of metaphysical ideas. The group allowed William, who was trying to formulate links between metaphysics and the new experimental psychologies, a venue for testing his developing theories on mental processes. In 1873 he drafted an essay, "Against Nihilism," that critiqued Wright's and Holmes's Darwinist materialism. William was troubled by philosophers who believed that consciousness could be reduced to physical processes.[44]

William's spirits remained relatively high from the fall of 1872 to the spring of 1873. Imagining sunlit waves, skimming gulls, and blooming flowers near the Amazon kept him going when his spirits were low.[45] Even though he felt he was not well enough to undertake a relationship, he began to long for a mate.[46] He dallied with Sara Sedgwick, Charles Eliot Norton's wife's sister, and he confided in Henry that the two Misses Wards, whom he met during a visit to the Isles of Shoals, were "not devoid of the principle of sexual fascination," though there is no evidence that these were anything more than passing fancies.[47] His mother still found him difficult, despite his improvement. Mother James complained that after just two or three hours of study William's head gave out and the strength went from his legs. She announced to her favorite son, Henry, less than three years before William met Alice:

> This necessity he [William] is under here to measure his strength every day, keeps his mind constantly fixed upon himself which is the worst possible thing for him. You will find him very much improved in appearance looking as well as he ever did I think, but still very morbid, and much more given than he used to be to talk about himself. . . . If dear Harry you could only have imparted to him a few grains of your own blessed hopefulness he would have been well long ago.[48]

Though reportedly his first semester's teaching was a success for himself and for his forty-five students, William was exhausted, but he had done well enough that one hundred students would enroll in his course for the fall of 1873, more than he felt he could handle. Although Eliot was unwilling to divide the physiology class into two sections, he was willing to grant William leave for a year, giving him the option of returning to his teaching in 1874.[49] At first William proposed traveling with a student who would pay his own expenses, but he decided instead to ask Aunt Kate for a loan of $1,000, promising to repay her out of his future yearly salary.[50] So back to Europe he went, close to the time when Alice Gibbens returned to take up her teaching duties on Beacon Hill.

This time William's European sojourn was a shorter one. His and Alice's paths nearly intersected in Florence. William found the Florentines debilitated and malformed, the city small and dusky, though his spirits improved on sunny days and while socializing with other Americans who wintered there.[51] He rode the omnibuses about town over the stone pavements and read Jakob Burckhardt's *Die Kultur der Renaissance in Italien* (The Civilization of the Renaissance in Italy).[52] For a time he stayed with Henry in Florence. Still entertaining thoughts of marriage, William told Wilkie, "At present Harry is my spouse."[53] In addition to an interest in marriage, he thought he had discovered a paternal instinct, although at present it would have to be gratified by Bob's newborn son.[54]

Then they traveled to Rome, where William was overcome by the nightmare of the Coliseum and found St. Peter's "a monument of human pride."[55] He was imbued with the moral view. Soon after reaching Rome he declared to Catherine Havens, "I find I have little heart for this loafing life."[56] He ate roasted chestnuts, abstained from liquor, and explored ruins.[57] After William contracted a fever, the brothers returned to Florence, where it was Henry's turn to be sick.

Whatever William lacked, he had not found it in Europe. If for no other reason, he was driven home by boredom. He sailed from Bremen to New York at the end of February 1874 and resumed his teaching during the autumn of that year, offering classes in anatomy and physiology. William professed to be on sounder footing upon his return to Cambridge, advising brother Bob to follow the credo he was developing: "First comes in all active spirits I imagine, a theoretic crisis, the need of knowing the truth, which after reaching a greater or lesser point of distress terminates in a faith—and then instead of perpetually reinvestigating the warrants for that faith, the sound thing to do is simply to go on living with it inside of you as a motive and an inspiration."[58] His parents, however, found him still battling depression.[59]

During 1874–75 William taught Natural History 3, a combination of biology, physiology, and anthropology. He also took over the Museum of Comparative Anatomy after director Jeffries Wyman's death in September.[60] Before fall term commenced he was apprehensive about his strength, worrying that eight months' steady work might strain him.[61] He made time for diversions, though, going to the opera, socializing with friends, attending his men's dinner club, and participating in Metaphysical Club sessions. More stable emotionally, still he complained of fatigue to Catherine Havens in February 1875.[62] That summer he traveled to Wisconsin to see Bob and Wilkie, acquiring a setter pup named Dido on the way home. He read Walt Whitman, whom he found coarse; nonetheless, the poet renewed William's rapture for nature and poetry.[63]

The fall term of 1875 found William more focused and confident, and by November he could work productively.[64] As his interests expanded beyond the physiological, he offered a graduate class, the Relations between Physiology and Psychology. The course marked the start of what we now call psychology courses in the United States.[65] In 1876 Harvard made him an assistant professor.[66] He had begun writing professionally, turning out seventeen book reviews for the *Nation* in a matter of months.[67] He was ready to consider the steady state of matrimony.

Maybe, just maybe, it was William who found Alice first. On 21 January 1876 he attended an "esthetic tea" at Mrs. Sargent's home, where the Radical Club met. He informed Henry, "The chief reason why I went, after having gone once to escape the importunities of Mrs. Sargent is that on that first occasion I had found a most particularly delightful young woman whom I also found again on the second occasion with a still more lovely sister. But I don't think even their charms can take me a third time."[68] If these lovely sisters were Alice and Mary Gibbens, then it took a friend's and a father's wish to make William go the third time—but that third time was the charm.

Alice liked William right away. She told her mother she had met the man she wanted to marry.[69] Although she had attracted men in Weymouth and in Europe, she had been so burdened by emotional and financial family duties that she had had little time to think of romance. Her overabundance of common sense kept her from any rash liaisons, and her close relationship with Whittier allowed her the pleasure of an admirer without feeling the pressure a formal suitor might apply.

Shortly after their meeting at the Radical Club, Alice sent William a copy of Katherine Sherwood Bonner's poem satirizing the group. The poem, "The Radical Club: a poem, respectfully dedicated to 'the infinite' by an atom," also parodied Edgar Allan Poe's "The Raven."

> But, dear friends, I now must close, of these Radicals dispose,
> For I am sad and weary as I view their folly o'er;
> In their wild Eutopian dreaming and impracticable scheming
> For a sinful world's redeeming, common sense flies out the door,
> And the long-drawn dissertations come to—words and nothing more,
> Only words and nothing more.

William shared the poem with his family and claimed that all of them found it amusing. He kept Alice's copy and sent her the newest edition of Bonner's satirical work.[70] But while William found himself attracted to Alice, he continued writing to Catherine Havens. He complained that she had failed a little test in comparative anatomy he had sent her (a drawing of a dog, which she was supposed to label), and he worried about her health. In this long letter he derides William Dean Howells for writing an "unmasculine book," a strategy that emphasized his own healthier masculinity.[71] He boasted of the raise to $2,000 that Harvard had promised him for next year, pronouncing himself still easily tired but more attracted to philosophy.[72]

At first William's courtship of Alice proceeded as courtships did in the nineteenth century. They saw one another frequently in the spring of 1876, William calling on her at Tremont Street. They took walks together on the Boston Commons, they exchanged books, they went riding together, and they wrote one another letters. Both particularly liked Robert Browning's poetry.[73] At one point Alice sent her photo to William, the image of a very earnest young woman in a black dress with a white ruffle at the top of her collar, her hair pulled back from her face in soft waves.[74] Sometimes, he thanked her just for being born.[75]

Alice soon learned, however, that this was no conventional courtship. William's courting involved more than just winning her hand. He had to justify their union psychologically and philosophically. Even if theirs was a case of love at first sight, that did not mean there were no obstacles to the marriage. Most of the obstacles came from his hesitancy to commit himself to a relationship when he was still by no means certain who he was. Alice had far fewer choices than her suitor and thus experienced little metaphysical anguish about her feelings. She was the more mature of the pair, a maturity hard-won. Though she was only twenty-seven when she met William and he was thirty-four, she had already known more difficulty than some people experience in a lifetime. His two-year-long courtship demanded all her patience.

The first summer of their courtship Alice saw little of her erstwhile suitor. She went with friends to the Isles of Shoals off the coast of New Hampshire, near Amesbury, Massachusetts, where she planned to see

Whittier.[76] William went to his Newport relatives, the Tweedys, for four days; then to Stamford, Connecticut, where he took a "long and beautiful ride" with Catherine Havens; next to New Rochelle to cousin Henrietta Temple's wedding; and finally to Philadelphia for a day-and-a-half tour of the Centenary of American Independence Exhibition.[77] The last month of his summer holiday he spent in Keene Valley in the Adirondacks at a small ramshackle dwelling on land called Putnam Camp he now owned with Charles Bowditch, Henry Bowditch, and Dr. James Jackson Putnam, who later became Alice's doctor.[78] In September Alice received a letter with a declaration of his feelings. "I am in love, und zwar [German, "that is"] (—forgive me—) with Yourself."[79] She was to tell him if any real (or imagined) obstacles existed to their union.

That autumn Alice returned to her teaching duties, still at Miss Sanger's school. When William returned to Cambridge, he fell ill, and he alluded to fatigue that spring; he was not cured of the malaise that had plagued him for years.[80] Perhaps this illness was caused partly by his anxiety over his new job as assistant professor of physiology but perhaps also because of his strong feelings for Alice, feelings he could not confine or control.[81] After he and Alice took a boat trip he wrote her a letter in which he laboriously defined his views on marriage. Probably because of his depression and anxieties, he decided that their marriage would be an unnatural one. Only an extraordinary appeal to "some metaphysical world 'beyond the veil'" could justify a union such as theirs. "But to the healthy Natural sense such a world is problematical. Whoever falls back on it for justification of what is outwardly a social crime, does so at his peril, and, should expect no countenance, perhaps even no tolerance from public opinion. To wander from the outward order that keeps the world so sweet is in a word to throw yourself upon the Tragical."[82]

When Alice read his tortured letter, she must have realized what a risk she took if she married William James. Eliza Gibbens encouraged the match, and Alice believed her suitor to be generous and modest, but now she questioned the rightness of such a union.[83] Although he now had steady employment, William was by no means a healthy man, as his letter attested.[84] As a child Alice had suffered from her parents' unhappy marriage, and she knew well the fatal consequences of loving a man who was prone to severe depression. William not only experienced deep depression, he also exhibited manic behavior. In this letter, written with few romantic overtones, he declared that Alice could marry him only if "she find[s] it spiritually laid upon her as a tragic duty, to do so." At the end of the letter, written when he should have been sleeping, he announces that he is free of her forever. Writing to her "is only an example of my general mania for theorizing at unseemly hours, & annoying innocent girls by my scholastic and pedantic way of taking simple matters."[85] Alice had a great deal to think about, not least that the man who wanted to marry her viewed their love as a form of philosophical torture.

When Alice tried to tell William of her own beliefs, he proved a poor listener. She wanted to convince him of the need for a religious outlook, but he remained confirmed in his skepticism, though he acknowledged to her the possibility that religion might be humankind's last refuge. Though she had not converted him to her own views, he wished he had listened to her more, as he envied her belief.[86]

Just before Thanksgiving 1876, William told Alice that he hoped to merit "certain goods" but that she need not acknowledge him outwardly. She only needed to recognize, to understand, what he was.[87] For a woman working full time and also helping a widowed mother, this may have seemed an overwhelming demand. By Christmas Alice remained unable—or unwilling—to convince William that she cared for him. He complained to Thomas Ward, "She cares no more for me than for a dead leaf, nor ever will; and viewed in the light of my health since the fall, I must say objectively that it is fortunate she does not. Subjectively, the measure is different."[88]

Although William and Alice did not see one another daily or even weekly during these two years, their letters detail the awkward, lengthy stages of their courtship. Letters frequently substituted for face-to-face intimacy in nineteenth-century courtship rituals.[89] William's ability to bare his soul on paper told Alice much about him. She was a highly literate woman and a first-rate writer herself, but again and again she read his letters, trying to comprehend his self-imposed dilemmas. Above all, he was very anxious to be sure that Alice understood him before they made a lifelong commitment to one another. In this sense William resembled most nineteenth-century lovers. Etiquette books stressed sincerity as the most important quality in a relationship; lovers were pressured to be unfailingly honest with one another.[90] In this area William excelled, leaving none of his bad qualities to Alice's imagination.

Aligned with this was another dominant feature of the era's courtship rituals, the test. Here again William took the lead, providing Alice with psychologically intricate tests designed to prove her stamina. Alice, like the hero of a fairy tale who has to face physical trials of beast and battle to win the heroine, had to run a psychological gauntlet before she and William could make the fateful decision to marry. In this particular courtship, though, gender roles were reversed. Often nineteenth-century women devised tests for men to prove their love, tests frequently more difficult than the tests men set for women. Men initiated the formal phase of a courtship, but then women were expected to test their suitors and to decide when it was time to announce an engagement.[91] Despite his insistence upon his masculinity, William took the more typically feminine role in devising and conducting these demanding ritualized tests. In spite of his constant testing Alice knew her own mind: she did care for him, more than she cared for dead leaves. That winter she told him that she "recognized" him, giving him the empathy he had demanded in the fall. That recognition gave him a focus.[92]

Perhaps encouraged by Alice's willingness to tolerate her son's demands, Mary James tried to advance their courtship. In March she and sister Alice invited Alice to come to their home on Quincy Street for a luncheon hosted by a club known as the Bee, the sewing circle sister Alice had joined in 1867 that included her closest friends. Mrs. James Sr. hoped Miss Gibbens might make "some pleasant acquaintances among her [daughter's] friends."[93]

While William vacillated, agonized, and analyzed their love, Alice followed her own pursuits. She heard Harvard professor Francis James Child's lectures on Chaucer, pronouncing them fine, and she continued to see John Greenleaf Whittier, whose friendship sustained her.[94] William focused on his own needs, on how he understood the nature of commitment and marriage, but Whittier thought about Alice. The same month Mary James invited her prospective daughter-in-law to the Bee luncheon, the poet admonished her: "I was pained to learn from Mrs. C[laflin] that thee are getting too tired with thy school labors."[95] He thought Providence meant Alice for something better than her present life afforded her. That winter she made him a piece of needlework.[96]

The courtship dragged. It was a year since Alice and William first met, but they made little progress in settling their relationship because he was not ready to make any decisions.[97] Katharine Hillard, Alice's friend and fellow teacher, invited her to go to England that summer. William encouraged her to go to discourage gossip about their relationship, but on 15 April 1877 he again thought she misunderstood him. "Some day, God willing, you shall read the bottom of my heart. Until then that you neither doubt nor judge me, is the sole hope of W.J."[98] He vacillated from day to day: she should go, she should not go. Katharine thought Alice should take the trip and reconsider the relationship, but she finally decided to remain at home.[99] On 21 April she went riding with William. Afterward he sent her a photo taken for that year's Harvard graduation. He looked handsome and pensive, sporting a full beard and sideburns and wearing a loose polka-dot bow tie. In the letter he urged her to respect herself, as it would be the best way of respecting him.[100]

Alice thought William would visit her on Tremont Street in late May.[101] Although she told him not to come to call on her on Decoration Day, she expected him the weekend after. Again he disappointed her: he was not going to call as he had promised. She might not see him at all before he went away. He told her that their peaceful rides disturbed him because they were too peaceful.[102] William went to Newport before seeing her, but once there he harangued her for not writing. In a long letter he explained her importance to his life and work, setting up a pattern he would follow throughout their marriage. "I find myself always mentally turning to you for corroboration or approbation when a new thought or plan occurs to me—even when, as I said last time, the plan seems that of turning away from you. This is so invariable, so automatic in its precision that it often amuses me to catch myself doing it. It shows how deeply a man needs the corroboration of the woman whom he respects, how something is missing till he gets it." He also confessed his anxiety about brother Bob's arrival.[103] Bob would haunt them in years to come.

Exhausted from her year's teaching duties, from Boston's heat, from William's erratic behavior, and perhaps even from thinking about the crucial role she now played in his work, Alice decided not to see him that summer. Though she promised to write, she refused to say when she would see him again. William defied her wish. "Your recommendation that I should not come to see you for an indefinite time but communicate with you by letter after my return is slightly amusing. Don't think either that you shall escape the future rides which it is your doom to take with me."[104]

He sent Alice drafts of his essays, one on the mystery of existence and another on optimism and pessimism, claiming that he thrived on uncertainty, testing, and difficulty. The attitude that most characterized him was one that "always involves an element of active tension, of holding my own as it were, & <u>trusting</u> outward things to perform their part so as to make it a full harmony, but without any <u>guarantee</u> that they will."[105] While William ate lobsters and drank beer at a Cambridgeport hotel, Alice pondered his words. Marrying William James would mean a commitment to his evolving work. It would be impossible to live with this man without pledging herself to him, body and soul, and while she believed in sacrificing for great causes, she must be very careful, because this commitment would be for life.

Weary of his courtship with its metaphysical agonizing, Alice acted: she decided to leave William for the summer. With her youngest sister, Margaret, she went to Sabrevois, a small village outside Montreal near the Richelieu River. The village was characteristically French, family centered with a Catholic church at its heart. A picture in her photo album shows Judge and Madame Papineau of Montreal, either a couple recommended to Alice before she went or friends she made while there.[106] Although Alice was an outsider in Canada, she was physically removed from her tormenting suitor. She loved William, but she feared marriage would tax his unstable character.[107]

Alice's imminent departure plunged William into the agony and tension he claimed were the core of his inner self. Her words were "like the touch of red hot coal to gunpowder."[108] He begged her to reconsider and go to Beede's Hotel in the Adirondacks, but, unlike William, when Alice made up her mind, she was immovable. Her feelings ran deep, and they had been bruised by his repeated handling. Alice went to Canada and William to Beede's, where Alice's sister Mary and their aunt Susan Webb, Eliza's older sister, spent the summer. Every night he walked into town for the mail, but no letters from Alice came.[109] In mid-September he told Bob their relationship was over.[110]

On 23 September Alice saw William again. She had a cold, and her face was pale.[111] While he did not expect her to see him often, somehow the courtship resumed. Who knows now how Alice regained her confidence in this eldest James son? She loved William: he represented a chance for her to experience emotional and physical passion. Perhaps she decided that he differed enough from her father that she need not fear marrying him. Swedenborg insisted that charity is not just a right religious practice, it is the centerpiece of what it means to be good. Those who faithfully practice charity channel God's divinity into their lives and into the lives of those around them.[112] Her marriage would demand extraordinary acts of charity, thus allowing her to manifest God's presence daily. Whatever the reasons, however, the decision was made, and Alice cast her lot with the Jameses.

In 1877 William sent Catherine Havens a Christmas present. The two previous years he had given her a subscription to the *Atlantic Monthly*, but this time he sent a seltzer water bottle handpainted with flowers by Mrs. Celia Thaxter, a contemporary American poet. It was William's final gift to Catherine.[113] Perhaps it was meant as a farewell, because in February 1878 William insisted he and Alice should not sacrifice the love and faith they had in one another.[114]

Few women could have tolerated William James's courtship, the suit of a man who could not love without analyzing every nuance of the relationship. The fragments he sent Alice of his nascent ideas were complex, even convoluted, but she had been exposed to the best minds of the era at the Radical Club and had participated in, or at least heard debates on, the latest ideas in theology, philosophy, and natural science. Further, some of his evolving beliefs matched hers: William's insistence on acting for the good came close to her perfectionist convictions. Alice held her breath as she watched William puzzle out what they meant to one another. If she were wrong about his essential goodness and stability, she would be doomed to repeat her mother's tragic mistake.

Alice gambled when she married William, as there was no certainty he could cope with the demands of a wife and family, but she was not gambling financially. She knew that Henry and Mary James would make some provision for their eldest son and his family should William prove unable to earn a living. By 1878 Mary James was weary of William's emotional demands, so she welcomed his engagement to Alice Howe Gibbens. But more even than financial security, important though that must have been to her, Alice saw in William the chance for a love affair. She might experience the kind of romance found only in fairy tales and sentimental novels.

On Friday, 10 May 1878, Alice and William became engaged. She took the chance that their future life together would be happy, not tragic. Preserved in the James family papers is a one-word note to Oliver Wendell Holmes Jr. penned on 13 May 1878 and signed by Alice Gibbens and William James: "Engaged!"

4 Alice in Jamesland

WHILE MARY AND HENRY JAMES SR. had already made it clear they would be delighted if Alice undertook the task of marrying their eldest son, Henry James Jr. also welcomed her. No one knew William's intense physical and intellectual hungers better, hungers Alice would have to appease. Henry told Alice that William was "sensibly improved," which probably meant that he was no longer suicidal or severely depressed. Gently, he warned Alice that in marrying William she was taking on not only a man whose past emotional history could at best be labeled unstable but the entire James family. Her vocation would be a wider one than she might have imagined: "I have an idea, too, that since I left America he [William] has sensibly improved. . . . I hope you are seeing a good deal of the rest of them—for I hold it to be part of the bargain that you are engaged, more or less, to the whole family."[1]

William's youngest brother, Bob, wrote to Alice from Wisconsin as soon as he heard the news: "I can conceive of his vision as only being realised among the goddesses." Like Henry, he suggested that Alice would have to be responsible for more than one James: "I owe very much more to Willy than is the lot of most men to owe a brother and it is a pleasant thing for me to believe that in time to come I may be allowed to owe his wife a great deal also."[2] Wilkie also welcomed Alice warmly. He considered William's

54

engagement to be the most important event that had ever happened in the James family. He knew how deeply his brother cared for Alice: "Willie was a born martyr, and if you had not reciprocated his affection, he would have loved you I firmly believe until the end of his life: he would in all moral aspects have been wedded to your being."[3] There remains no record of a welcoming letter from sister Alice. At the same time the engagement was announced she took to her bed.[4] Mother Mary told Bob that her daughter's illness was "'a nervous breakdown of a very serious character—an aggravated recurrence of her old troubles.'"[5]

If she hadn't already realized just how high a place the James family held in Cambridge and Boston society, Alice must have known they were an important family within weeks of announcing her engagement. There were brilliant elements in her union. No less a personage than Harvard's president, Charles William Eliot, with his wife, Grace Hopkinson Eliot, called on her to extend their congratulations.[6] Though Alice came from an unknown family in unknown Weymouth, no one, perhaps not even her future sister-in-law (whose thoughts were never officially voiced), objected to her marrying William.

Alice's childhood friend Kate Putnam, still in California and now Mrs. John Hooker, visited Cambridge the month before the wedding. Kate found Alice beautiful and lively, even prettier than her younger sister Mary.[7] Alice would make a lovely bride.[8] Elizabeth "Bessie" Glendower Evans, who knew Alice during the 1880s, described her thick, soft hair, her great, deep eyes, her heavy features, and her youthful, "wild-rose complexion," a combination that together made her quite beautiful.[9] Kate tried to persuade Alice to marry before Kate went home to California. The child who befriended Kate in 1856 had become a remarkable woman. "In fact, I am in love with her, and quite envy Dr. James," Kate announced to her sister Minnie.[10] Alice planned an autumn wedding, but the couple decided to move the date forward to 10 July, perhaps so William could not change his mind one last time, or perhaps because Alice had misgivings about leaving her mother and sisters and did not want to wait any longer to make this momentous change, or perhaps even so Kate could attend.

Despite her lively manner Alice showed the sobriety that had characterized her as a teenager. As she rushed to prepare for the ceremony she was glad to be busy, "for the leaving home and solemn change makes these last days very grave ones," she told Whittier.[11] She hoped to take William to meet her friend before the wedding, but at the end of June she wrote to decline the poet's invitation. The ceremony was imminent: there was no time left for a final visit to Amesbury.

On 10 July 1878 Alice and William were married at the 153 Boylston Street home of her grandmother Mary Gibbens, still a prominent member of the Chauncey Street First Church. Most weddings during this era took place in the bride's home or the home of one of her relatives. As Eliza Gibbens still lived in rented quarters in Cambridge and sister Alice remained ill, the elder Mrs. Gibbens's home was the practical choice for a parlor wedding. Rufus Ellis, who had shepherded Daniel Gibbens through his stormiest years, married them, William paying him $25. Mary and Henry James Sr. were on hand to give their blessings, but none of William's siblings attended. No pictures remain of the ceremony. Nineteenth-century brides were not usually photographed on their wedding day, and also all her life Alice disliked having her photograph made. Years later she confessed to weighing 180 pounds that day, while William weighed less than 140.[12]

After the brief morning ceremony the newlyweds boarded the afternoon train to New York, where they stayed in the Windsor Hotel for a night.[13] The next day the couple went by rail to Saratoga Springs, to the newly renovated Grand Union Hotel, a resort hotel in the European style.[14] It had an enclosed court with elm trees and vast marble floors. William had reserved a room there for his bride, a luxury for a woman who had lived in modest pensions and boardinghouses for years.[15] They spent another night at the Fort William Henry Hotel on Lake Champlain, where William left his brushes and slippers behind, perhaps because he was so excited at his wife's closeness.[16] Years later William recalled how they truly came to know one another when they were finally alone at Putnam Camp in Keene Valley.[17]

The honeymoon was a long one: William had the summer free, and Alice had left her paid work forever. After they left Putnam Camp they boarded at Beede's Hotel, which commanded a view of Mt. Marcy, "the Giant of the Valley," and Dix's Peak (now Dix Mountain). This large, two-story building had a wide veranda for enjoying the spectacular scenery.[18] Keene Valley, located along the East Branch of the Ausable River, provided an unspoiled locale for this too short interlude in their lives.

Heavily wooded with spruce, hemlock, pine, and hardwoods, the area has a striking combination of valleys and rugged mountains. The newlyweds took long walks through landscapes threaded with massive rocks and deep green foliage. The valley made a habitat for abundant fauna: white-tailed deer, river otter, bobcat, snowshoe hare, moose, porcupine, beaver, red fox, black bear, and many songbirds.[19]

By July the black flies, mosquitoes, and midges had abated, allowing the honeymooners to spend hours outside without being eaten alive.[20] They spent their days reading, swimming, and walking, Alice often wearing a green plaid dress and laughing at William, her nostrils dilating.[21] Sometimes the honeymooners climbed down from a roaring waterfall and then walked across Dixwell's Folly Brook (which William later called "our old brook") to Chapel Pond Road.[22] One evening they sat on a fallen tree near Sandy Gap Brook, blew out the lantern, and returned to camp late.[23] Having finally committed himself, William became an impetuous and ardent lover, indulging in an intense physicality that counterpointed his mind's frenetic pace.

In the evenings Alice helped her husband with his work. Since his eyes were still weak, he dictated essays and letters to his wife. She was both an amanuensis and a respondent, allowing him to further define his evolving ideas. One article, begun before they married but still in progress, was "The Sentiment of Rationality," which appeared the next year in *Mind: A Quarterly Review of Psychology and Philosophy*, a British journal edited by George Croom Robertson. In this essay William defends the needs of our logical natures to philosophize, to find a metaphysics that provides both unity and clearness in its explanations of reality. Toward the end he concedes that persons of deep religious convictions could cut through metaphysics by searching in the heart rather than the head. "To religious persons of every shade of doctrine moments come when the world as it is seems so divinely orderly, and the acceptance of it by the heart so rapturously complete, that intellectual questions vanish, nay the intellect itself is hushed to sleep."[24] He saw these convictions in his wife, telling his brother Bob on the eve of his wedding that he took Alice for her moral more than her intellectual qualities.[25] She joined his lifelong efforts to explain reality and truth, focusing them through her own uncompromising humanitarian lens.

But she may have done more than provide a moral lens. Longtime James family friend Francis James Child claimed that William began his great work, *The Principles of Psychology*, on their honeymoon, but he did not begin it alone. Alice was immediately central to this important project. Child told a friend, "'William has already begun a Manual of Psychology—in the honeymoon;—but they are both writing it.'"[26] William claimed she loved learning about the latest research in behavioral psychology, new to her and quite different from what he teasingly called her mystic and superstitious beliefs.[27] Her metaphysical concerns tended toward the spiritual and toward immortality. Many of her ideas came from Swedenborg, and some of them became part of her husband's mental map, though it would be years before he explored religious belief seriously. Like Swedenborg, William came from a scientific (and in his case a behaviorist) position before turning his analytical lens on religious philosophy.

While Beede's had far fewer guests than he anticipated that summer, Alice and William knew a few of them. Katharine Hillard, her sister, and a Miss Cushing were all in residence at the hotel. They helped make a lively group at mealtimes. Toward the end of their honeymoon Alice invited Kate Putnam Hooker to visit. She told Kate that while it had rained most of the time, she was utterly content, despite the weather.[28] Together, Alice and William told Francis Child, "We have spent a ballad-like summer in this delicious cot among the hills. We only needed crooks and a flock of sheep. I need not say that our psychic reaction has been one of content—perhaps as great as ever enjoyed by man. (and woman! A.H.J.)."[29]

On their return to Boston in early September the couple boarded at Sarah Humphrey Hale Hanks's boardinghouse on the corner of Harvard and Ware streets. They bought furniture for their rooms, but for the most part Alice was free of household duties.[30] Her transition into what would become an exhausting life was an easy one; she had time to pay calls, read, study, and admire her wedding gifts.[31] She and William visited his family frequently, and sometimes sister Alice strolled to their quarters at dusk.

Soon after their return William delivered a series of six Lowell Lectures entitled "The Brain and the Mind," talks based on ten lectures he had given in Baltimore in February 1878. The bulk of the outlines and fragments of extant drafts are in Alice's hand. These manuscripts contain ideas on consciousness as an efficacious evolutionary adaptation; notes on habits, perhaps deriving from the habits he was currently establishing as a result of married life ("The great thing is to form habits which then leave hemis[pheres]. free for higher flights and in forming habits, to keep them unbroken"); ideas about the operations of memory in the nervous system and the mind; and a description of a positive view of consciousness as an active entity that transcends determinism.[32] To say that she was only an amanuensis confines Alice to the role of a mute stenographer, but her inquisitive mind must have expanded and responded to the ideas William presented.

It did not take long for sister Alice to echo her parents' praise for wife Alice. Sister Alice taught history for the Society to Encourage Studies at Home, a correspondence school for women, and she had a rewarding relationship with Katharine Peabody Loring, a fellow teacher.[33] Her illness during the spring when William announced his engagement may not have been caused by jealousy. Though thirty-year-old sister Alice disapproved of many of her peers' marriages, she thought this union entirely satisfying. She found that the marriage added a welcome dimension to her life, and she asked her friend Fanny Morse why she had never congratulated her on "the real joy that has been brought into life by William's marriage? A happiness which grows day by day as we get to know our dear Alice better. How William can have been so fortunate a man, we cannot any of us understand, and he himself less than the rest of us. She is a healthy lovely being so sweet and gentle & then with so much intelligence besides."[34] Sister Alice sensed that her brother's wife, who was sane and perennially positive in her outlook, would balance her brother's tendency toward depression.[35] No other immediate member of the James clan could do that for William.

These months allowed Alice to know her in-laws better and also learn more about William's work. She continued reading to him and taking dictation in the evenings. While rapidly changing urban American culture moved toward a separation of home and work, sometimes resulting in a male-gendered public sphere and a female-gendered private one, this was not always the case. Many Victorian husbands and fathers were closely involved with daily family life, as was so with the Jameses.[36] In addition, because William worked at home it was natural for him to share his ambitious intellectual projects with Alice. While he was not a relaxed or an easy man, her calming presence reduced his anxiety, and she in turn gained an understanding of recent developments in psychology and other intellectual matters, a substitute for the Radical Club's heady atmosphere.

Personal and professional finally merged as William found new directions for his work. While he had published forty-odd reviews and essays in the decade before his marriage, in 1878 he published three important articles setting forth the seeds of his life's work. Just a month before his marriage he signed a contract with New York publisher Henry Holt to write a book on psychology for the firm's American Science series. He anticipated finishing it by 1880, although Holt hoped for it sooner.[37] During the next decade Alice and the children she bore would provide William with ample opportunities to study human growth and development. His life and work finally had come into focus.

In January 1879 another article revealing his rapidly evolving ideas appeared in *Mind* entitled "Are We Automata?" Except for the first four pages, the fifteen-page manuscript is in Alice's hand, with an occasional note inserted by William, making a kind of visual tapestry.[38] In this essay William inveighs against the doctrine of contemporaries like Thomas Huxley and William Clifford, who tended to treat humans as decapitated frogs whose reflex actions become automatic.[39] Feelings, which William equated with consciousness, simply had no place in these scientific investigations. William claimed instead that the conscious mind exerted a powerful force on reality. There is something in us that understands our own experiences: "This self-transcendency of data constitutes the conscious form. Where we suppose it to exist we have mind; where mind exists we have it." He held out, as he would time and again, for the possibility that human will could transform an individual's life positively. We must view "our conscious selves as actively combating each for his interests in the arena and not as impotently paralytic spectators of the game."[40] In the manuscript the last sentence is in Alice's hand.

Other early manuscripts show her hand weaving in and out of the ruled pages, a testimony to her willingness to help her husband succeed in his labors. In addition, their evenings spent working together may have helped him develop automatic, habitual customs that, paradoxically, allowed him more latitude for creativity. But unlike Dorothea in George

Eliot's *Middlemarch*, whose help with her husband's *Key to All Mythologies* yielded her no happiness, Alice was rewarded by William's passionate love. His essay "Absolutism and Empiricism," published in *Mind* in 1884, in which he insists on the role our emotional as well as our logical faculties play in constructing philosophies, asserts, "Husband makes, and is made by, wife, through marriage; one makes other, by being itself other; everything self-created through its opposite."[41] There could be no better description of what marriage did for both.

Just ten months after their wedding, on 18 May 1879, Alice gave birth to a son, whom they named Henry James and promptly nicknamed Embry (he was later known as Harry). He weighed eight and a half pounds. The delivery went well, and she nursed the baby successfully. A picture taken soon after his birth shows Alice's smooth face and her hair pulled into a double bun; she holds a healthy-looking baby with abundant dark hair. Her old friend Whittier congratulated her: "The best that I could wish for thee has come, with the beautiful spring."[42] With her first child, however, came changes in her marriage. Alice subscribed wholeheartedly to nineteenth-century idealizations of motherhood, taking on the role with relative ease. Even liberal commentators like Mary Tyler Peabody (Mrs. Horace Mann), who thought the unmarried state could be better for women because they would be able to develop themselves more fully as human beings, thought all women were inherently maternal. A woman without a maternal instinct, married or single, was abnormal.[43] Alice now had a definite purpose and a sense of security that came from this all-absorbing, socially mandated task.

In the first weeks after their son's birth, one or the other parent sometimes became short-tempered. William could do little reading or writing at night, as his eyes were still weak, but Alice had little free time to help him. Although this change in a routine just established disturbed her husband, she held her own when William lost his temper, even shouting back at him on occasion.[44] Given the couple's intelligent minds and strong wills, plus their shared aspirations for William's career, a certain level of conflict was inevitable. Alice occasionally erupted when she was fatigued, as she was now. She had not lived with men since she was nine years old; now she had two to accommodate. She had her husband's total approval and emotional support, but she did not always have his patience or his presence. Though she was committed to her new life as a mother, that did not mean her adjustment was effortless.

In late July William left for three weeks, coming back in August to take Alice and baby Embry to a house he had rented on the Maine coast.[45] The change seemed to disagree with the infant, however, so William returned his wife and son to Cambridge. He then spent two weeks in Oak Hill, where he wrote a review of Herbert Spencer's *The Data of Ethics* and worked on his chapter "The Perception of Space" for *The Principles of Psychology*. He reclined on a ledge, watching the moonlight and listening to the sea crash on the rocks below. And he slept like the gods and looked for letters from Alice, who was walking now and having checkups with Dr. Putnam (who told her too little, she thought).[46] A dried brown fern William sent her that summer remains in the Houghton Library preserved in a small envelope, still curving and graceful.[47]

This pattern prevailed throughout their marriage: each time Alice gave birth, William left. When he disappeared periodically, sometimes briefly and sometimes for months, she returned to her comfortable matriarchal arrangement. Not only did Alice have help from two Irish servants, Jennie Sullivan and Annie O'Collins, she had devoted relatives who adored her children. In addition to Alice's mother and two sisters, her aunts Susan Webb and Nancy Jackson and occasionally her cousin Louis Webb lived with the extended family group. At the time they were still in rented quarters, probably at 11 Quincy Street.[48] Finally, William's absence was the most dependable form of birth control then available. Condoms (sometimes called "French letters"), pessaries (diaphragms), douches, and sponges remained widely available despite the passage in 1873 of the Comstock Act, which made it illegal to import, mail, or transport interstate any item designed for the prevention of conception or to aid abortion. Some couples also employed a form of the rhythm method, abstaining from relations for a week to ten days after the cessation of the menses, and while there would have been some limited success with this method, there was no guarantee it would consistently work.[49] No record remains concerning whether or not Alice and William employed any of these methods, though the record does show how frequently he was away from home.

During her husband's absences Alice also had her in-laws for company.

Soon she felt strong enough to take the baby to visit the James family at 20 Quincy Street daily. Sister Alice warmed to Embry. "He is a dear little soul and we have a delightful visit from him every day. The day seems quite lost if we don't see him."[50] Though she made the trips to Quincy Street, this new mother was tired: during the summer she had been ill, and the baby had stomach problems. When she remained weak that fall, sister Alice wrote her thank you to Fanny Morse for a gift of a baby sacque.

After his return that fall, William, like Darwin and other scientific thinkers of the day, became passionately curious about this child, using his observations to help formulate his ideas on sensation and reality. He told Fanny Morse that the baby "is the most interesting little animal I ever observed."[51] He was in step with his times, as childrearing had become more scientific after the 1870s with the rise of behavioral studies on children's health and development.[52] Gentler methods of childrearing were advocated in order to raise more enlightened, moral, and happier children, the kind of ameliorative philosophy compatible with William's belief in our ability to influence our own destiny positively. Though his children tried his patience, he was a loving father.

He left Alice and Harry again during the baby's first Christmas to visit his Tweedy relations in Newport, taking along the memoirs of Catherine II of Russia.[53] His thoughts of Alice mingled with ideas for a letter he was writing to philosopher Charles-Bernard Renouvier. "As I lay abed this A.M. . . . mitten [German, "midway"] into my strong and strange consciousness of your existence and essence, came the notion of an improvement in one of the paragraphs of my letter to Renouvier. So copy it but don't send it. When I get back, I can easily rewrite that paragraph.—Dearest, I do feel as if I were related to you by a peculiar kind of tie."[54] Already she was inseparable from his evolving work, always in tune with what William was thinking, writing, reading. Years after his death, as she and her eldest son, Harry, prepared an edition of William's letters, she suspected he did not know a particular French text, the *Réflexions* and *Maximes* of Vauvenargues, because he had never mentioned it to her.[55]

By January 1880 William had verbalized the difference his son made in his marriage: he complained that Embry prevented Alice from helping him.[56] On the other hand, despite his dissatisfaction at having to share her with his firstborn, William informed philosopher Josiah Royce that marriage had brought him a peace of mind he had never known. He wished he had married Alice ten years earlier.[57] When William traveled to Europe during the summer of 1880 to learn from the German scientists who were making advances in experimental psychology, Alice and Embry did not accompany him, so Eliza Gibbens invited her daughter and the baby to move back in with her during William's absence.[58] Alice realized that William must meet prominent men in his field, most of them in Europe, in order to advance his work. Furthermore, he could not categorize and formulate his observations without extended absences from home, when he could analyze and write up what he had observed. William knew that his wife rested better when he was gone, even though his absence made her the pater familias she had been more than fifteen years before. She was the acknowledged leader of the Webb and Gibbens women, who relied on her cool judgment, strength, and warmth.[59] The resolve she had acquired when she was a girl allowed her to juggle children, relatives, and William.

No sooner had William passed the coast of Ireland than he was overwhelmed by his separation from his wife: "It is the queerest renovation of my old lovesick days, and the queerest repetition of my old bachelor outward circumstances with the pervading inward sense of this wonderful & precious piece of property safe in my possession."[60] Once he arrived, though, he debated staying abroad longer. He asked Alice to assess their finances. If their bank balance allowed it and if his physical condition continued to improve, then it might be best for him to remain through the winter.[61] While Harry learned to climb stairs and talk (he could say "barn" and "mooley-cow"), William stopped in England to visit Henry and socialize with British notables.[62] He then went on to Germany. In Switzerland, vacationing before returning home, he had what he described as a "moral revolution," when thoughts of Alice and the beautiful surroundings made him cry: "Over the right-hand near mountain the milky way rose, sloping slightly towards the left, with big stars burning in it and the smaller ones scattered all about, and with my first glance at it I actually wept aloud, for I thought it was you, so like was it unto the expression of your face—your starry eyes and the soft shading of your mouth."[63] While William explored his emotions, Alice coped with Harry's intestinal upsets, her mother's sickness, and her own colic.

William did not spend the entire year abroad, even though his father thought he should spend a full year there. However, Henry Sr. knew how much Alice and young Harry meant to William. Henry deferred to Alice's authority, advising William to follow his wife's advice and showing respect for her proven ability to steady William's son.[64] Longing for home, William took a berth on the *Parthia* for 25 August.[65] Not the least of his reasons for his return was that he needed Alice's help. His eyes had broken down in Switzerland. He hypothesized an inverse relation between walking and vision: when he walked a lot, his eyes got worse. He needed his scribe desperately.

After his return to America William could not find separate lodgings for his family in Cambridge. Finally, he located rooms at a house in Louisburg Square, on Beacon Hill.[66] He again entertained the possibility of a position at Johns Hopkins University in Baltimore under President Daniel Coit Gilman, but that position never materialized.[67] Each time the possibility arose but he was not offered the job, he consoled himself with the fact that Alice needed to be near her mother and sisters.

As William's reputation grew, he relied more and more on Alice to negotiate family relations and crises. A speech he gave to the Harvard Natural History Society two years after their marriage entitled "Great Men and Their Environment" stresses that powerful individuals who alter the course of human history have to live under conditions that allow them to develop their full potential. In a Darwinian sense the environment selects these men: "And whenever it adopts and preserves the great man, it becomes modified by his influence in an entirely original and peculiar way."[68] Though he makes no mention of Alice or of his work in this speech, she had created an atmosphere where William could develop his genius. Despite the demands of pregnancy and childbirth as well as her service to the Gibbenses and the Jameses, she kept close to his work. When Thomas Davidson recommended a recent sociological book to William, Henry George's 1879 *Poverty and Progress*, a response to the outcry over the 1873 panic, he wanted Alice to read it as well.[69] If she did, she would have read an important text in the Social Gospel movement, a continuation of earlier antebellum reform movements, as George was one of the main proponents of social Christianity. The book was an indictment of the American social system and the Marxist system, too, and offered a solution to be achieved in part through a single tax.[70]

Although Alice quickly became an intimate part of the Quincy Street circle, as yet she and Henry James knew one another only through letters. The stout, balding bachelor looked forward to meeting her when he came to America in November 1881, hoping to find her "fat and brown & lusty."[71] Their initial meeting at Quincy Street went well: they liked each other.[72] Quickly bored in Cambridge, though, Henry soon left for Washington. During his absence Mary James died on 29 January 1882, so he returned and stayed until May, but still Alice saw little of him. She was pregnant again.

On 17 June of that same year Alice gave birth to her second son, William James II, or William James Jr., known as Billy. After the baby's birth William left for New York to see his publisher, Henry Holt; *The Principles of Psychology* was far from finished. From the Everett House, a hotel on Union Square, William shared with Alice his worries about his youngest brother, Bob, now very unstable. He could not stop drinking. William thought they should give Bob money and then insist that he leave them alone.[73]

When William returned from New York in mid-July, he complained that Alice's doctor, Emma Louisa Call, would not let him near Alice. One of the first five women admitted to the University of Michigan medical school, Dr. Call was a pioneer in the medical field, but Alice was open-minded enough to trust a lady doctor.[74] The nurse, Miss Lespierre, had stayed on to help, and William worried she might keep him from his wife's bed at night, so he left again immediately, visiting the Morses at Beverly and then the Tappans at Tanglewood. Late in the summer of 1882 he sailed back to Europe. Alice and the children remained with her mother, who had just purchased a house across from the Harvard campus at 18 Garden Street. The money the couple saved on rent helped pay for William's trips abroad, trips essential for his research.

This time, though, Alice not only had children to care for, she had Henry James Sr. as well. When he and sister Alice returned from a summer at Manchester, New Hampshire, he visited his daughter-in-law and grandchildren often, taking great pleasure in their company.[75] He thought Alice was sweet and the boys the most interesting children he had ever seen.[76] Despite these new interests, the aging patriarch declined quickly after the death of his Mary. Long a controversial public figure, writer, and lecturer, Henry Sr. had earned Alice's devotion. Both temperamentally intense, they shared a belief in William's genius.

That fall Alice considered doing without a nurse for the new baby. Perhaps she thought her mother and sisters would be help enough, but William was concerned that her health might suffer during this experiment. On 3 October 1882 he announced that she should try to find a permanent nurse.[77] As Billy was only a few months old that fall, Alice still nursed him. Physicians (and mothers) debated the best age for weaning, but most infants were not partially weaned until eleven months, so the physical demands upon a woman's body could be enormous.[78] Her nurse-less experiment did not last long, however. By October she had decided to find help. William feared she had impaired her health: "I only wish I could believe you hadn't quite used yourself up before you gave in. What you write of the day when [George Herbert] Palmer called and found you in bed makes me think it otherwise."[79]

During these trying months emotional support for Alice came from an unexpected source: Henry James Jr. In October she received his sympathetic letter from Bordeaux: "Abandoned by your husband who leaves you two Royces in his stead, you seem to me, dear Alice, very greatly to be pitied."[80] Josiah Royce was William's new colleague in the philosophy department, here from Berkeley as his sabbatical replacement but destined to stay. Alice was by no means certain she liked either Mr. or Mrs. Royce. Henry viewed her situation as unnatural, fearing she would feel bewildered and abandoned. She would need his reassurance in the weeks to come.

On a late fall morning in 1882, dressed in a black bonnet and black dress, Alice traveled by horsecar from Harvard Square to Charles Street, small Harry and baby Billy with her. Not long after Mary James's death, Henry Sr., sister Alice, and Aunt Kate had moved from 20 Quincy Street to a small brick house on 131 Mt. Vernon Street, on Beacon Hill.[81] While Alice slowly recovered from her second pregnancy and birth that autumn, Henry Sr. gradually grew weaker until he could no longer visit Alice and his grandsons in Cambridge. She must travel to him.

The trip was not an easy one for Alice. The horsecars, large trolley-type cars with flat roofs and open windows, were not always clean, and there was no heat in the cars to warm her and the boys on cold fall days. Sometimes called streetcars, horsecars had been one of the main forms of transportation between Cambridge and Boston since 1856 and were not replaced by electrical cars until 1889.[82] Once she stepped from the cars on Charles Street, Alice walked up the hill to her father-in-law's home. She brought the children in the morning to see their grandfather and then returned in the afternoon to listen to a report from Dr. Ahlborn, Henry Sr.'s physician. She made the trip many times that fall and winter.

Not only did Alice help this second father pass from the world, but she calmed sister Alice. The first task was a sad but rewarding one to her, as she realized how much she loved this Swedenborgian patriarch; the second task was more challenging. It took all her patience to cope with this querulous invalid. Although the two women had made friends three years ago, sister Alice remained a difficult woman. She thought her father had grown indifferent, showing no affection for her now.[83]

Henry Sr. prepared and signed his will on 21 November 1882, and after that he declined rapidly. Aunt Kate provided steady nursing care, but sister Alice still avoided the sickroom. Alice helped Aunt Kate do everything possible to ease the old man's passage. When he would not eat the calf's-foot jelly that Mrs. Gurney brought him, Alice proposed making jelly that he might like better. His irritability did nothing to dissuade her from her visits. At the end of November he had an attack of nausea and fainting, waking at times to take teaspoonfuls of brandy and water.[84] Alice listened to him patiently in his dark room as he tapped his cane on the floor with his crippled hands, his fingers too weak to grasp it tightly. He sipped mandarin orange juice but took little food.[85] Occasionally, he ate baked apples, baked potatoes, oranges, and bread and once even asked for quail, but most of the time he refused to eat. It seemed he was starving himself to death. Alice was angry with the doctor for trying to force-feed Henry Sr.; she called the doctor an idiot. She knew force would have no effect on this proud man, that his death must be his own.[86]

Though he refused food and had lost his will to live, Henry Sr. declared that he would not go until Providence appointed.[87] Despite his fatigue and general debility, he retained some of his old fire and energy. The doctor said that all his sleeping did not mean softening of the brain. When Aunt Kate said he was getting well, Henry Sr.'s response was "Ridiculous!"

However, the doctor's news, combined with Aunt Kate's chest massage, made him fall asleep contentedly, repeating the word "delicious."[88] On 13 December Alice stayed away, weary and fearful of disturbing sister Alice and Katharine Loring. Instead, she sent her sister Mary to knock at the door and ask for an update.[89]

As she nursed her father-in-law Alice nursed her baby. In late November Dr. Folsom advised her to stop nursing the baby on demand at night. No matter how much Billy cried, she should not feed him between 10:00 P.M. and 6:00 A.M. After three weeks of this regime Alice and the baby were both miserable. The same day that she stayed away from Mt. Vernon Street she made up her mind to ignore the doctor. "I concluded after much thinking that it was our own affair, Babe's and Mine, and so to the great joy of the poor little thing I let him nurse just as often as he chooses. He is content, and so am I. He cries no more, and is happy as he is well."[90]

Tired as she was, every night Alice sat up late to write reports to William of Henry Sr.'s health. She sincerely believed it was better for William to stay in England, and she hoped her letters would keep him abroad. Nursing one infant, caring for a toddler, and ministering to a dying man, she was fully occupied. William was not dismayed to miss his father's last days. Their relationship had been a loving but difficult one. For years Henry Sr. tried to convince his philosopher son of Swedenborg's truths, theological truths far removed from William's emerging ideas. Therefore, William let his wife bear these burdens in his place; he knew she could withstand them better. Sometimes, though, she vented her worries to her husband, confessing, "The anxiety about your father has kept me in a state of tension till now; not my least anxiety has been whether or no to write you. I hope I have done right. I will write tomorrow. Goodnight. Sleep well!"[91]

On 6 December sister Alice telegraphed Henry to come home. She did not want to face the aftermath of her father's death alone, and she wanted Henry, not William. The same day Alice expressed sympathy for her brother-in-law: "I grieve for your Harry in London alone with his bad tidings tonight."[92] A few days later she empathized with what he could expect upon his arrival. It would be a desolate homecoming.[93]

On one of her longest days that winter Alice dressed the children and walked with them to Harvard Square to board the horsecars for Boston. William wanted pictures of the boys and of Alice, though she disliked being photographed. When she reached the photographer's studio, she found the children's picture had not come out. She would have to have it retaken. She reboarded the cars and this time dismounted along Charles Street, by now her burdens even heavier, and walked up Mt. Vernon Street to number 131. This errand did not succeed, either. When she took Harry and baby Billy to their grandfather's room, Billy took one look at the dying man and cried. Henry Sr. weakly thundered, "'Oh, take him away!'" and then fell asleep.[94]

As Henry Sr. faded from the world, sister Alice took to her room, where her companion, Katharine Loring, administered large doses of opium to calm her jangled nerves, countermanding the doctor's orders that she not have it. The sick woman resented her sister-in-law's interference and was annoyed when Alice interrupted her tête-à-têtes with Katharine.

By mid-December Henry Sr. refused to take any food and did not even want water. When he awoke, he was startled to find himself still alive.[95] On 18 December he called out his last words, "There is my Mary." Aunt Kate heard them, but Alice was not there. She was in the next room trying to calm sister Alice, who could not bear to witness the old man's death.[96]

After Henry Sr. was gone Alice regretted that she had not told him how much she loved him. She had feared that this strong-willed, intelligent man would find her sentimental, but in the end that did not matter. She only knew how much she had cared for the person who had chosen her as his son's wife. Before his death she confided, "Oh William dear, your father and mother have been so dear to me, so endlessly kind to me and mine, so gentle in judgment and patient with my failures, and they do now so <u>belong</u> to me through you and the babies that I am losing a part of my own life in this dear old home of yours."[97] She was surprised to learn that Henry Sr. had asked Aunt Kate to give her his paper cutter and chest of drawers, things he used daily.[98] The patriarch's death had multiple meanings, emotional and financial, for his children, but to this adopted daughter it meant the loss of another loving father.

Alice represented William and herself when she stood next to brother Bob at the Cambridge Cemetery on 21 December as her father-in-law was buried next to his beloved Mary. A small group gathered while sods were piled atop the coffin. That night she lay in bed thinking, "And now the white moonlight shines over the two mounds, side by side."[99]

Alice felt empty.[100] Again facing a great loss, she had little time to grieve. She kept busy preparing Christmas for her family, buying a sled for little Harry. On Christmas Eve she tended a sick baby, but despite her exhaustion and depression she had a deepening, comforting awareness of a spiritual world.[101] She told her husband, "If one impression, stronger than all others is left to me from those days, it is the unutterable reality, realness, nearness of the spiritual world. Death to that man was as he said 'nonsense'—the change he panted for was more life."[102] This unwavering belief in a corresponding spiritual world was an unshakeable part of her personal theology.

The situation at Mt. Vernon Street deteriorated further. After the funeral sister Alice asked Aunt Kate to leave. She had found Kate destroying Henry Sr.'s papers, but animosity had built between the young woman and the older one for years. Although Alice was angry to see William's aunt treated this way, she felt helpless to intervene. She told William that she was determined not to alienate her sister-in-law. "Her laws are not ours, and her suffering should make us merciful. I don't think it possible that she herself can know how hard she has been."[103] The next day she repeated her thoughts, almost as though she were convincing herself. "Alice had decided everything. I think she rules Katharine [Loring] as well as every body else and Katharine has caught much of Alice's imperativeness of speech and manner. They neither of them have had any mercy for Aunt Kate." But she would try to befriend her sister-in-law for her parents' sake, "to be a sister to her if she wants me. I am finally sure of this: she is not made as other women."[104]

By December's end she felt her efforts were working.[105] She hoped Henry would ease the tension that had developed between Aunt Kate and sister Alice, and she shared those hopes with her spouse. "Alas for Harry [Henry] who comes tonight! He will need every kindly art at his command to smooth the troubled waters."[106] She intuited that he best understood his brilliant but difficult sister. As his father's executor he would have to negotiate and settle the will, which left Wilkie out altogether and made only a slight provision for Bob.[107] He also must help decide future living arrangements for Aunt Kate and for sister Alice.[108] Perhaps Henry did still the waters, because by mid-January Alice found sister Alice improved and on an independent footing.[109]

Henry arrived in Boston on 21 December but was too late to attend his father's funeral. Alice nearly missed meeting him. She had gone to Boston while Henry had gone to her home in Cambridge, so she stayed at Mt. Vernon Street until her brother-in-law returned from Eliza Gibbens's house. He had the worst headache he had ever experienced.[110] This second face-to-face encounter with Henry involved a small shock of recognition: she saw her own fatigue mirrored in a fellow human's face. She told William that Henry looked "dreadfully used-up. I saw him for a few moments in town after waiting a while for him to come back from Cambridge."[111] He looked strangely middle-aged to her. When Alice told him that no one had telegraphed William with news of their father's death, Henry was so troubled that he wrote to his brother the day after Christmas explaining this curious lapse.

Two days after Christmas Alice went to Boston to again have photographs of the children made for William. On her way back to Cambridge she stopped at Mt. Vernon Street. Henry made friends with the baby and insisted on escorting them to the cars. "Imagine my feelings as we ambled down Charles St. looking like a nursery in which Harry [Henry] had, by some fatality, been caught."[112] Though she saw his innate goodness, she was bewildered by the attentions of this confirmed literary bachelor. Henry (no longer a junior) tried hard to befriend Alice and her brood. At first his namesake, Henry James II, did not know what to make of this reserved uncle, who stared at him. Finally, the boy shouted "<u>Boo</u>!"[113] Later Harry warmed to Henry, reciting "The Owl and the Pussycat" to him.[114]

By New Year's Day Alice had switched in her letters from a comic tone to one of hesitation about her new relationship with Henry. She shared her doubts with William. "I think your brother Harry makes one miserable in a fine, inexplicable fashion. He is trying all the time to do his whole duty by me, but I know it is adverse fortune which thrusts me upon him, and though I try to temper myself to him and be as slight a shock as possible, I am constantly diverted by my want of success. How wide these differences of nature are, and how I thank God for yours—your nature darling—which shelters mine so warmly."[115]

Henry kept reaching out to Alice, even when she seemed intimidated by him. On New Year's Eve, after his visit to the cemetery, where he read aloud William's oft-cited farewell letter to their father, he visited her in

Garden Street.[116] He spent the day enchanting her with tales of his friends and fellow writers, Ivan Turgenev and the inimitable Gustave Flaubert, who was put on trial on moral charges in 1857 after the publication of his novel *Madame Bovary*, which was considered scandalous.[117] She thrilled at this firsthand report of these famous international authors. In only half an hour Henry awakened her intellectual curiosity, muted since Harry's birth.[118] Though she found Henry formidably reserved, within weeks Alice felt easier with him.[119]

With Henry's sympathetic aid Alice accepted the loss of Henry Sr. and continued her busy life. She enjoyed charades at the Childs' home, where the players wore the faces of animals in Paradise, perhaps a Swedenborgian exercise, as animals on earth would have corresponding spiritual counterparts in heaven. That same afternoon she patiently listened to gossip about Miss Annie Longfellow's evening visitor and to Mr. Paine's opinion of the conductor Sir George Henschel of the Boston Symphony: Paine thought Henschel the worst conductor who ever held a baton.[120] She saw Gilbert and Sullivan's light opera *Iolanthe*, and she read German writer Karl Emil Franzos's short story collection *Die Juden von Barnow*.[121]

Alice resumed her duties as a faculty wife, advising Josiah Royce's wife, who lacked Alice's social skills, on hiring servants and adjusting to Cambridge. Alice also counseled Royce on his teaching, telling William of the incident: "I shall give Mr. Royce a hint of that criticism about fast talking—he told me he felt so terribly in the dark about what the students might find wanting in his teaching. It doesn't amount to anything but I will pass it on for what it's worth."[122]

Neighborhood affairs, too, claimed her attention. She still had the same acute sense of justice she had had at age ten, when she agonized with the abolitionists. When the family dog, Sandy, caused a contretemps with their neighbor Dr. Wyman, Alice wrote him an angry letter.[123] Ailing Sandy had been so patient with the baby, letting Willy poke his fingers in Sandy's eyes, that Alice was determined to defend the animal.

Most of all, Alice found contentment and purpose in her life with her children, a new relationship that helped form a substitute for her romantic union with her absent spouse. Now the baby was a young bird, flapping his arms and opening and closing his fingers.[124] She promoted young Harry's moral development. At three and a half he was a bright, serious child with a mind of his own. She worried that her firstborn told lies, though William advised her that everyone tells stories. She saw the boy's strengths, too. He had "outgrown his old sweet ways and is become conscious and boyish."[125] Although he did not always mind nurse Lizzie, when confronted he went alone to his room to think.[126] William pushed his young son toward responsibility, telling Harry to take care of his mother while his father was gone.[127]

Though William longed to return to his wife's bed that winter, he realized he must leave her longer to her nursing infant. The couple debated when he should return. Alice thought that the book would go better if she were with her husband, so she suggested spending the summer in England, with or without the children, to help him with *The Principles of Psychology*. She was firmly committed to the project's success: "I want the Psychology to outrank in importance everything but your health."[128] If he did not want her to come to England, she offered him her sister Margaret's room at 18 Garden Street for a study if he came home. He would have to sleep elsewhere, though, as there was no additional sleeping room at Eliza's home. The house itself had drawbacks for someone with work as crucial as William's: it was very noisy.[129] Although she was concerned about the unsuitable living arrangements, Alice also knew that if William returned, she risked another pregnancy, and another pregnancy now would be difficult for both of them. On New Year's Day, 1883, she told him to stay in England. And she agreed with him: two children were enough.[130]

When Alice met her brother-in-law again, they held intense discussions on whether or not William should come home, conferring as conspirators who knew his welfare better than he did. When William proposed sailing home on 12 February, they urged him to stay in London. They knew he would be of little practical assistance during this time of emotional assessment and regrouping in the family circle. Henry advised his brother to complete his sabbatical, using Alice's feelings as one rationale: "Your wife strikes me as distinctly <u>distressed</u> at the prospect of your return, & she could not restrain her tears as she spoke of it to me today."[131] Immediately, William resented the pair's interference with his plans, protesting that he and Alice had worked out their arrangements long before Henry arrived on the scene.

Beneath these protests lurked an odd sort of jealousy. William had shown no eagerness to come home when he read his father's funeral notice in the *London Standard*, but now he insisted that if he returned it would be to everyone's advantage and would make no disruption either in his life or in Alice's.[132] He suspected that Henry and Alice were conspiring against him, albeit with the kindest of intentions, and his muted jealousy was for their imaginative, not their sexual, intimacy. In one letter to Henry his parting salvo—"You know my Alice tells me everything, & will tell me any messages you send"—summed up his bid for mastery.[133] Henry retorted, "Alice reads me & sends me everything possible."[134]

While William struggled to assert his marital control from England, Henry thought of Alice. Urging William to remain abroad, he suggested she spend the summer with her husband in England in the picturesque fishing village of St. Ives, Cornwall. The same day that Henry wrote to William with his advice for their living arrangements, 11 January 1883, Alice revealed to her husband a suggestively sexual response she had had to her brother-in-law, feelings she would not have acknowledged consciously. "My depression last night was not for your postponed return. No dear! it was the after effect of Harry who is to me like a strange perfume, very pleasant but leaving a curious lassitude behind. And he is so good!"[135]

William missed Alice more and more that winter now that Henry reaped the benefits of her soothing companionship. William hungered for Alice's presence. He thought that their marital bond had grown stronger during the time they had been apart: he felt they were now as one person.[136] He often referred to Alice's physical appearance. She was "so rich, & crimson."[137] He talked of her "angelically slumbering form," "her large eyed delight," and her "stately delicate beauty, with [her] magnificent black silk dress on."[138] When he thought of how she looked, he had thrills and convulsions.[139] Although he never said so, William was perhaps disturbed by Alice's implied erotic feelings for Henry. William's rhetoric became increasingly sexualized: "I shiver through & through with longing to be with you & never to leave your side, to melt into your being, to be rolled in your arms & silent in a last embrace."[140] His language of possession and control also increased, as he addressed Alice as his "Child Wife," infantilizing her while she tended their children.[141] However, Alice formed her own ties while he was gone, first with Henry Sr. and sister Alice and then with Henry. She was not to be so easily subdued.

In addition to missing her physically, William missed Alice's help. In February she sided with French philosopher Renouvier instead of her husband, surprising him a bit by her departure from her typical adherence to his ideas but making him realize just how strong their marriage was.[142] Finally, on 17 March 1883 William took passage for home on the *Servia*. He advised Alice not to meet him in New York, but he hoped they would find a private moment at Eliza's home.[143] He had advised her earlier not to give away any baby clothes, reminding her that accidents had already happened to them twice.[144] Henry remained in America until August 1883.

Henry's fiction following his stay in America bears faint but unmistakable traces of his encounters with Alice. "The Impressions of a Cousin," one of the tales Henry wrote following his American stay, published in the November–December 1883 issue of *Century* magazine, reveals her shadow. He adopted a female persona in this tale, that of an artist, Catherine Condit, who writes both her own story and the story of her orphaned cousin Eunice. Just as Henry watched his sister-in-law Alice, so Catherine Condit watches her cousin Eunice, who bears the imprint of Alice's steadfastness in caring for all the Jameses: "For her conscience is so inordinately developed that she attaches the idea of duty to everything—even to her relations to a poor, plain, unloved and unlovable third-cousin."[145]

The story's orphan, Eunice, after returning from Europe, is manipulated and betrayed by her financial adviser, Mr. Caliph. That had happened to Alice Gibbens while she lived in Europe with her mother and sisters: family funds shrank during her absence. Mr. Caliph, in trying to marry Eunice to his stepbrother, mimics Henry Sr.'s role in promoting Alice and William's marriage: "There are far too few among Americans who marry, that we are the people in the world who divorce and separate most, that there would be much less of this sort of thing if young people were helped to choose; if marriages were, as one might say, presented to them."[146]

Even the diametrically opposed philosophies of suffering held by Catherine and Eunice recall how Alice and her brother-in-law Henry dealt with the difficult members of the James clan: Alice comforted them and Henry wrote about them. Catherine's observations of Eunice suggest Henry's views of his sister-in-law after spending months in her company: "If I am not mistaken she [Eunice] is capable of the sort of affection that is expected of a good wife. The longer I live with her the more I see that she is a dear girl. Now that I know her better, I perceive that she is perfectly natural."[147]

The tale also contains a dry aside on the need for a woman to mediate the relations between men. Already Alice played this role of mediator in the triangular relations among Henry, William, and herself, a role Miss Condit (a conduit?) describes in her journal: "I don't think I care at all for the relations of men between themselves. Their relations with women are bad enough, but when there is no woman to save it a little—merci!"[148] While we don't know how much Henry knew of Alice's financial struggles to support her family after Dr. Gibbens's death, it seems reasonable to assume that William discussed at least the outline of his bride's economic situation with his closest brother. When Eunice, like the younger Alice Gibbens, suffers major financial reverses, she bears her burdens with dignity and resolve. At the tale's end Catherine Condit returns to the Rome she loves, leaving Eunice to work out her relationship with Mr. Caliph, just as Henry returned to England, leaving Alice to work out his family's relationships as best she could.

Like the psychic presences William later investigated, Alice reappears in two subsequent tales, almost as if Henry could not quite bear to leave her behind metaphorically, even though he had left her literally. In "Pandora," which appeared in June 1884 in the *New York Sun*, Henry includes an American family with three daughters living in Dresden. In "Lady Barbarina," serialized in the May–July issues of *Century* magazine that same year, the Dexter Freers economize by living in Dresden and Florence, just as the Gibbens family did a decade before. Alice's early years had captured Henry's imagination.

Henry may have learned from her and the Gibbens women details of the contemporary American Spiritualist movement, a movement he parodies in *The Bostonians*. Spiritualist Selah Tarrant and his wife live in a small home in Cambridge with their daughter, Verena, the prize in a battle to possess her. Henry uses his amusing characterization of "Doctor" Tarrant, with his waterproof and his sense of self-importance, to satirize the growing Spiritualist movement, a movement his brother would soon investigate from a purportedly scientific perspective. And like Verena's two would-be possessors, Olive Chancellor and her Southern cousin Basil Ransom, Henry and William both tried to control Alice that winter.

William had his own opinion of *The Bostonians*, an opinion consistent with his views of his younger brother's fiction. Alice often read Henry's latest work aloud to William at night, but even her persistent championing did not change her husband's negative evaluation. William thought that this novel could have been a bright, sparkling, one-hundred-page story, but instead Henry had "worked it up by dint of descriptions and psychologic commentaries into near 500,—charmingly done for those who have the leisure and the peculiar mood to enjoy that amount of miniature work,—but perilously near to turning away the great majority of readers who crave more matter & less art."[149] Alice continued to promote her brother-in-law's writing despite her husband's reaction.

Henry James Sr.'s two eldest sons reaped the returns of the marriage that their departed father had helped engineer. No matter how William had worried and tested Alice, she retained her good spirits and equilibrium. William now thought his wife's soul was the color of crimson, a word he used more than once to describe her, and Henry had met the family that would become his greatest resource in his last years.[150] Thus far, Alice had earned her bride-price. She would prove her worth over and over.

5 The Grief Child

THE END OF 1883 SAW THE death of yet another James: Garth Wilkinson James died in Milwaukee on 15 November at the age of thirty-eight of Bright's disease (a chronic kidney disease). Henry visited him in February of that year, and William visited him in October.[1] Alice had met Wilkie only briefly, but his death was one more in a series of losses for the James family.

On 31 January 1884, just ten months after William's return from Europe, Alice gave birth to her third son. William and Alice had had the "private interview" at Eliza's house (or somewhere else) William had longed for. Despite their decision to have only two children, she had responded to her husband's passionate need. She came through the delivery well, but her recovery was slower this time. William thought the baby was "Jewish-looking."[2] He asked Henry to help find an English nurse, and he promised to try, though he feared that a real upper-servant Englishwoman would prove to be a Tartar and expect a nursery maid under her.[3]

Months passed before William and Alice named their son. At first he had considered Tweedy, after his Newport relations, but he decided against it.[4] Lover of words that he was, Henry had pronounced opinions on the naming of Alice and William's children. He hoped that the child would have only one name, with no middle name squeezed in, and that it would be the child's own name, not a name that already belonged to someone else.[5] The baby became Hermann Hagen James, after the German entomologist Hermann August Hagen, a professor at the Lawrence Scientific School at Harvard.[6] As William admired the scholar but had no relationship with him, Henry could not understand this choice. He approved of Hermann, which he found pretty, but he protested that the middle name, Hagen, spoiled the first name.[7] He preferred a Shakespearean moniker—Sebastian, Valentine, or Benedict—and would have named his own child Roland James.[8]

Alice was not happy with Hermann Hagen: "'That name is like a hair shirt. Let's take it off the poor child and give him one that suits him.'"[9] The two older boys decided to call their new brother Hummy. The baby was oblivious to these rhetorical debates, however. With devoted parents, siblings, and loving Gibbens women surrounding him, Hermann was a happy, thriving baby.[10] At ten months he crawled like a turtle.[11]

Sister Alice wrote to Alice on her delivery of a third male. "I am sorry that he has chosen the inferior sex, though I suppose it is less on one's conscience to have brought forth an oppressor rather than one of the oppressed, and you won't have to look forward to evenings spent in Lyceum Hall trembling lest he should not be engaged for the German [a dance] or left dangling at supper time."[12] She did not hesitate to share her feminist sympathies with her sister-in-law.

William accomplished little that winter between a new baby and a demanding teaching load. His eyes still bothered him, but once again Alice could not read to him. Eliza Gibbens did her best to accommodate his needs at the Garden Street house, carving out space for a study for her adored son-in-law. It contained a small alcove adorned with a photograph of a bust of Plato and a corner behind his desk in which stood a cast of Michelangelo's *The Dying Slave*. With Eliza, Mary, and Margaret Gibbens plus one or two extra Webb relatives, a young Irish maid named Lizzie, and a pug, Jap, in residence in addition to his own group, William needed a quiet corner.[13] As spring began he told Thomas Davidson that he had completed almost nothing other than writing a new lecture on freedom of the will.[14]

Despite their responsibilities to their family and to his work, Alice and

William still had a profound love affair. What Alice gained when she gave in to William James was the chance to be loved as few women have been loved. His searing feelings came from the depths of his soul. He called her "bride-guide," "dearest bride," and "Beloved heart." He thought they must adjust to one another; the burden was not hers alone.[15] Even if he didn't believe in Alice's God, he believed unreservedly in what he and his wife shared. He was temperamentally incapable of doing anything halfway or dishonestly.

After moving into their own rented home at 15 Appian Way, the Jameses spent their summer vacation in upstate New York at Springfield Centre. William settled Alice and the three boys in a clean boardinghouse run by a lady and her daughter. They were near Otsego Lake, and the village was just nine miles from Cooperstown. The two older boys had a barnyard with chickens, which delighted Alice. All three boys would benefit from the fresh air. Cambridge was hot and humid during the summer, not a healthy climate for young children.[16]

William planned to stay with his family until the end of August and then travel home through Keene Valley, spending a week or so at Putnam Camp. In July, though, he returned to their quieter Cambridge home via Richfield Springs instead, leaving Alice behind with the boys and her youngest sister, Margaret, to help. He had taken time from his precious *Principles of Psychology*, still six years from completion, to edit his father's papers, but working conditions had not been ideal in Springfield Centre.[17] Relying on her opinion, he sent Alice summer homework, asking her to read Edmund Gurney's article in *Mind*, probably "What Is an Emotion."[18] In August he went to Saratoga Springs and then to a spiritualist camp meeting at Lake Pleasant, spending a night there before going on to another circle of spiritualists. He thought that most of what he saw, including a mesmerist performance, was nauseous, though he longed for Alice's opinion on the mediums' performances.[19]

The proofs of *The Literary Remains of the Late Henry James* arrived that summer, about the time that the family dog, Dido, chewed off part of a table leg.[20] William struggled with the proofs, determined to honor his father's memory though still opposed to most of his ideas. While he thought that the book's sales would offset the printing costs, the book sold dismally. William gave copies to Henry Sr.'s friends and contemporaries, but most did not even acknowledge the gift.[21] Still, Alice's father-in-law had left her a legacy of love, good memories, and the comforting knowledge that he had shared some of her convictions.

William feared Alice had immolated herself by marrying him. She had become an archetypal mother to him, and he longed "to nestle and vegetate" by her "sulphurous" side.[22] Although he felt guilty at abandoning her, he reveled in his time alone. When he visited Saratoga Springs, where they had stopped briefly six years before, he wrote to Alice of his memories, recognizing her dedication to him and his work: "Methinks I shall shed a tear tonight as I think of the little girl then buried, who buried herself, caring nothing for it, that I might be."[23]

Although Alice's was a metaphorical burial, it sometimes seemed a real one to her during the years of repeated pregnancies and childbirths. Only working with William kept her mentally alive. They were so intertwined by now that their lives were inseparable. He confessed to his wife, "I think of you all the time, of that ceaseless give & take, first thee, then me, of the intellect, of the heart, of worldly wisdom & practical sagacity, of which our wedded life consists, and without which 'tis well nigh impossible to live!"[24]

In September 1884 Alice returned to Cambridge with her three sons. William took five-year-old Harry with him to Putnam Camp in Keene Valley to alleviate his wife's burden. The fall brought more challenges. That summer Bob, who would become more and more of a care for the Jameses, had left Milwaukee for Boston just before sister Alice left for England. Bob telegraphed William to expect him that evening. His three-month job as curator for the Milwaukee Art Museum had not worked: the museum proved to be a very small affair located at the rear of a store. When Aunt Kate wrote to Bob's wife, Mary, she learned that Bob had had an affair with another woman, probably the main reason for his departure. Although Aunt Kate and sister Alice were so disgusted with Bob that they wanted nothing to do with him, Alice and William tried to help. By December 1884 Bob was living across the street from them and boarded with them for $5 a week. William told sister Alice that Bob made himself useful running errands and handling the correspondence concerning some commercial buildings in Syracuse the James children had inherited from Henry Sr.[25]

As if Bob's problems weren't enough to bear, in November diphtheria threatened Harry. Alice had reason to fear. Diphtheria was a serious and highly infectious disease. The bacillus for the disease was discovered in 1883, but an antitoxin was not discovered until 1894. The mortality rate was 35 percent and as high as 90 percent if the disease reached the larynx.[26] But Harry weathered this threat. This crisis over, William told Alice he had enshrined her in his mind: "Your eyes (like two brown moons,) your rich red smile, the rich graciousness of your manner, the faithfulness of your heart, the justness of your intellect, the morality of your life, oh!"[27]

The year 1885 promised to be an easier one for the Jameses. While their plans for a new house had been put on hold due to the expense of building, William was promoted to full professor at Harvard in March, with a five-hundred-dollar-a-year raise. Bob had moved to Concord, where he seemed to be doing well.[28] Alice could feel confident in their future.

In March 1885, however, Alice contracted scarlet fever. She was in bed nearly six weeks, quarantined in her room.[29] Scarlet fever is usually contracted by children under eight; it is unusual for an adult to have the disease. Initial symptoms include vomiting, chills, high fever, rapid pulse, sore throat, and, after a day or two, a scarlet-red eruption on the skin. The disease can damage the heart, kidneys, and hearing.[30] Alice sent the three boys to her mother at 18 Garden Street while she convalesced at 15 Appian Way.

Once the immediate danger was past, Alice enjoyed her isolation, the only true vacation she had had in seven years. Paradoxically, her imprisonment meant freedom to indulge herself in study and rest. Servants put coal, food, water, papers, and books outside her door, which had cotton stuffed in its cracks. She then took these offerings into her room, "like an antique leperess." When she was done, she threw her reading material into the fire.[31] William read letters to her through the door; one was a congratulatory letter on his promotion that delighted her.[32] By April Fool's Day William reported that Alice was recovering, looking like a rosebud.[33] Her ability to indulge herself without guilt when the occasion offered itself signified her psychological soundness.

Alice emerged from her cocoon to a cold and dry spring. She and William planned to take a house at Pocasset, on Buzzard's Bay, for the summer, where they all could recuperate from the long winter. In April William cleaned up the James family plot at the Cambridge Cemetery, arranging to have a pine tree replanted and the dead sweetbriar and barberry "renewed."[34]

But ill health struck Alice's family once again when Eliza Gibbens developed bronchitis. In addition, her heart was weak.[35] When doctors told her to seek a warmer winter climate, she made tentative plans to go to Italy in the fall with Mary and Margaret. Upon their return from the summer's holiday the Jameses would move into the Garden Street house to save money for their own house. Her plans for next year fixed, Alice looked forward to summer and warmer weather.

Alice's bouts with illness were not over, though. In early June, before the family started their vacation, Hermann contracted bronchitis and then whooping cough, which he transmitted to his mother through the droplets he sprayed into the air when he coughed. Like scarlet fever, whooping cough is a disease usually contracted by children, but Alice was weak from her recent bout with scarlet fever. This respiratory tract infection causes a deep cough that is followed by a high-pitched whoop. Before immunizations were available several thousand children a year died from the illness. Today children are vaccinated against whooping cough, but in 1885 the only recourse was to try to keep patients from becoming dehydrated, because the coughing spells frequently ended in vomiting.[36] William kept sister Alice abreast of Alice's and Hermann's health and sent her a few leaves from the James cemetery plot, where the roses, barberry, and new pine tree were flourishing.

In mid-June Margaret Gibbens and William took the two older boys to Jonas Cutter's rooming house in Pottersville, New Hampshire, to search for a summer home while Alice and Hermann recovered. Writing from a tombstone near the farmhouse, William told Alice of his search and of his offer to let Margaret take three-year-old Billy to Italy with the other Gibbens women in the fall.[37] He found a place at Jaffrey and planned for his wife and son to join the rest of the family in July.

In many ways William James was a wonderful father. He enjoyed playing with and observing his children. Though taking care of them without Alice exhausted him, he kept in high spirits. Billy slept soundly, and Harry was in peak form. William told Alice:

Active entertainment all day long, leaving no chance for pleasure of any kind,—enough to break the back of Hercules. I exagerate about Harry, who, it is true will take care of himself a little. I am just home with them from a neighboring pond, where we have been for 2½ hours, going in bathing, among other things. Harry has lost the fear of the water which he showed last summer, & splashes about splendidly, and it was a pleasure to see Wm's. little waddling form imitating him. Yesterday we had another good ride in the afternoon behind the old horse, whom Harry drives most of the time.[38]

William missed Alice, though, despairing that they would never enjoy one another again.[39] They had been separated for four months, their living arrangements constantly in flux. Their physical separations frustrated him, his hyperactivity increasing. Part of her ability to steady him came from the relief their physical relationship gave him, a counterpart to his mental activity. Their intense longing swirled around the sick child, William with a hard, unrelenting ache, a yearning, for her, and she eaten with anger and jealousy by something spinster Grace Norton had written in a let-ter.[40] But by late June Hermann seemed better, and they looked forward to resuming their marital relations.[41]

But on 29 June William returned alone to Eliza Gibbens's house at 18 Garden Street: Hermann was in critical condition. Alice expected "the flower of the flock," as William deemed him, to be taken away at any minute.[42] William declared himself ready to accept cheerfully what might happen; it would make the other children more precious to him. But Al-ice might not have been so resigned. Her crawling turtle, her little Jew, her finest flower—Hermann was her dear child and her heart's content. The child lingered nine more days, fighting for his life. Alice nursed him round the clock, never sleeping herself. After four separate convulsions, on 9 July he died in his mother's bed.

On 11 July 1885 Alice and William buried their small son beneath the little pine tree William had planted that spring, just a space away from Henry Sr. The tree had proved stronger than their eighteen-month-old child. At sunrise the day of the funeral the couple drove in their buggy out to Waverly, where they gathered pine, oak, and birch leaves, wildflow-ers, and ferns and grasses to decorate the tiny coffin. They nestled their

Hermann Hagen in a wicker cradle covered with white Canton flannel, placing leaves about his head, flowers at his waist, and ferns and grasses at his feet. Unitarian minister Andrew Preston Peabody gave a short service at home and then a tender prayer for the baby's unblemished soul at the graveside. The wicker lid was closed and covered over with more branches and flowers.[43]

Some stories are told so many times that they gain near-mythic status and hence become truth to listeners. That is what happened to the story of Alice's reaction to little Hermann's death. William thought she accepted this tragedy calmly, telling his cousin Kitty Prince, "She is so essentially mellow a nature that when the excitement is gone and the collapse sets in, it will be short & having nothing morbid about it."[44] That remark has been repeated so often that no one disputes it. William did adjust fairly quickly, though he spent a sleepless night at Garden Street at the end of July thinking of his son going through that "dark portal, & becom[ing] that changed little form gasping for breath on this bed."[45] The beliefs he had struggled to articulate during their courtship were now tested. Allowing himself no faith in a personal god, he needed to believe in a moral life that would let him go forward. "Ah! Alice, through it all it is good to feel the reality of the moral life, which at other times we press so little against we may doubt if it's there. This has brought me nearer to you than ever before, so near that it is almost absolutely near."[46]

However, William had spent only a fraction of the time with the baby that Alice had, and he never enjoyed the physical closeness to the child that childbearing and nursing bring. His analytical habits still operating despite his sorrow at the loss of a fine son, he watched his wife. He had already commented on how tirelessly she had worked to try to save Hermann. Years later he generalized from his observations. Containing the experience of losing a child in a box called "Psychology of Belief," he wrote, "If there is anything intolerable (especially to the heart of woman), it is to do nothing when a loved one is sick or in pain. To do anything is a relief."[47] Alice's reaction was different, but her psychologist husband never understood how deep her grief ran. According to Swedenborg, all infants who die are adopted by God and become angels, so she knew Hermann was in heaven, but that knowledge did not make her loss any less painful.[48]

She had always been self-reserved and self-contained, used to bearing others' burdens. She had borne more than her share since she was sixteen. Though William made her happy, she could not turn to him with her troubles. Eliza Gibbens loved Alice, but she lacked her daughter's psychological and physical strength, and now Eliza was seriously ill. Though Alice buried her sorrow deep within herself, it never disappeared. Her brother-in-law Henry sent her his deepest sympathy.[49] Unlike his brother William, who thought that his wife had dealt quickly and finally with her son's death, Henry knew that Alice would never fully recover. In a photograph taken around this time her eyes and mouth lack their usual brightness: she looks much older than her thirty-six years. Twenty years later her sorrow surfaced in a dream that she shared with William: "I have such curious dreams, and one unhappy thing keeps recurring. I seem to be wandering in difficult places (last night it was over a trellis work built above the water) and always I am carrying in my arms a baby, whose I know not, a weak ailing child whom I cannot get rid of or lay to rest."[50]

After the baby's funeral Alice, William, and the two boys retreated to the Lawrence family farmhouse in Jaffrey. It seemed best to be away from Cambridge. Both children were happy, thinking they helped with the farmwork. They kept busy all day about the place. Alice could not get Harry to come to supper at night until he saw the cows come home.[51] The boy worried about what had happened to his baby brother, but Alice reassured him that Hummy had gone to a beautiful place.[52] Later in his life Harry recalled little of his mother those months, except that she stayed with him and his brother Billy until they went to bed. She was drained of her vitality. Toward the end of August William returned to 18 Garden Street, leaving Alice and the children awhile longer in New Hampshire. Finally, she had her evenings to herself.

William did not feel well on his return to Cambridge. He, too, was exhausted from the summer's stress and sorrow. One August night he walked past their house on Appian Way, gazing up at the shuttered windows of the room where Hermann was born. He thought of how quickly it had all been over, and he again told Alice they were now closer because of the tragedy: "As I gazed up at the closed shutters of the room in which our little one began his career, and thought what a queer little fragment it was, how quickly over, and how near at hand his death-bed was, and his grave, an awful sense of compassion came over me, and of close drawing to you, as if we were indefeasibly one through the little life having proceeded from us."[53] In a curious twist of fate William found a real turtle walking in Eliza Gibbens's yard on Garden Street. He kept it for Harry in a tub in the cellar.[54] The pet distracted this six-year-old from the loss of his baby brother, but the living turtle would not distract the baby's mother from thinking of her own turtle, who had learned to creep less than a year before.

Even through her sorrow, lacking her usual strength, Alice helped others. She comforted William. "'I know how you are feeling, but a second youth, in some ways better than the first one will come as soon as the first one has passed out of sight. I know, for I have been going through it the last two years, and very black it made the world look sometimes. Now I feel a young <u>middle</u> <u>aged</u> woman, and it gives me back a sort of courage that I thought had gone never to return.'"[55]

At the end of the summer Alice returned to Eliza Gibbens's house as Eliza, Mary, and Margaret prepared to leave for their winter abroad. Their departure was delayed, though, when Mary Sherwin Gibbens and philosopher William MacKintire "Mack" Salter decided that they would marry in December.[56] Now Eliza would have only one daughter to take her away from Cambridge's cold winters. Alice and William welcomed the marriage, though he commented to her, "A woman can <u>never</u> understand a philosopher before marriage, — rarely after. I don't say that the same relation does not also obtain between a philosopher and a woman!"[57]

Trouble with Bob again loomed for Alice and William. He erupted in their lives at the worst possible times, this time less than a month after the baby's death. William received a letter from him on 2 August, a letter that made him think Bob had started drinking again. Alice proposed that they buy Bob's share of the James family properties in Syracuse, but William thought they couldn't afford the expense. He wished Bob's share could be placed in a trust, which would give Bob (and William) peace of mind.[58] They both coped as best they could as Bob swung from one extreme to another; they were exhausted from the ordeal. William confessed to Alice his anxieties over Bob's future, given his brother's mental instability.[59]

When Alice returned to Cambridge, her responsibilities distracted her from her own grief. She still had her mother as anchor; Eliza Gibbens's gentle, loving support helped Alice survive this difficult time. Harry started school that fall, writing his name on every available surface.[60] Grandmother Gibbens helped him learn to read and started him on his math, spending a few minutes with him every morning studying Warren Colburn's method of mental arithmetic. At the end of each lesson she rewarded Harry with a piece of candy.[61]

Alice spent Christmas 1885 without Hermann Hagen and without William, who had gone to Newport to be with the Tweedys and the Emmet cousins for the holiday, Alice observing the day with her Gibbens relatives. Christmas was not the important holiday it is today in American culture, but it took on greater significance toward the end of the nineteenth century. William was sorry he had not brought young Harry to enjoy being with the Newport children, but he thought to take him in the spring. After Newport he went to New York to visit the Walsh relatives and help Eliza and Margaret Gibbens off on their European voyage. Still hoping to secure a position at Johns Hopkins, he continued on to Baltimore. Alice endured a persistent headache that holiday season.[62]

In addition to entertaining Webb relatives and managing her household, Alice helped her dear friend Ellen Gurney cope with the death of her sister, Marian "Clover" Hooper Adams, Henry Adams's wife.[63] Suffering from overwhelming depression, Clover committed suicide by drinking the potassium cyanide that she used to develop her photographs. Ellen's loss was one more sorrow for Alice at the end of a hideous year.

Clover's sister Ellen had been a friend and admirer of Henry Sr. and a companion to sister Alice. One of the first friends that Alice made in Cambridge, Ellen was an intelligent, sensitive person. Both women were reserved and self-effacing. They shared books and poems, Ellen sending Alice a poem written by her mother, who had died at age thirty-six. When Alice was a newlywed, Ellen shared her aunt's recipe for potted ham. She recommended it highly for tea sandwiches: "Chop hock and dried pieces of ham: to a pint of ham one tea-spoonful of flour, 2 of mustard, & piece of butter the size of an egg, cover it with water, and let it scald. Mould it in a form."[64]

Now Ellen's thoughts were for others' suffering: "I have never felt so strong & rested and feel the strain of the shock is largely for Clover's friends to bear and we only long to shield them."[65] She told her friend not to grieve for her, though she needed her empathy—Alice of all people knew the aftermath of suicide. Ellen confessed her desperation at losing Clover, her failure to help her sister, her own "wanton arrogance and hideous blundering in playing ill my last, only card in a tremendous game—I blindfold—the universe—laws of nature, God, fate everything, pitying or not."[66] Though she was not ready yet, she clung to the thought of seeing Alice.[67] Now childless Ellen craved solitude, but later in the spring she and Alice took drives together.

In April William left for Washington DC, worried at leaving his wife while her mother and sisters were gone.[68] Eleven months after her child's death and without the support of her mother and sisters, Alice faltered. She rested on the couch most of the day, letting William's cousin Kitty Prince watch the two older boys, now ages six and nearly three.[69] She manifested classic symptoms of depression, and her collapse was not a short one. Though William assured her she would one day be rewarded for her maternal duties, she did not bear her burden as beautifully as he claimed the summer before.[70] Only the healing flow of time would allow her to return to her work of nurturing her family, promoting her husband's career, and maintaining her sense of self.

6 New Directions

AS ALICE SLOWLY RECOVERED FROM her loss, William's work took new directions. His first recorded interest in psychic phenomena came in 1869, when he reviewed a book by Epes Sargent, *Planchette, or the Despair of Science*. (A planchette, a triangular piece of wood mounted on two wheels and with a pencil at one point, was used for spirit communication. A medium would place one hand on the device, which was placed on a piece of paper, and then allow a spirit to move it, sometimes producing coherent messages.) William critiqued Sargent for his failure to conduct scientific investigations "in which pedantically minute precautions had been taken against illusion of the senses or deceit."[1] William visited a medium as early as 1874 to investigate her claim that she could raise a piano. Though he found her a deceiver, he wondered whether there yet might be some force unknown to us or if such accounts revealed "universal human imbecility."[2] Such psychic phenomena were of great interest at the time, both abroad and in the United States.[3]

Now William's interest in psychic events intensified. In 1885 he established a psychophysics laboratory at Harvard, and he also began experiments with hypnotism, which eventually became an accepted part of medical treatments.[4] Investigating both physiological and psychic phenomena, he helped develop a questionnaire on trance and hallucination that elicited

17,000 responses.[5] Like Alice, he took these matters very seriously, but he approached spiritualism differently than she did—in a scientific spirit, he believed. Ultimately, he wanted to find a middle way between religious and scientific attitudes toward psychic phenomena.[6] Through his mother-in-law he discovered a Boston medium, Leonora Piper, whose work he investigated for decades. She was a strikingly lovely woman, her beauty surely a part of her appeal.[7] He saw her before Christmas 1885 and thought she was honest; though he would have to pay her for her help, she was well suited for his research.[8]

After hearing of the medium through a friend or a friend's servant, Eliza Gibbens had attended one of Mrs. Piper's séances.[9] Eliza was impressed with this woman, who gave her many details about the Gibbens family, including her husband, Daniel Gibbens. Eliza told her daughters, and one of them went immediately; then mother and daughter suggested that William and Alice see Mrs. Piper. When Alice and William attended, Mrs. Piper mentioned a "Niblin" or "Giblin," words reminiscent of "Gibbens." They were also impressed. Not only did the woman hear from Niblin/Giblin, she uttered a variant of Hermann's name: Herrin.[10] Alice was sure the baby was calling to her from behind the gossamer curtain of eternity. She had not been able to reach her child on her own, but this medium had contacted him the first time Alice visited her.[11] Hearing this one name was enough to make her Mrs. Piper's disciple for the rest of her life. Years later she confided to her friend Bessie Evans, "It did make me reconciled and happy just that one flash of light over the undiscovered country."[12]

Mrs. Piper intuited just how effective communications concerning children (living and dead) were to mothers. In one sitting she advised Alice on how to deal with Billy's tantrums, and later she alluded to Hermann's ghostly presence at 95 Irving Street, the home where the Jameses lived after 1889, "how a certain rocking-chair creaked mysteriously."[13] And after Mary and William Salter's baby, Eliza, died in 1889, Mrs. Piper sent messages from the child, reporting that she died of diphtheria and that one of her last actions involved playing with her father's knife. Mary Salter tried to recall whether she had spoken to Mrs. Piper about the knife incident, finally deciding neither she nor her sister Margaret had mentioned it. She noted the grief that recalling the child's death engendered. "And, indeed, my baby's illness is something I can speak of to no one. Time for me only adds to its pathos."[14]

Just before Hermann's death William had grown tired of the whole psychic business. In June 1885 he told his skeptical sister that he found his investigations loathsome and intended to give them up the next winter and return to his work on *The Principles of Psychology*.[15] But now he continued his research, which had taken on new urgency for Alice. She was desperate to reach her baby, by now an angel. Swedenborgians believe that angels are very close to us, their physical being exchanged for a spiritual existence. Some angels even visit earth, according to Swedenborg. This conviction sustained Alice. Until the end of her life she frequently participated in séances, trying to contact her lost ones. She believed that she could receive messages from them with a medium's help. Ghosts and various psychic presences became important members of the James household.

William's turn toward the spiritual realm started while he was writing *The Principles of Psychology*, which was heavily influenced by contemporary work in behavioral psychology. In 1937 Horace Kallen, who had been William's devoted student at Harvard, asserted that Alice's influence was far greater than anyone had yet acknowledged. He also notes that because of Alice, William began to reflect his father's Swedenborgian spiritual beliefs, albeit subconsciously. Reviewing Ralph Barton Perry's 1935 two-volume biography of William James, Kallen disagrees with Perry's assessment of Alice's role. "'She was not only the exemplary wife and mother . . . she exercised a very positive intellectual influence in her husband's life. I am inclined to believe that the unconscious redirection of William's thought toward that of Henry, the elder's would scarcely have gone so far as it did without the conscious as well as continuous reaction upon it of Alice James; that role in the mutations of William's thought was far greater than that of many correspondents to whom Perry gives Chapters.'"[16] Although Alice's son Harry disagreed that her influence was purposeful, he was ashamed of William's psychic research and might not have wanted to admit the importance both parents attached to it. It is plausible that Alice helped persuade her husband to scrutinize the realm of the dead. During the winter of 1885–86 William, sometimes accompanied by colleague George Herbert Palmer, attended a number of Saturday "Cabinet Séances" at Mrs. Piper's home on Pinckney Street.[17] By the summer of 1886 William had summarized his investigations of her for the inaugural volume of *Proceedings of the American Society for Psychical Research*.[18]

In a séance participants try to communicate with the dead. The mediums conducting the sessions claimed that strong light hindered communication with these spirits, so rooms were kept dark. (Thus, participants were less likely to notice any suspect movements or actions.) Sometimes a voice spoke through the medium, sometimes a ghostly apparition appeared. Communicants might hear music, or objects such as a table might move for no apparent reason. Other means of reaching the other world included automatic writing or the use of a Ouija board. In these instances participants claimed they relinquished all voluntary muscle control. Their fingers were guided by the spirits, who then relayed messages. In *The Principles of Psychology* William deemed automatic writing the "lowest phase of mediumship."[19] Twenty years later he judged it less harshly as "one example of a department of human activity as vast as it is enigmatic."[20]

Skeptics took elaborate steps to expose the trickery practiced by unscrupulous mediums. Sometimes they conducted personal searches of mediums, though William and his colleagues tried to avoid such embarrassing procedures. Frequently, though, a medium's rooms were searched to see whether there might be secret openings in papered walls or carpeted floors. (In rented houses these searches were considered unnecessary, as it would be unlikely that the medium would alter someone else's house to such an extent.)[21]

Mediums were frequently women who invoked male controls, spirits who the mediums claimed dominated them and relayed messages from that other world. Mrs. Piper's control at that time was a French physician, Dr. Phinuit, a loud, aggressive man who lectured participants on morality.[22] Leonora Piper's popularity lasted for decades. William became convinced that even if other mediums were fakes, she was honest—the one white crow among all the black ones. Later, in his 1896 presidential address to the Society for Psychical Research, he declared, "If you wish to upset the law that all crows are black, you mustn't seek to show that no crows are; it is enough if you prove one single crow to be white. My own white-crow is Mrs. Piper."[23]

Many mediums used elaborate props to convince their clients of their veracity. They played trumpets or bells, used red lights, placed chairs in circles, sat in cabinets, anything to set an atmosphere conducive to seeing and/or hearing spirits. Mrs. Piper, however, was subdued. She did not levitate tables or exude ectoplasm, a viscous substance coming from the medium's body, or engage in other dramatic practices. She was the right medium for Alice, as Alice was too sensible to appreciate other worldly histrionics. Mrs. Piper became a lifeline for this bereaved mother.

On a starry night, Monday, 5 July 1886, Alice and William visited Hermann's grave.[24] From the knoll where their baby lay they could see the distant Independence Day fireworks. Here, Alice could see new life where a year before she had seen only death: the young pine tree was growing, the barberries looked healthy, and the rosebushes bore white roses. The couple renewed their marriage, which had been sorely tested by this loss. By August 1886 Alice knew that she was pregnant again. William had made his way back into her bed, with the inevitable consequences.

The James family went to Jaffrey, New Hampshire, again that summer to escape the heat of Cambridge. Alice's sister Mary and her husband came along, keeping Alice company when William left looking for land for a permanent summer retreat near Kittery Point, Maine. Aided by Harry, Billy learned to make wooden boxes, both boys sawing and nailing. Perhaps because of all his activities in the fresh air, Billy was less prone to fits of temper that summer.[25] By early August Alice told William, "'Hopefulness and youth have come back to us somehow.'"[26] All summer, as she contemplated her loss of the previous year, she continued her soft but relentless pressure to persuade William to think about religion and the deity who comforted her.

Finally, William announced to his wife, "I have really to take up with a new <u>God, your God</u>, who really is very different from my old one, and it is no easy thing to do right off. But with you for his prophet, what god would not prevail in the long run."[27] This decision, made at Alice's behest, helped shape the direction of his future work on religious experience. Nearly all his major works include a meditation on the "religious hypothesis," as he often called it. Alice probably envisioned a deity who combined Congregational and Swedenborgian attributes, but whatever her vision was, her husband sometimes took this deity under consideration.

Before Harvard's fall term started, William traveled to New Hampshire to look for land. This time he went to Chocorua, a village with a lake nearby nestled beneath the mountains. Nearby Mt. Chocorua was 3,500 feet high.

This scenic area was approximately six miles from the nearest train station and a four-hour train ride from Boston.[28] For $1,000 the couple could buy a house and barn with fifty tree-studded acres and a view of Chocorua Lake. William looked again and found a place he liked even more: seventy-five acres of land, two houses, a barn, a mineral spring, an oak tree, and pine woods—all for sale for $900 or less. One house had fourteen doors opening outward, he claimed.[29] He finally bought the parcel for $750.

Alice was not ready to leave Jaffrey that summer. While she planned to stay there until October, she returned to Cambridge for a pragmatic reason. "Today we are enjoying the most exquisite September weather, and the vacant house is so pleasant, the boys so happy I hate to think it must come to an end in one week more. This morning with ladders and big baskets hung from the boughs, Mr. Lawrence is gathering apples and Harry helps. Billy did till he said his 'back got tired of bending.' I should stay till October," she informed her sister Margaret, "but for Miss Farland who can only come to me the last week of this month and not again till December. She is to make over my serge which has been dyed black."[30] Her strength began to return, as it had done as a young girl when she was confronted with tragedy.

Alice eagerly awaited her mother and sister's return. Eliza and Margaret were still abroad, spending this past summer in Germany. Alice's brother-in-law Henry had entertained shy Eliza and her lively daughter graciously when they visited London. The pair had planned to visit sister Alice in Leamington, too, but she returned to London on 1 November, sparing them an extra trip. In the end, sister Alice was not able to see them, but Henry performed his duties as host most competently. All boded well for their voyage, but the trip ended in near disaster when the *Pavonia* was almost into the Boston harbor. On 19 October 1886 Eliza and Margaret Gibbens left Liverpool, where Eliza's husband had embarked for home a quarter of a century before. These fast passenger ships crossed the Atlantic in ten days in good weather. The *Pavonia*, though, grounded on a sandbar off Duxbury Beach. Passengers disembarked sooner than expected, climbing down rope ladders to the lifeboats. William told Henry that Margaret had fallen into the sea, where someone held her up. Henry worried, "Who was holding up her mother?"[31] But aside from their wet and salty steamer trunks, mother and daughter suffered no damage and arrived at 18 Garden Street in good health.

That same fall sensitive Ellen Gurney lost her husband. She remained in good spirits, but losing both her sister and her husband within a year took its toll. Alice told Margaret, "He failed so rapidly after they got him to Beverly that there was no chance to hope. She has been wonderfully patient, with a sort of pathetic cheerfulness that went to my heart,—and now the blow has fallen! It was their moving in to their new house which both had been so interested in. She has her brother and the children, but still she seems to me terribly alone."[32] When Alice returned from Jaffrey in early October, she stayed with Ellen overnight to comfort her, as the woman came closer and closer to a nervous breakdown.[33] Sister Alice also worried about Ellen, but she was thankful her sister-in-law offered Ellen so much comfort.[34] By now the James family depended on Alice's good sense and her ability to navigate most crises successfully.

This Christmas season it was Alice who traveled. She took young Billy to Newport to see the Tweedy and Emmet relations, while William stayed behind with Harry. In a letter written before Christmas, sister Alice sent her approval of this next pregnancy on the condition that the baby would be a girl. She wished the baby would have Alice's eyes and soft outline.[35]

By now, Billy, a high-strung four year old with symptoms of asthma, required a great deal of Alice's time. Taking no risks with her remaining children, she asked her mother, who had been visiting the Salters in Chicago, to take the child to Aiken, South Carolina, for the winter. A trip to a milder climate would be beneficial for grandmother and grandson, and Alice could await her next child with calmer spirits. Margaret Gibbens went along to help, and the trio planned to stay until May.

After their departure Alice had only Harry to manage. A serious, dependable child who loved his books, he was little trouble. That winter Alice and William read *The Iliad* and *The Odyssey* aloud to the boy; Homer's epics were among his favorites. The weeks before her delivery were peaceful ones: she was reconciled to the loss of one child and anticipated the next.[36] By 1870 couples had begun to limit their families—but not Alice and William.[37] She wrote to her mother of the peace she felt:

> I rest the live long day, most of the time in the library with William. All that soreness and stiffness about the hips and loins has gone and most wonderful of all, the hurried, harassed feeling that had grown

so uncomfortably natural to me, has gone too. I don't know myself, or rather I seem to have gone back many years to an inward attitude of quiet and reconciliation which has long deserted me. I mean to keep hold of this good thing and be inefficient if need be, but at least not again get tired to the very spirit's core.[38]

On 24 March 1887 Margaret Mary James was born, the Jameses' first daughter and fourth child, named after Alice's sisters. Alice labored for just two and a half hours; the delivery was an easy one, with no complications. Dr. Call assisted at the birth, giving her strong-willed patient very little ether. This baby was healthy, with a long nose and a resemblance to her mother.

Both Alice and William rejoiced to have a girl, as did sister Alice, who told her sister-in-law, "That 'he is a girl' delights me, it will be so good for the boys, elevate the tone of the house and be some one for me to associate with in the future!"[39] She knew William's tendency to study his family, so she hoped to return to "protect the innocent darling before she is analysed, labelled and pigeon-holed out of existence."[40] Sister Alice liked the name Margaret; she hoped the little girl would then be nicknamed Peggy, and she threatened to disinherit the child if she did not have Alice's lustrous eyes.[41] From Venice, Henry congratulated them on their "little feminetta."[42] William was already anxious about his daughter's matrimonial prospects: he began saving for her dowry.[43] Engrained as she was in nineteenth-century gender typing, Alice thought this baby was different from her boys. Peggy was unselfish, tactful, sedentary, and possessed of a beautiful voice, like her mother's.[44]

By the time Peggy was born, Alice and sister Alice were friends, a friendship that continued until sister Alice's death. Sister Alice was firmly established in England, Katharine Loring with her most of the time. A confirmed invalid who seldom left her rooms, she established a circle of friends and an interest in politics that sustained her. She held a sort of salon at her London lodgings at 7 Bolton Street, just minutes from Henry. A voracious reader, she became noted for her cynical, erudite conversation. During the summer of 1886 she began visiting health spas at Leamington, eventually taking rooms there in July 1887, because she had found the London scene too stimulating. In Leamington she could nurse her unpredictable health, receiving only occasional visitors. It was here that she began keeping her diary, a brilliant record of her life.[45]

Alice and sister Alice had learned to trust one another, each providing moral support for the other. Henry, too, admired and lauded Alice, but at this stage in their long-distance relationship he thought of her primarily as William's wife rather than as the prized friend she would later become. He envied William having a partner who could transact the business of daily life for him.[46] It was sister Alice who could best see Alice for who she was, an intelligent, thoughtful, loving woman with a great interest in literature and liberal politics. As different as the two women were, one with children and ensconced in a heterosexual relationship, the other childless and partnered with a woman, both were keen observers of people. They were friends, albeit epistolary ones.

After her removal to England, sister Alice wrote fiercely funny letters, sharing her views on people (longtime James family friend Grace Norton was a prudish spinster, cousin Ellen Temple was narcissistic). She shared her intense interest in politics, sending Alice a liberal publication, the *Speaker*.[47] Finally, she stood up for Alice's rights: she did not have to like Grace Norton just because William did. In turn, Alice confided in her sister-in-law, confessing her secret dislike of Harvard president Charles Eliot. A man of principle and an educational visionary, Eliot was personally reserved and sometimes even stern.[48] When she and William went to dinner at his home, Eliot told Alice he had seen her boys playing with two ragamuffins near Harvard Square. Distressed by his remark, she explained what really happened. "Then I remembered what you [sister Alice] once told me that President Eliot was always telling people something disagreeable about themselves."[49] And she complained of Mrs. Royce: "Mrs. Royce is as fierce and sharp-tongued as ever & their three children most unruly." She wrote news of Cambridge engagements and marriages, of people sister Alice had known all her life. She added a postscript: "I hope you burn my letters, with their gossip and stuff." Now Alice was part of the women's lunch club sister Alice had started years ago with Mrs. Ames, Mrs. John Brooks, and Mrs. Scudder, whom she deemed silly.[50]

One of Alice's best stories (her son Harry claimed she recounted stories in the most wonderful way) involved Elizabeth Palmer Peabody, noted Bostonian reformer and allegedly one model for Miss Birdseye in Henry's novel *The Bostonians*.[51] In an earlier letter to sister Alice she shared the tale, full of pathos and humor. Alice had spent the morning with Horace Scudder, who had just finished reading *The Bostonians*, and he told her the story:

> She [Peabody] was wandering about Buckingham St in search of the Baptist minister in whose church or vestry she was going to speak that afternoon. Mrs. Scudder in pity, offered to accompany her hither. A small audience had assembled and the poor old lady began her address: "I was 6 years old when I saw an <u>Indian</u> for the first time" and then she rambled on, slowly traveling down the years till her exhausted auditors had one by one all stolen away, and the winter twilight came to hide the vacant room from her poor dim eyes, as she sat holding Mrs. Scudder's hand, talking still. Her closing words were: "What I want is 300 dollars, and I appeal to you for aid in raising this sum."[52]

Two weeks after his daughter's birth William returned to Chocorua to prepare the place for summer occupancy. He estimated it would cost $2,000 to renovate the place to their liking. The house was to have ten large rooms and three small ones, not counting the kitchen and pantries.[53] In June Eliza Gibbens and William took the two boys and headed for Chocorua, where they stayed at Nickerson's Inn, leaving Alice and baby Peggy in Cambridge with Margaret. The baby had an abscessed ear, so Alice stayed in Cambridge until Dr. Clarence John Blake, Boston specialist in ear diseases, pronounced her out of danger, but she was anxious to have Billy in the country because he stopped wheezing as soon as he arrived in New Hampshire.[54] William took the boys boating and supervised the carpenters.[55] He looked for a horse, though he had one already, Lucy, and he planted potatoes. He ordered presbyopic spectacles for reading: Alice was too pressed to help him that spring.[56]

On 11 July Alice and Peggy traveled to New Hampshire, arriving tired from the trip. William journeyed back and forth through the summer from Chocorua to Cambridge, leaving Alice responsible for daily farm and household tasks. She was not unhappy, despite the work involved renovating a house and planting a garden, and she took satisfaction in establishing family routines. At the end of August William left for Putnam Camp for his annual vacation. Work slowed at the farm, as the carpenters were away, though the painter had worked hard and finished on 1 September. Some days the baby was demanding and fretful, so Alice napped when she could, adjusting to the easier rhythms of life in the country.[57]

Alice's practical letters, which she feared were dull, showed flashes of her insight into human nature. She was not upset when her hired man, Frank, and two women went to hike up Mt. Chocorua, leaving her to get her own dinner. She began to make friends among the neighbors and village tradesmen. Her occupation with practical matters turned her thoughts from her losses: these homely affairs were part of her honest essence. "The baby is much better, digesting so beautifully that I cannot think of moving her. I have been out of doors for nearly 2 hours superintending the strawberry bed and Ross's work—all as far as I can see, very satisfactory. The strawberry plants came yesterday noon, before the bed was ready for them," she told William. "I had Frank open the boxes, sprinkle them with water (they came packed in moss) and put them in the cellar for 24 hours. We had a great excitement about manure—Lord's man wouldn't sell—my book says good stable manure is an essential, but at the crisis of affairs Ross's son-in-law caved in and I have a cord of the stuff from him. Before night the plants will all be in. It is a cloudy day fortunately."[58] She could even keep chickens.

While she missed her husband, Alice was content when he was in good spirits; the depression that sometimes still plagued him was absent now, making her life easier. She reported no headaches that summer. After William left Putnam Camp to go climbing in the Adirondacks, she confessed to him, "I really pity you, to be receiving these dull lines from me—but I can do nothing better. You will know from them that we prosper especially the baby and Billy. We miss you tremendously, but I am easy in my mind about you, and so thankful to have you away. We jog on very successfully. With love always, my own dear William, Alice."[59]

As their Chocorua summers went on, Alice and William slipped into an easy routine, habits he welcomed because they allowed him to work. In the morning Alice went to the kitchen to make sure all was in order while William bathed in the cold stream nearby. They breakfasted at 7:30 a.m. The first weeks of vacation William tried to have prayers and a Bible reading after breakfast, perhaps at Alice's behest, but that habit soon vanished. William spent the rest of the morning writing, chopping wood, walking, or driving. Alice was busy with household tasks and the children, superintending affairs from her china closet—her "quarter-deck," according to Harry. The older children did lessons with their efficient German governess. Alice was particularly careful to keep the cook happy. Though her husband was the experimental psychologist, Alice had her own genius for understanding people. If she could discover what was on the servants' minds, she could keep them in order.[60] It was hard to find outdoor laborers, so at times she felt like a suppliant.

Despite the work, it was a nearly idyllic life, a summer Eden. On afternoons the family plus guests often drove out with a picnic lunch to one of Chocorua's scenic hills. More often than not Alice stayed behind, glad to have a few moments alone or with her mother. She longed to climb Mt. Chocorua, but she feared that her slow pace would hold the others back.[61] She could honestly tell Henry that things went well for her, though he worried that she worked too hard those long summers. Determined to play a role in his brother's marriage, Henry continued the solicitude for Alice he had manifested since he first heard of her engagement. Alice did work hard, but she enjoyed life in Chocorua. While she often disparaged her writing style (besides her innate reserve, the need to appear modest was a nineteenth-century rhetorical convention), she mused on the peace and poetry she found in these mountains. She told William, "'The land is so mysterious, purple, brown and gray; sad too in a lofty compassionate way as if the secret of its own sorrows had long since ceased to burden its deep heart.'"[62]

Even before the first summer and the renovations were over, friends and relatives sought out the companionable Jameses at Chocorua. The Gibbenses and Salters came and went regularly. In addition to William's Harvard colleagues, James relations and Cambridge neighbors would arrive, sometimes staying a week or more in the roomy house. Usually, Alice loved company and became animated when entertaining guests she liked. She had antipathies, though.[63] When a Mr. Merriman and his wife and their friends stopped by looking for William, Alice "was struck by their dull aspect, they wore a strained look too, as of people who have smiled too long at will," thoughts she shared with her absent spouse.[64] Another antipathy concerned an artist whom William had known at least since the early 1870s, a Miss May Whitwell. Once he had teased sister Alice that he might propose to her.[65] William tempted fate in sending her to Alice late one summer.

William invited May Whitwell to go with him to Keene Valley in September 1887. He found her intellect weak, but he sent her to Alice that same month after the Keene Valley trip ended. The artist decided she would stay to paint infant Peggy's portrait. When October came and William returned to Cambridge, May Whitwell was still at Chocorua, still painting. Alice thought she overstayed her welcome.[66] She called May a metaphysical hen, a phrase William agreed was an apt one.[67] With three young children, an aging mother, and a large country place to renovate and manage, Alice did not want to host an itinerant artist who painted for room and board. She did not hesitate to let her husband know her wishes, holding her own in this argument as she did in many others. Though he knew Alice was tired of her houseguest, William professed his enchantment with the artist and tried to persuade his wife to appreciate May.[68] He visited May in her rooms when she returned from Chocorua to get news of Alice and the group, determined to remain friends with her despite his wife's frustrations with (and even possibly jealousy of) her.

That fall, despite her guest, with her hired help Alice planted apple trees, currant bushes, Cuthbert raspberries, Greg raspberries, English gooseberries, bush roses, Ayrshire climbing roses, hollyhocks, and Virginia creepers. The currants had to be planted as soon as they arrived so that their roots didn't dry out.[69] William sent her grass seed and paint and wondered whether they should buy Sam Scudder's hen coop.[70] She chose wallpaper, ordered wood, and tried to decide where to plant the apple orchard. She had her help dig a drainage ditch around the house to keep water from the pond from damaging the foundation in the spring.[71] Finally, she had to decide whether to sell their horse, Maggie, that fall or board her at a cost of $40 for six months.[72]

William wanted more land and more children. "I do so much wish you were alone in the house with me tonight! Perchance when you wean the baby, we may accomplish it! The sudden thought so intoxicates me that I almost begin a new sheet of paper!"[73] He did not fear another pregnancy.[74] He missed Alice acutely, while she, still nursing their daughter, seemed less eager to resume their physical relationship. After he returned to his teaching Alice remained in the country, toiling on their farm and tending three children. William chided her when her letters were not romantic enough. After a long discussion on various stains for the farmhouse he announced, "Meanwhile, I wish you might express a little more sentiment in your letters! No matter I trust to find it when you come."[75] Theirs was again a fully embodied union. Their marriage had survived the death of a child, and they began calling Chocorua their "nestling hamlet."

After Alice returned to Cambridge she and William read William Salter's lecture "The Cure for Anarchy," debating its ideas. By the 1880s various small labor unions had attempted to legitimize themselves and reduce the most glaring worker abuses of the Gilded Age, but with little success. The federation of organized trades and labor unions in the United States and Canada set 1 May as the day when an eight-hour workday should become law. On that day workers' rallies occurred all over the country, the largest of them in Chicago. There, the McCormick Harvest Machine Company was surrounded by strikers, who fought with "scabs" crossing the picket line. The Chicago police laid siege to the strikers, killing four. The working community was horrified.

Local anarchists called for a rally at Haymarket Square for 4 May. The demonstration was peaceful, but as the police moved in to disburse the crowd, a striker threw a bomb and killed a policeman. Fellow police opened fire on the crowd, and the strikers shot back. Seven policemen and four workers were killed. The eight men allegedly connected with the anarchists who organized the rally were arrested for the murder of the policeman killed by the bomb. While the prosecution failed to connect the eight with the bombing, it argued that the defendants had ordered the detonation. Three of the leaders were hanged in November 1887, and another committed suicide in his cell. Later evidence proved the bombing was the work of the Pinkerton Detective Agency.[76]

The incident caused a resurgence of secret patriotic fraternal organizations that were antiradical, anti-Catholic, and anti-Semitic.[77] William told Henry that this meaningless anarchist riot was "the work of a lot of pathological germans & poles."[78] He refused to sign his brother-in-law's petition for clemency for the men arrested, as he felt that punishing them might help prevent future anarchist violence, but Alice was terribly disappointed in his refusal to support these men.[79]

Although her return comforted William, it brought sorrow for Alice. Ellen Gurney, who suffered from depression after the deaths of her sister and husband, wandered away from her house to Cambridge's Fresh Pond, where she was struck by a passing freight train. She was taken to Massachusetts General Hospital in Boston and died that evening.[80] Alice told sister Alice in England of Ellen's fate. Sister Alice was horrified at her friend's violent end, though she was glad Ellen's suffering was over.[81] "How noble she seems and what a desolate void her going makes for you. Beside our silent and dignified dead, how trivial we living folk seem, do we not?"[82]

Besides coping with the loss of Ellen, Alice had worries about Billy: his asthma, which improved in the high clean New Hampshire air, worsened when he returned to Cambridge, where the air was sullied from horse cars, bituminous coal fires, and industrial pollution. Cambridge had industrialized rapidly during the second half of the nineteenth century and was now a large manufacturing center, aided by proximity to good railroad and water transportation. In 1845 the small city had 94 manufacturing firms, but by 1885 there were 578, manufacturing such diverse items as soap, bicycles, telescopes, musical instruments, iron, carriages, rubber goods, and candy.[83] Cambridge was also home to Ginn and Company's huge Athenaeum Press, which produced many of the country's school textbooks.[84]

Alice finally decided she needed to take the children to Aiken for the winter. William hoped that Margaret would go again, but this time Alice insisted making the trip. In South Carolina she could board, freed from household responsibilities to concentrate on her children. She had not been so far from home since 1873. She had another motive in leaving, however. William hoped to finish *The Principles of Psychology* that winter, and he could work more productively when his family was gone.

Although Harry was seasick, the group arrived safely in the South before January was over. They had taken a steamer to Charleston and from there a direct train to Aiken. After the Civil War the town became a popular resort for Yankees. Though near the Savannah River, Aiken was not too humid until summer. The winter months were mild and the springs lovely, with dogwoods, redbuds, azaleas, and myriad other flowers blooming. The woods, too, were beautiful, full of longleaf pines and live oaks with twisting branches draped with mistletoe, quite unlike New Hampshire's forests. They stayed at the Townsends' boardinghouse, where Alice had the help of a German governess, Fräulein Hunersdorf.[85]

The separation was not without its problems. Usually, William went away, not Alice. He was restless during her absence, roaming the house and having difficulty sleeping. No sooner had his wife's boat pulled from the dock than William visited May Whitwell. When he saw her light on at 9:00 p.m., he could not resist going up to her rooms. They talked about the baby's portrait, which was out being framed. She wanted to show it at an exhibition, and William quickly concurred. On the same day he wrote to Alice he also wrote to Theodora Sedgwick, "You may be sure that now that the cats are away the mouse will play."[86] On 31 January he went to a party in Concord. He told Alice "<u>one</u> beautiful girl is enough to make a party pleasant, & one was there raven hair, coal black eyes." He even admired Tom Ward's thirteen-year-old daughter.[87] Though he was sincere in his protestations of undying love, he was too interested in human behavior to avoid people. He took Alice's understanding for granted, so much so that he told her everything. Surely, she must understand how much he loved her; these other women were only passing interests.

But Alice did not always understand William's flirtations, harmless or not. Later that spring sister Alice warned her that William's attraction for other women had grown as his reputation increased, something Alice must have already guessed. At least two Englishwomen, Mrs. Gurney and Mrs. Pollock, had crushes on him.[88] Later, sister Alice advised, "Every woman, wife or maid, knows that her fellow man, is to <u>flattery</u> as blotting paper to ink, he soaks in it, in no matter how crude a form or how wreathed about in mouthing ineptitudes, with endless ecstasy!"[89]

Alice was far from home, struggling with young children, one with bad ears and one with asthma. She may have been a saint, but she was a human one. In February she confided her loneliness, Harry's occasional rudeness to strangers, and the baby's sleepless nights, but William only counseled, "Patience! Patience!"[90] When she was sad during those winter months, he thought it was "just one of those autumnal moods."[91] He expected her next letters to be cheerier. Perhaps reluctant to leave her darker side on record for posterity, Alice asked him twice that winter to burn her complaining letters. William refused. "Our children's most precious heirloom! never!"[92]

This winter Alice was relieved temporarily of one family responsibility. Not long after she departed, Bob erupted again. By now his wife, Mary, and his two children had moved to Concord, but Mary and Bob remained estranged. This time, William learned, he had spent a night in Boston getting drunk, cutting and bruising his face. He claimed he was really insane and begged to be confined. William took him to Hartford, Connecticut, to Crothers Institution for Inebriates.[93]

During their winter's separation, William began to ask questions about his wife's past.[94] During their courtship the focus had been on his tortured consciousness and almost never on Alice. He may have never known the full circumstances surrounding her father's suicide. And while he teased her about jealousy, he forgot that she might be genuinely jealous. He constructed her as a model of maternal devotion and a loving wife, but that model sometimes prevented him from seeing her. When he wrote a note to May Whitwell about a new portrait of hers he had seen displayed, he told Alice that he had done so. "I hope you will permit that!"[95]

At the end of the first week in February William found their maid, Lizzie, who was about to leave their service, so amiable that he confessed his urge to kiss her when she came to say good-bye. He blithely informed his wife of his desire. "In fact I should be less than human and unworthy to be your or any one else's husband without such an impulse on that occasion. Wherefore send your consent, so that if it takes place [the kiss] it shall be with a good conscience."[96]

It didn't take long for Alice to tell William that her depression was because of him. As she coped with Billy's fever, Harry's fall off a horse, and Peggy's sleeplessness, she had to think about her husband kissing her maid. She was not convinced of his innocence when she read a letter dated the day after Valentine's Day explaining that his impulse to kiss Lizzie was "merely a natural expression of passing tenderness and cordiality."[97] To add insult to injury, he forgot her birthday that month, backpedaling by claiming he thought of her that day constantly but did not remember to write. He told her he thought she was still twenty-seven. (She was thirty-nine.) Determined to have the last move in this game, he kissed Lizzie when she came to say good-bye.[98] What could Alice do with a man who was so honest and who left behind his frogs for a laboratory experiment in a box at the St. Botolph Club dinner?[99]

While William's irrepressible energy and antics tired Alice, their skirmishes made William relish marriage. He thrived on conflict. During her absence he reread their courtship letters, reflecting on how sick and tormented he had been yet how right marriage had been for him. He found her more substantial now, though he hastily assured her he was not thinking of her expanded waistline. He told her she had wrought "my transformation into the normal man and husband you have now. . . . As God made me, as I then made myself, so have you re-made me."[100] He knew full well how much she had contributed to his improved psychological health, a health that allowed him to work.

Even though he affirmed her importance to him, and she knew that William was utterly sincere, Alice told him that she worried that she had not been the right woman for such a brilliant but demanding man. "Deep down in my heart has lain so long the sad doubt of your well-being and a thousand times I've trembled before the thought that I had been over sure of your need of me and that you might have chosen better if I'd never crossed your path. It's a long, long story, all this morbid pain, but it was in the bond, and not wholly unforeseen by me in those days and weeks of rapture and heartbreak when you were writing me those letters."[101] Despite her doubts, a decade after their wedding she told William that he was her universe.[102] In March she sent him a letter in which she made allusions to their courtship and included a sprig of jasmine.

During his family's absence William looked for another place to rent when they returned, one with more room for the two families, the Jameses as well as Eliza and Margaret Gibbens. Also, Alice remained convinced that the dwelling at 15 Appian Way, where Hermann died, was unhealthy. While William did not believe this, nonetheless he searched for another house, a fruitless effort, as he found nothing suitable for them.

By spring the couple had stopped quarreling in their letters, and Alice was again William's angel. They hoped to spend a week together in April, but their plans did not work out. Alice was delayed in Aiken by Peggy's teething until William's limited patience was sorely tried. Alice gained weight that winter, but fortunately, due to her long absence, she was not pregnant again.[103] She had time to take a deep breath before starting the next pregnancy, nursing the next baby. Her three children had done well in Aiken: Peggy learned to crawl, Billy's asthma was under control, and Harry drew pictures of cotton gins.

After a few more epistolary contretemps and sleepless nights the Jameses reunited in May, Alice improved after her winter in the South. She was becoming herself again; she had that "je ne sais quoi" about her, that dry and practical air William loved.[104] Former abolitionist Alice brought two African American servants back, Louise and Andrew. During the Reconstruction many former slaves worked as servants and found conditions better in the North. Although servants were increasingly difficult to find in the Boston area, William doubted the wisdom of this plan. Andrew, while an expert with horses, might not be good at gardening and chopping, and Louise might not do well sharing a room with a white maid at Chocorua.[105] But he gave in because he wanted his family back. Andrew at least proved to be an exemplary servant, far superior to the New Hampshire Yankees.[106]

No sooner had Alice arrived in Cambridge than it was time to go to Chocorua. Renovations and landscaping were far from finished. She stayed on at summer's end to supervise the laborers, from six to ten men at a time. By now their lives revolved around what their senses could apprehend: wallpaper, floor varnish, earth moving, potash, planting. William's letters now toggled between the practical ("Also get the lime-barrel now under the 'lean-to' where it leaks, under a less leaky place") and the romantic ("I exult in you").[107]

Alice was tired at the end of her long summer, sometimes doubting the wisdom of the purchase. While she had loved Chocorua during previous summers, right now the farm seemed foreign to her.[108] Her winter spent in a boardinghouse may have made her disinclined to shoulder such a heavy workload again. William and Alice spent a day and a half together toward the end of September, he enthralled by his "bride." With her help he planned to increase his reading program that winter. Peggy demanded less of Alice, but William demanded more. He wanted her to read aloud to him at night again.[109] He teased her that he had learned the secret to dominance in their marriage: "I shall know the secret hereafter:

speak to you with cold cruelty, as on that ride, and you instantly become absolutely plastic in my hands! Heaven bless you for it, you gentle submissive thing."[110]

The long summer and all its demands did not submerge Alice, however; her intellect and curiosity remained sharp as ever. By Christmas sister Alice had relayed a compliment to Alice. A friend reported that whenever she visited "Mrs. William," "'Mrs. Alice's face very sweet and handsome and I like to talk to her when we can really have time to say a great deal, I carry home always something to Joe when I have called there.'"[111]

Like sister Alice, William admired her, praising her strength. He did not wholly ascribe to his culture's gender role definitions: "You can't tell how the sight of you bossing the work made me admire you."[112] He would rely on Alice's strength more and more in the coming years.

7 95 Irving Street and Beyond

BY THE FALL OF 1888 the Jameses had realized that it was time for them to find more permanent quarters. William had a solid position and modest income at Harvard, but even with the Syracuse rental income they lacked funds to buy a home. In March 1889, though, William's Aunt Kate died, leaving him a bequest of $9,000. This made their decision to build a home certain.[1]

Earlier that winter William had found a lot on Irving Street, just blocks from 20 Quincy Street, where the James family had lived for years. It was close to the Harvard campus, so that he could walk to classes. In 1887–88 financially pressed Charles Eliot Norton asked landscape architect Charles Eliot, son of Harvard's President Eliot, to draw up a design for subdividing his beloved estate, Shady Hill.[2] Eliot planned a curvilinear street pattern similar to Frederick Law Olmsted's designs, with large, single-family houses set back from the streets. The Shady Hill development was part of the movement north and northeast from Harvard's campus, as there was no more room for professors to build near the university, and existing property was expensive. Shady Hill and Dana Hill, originally part of Cambridgeport, became virtual extensions of Old Cambridge.[3]

These developments were just one example of the growth that threatened to overwhelm Cambridge during the second half of the nineteenth century, when it moved from being a colonial and revolutionary village to an incorporated suburban city. Some of the growth came from professional and merchant families moving out from Boston, but it also came from the many immigrants drawn to work opportunities in the factories. The city's population nearly doubled between 1880 and 1910, when it reached 100,000 people, and its population density was 25 persons per acre, a higher density than Boston and even than most American cities of that time. When beloved writer James Russell Lowell returned to the city from Europe in 1889, he felt as if he had been brought in to a world of ghosts, as Cambridge had changed beyond recognition.[4] By the time of William James's death in 1910 there were calls to suppress pollution and regulate growth.[5]

Building the Irving Street house proved a formidable undertaking, and the Chocorua retreat was not yet finished. The worst of overseeing the construction fell to Alice. During the summer of 1889 William decided he needed to go abroad again to see his ailing sister Alice and to attend an international conference of physiological psychologists that would be held in Paris. He had promised his wife that she could come on his next European trip, but, fatigued and frustrated, he put her off one more time. It was not possible for both to be gone at once just then, and, in addition, the cost of taking her would be prohibitive while they were building a new home. On the spur of the moment he decided to go alone. He was still, as sister Alice described him in her journal, "a blob of mercury."[6] William comforted Alice: "Only heaven reward you for all you're doing for us."[7] Sometimes it must have seemed that only heaven did reward her.

It was the same old story: absence makes the heart grow fonder. William said it himself, telling Alice, "What a wonderful effect absence has in quickening and at the same time simplifying one's impression of the absent one."[8] But while his desire increased when they were apart, they argued by mail, this time over a lift. William loved the idea of an elevator, but Alice wanted a large linen closet. He tried to compromise. They could have both lift and linen closet by shifting other rooms and closets around. He promised to make the elevator childproof, as one of Alice's objections had been her fear of the children getting hurt playing in and around it.

Finally, he threatened: "For once I'll assert my supremacy in this marriage!"[9] But in his next letter he told her that he was going to investigate three Boston houses with lifts. Unless those homeowners unanimously recommended the innovation, however, "out of love for you and your horrid little midgy nature I will not put it in."[10]

During his voyage out on the *Cephalonia* William analyzed his marriage with its seemingly unavoidable conflicts. He sifted his guilt at leaving, his veneration for Alice's faithfulness, and his anger at not taking her along. Alice took a more direct approach. She cried when he left and then went about her duties. His departures were always stormy: he never left himself enough time for last-minute tasks, so she hovered nearby, trying to help. Inevitably, pressed and stressed, William lost his temper.[11] Once gone, though, he missed his wife, particularly her observations, as her vision was sometimes greater and bolder, he thought. There had been a gender-role reversal in the marriage, "I the so-called woman, you the man," he confessed to her.[12]

That summer he soaked up impressions and took his pulse. While she struggled with houses and children, he was so confident in her willingness to let him travel and study that he told her, "Really this life is just like Heaven. No duties, perfect weather, even the cabmen polite, and feasts for the eye on every side."[13] When he could not find suitable jewelry for her in Paris, he promised to bring himself back instead. Theirs was now the complete moral union he had feared was impossible to achieve during their courtship.[14] As he wrote of his heavenly Parisian life, Alice sprained her ankle, exhausted from her Chocorua chores.[15]

During his absence the builders made real progress. Noted architect William Ralph Emerson had designed the house with input from the Jameses, particularly from William.[16] His absence that summer saved the family at least $2,000, according to the builder, because he was not there to tinker with the plans.[17] In the end the house cost $15,000 in 1889 dollars, approximately $340,000 in today's currency.[18]

After William returned and just before the house was completed, Mrs. Piper visited Chocorua for a week. Perhaps the Jameses wanted the comfort of her presence before making the move to their new home. William was now completely convinced of the medium's honesty, but presumably during her visits she gathered additional information about the family that she could use in later séances.[19] In one sense she acted as a counselor to the couple. Occasionally, her control, Dr. Phinuit, gave them long lectures on "our inward defects and outward shortcomings, which were very earnest, as well as subtile morally and psychologically, and impressive in a high degree."[20]

Late in September 1889 the workers were ready to paint, estimating it would take them a month. On 7 October William spent his first night in the house, in Alice's bedroom, though the plumbing was not done and the painting not completed.[21] She remained in Chocorua until the house was finished. Her California girlhood friend Kate Putnam Hooker was in town, but William was not eager to see her. His memories of her visit during his and Alice's honeymoon were not good ones.[22]

That fall Alice knew that she was pregnant again, but before the end of October she miscarried. She was shocked and depressed.[23] William reassured her, trying to comfort her, in a reversal of their typical roles.[24] She had lost another child, albeit a scarcely formed one. She confided to Henry, "'The fact is, that for these past two years, I have lived from day to day, trying to meet the urgency of each hour and somehow tow the children through.'" But again, her inner resolve steadied her. Despite all her other responsibilities, she vowed to nap each afternoon so that she could stay awake at night and read to William.[25]

In November all five Jameses moved into the 95 Irving Street house, a large, shingled, three-story dwelling that would be Alice's primary home for the rest of her life.[26] The front door opened into a large foyer and reception area that featured a wide oak stairway making ninety-degree turns to the second-floor landing. All the rooms in the house had interior doors to insure privacy. On the left side of the ground floor were the drawing room and William's library. The small drawing room featured a Colonial Revival fireplace mantel, carved with garlands, and a door to the outside, leading directly into the garden. The library, twenty-two by twenty-seven feet, was designed to be the most welcoming room in the entire house. Its walls had floor-to-ceiling bookcases. The room's focal point was the fireplace, set to the left of the door. The mantel was made of a single pine slat two feet wide, supported by double Doric columns. In this room the couple wrote letters in tandem at William's large desk, reading one another's correspondence. Facing south, the library had one large window in back and three windows overlooking the side garden. To the right of the entryway was the dining room, a butler's pantry leading from it, and then the kitchen and more ample pantries.

The master bedroom, the same size as the library and also with a fireplace, was on the second floor and included a private bath and three large closets, one of which was a hidden cedar closet entered from one of the other closets. The second floor had two other bedrooms with fireplaces and a servant's bedroom at the back. Third-floor bedrooms featured gabled ceilings. At the front of the third floor Alice had a sewing room with a wall of built-in drawers and cabinets, a sort of counterpoint to William's library with its walls of bookshelves. There was a roomy attic fifty-two feet long above the third floor furnished with a table, a standing desk, and an armchair. The attic's many windows let in light year-round, and William sometimes wrote there. A back stairway led from the service area of the house to the smaller bedrooms above for the servants. The house was heated by coal, with a large furnace in the unfinished basement.[27] There was no lift in the house.

A few months after she moved in Alice was pregnant again. The demands of the new house plus the fatigue from the first trimester of pregnancy made her short-tempered. In May she wrote from Chocorua to William angrily, summarizing everything that had gone wrong during the last year. But, having unloaded all her frustrations in a letter, her mood passed. He warned her, "Don't let yourself get mad again."[28]

During this demanding time Alice became jealous of Boston artist and socialite Sarah Wyman Whitman.[29] It was no wonder: she was pregnant for the sixth time, while Mrs. Whitman was a powerful, beautiful woman. A portrait done by Helen Bigelow Merriman, now hanging in the Schlesinger Library, shows an elegant, proud woman holding a palette of bright purple, green, yellow, red, and white paints with three paintbrushes in her left hand. Sarah Whitman adored William and entertained him frequently in her summer home, Beverly. They had met in the late 1880s at a philosophical club she hosted.[30] He reassured Alice: "You have no call to be jealous, my darling darling generous-hearted wife, for she is as remote from me <u>personally</u> as Sarah Bernhardt would be were she here."[31] Not long after he wrote these words to Alice, however, he spent time correcting proofs in Mrs. Whitman's studio, she helping at times, though he insisted to Alice, "<u>My</u> wife is <u>you</u>."[32]

In the spring of 1890 William shipped his 2,970-page manuscript, "Principles of Psychology," representing over a decade's work, to Henry Holt, and Holt steadily mailed the proofs back as chapters were ready. William predicted it would be a big book in terms of both sales and reputation, and he was right. For decades it was considered the most important academic text on psychology. Later it came out in a shorter version, and the royalties proved to be substantial. It made William's reputation—and Alice's finances—secure. While by far the majority of the pages in the extant manuscript fragments are in William's hand, there is a very tidy diagram on "Feelings & Domains on Planes of the Mind" executed in Alice's hand.[33] William spent most of that summer alone in Cambridge correcting the page proofs of his massive text, leaving his spouse at Chocorua with the children. They had incurred many expenses building the new home, and now there would be another child to provide for. The book's royalties would be welcome.

Though William's book was not quite finished, Henry had completed another long novel, the fourth of the realistic novels he composed during the 1880s. At this point Henry's reputation far eclipsed his older brother's. One of Alice's pleasures that spring came from reading *The Tragic Muse*. The text features three strong heroines: modest and eager Biddy Dormer, an aspiring sculptress who finally achieves a happy relationship; the imperious, ambitious widow Julia Dallow, who uses her wealth to persuade Nick Dormer, a would-be painter, to enter the political world as her surrogate; and finally, Henry's wonderful creation Miriam Rooth, an actress of Jewish origin who marries Basil Dashwood to advance her career. This intricately plotted novel, with its detailed scenes of Paris and London, features minor characters like aesthete Gabriel Nash, whose complex portrait deepens the story. Alice might have recalled parts of her first European sojourn in the story of Miriam Rooth and her mother, who moved from one country and pension to another to conserve their meager funds. It was only Miriam's relentless determination that allowed her to develop her voice and achieve the theatrical triumph she hungered for.

Alice had an unmitigated appreciation of her brother-in-law's genius. "You seem to me to have crossed the border into the kingdom of the Great, into the land where the few, the Masters live and create by laws and immensities of their own. The book is new, unlike any other—so new that perhaps people won't take it in today or tomorrow, but its own day is waiting for it. The delightful talk, the serene good nature, the revelation of the artistic nature—it's all wonderfully fine," she exclaimed to Henry. "And it all fits and rests in its own whole. I mean the feeling of structure which it gives me, as does a beautiful piece of architecture. The sensation is rare enough to be reveled in when at last it is vouchsafed."[34] Then she confided how difficult the winter had been, building the house, paying the bills, and "a larger number of melancholiacs than usual to be pulled through by poor William."[35] "I wish, dear Alice, that you were tasting as much as I, this summer, of the irresponsible," Henry wrote from Italy.[36]

Relations among Alice, Henry, and William had gradually shifted over the last decade. Through their correspondence Henry learned more from Alice than he did from William about his older brother's family. The two knew that they were more like one another than either was like William. Henry gently chastised his brother for his failure to communicate: "Give Alice much love from me & tell her she shall lose nothing by waiting a little longer for an answer to her letter. SHE told me, in some detail, about the house."[37] He could depend on Alice to help him remain part of his brother's world.

That summer she was moodier, sometimes teary and occasionally short-tempered, yet still she managed Chocorua successfully. In August Alice had a terrible head cold, and toddler Peggy said her mother's nose was worn out.[38] Weary of it all, Alice told William she would not be giving birth to the second Messiah.[39] They had ordered a tombstone for Hermann, William reflecting on the baby's short life: "Poor little Humster! How I should like to hold him in my arms once more."[40]

Alice capped off her summer by reading the proofs for *The Principles of Psychology*, a hefty 1,400 pages. During the second trimester of her pregnancy, despite varicose veins and headaches, she came back to Cambridge to help with the corrections. She had championed the book for over a decade, and she was determined to see the project through to its end. First she attended a Webb family celebration at South Weymouth with her mother, and then she spent a week helping correct proofs. After she returned to Chocorua, William, trying to lift her depression, reminded her how much she had influenced his life: "Darling in all seriousness you have lifted me up out of lonely hell. . . . You have redeemed my life from destruction and crowned me with loving kindness & tender mercy, and my fortunes are eternally linked with yours."[41]

She deserved her husband's praise. Her direct contributions to *The Principles of Psychology*, whether or not she did help him write it during their honeymoon summer or just took dictation and responded to his ideas, may have been few, yet she had provided him a steady emotional counterweight and intellectual companionship during the past turbulent years.

While William studied the work of European behavioral psychologists, analyzed the ideas of previous theorists on the brain and its conscious processes, started an experimental laboratory at Harvard, and looked deeply into the workings of his own mind, Alice kept her practical focus on the world of experience that he analyzed: her mother, her sisters, her children, her in-laws, her neighbors, her houses, her strawberry plants, her chickens. In addition to hundreds of lively examples drawn from both the animal and human worlds, examples explained in an intelligible and sometimes humorous manner, some observations in *The Principles of Psychology* derive from what William had observed watching their children, particularly in chapter 24, "Instinct."[42] He describes the complex mechanism whereby babies learn that fire is hot by touching a candle flame; babies' deep sleep in the first weeks after their birth; and why a child born in Boston does not realize he is in the third story of the house or at longitude 72° west and latitude 41° north. Near the end of the second volume he refers explicitly to his own experience. Babies make "a peculiar *sound expressive of desire*, which, in my own three children, was the first manifestation of speech, occurring many weeks before other significant sounds."[43]

In his clearly written compendium of recent experimentation on the sensory organs and brains of animals and humans, William supplements that research with his own fresh analogies of mental processes, analogies that include his famous "stream of consciousness" description, which became an important trope for subsequent philosophers, psychologists, and literary theorists. These explanations demonstrate his genius in explaining the complex relationships between mind, body, and external reality. Rejecting both transcendental and associationist theories and holding to some of Darwin's principles of accidental variations while refuting most of Herbert Spencer's social Darwinism, William speculated that the brain receives sensory input from experience, but then these experiences, through individual processes of memory, help mold our perceptions of subsequent experiences. Thus, the mind cannot be explained only as a template stamped by its apprehension of the physical world. Accidental and spontaneous variations, what he called "secondary internal processes," allow us some free mental play. Mathematical systems, logic, aesthetics, even metaphysics cannot be explained on an atomistic level, though William stops short of ascribing these abstract operations to a transcendental agency. In short, we are more than the sum of our parts.

Just three days before Christmas 1890, Alice's last child was born, not long after William received the completed *Principles*. She had another boy, who weighed eleven pounds. The baby was not named immediately, and, in fact, his name changed at least twice before he reached his teens. The proud papa told Henry, "It all went off most beautifully—One doesn't see why it mightn't happen every week."[44]

Again, William picked a name Alice disliked, and Henry complicated the process by his own opposition to William's names. By February 1891 the child was still nameless. William liked Francis Tweedy or Francis Temple. "Francis" came from an old James family friend, Francis Child, "Tweedy" would be a nod to the Newport Tweedy relatives, Edmund and Mary, and "Temple" came from William's orphaned Temple cousins, one of them Mary "Minny" Temple, whom Henry later immortalized in *The Wings of the Dove*. Henry objected violently to them all. Referring to "the unspeakable or unnamable babe," he suggested Alexander Robertson James after their maternal great-grandfather.[45] Then he apologized to Alice for stirring the familial waters: "I am very sorry my suggestions raised a gust—they were intended only to still the breezes—& I thought the matter still open for discussion as the child had not, as I suppose, been Christianly baptized & registered." He assured her he would accept their decision.[46]

Francis Tweedy it was. For years Alice called her son Francis, while William called him Tweedy. At some point the little boy called himself John, as he did not like either name. Finally, in 1902 William officially named his son Alexander Robertson, using Henry's suggestion, though Alice and her daughter Peggy continued to call the boy Francis or Tweedy for three years more.[47] Therapists might question the effects of a name change upon an eight year old, the child of America's first psychologist at that.

Alice's last child was a happy baby who gave his mother relatively little trouble, and William found him the most promising of all their children.[48] By now her habits of baby tending and nursing were second nature. She was an expert at managing babies: she knew how to put them to sleep by suddenly adjusting the gas flame in their lamp either up or down. She believed the sudden change in the light hypnotized little ones.[49]

Though she was content, Alice felt more tired than ever in 1891. She had trouble finding suitable servants for the Irving Street house, and now she had one more infant to add to her load. To top it all off, Peggy had minor surgery that summer. By the end of the summer William was also tired after completing the shorter version of *The Principles of Psychology*, called *The Briefer Course*. In condensing the book he expanded some sections, including a greater emphasis on sensory perception and the will.

He decided to travel to the North Carolina mountains, near Asheville. Like all his other absences, this one made William's heart grow fonder. Alice was bathed in sweetness "like a baby bee drowned in the honey of its cell!"[50] He returned with renewed energy and enthusiasm for his marriage, while she could be nothing but tired. The winter of 1892 found them fighting again, this time over chickens. William was remorseful afterward for making Alice's duties even harder.[51]

No sooner had William returned from his vacation than Henry called him to London. Sister Alice's time was drawing short. Her health had declined during the past few years, as she experienced cardiac complications, spinal neurosis, and gout, and by the summer of 1891 Dr. William Baldwin had diagnosed a lump in her breast as a malignant tumor.[52] William debated going to her. At Chocorua he said it was the devil tempting him and he would not go, but the next day he changed his mind. Not only was his sister dying, but Henry's first play, the dramatic version of his early novel *The American*, revised to give audiences a happy ending, would be performed that fall.[53] In mid-September William made a brief farewell visit to his sister, musing afterward to her that they had not had the deeper talks he had hoped for and noting that he felt the same way after he left his wife: "It seems as if in the past twelve years I had had no opportunity to have any particular talk with her about the innumerable things that are of most importance."[54]

On 5 March 1892 sister Alice sent William's family a final telegram:

"Tenderest love to all farewell Am going soon. Alice."[55] After her sister-in-law succumbed to breast cancer the next day Alice wrote empathetic letters to Henry, sharing her memories of his sister and his parents, Mary and Henry Sr., and voicing her generous wish that she and sister Alice could have become closer friends had fate allowed. "For years I have looked forward to seeing Alice again, to being something to her from out the larger knowledge that life brings to us all, but it was not to be and the loss is all mine."[56]

Sister Alice left William a legacy of $20,000, a liberal bequest that made possible a European family trip during one of William's yearlong sabbaticals. Family dynamics changed again, too, with her death. Freed from the draining care of a chronic invalid, Henry could take a greater interest in Alice, William, and their children. That spring Alice tried to reach the dead Alice in the spirit world, visiting Mrs. Piper, who claimed to have received a message from the departed woman.[57]

Alice had long anticipated a trip to Europe, but now that it was really possible, she had reservations. On 22 March 1892 she shared her qualms with Henry. "I confess the undertaking looks formidable but I have a good nurse and I am a fair sailor myself." While her German nurse promised to stay with the family for at least two months following their arrival in Europe, Alice knew making the trip would require great physical and mental strength. One bonus for her efforts would be a renewed acquaintance with her brother-in-law, whom she had not seen face to face in ten years. "I long to have the children know you," she told him.[58] William knew she needed this vacation.[59]

As he would make his summer plans around theirs, Henry awaited the final word on the Jameses' itinerary. Alice lamented the improvisational nature of their trip. "William's soul rebels at any definite plan," she told Henry. "So, though I would fain make choice of a place to aim for, burdened as we are with our four children, I try to keep an 'unbiased mind' and trust to providence."[60] While this sort of planning fit nicely with William's propensity for acting on the moment, Alice felt that some contingencies could be addressed in advance.

As of 16 April 1892 William did not know whether his long-overdue sabbatical trip would take place or not. Uncertainties remained: George Herbert Palmer, William's replacement, had been offered a permanent job at the University of Chicago, and William did not have a tenant for the Cambridge house. On 6 May Palmer announced that he had declined the Chicago offer and could take William's teaching duties. A Thaw family took the Chocorua place, but when it came time to depart, the Jameses still did not have a tenant for 95 Irving Street. Eliza Gibbens, though, now lived in her own house at 107 Irving Street and would continue to search for renters for William and Alice.

Still Alice worried, because once they arrived in the Old World they had no set program: no lodgings reserved in advance, no fixed travel plans, no schools for the children. She had taken her mother and sisters to Europe in 1868 under much the same conditions, but she was older now and had small children, not adult female relatives. They planned a ten-day stay in Germany and then a trip to Switzerland, where they hoped to summer. From there they would trust to Providence. Alice believed in Providence; William did not. Despite these difficulties, she resolved to spend this year abroad. She had preserved one desire all her own: to set foot in Europe again.

8 On Sabbatical

ON 25 MAY 1892 at 4:30 p.m. the SS *Friesland*, pulled by tugs, moved slowly from the docks at Jersey City, all six members of the James family plus a nursemaid aboard, their total fare $460. Long and narrow, the steamer was an astonishingly sleek-looking craft, given that it weighed 7,116 gross tons. Its black steel hull sat low in the water, four rigged masts punctuating its length at uneven intervals. The Red Star Line ship's first-class quarters held 226 passengers, with 102 in second class and 600 in third class. Once on the ocean, the *Friesland* obtained a maximum cruising speed of fifteen knots per hour. The boat was the only clipper-bowed ship the Glasgow line ever built and its first powered by triple expansion engines. The vessel represented the best in late-nineteenth-century naval engineering know-how.

Though the ship was beautiful and the James family enjoyed well-appointed staterooms, it was not an easy passage. The voyage proved taxing, despite Alice's careful preparations: she brought bottles of milk for the baby, ginger for seasickness, and her aunt Nannie Webb's jersey to wear under her winter jacket so that she could take off her corsets and lie down whenever she had a chance. The first day at sea all three older children were sick. Alice, too, felt queasy from time to time. When Peggy and Billy recovered, Harry got sick all over again, and finally William succumbed. "The ship is in rough seas today," she wrote to her mother, "so we keep Billy & Peggy in their berths. But they are much better. Poor little Peggy eats valiantly what she sees Billy take, vomits within ten minutes as a matter of course & nibbles her lump of ice without complaint. Billy is in the deeps, loathing the ship & Europe. The first night of his sickness he laid motionless looking as William said, 'like a dead Crusader.'"[1]

Although his reputation did not keep him from seasickness, William enjoyed the respect of the students who were aboard. *The Principles of Psychology* had earned him a solid international reputation. Not everyone knew him, however, despite his academic credentials: when he took the baby on deck for a turn while the nurse went to breakfast, William told a bystander he would look for a job as a nursemaid upon reaching Europe. The man replied, "'I thought you was always so.'"[2]

Alice told Eliza that her husband was now "a form of use," which is what he usually said of her: Alice is a form of use. This phrase has at least a double meaning: it connotes someone who performs the practical daily functions that allow us to lead orderly lives, but in Swedenborgian doctrine it has a specific theological connotation, that of humans' potential to correspond to a higher spiritual order. Henry James Sr. expounded on this in his *Society, the Redeemed Form of Man*: "It is the unfailing attribute of natural existence to be a form of use to something higher than itself."[3] Both parents had no choice other than being useful during this trying ocean voyage.

The ship docked at Antwerp, Belgium, on Sunday, 5 June, and the weary group disembarked in the pouring rain. Their sea voyage over, the Jameses began a fifteen-month sojourn abroad, a time of discovery and vexation. Alice had finally returned to the continent where she spent five youthful years, years that played a key role in forming her character. The trials she endured then would stand her well in the weeks to come.

The first hotel where William inquired for lodging, the Hotel de Hollander, proved full, to weary Alice's disappointment, but he soon found comfortable rooms at the Hotel Ernest. The group spent a day exploring Antwerp, and on the third day the family rode the cars to Cologne, Germany. Francis grew cranky with the heat, the first time he had fretted during the entire two weeks away from home.[4] Harry showed no interest in Cologne Cathedral, asking, "'Are we never going to get out of this?'"[5] Next, the group traveled by riverboat to Freiburg im Breisgau, a German city near an entrance to the Black Forest. Their trip down the Rhine was surprisingly pleasant, although when William tried to show Billy, just turned ten, the castles along the way, he insisted on counting the cars on the passing freight trains instead.[6]

Freiburg enchanted them all. The impressive central minster with its slender spire, one of the finest Gothic churches in Germany, featured stained-glass windows and Holbein paintings. The outstretched pigs with their flapping ears on the cathedral buttresses must have delighted the children, though the street where the family stayed was dark, and it rained often that month. While Alice found Freiburg suitable for the children, her labors continued: the boys teased Peggy continually on days they could not go out, and the baby cried. Her children missed their daily routine, and so did Alice: she could not extricate herself from the *Kinder Schaar*—the mob of children.[7] Though tending children was harder here, she was grateful to be back. She met an old friend, Miss Papendick, who had known the Gibbens women during their four-year stay in Germany twenty years ago. She invited Alice to tea.[8] She felt at home among the Germans once more, but William had a less positive reaction. Already tense from the stress of the trip, he suffered from insomnia.

William and Alice considered spending the winter in Freiburg, as their Cambridge friends the Brookses had found a good school for their own son. Helen Lawrence Washburn Brooks and her husband, former Unitarian minister John Graham Brooks, could be a valuable source of information on schools and domestic arrangements. But finally, William decided that Freiburg was not important enough for his work, even though a number of university students sought him out when German psychologist Hugo Munsterberg, who would begin teaching at Harvard the coming fall, announced that the author of *The Principles of Psychology* was in town.[9]

The Jameses debated moving to France or staying somewhere else in Germany for their European winter: they could not arrange for the boys' language lessons until they had chosen a country and thus a language. This time Alice was less patient with William. She felt anxious about their plans, perhaps because she was so far removed from her Cambridge support groups. She confided in Henry that she felt perplexed and distraught, even though the place was congenial: "Do you wonder why I sometimes ask myself why I brought them so far from home?" Yet she rejoiced at having set foot on the Continent again.[10] Alice kept in remarkably good spirits throughout most of this sabbatical year, only occasionally falling into depression.

Ready to move on, William decided to seek summer quarters in Switzerland, postponing winter plans temporarily. Alice would have stopped in Germany, glad to be back in her beloved adopted country, but her spouse could not be happy in the first place they landed. Recent research in psychology suggests that individuals with fewer choices are happier people in general. People who make a choice and then don't look back on the "what might have beens" are more content. Individuals who go to extremes to always find the best possible choice, called "maximizers," show borderline clinical depression.[11] William was a maximizer. He could not decide, and once he did decide, he continually worried over what he might have done instead. Alice, who in her early life had had few choices but learned to deal with them, knew that William's standards for their winter destination—he sought a place "rural, bea[u]tiful, neither too hot, nor too cold, not too high . . . not fashionable, yet not too primitive, and cheap"—were unrealistic.[12]

In mid-June Munsterberg accompanied William to Lucerne by rail. William found Hinter Meggen on the misty Lake of Lucerne inexpensive and charming and told Alice to bring on their band.[13] Lucerne, divided through the middle by the Reuss River, featured fountained squares ringed by the colorful facades of medieval buildings. William sent Alice specific directions on making the journey but did not meet her at the train station because of the extra expense involved. Instead, she hired someone to drive the group the two miles from the train depot to the pension in which William had taken rooms for the family. He urged her to bring a German fräulein to help.[14] Already the sabbatical tested their relationship. Just after he arrived in Switzerland William had written to ask Alice's forgiveness for his impatient and "unlovely" departure.[15] Thrust into his family's company in cramped quarters, he was less than thrilled with his new proximity to his children. He announced to Josiah Royce, "No one ought to travel with children, who wishes also to travel for his own pleasure: so much have the past weeks taught two simple adult souls!"[16]

At first, Alice, too, felt disheartened, despite the location's beauty, telling her sister Mary, "I came here from Freyburg on Thursday, tired and somewhat discouraged for the baby had been ailing and having poor nights, and I felt like a person treading water. I could not get on, in any way and we were so at sea as to our plans." Once she recovered from the trip, however, she adapted easily to the Pension Stutz, a chalet one hundred feet above the lake and two miles above the city itself. The older children ran on the balcony surrounding the house, and Francis had fresh cow's milk.[17] Alice was even happier with their accommodations when she saw hens in her yard. Their noisy presence added a note of home. She wrote enthusiastically to Eliza, "The hens are rolling about the house with the old friendly clucks and I am hoping that the Sister who keeps the yard in order will not see how far they have ventured and drive them away. Yesterday I went to market with one of the Sisters—there are four, and spent a delightful hour there in the town. The stalls spread under a long arcade skirting the river were the most tempting I ever saw—beautiful vegetables fruit and flowers and such butter!"[18]

After settling his family at the Pension Stutz, William disappeared, once again scouting more suitable quarters. No matter where he was, someplace else might be better. He confessed his guilt at leaving Alice with four children to amuse: "I am a selfish beast."[19] She survived, however. The baby seemed better, and young Harry gave up his diet of bread and water. That week William planned to go to Geneva to inquire about a school and family quarters in Paris (he hoped in Versailles).[20] Alice was to follow a week later with the children. She remained patient with his eternally seesawing plans, telling Henry that the splendid views all around consoled her: "And the beauty of these mountains! Never twice the same."[21] William merely warned Henry not to visit them as yet, as they were still too transient.[22]

Finally, the group left Lucerne on 7 July for the tiny village of Gryon. Seventy-five miles from Geneva, it was a tranquil mountain village with traditional eighteenth-century white houses. The Jameses planned to stay for a fortnight and then possibly leave the two older boys there for the rest of the summer. William found the village charming, and there was a pastor in residence to teach the boys. Harry studied French and Latin every day with the village schoolmaster while his father looked for a more permanent arrangement for the boys' summer lessons.[23]

Alice struggled to push the baby up and down Gryon's narrow, winding streets with their views of magnificent Alpine scenery, but the first days there she was glad to be back in Europe. She found a few peaceful moments to write to her mother: "I wish you could hear the organ in the little church opposite rehearsing the Sunday hymns. The solemn strain is so sweet on the morning air. And then the sun pours in and presently I shall take my stockings [to mend] and sit down alone and think of you and the girls and all that I should like to hear and tell about."[24]

But this spot would not do for either the children's schooling or William's work. He continued to complain, this time to his old Cambridge friend Grace Ashburner: "It seems to me that the most solemn duty I can have in what remains to me of life will be to save my inexperienced fellow beings from ignorantly taking their little ones abroad when they go for their own refreshment." His wife could tolerate the upheaval better than he. "Alice, if she writes to you, will (after her feminine fashion) gloze over this aspect of our existence, because she has been more or less accustomed to it after all these years and on the whole does not dislike it (!!), but I for once will speak frankly and not disguise my sufferings."[25] Just as they settled in Gryon and the boys began their lessons, William abruptly decided they should go instead to Lausanne, where he hoped cow dung and sublimity would not dispute for mastery.[26] Still seeking the elusive sabbatical Shangri-la, William went first, staying in the Hôtel Richemont. In one of his not-infrequent nods to Alice's needs, he felt diabolically mean to be enjoying himself so while she was cooped up with small children. He comforted himself that at least she had one burden less now that he was gone.

While Alice waited for her husband in Gryon, it rained seven days out of eight, and she had no fire and little hot water in her quarters. In addition, she had to break her vegetarian diet and eat meat because there were no vegetables available other than potatoes, and she refused to live on potatoes alone. During the late nineteenth century nursing mothers were advised to eat vegetables and avoid fatty, spicy foods, so perhaps Alice had adopted this habit during all the months she had nursed children, but it made another reason to dislike the village.[27] Despite her earlier encouraging message to her mother, she was more honest with her sister. She was tired of keeping four children occupied in unpleasant quarters while William wandered. She voiced her depression to Mary:

Imagine two large rooms on the village street, cold and dark with the low-hanging clouds, which hide the snow-covered peaks over against us. We have no fire and very little hot water, though to be sure my little Helène brought me a foot warmer this morning. In these two rooms the four children & I manage to live through these depressing days[,] our only diversion the painful one of trotting 3 times a day to our meals at the end of the village. The wet shoes, stockings, clothes etc. diffuse a permanent <u>dust</u> over our two rooms.[28]

Sometimes she disliked her entire existence, despite William's claim that on the whole she liked it. She was too vital and curious not to chafe at being confined to quarters. He mused to his wife what it might be like if she accompanied him on his solo forays: "I keep saying to myself, 'if Alice were only able to travel with me and have her mind enlarged and her soul uplifted by seeing all these delicious nooks, villages, streams, and heights, how much better it would be for both of us.'"[29] But he quickly told himself—and her—that it wasn't possible.

While William dashed here and there in search of the perfect arrangement, Alice devised her own sensible plan. The family would winter near Lausanne so the boys could attend the Collège Cantonnale. She located a house in Clarens with room and board for four francs a day, and for Peggy she had a governess, a tranquil, stout woman who spoke German, French, and Italian and charged sixty-five francs a month. Alice liked the woman. She would try to make William see the practicality of these arrangements.[30] She so loved the Swiss mountains that she hoped to bring him around to her plan.

On 21 July she and the children left Gryon for Lausanne. Alice thought she had come up a notch.[31] The city, located on Lake Geneva, had long been a favorite residence for foreigners. During her husband's short, frequent absences Alice took long walks when she could (with and occasionally without the two younger children), negotiating the city's narrow, winding streets and staircases from her vantage point along the rue Petit-chêne. The University of Lausanne had received university status the year before she arrived, making the city a growing center for learning and the arts, but at first Alice acquired culture only through osmosis. There was scarcely time even for reading or for taking dictation from William.

William found places for the boys near Lausanne so they could learn French, with the aim of putting them in school at Versailles that fall. Harry went to Pastor Cérésole's home at Vevey, where he shared a room with the pastor's youngest child, a ten-year-old boy. Madame Cérésole was Louis Agassiz' niece, and the couple had seven children.[32] Billy was lodged at Pastor Thélin's. He was homesick: he didn't like the food, and he shared a room with two other boys. Harry, on the other hand, sent his parents a cheery postcard.[33] Reading it, Alice cried despite its happy message because this was the first time any of her children had left her. Fortunately, Peggy calmed down, playing happily with the daughters of Swiss philosopher Théodore Flournoy, her father's colleague.[34]

Once he settled his family in Lausanne, William suggested Henry might meet them in Geneva, or he would meet Henry alone, leaving Alice to her child tending. He wanted his brother, now in Italy, to stay only twenty-four hours with them, fearing he would quickly tire of their child-centered conversation and cheap lodgings.[35] Henry arrived at the Hôtel Richemont in Lausanne on 29 July in the midst of a heat wave. Despite William's warnings against a visit of over a day's duration, Henry intended to pay his American family a good visit, but he was greeted by a family quarrel. The two older boys had come from the homes where they boarded to meet Uncle Henry, but Billy had skin sores, and William had lost his temper with Harry.

Just after Henry's arrival, William departed on a prearranged walking tour in the Engadine with his friends Frederick W. H. Myers and A. T. Myers of the British Society for Psychical Research.[36] He left Alice to entertain his brother, claiming that he needed the mountains and solitude to calm his nerves. He had not informed Henry of his plans and was perhaps secretly relieved to leave his wife to help ease him into uncledom. At any rate, William did not change his tour dates. After he left he asked Alice to convey his apologies for losing his temper: living with Billy and Peggy in a bedroom for two months had made him "explosive."[37]

This was Henry's first face-to-face meeting with Alice in a decade. While she found her brother-in-law staid, formal, and heavy to the point of obesity, she liked him immensely. On his side he fell into an easy friendship with her, although he regretted leaving Daniel and Ariana Curtises' Palazzo Barbaro in Venice, with its medallioned and arabesqued ceilings, its views of rosy dawns, and its supersubtle hostess, Donna Isabella (Isabella Stewart Gardner, who was renting the palazzo that month), only to find a scattered family. His nephews were treated as he and his brothers had been during their youth in Europe, placed here and there in different schools.[38]

But despite the family quarrel and William's departure, Henry tried to bond with Alice and her children, perhaps partly motivated by the loss of his sister that spring. He rescued Billy from Pastor Thélin, and they traveled by boat to visit Harry at Vevey, a kind gesture on the part of a bachelor who had spent little time in the company of children. Henry told his two nephews to embrace when the visit was over: they should not be afraid to show their feelings for one another.[39] He turned his back in order not to embarrass them. He told Isabella Gardner that he was pleased at "uncledom": "They [his nephews] are charming and the little girl a <u>bellezza</u>."[40] Henry had sent them thoughtful notes in the past, so the children were delighted to meet him in person.

The evening of 4 August Henry slipped away to visit his friend Henrietta Reubell at Ouchy. Henrietta, or "Etta," as Henry called her, was an intelligent, sophisticated, rich Parisian-American woman whom he found most agreeable.[41] He and Etta discussed Americans who drag their children around Europe. Henry mused on a plot for a story: a girl waits for a husband to take her abroad but the husband never comes, and the girl dies without seeing Europe.[42] As she had done in 1882, Alice provided him with a starting point for his storytelling. Henry knew how often William had promised to take her abroad and then changed his mind. This helped Henry construct a heroine who was disappointed in this way. Henry remained another week and a half with the beleaguered Alice before returning to his flat in London on 15 August.[43] Earlier, he had told Charles Eliot that he planned to spend a month with the family, but William's immediate departure had made him feel oddly unwelcome.[44]

After Henry left Alice went to bed that night feeling discouraged: William had abandoned the notion of Versailles and proposed going to Stuttgart instead, but she feared the place would bore them. She had her own methods of achieving results. Before she fell asleep she called mentally for help "with all that is within me" and then drifted off peacefully. When she awoke the next morning, she knew that they would go to Florence.

William had left the hotel early that morning, but when he returned at eleven o'clock she proposed Italy. He was delighted.[45]

Alice had spent months in Florence, so her memory housed images of its stone buildings, stone streets, stone churches. This was no abstraction she sought; she sought her youth, and it came to her in a dream state, so she was not responsible for the suggestion. Her husband explained in *The Principles of Psychology*: "It [consciousness] is always interested more in one part of its object than in another, and welcomes and rejects, or chooses, all the while it thinks."[46] She consciously selected a topic to focus on before she fell asleep: where to go for the winter. Then in her dream other mental processes took over, and the Italian city of her youth surfaced.

She was so confident her plan would work that she did not scruple at using indirect methods to persuade her spouse to adopt it. "William had gone to meet Myers so I did not see him till 11 a.m. but when he got here & I proposed Florence as my choice he was <u>delighted</u>. He had reproached me, justly with not having any <u>needs</u> for myself and it made me realize how starved & poor I should feel to go back to Cambr. having only tended the children, and done & seen nothing for myself! I don't think we shall change again."[47] These words to her mother proved to be the proverbial last ones.

Shortly after his return to London Henry reported to Grace Norton that he had been "near" William and his family rather than "with" them. He described their arrangements to her: "They have plans as numerous as the leaves of the forest, and much more various." But he approved their plan to go to Florence rather than to Paris or Stuttgart in the fall, mentioning Florence's Cascine as a sunny paradise for children.[48] He planned to visit them again—he hoped to have a real reunion with William this next time.

Plans for Florence came together quickly. Through American expatriate Dr. William Baldwin, who had befriended Henry in 1887 in Florence and attended sister Alice during her last days, William learned of an English school for the boys. Though he made no claims for its academic program, Henry thought it would have a little Latin and Greek and lots of lawn tennis.[49] And Alice could return to the beautiful city on the Arno, where she had studied music with Luigi Vannuccini years before. The decision for the winter made, she felt happier than she had in years. Her life was greatly simplified: she had virtually no housekeeping to superintend, as the house in Lausanne was unadorned and comfortable. She found the food plain but healthy: no sweet dishes at dinner, only fruit. Since her children were contented, she was.[50]

The Jameses stayed in Switzerland until mid-September, when bad weather made them suddenly embark for Italy. After stopping at Lake Maggiore for over a week, they reached Florence on 21 September. Although the children immediately became ill, fortunately there were furnished apartments available for the family: the fall tourist season had not yet begun. By 4 October the Jameses were installed in an apartment at 16 Piazza dell' Independenza, on the northwest side of the square. The square was close to the central train station, Stazione Centrale di Santa Maria Novella, with Santa Maria Novella church close to it. Built in the thirteenth century by the Dominicans, the church had remarkable fifteenth-century frescoes, some painted by Domenico Ghirlandaio and his assistants, one of them a young Michelangelo. The Galleria dell' Accademia, Alice's "Gallery," was just five blocks away: Michelangelo's carving of David had been moved there in 1873 from the Piazza della Signoria.

At first Alice found that Italy did not fulfill Henry's promises, though he comforted her that the city's charms would compensate for any hardship. Florence would soon "steal more & more into your affections & beguile you in to enduring certain domestic discomforts."[51] While the apartment's rooms were large and sunny and the kitchen's open hearth ten by six feet, there was no oven or any domestic conveniences.[52] The bedrooms were unheated, but the Jameses found sheet-iron stoves that vented through the chimney.[53] Unfortunately, they could only heat one main room, so William had no separate study that winter.[54] Evenings they crowded around the dining room table to read and work. At night they placed a wooden cage with an earthen dish full of hot coals between their sheets to warm the beds. Things improved, though, when Dr. Baldwin found Alice a cook for $2.50 weekly. Raphaello was creative and amenable.[55]

The indispensable Baldwin befriended many Americans abroad. He was a highly competent physician who had attended royalty, a magnetic, charming man with gray hair, clear eyes, and an aquiline nose. Before opening a practice in Florence he had gone to medical college in Long Island and then studied in Vienna. Besides treating the American expatriate community, he treated the peasants in the Abruzzi region, drawn by curiosity at their rare diseases but also motivated by humanitarian impulses. Like William James, Baldwin was a bright, active, ambitious man.[56] Alice wished they could have seen more of him that winter.[57]

Apartment life became easier in mid-October when the two older boys started at the English school the doctor recommended. Though Harry and Billy took French and German lessons, they did not learn as much language as they would have in a foreign school, but they played cricket and football and found friends.[58] Alice taught Peggy two hours a day and then took her to fencing and gymnastic lessons, but that was not enough for the energetic little girl. "Peggy's needs are not yet provided for but I hope they will be soon," she wrote to Henry. "She is growing so very active that two hours of teaching at home does not seem just the thing. . . . These rainy days she has a wretched time with no play, and the boys hector her till she gets wild with excitement." From Ruby Baldwin, who had seven children, Alice learned of a school just started by an English lady where she hoped to enroll Peggy.[59] Fortunately, she had help for Francis Tweedy: his Swiss nurse, Hélène, was devoted to the child.[60]

Just as Alice settled her children, William turned "vile."[61] He was without his frenetic Harvard routine, a routine that made his life and hers easier. Confined with small children, he found his misgivings about a sabbatical trip *en famille* fully justified. He desperately missed his Irving Street library. He decided to go to Padua and then to Venice, ostensibly to investigate a psychic occurrence for the British Society for Psychical Research, but his departure also undoubtedly owed much to their living arrangements. Alice was unhappy when he left, but William wrote to make amends, wishing she were with him.[62] He could not bear the demands of a daily household routine, and Alice could not leave the children to join him.

The couple fought often during their stay in Florence, usually over children and money. William confessed to Grace Ashburner that he found it impossible to economize while living abroad, pinpointing one of his own weaknesses exactly, though he could not overcome it.[63] When he brought a friend home for lunch and insisted on serving the Champagne Alice reserved for dinner, she was visibly upset. Another day he came home with paintings, an unauthorized purchase. When she protested, William took a pair of scissors and cut the landscapes into pieces while their son Harry watched in horror.[64] Perhaps his outbursts were triggered by his loss of conjugal intimacy with his wife, added to the stress of being constantly with children.

That winter the Jameses enjoyed music as an antidote to their marital spats: they attended performances, including new operas. In December they saw Pietro Mascagni's acclaimed *I Rantzau*, the libretto based on an 1882 novel entitled *Les deux frères* by French writers Émile Erckmann and Alexandre Chatrian.[65] A contemporary Florentine reviewer found the music far better than the plot. Alice's singing teacher, Vannuccini, was still alive, but there is no record of her visiting him.

By December the family had more or less settled in, but Alice experienced depression. William empathized with the monotony of her current life: he occasionally left the family during these months, while she was confined to quarters.[66] The boys liked their school, and the younger children kept healthy, although Francis Tweedy roused William and Alice between 5:00 and 6:00 a.m., and Peggy clung to them throughout the day.[67] Eliza Gibbens sent Francis *The House That Jack Built* for his birthday. He loved to hear his mother read the rhythmic, repetitive words.

Just before Christmas Alice reflected on her own past and on her current struggles with her children. She tried to control her character, writing to her aunt Nannie:

> You used to be so cheerful and I remember you and Mother laughing together—what about I didn't know but it was all the more delightful for the vague sense I had of our situation being by no means a light or amusing one. . . . [Y]et the "sphere" in the house was always a cheerful one. It has come to mean more than anything else to me. As I look backward I am so grateful to Mother and you two dear Aunts for never clouding our lives as I fear I do my children's and so I resolve anew to give up the struggle to accomplish this or that and try to be a more tranquil, cheerful mother and daughter and niece and keep a heart at leisure from itself to soothe and sympathize. It is a better ideal, for me, and it comes to me as one more good gift from those to whom I owe so much.[68]

On Christmas Day the children had stockings in the sitting room, which Alice had decorated with mistletoe and Vallombrosa holly she had purchased for thirty cents.[69] She described their celebration to Eliza Gibbens: "After coffee we came into the sitting room where the children had hung up their stockings. Peggy had a tea-set, a toy watch, three books[,] a fancy basket of candy, the little turquoise ring I have had so long (just fits her)[,] a straw hat for her doll and a pretty work basket from Miss Loring. The baby had a Noah's ark, blocks, two lumps of sugar which filled up the measure of his contentment. The boys had candy and two books a piece and I had a lovely ring from William, three beautiful perles." Though William would not go, she took the children to Christmas service at the American church, but the altars and bowing priests offended her Protestant sensibilities.[70]

During her six months in Italy Alice's good nature and empathy endeared her to expatriates and visitors alike. As if she had not given enough already to her family, she gave generously of herself to these virtual strangers. She needed a community of friends, even if they were sometimes demanding, to offset her constant family duties. Frank Duveneck, the husband of William's old Newport friend Lizzie Boott, who had died in 1888, called, as well as artist Frank Loring and his sister Mary. Even Mark Twain dined with them.[71] They found him delightful company and wished he lived in Cambridge. Alice celebrated the New Year by throwing a dinner party, inviting the Lorings, Baron Ostensacken, and Harvard graduate and art collector Charles Loeser. When she had the time and the means, Alice entertained brilliantly. She managed to produce Japanese umbrellas to screen the lamps, red skirts for the candles, and a flower arrangement for the table. The dinner was served by a servant hired for the evening. The gala went on until after eleven at night, and William hadn't made her dinner any more impossible than he made anything else, she thought.[72]

Still struggling with her weight, Alice continued to diet, but that did not prevent her from hosting dinners.[73] She did not expect others to follow her extreme weight-loss regimes.[74] In February she promised her husband she would try to improve her appearance: "You know your good theory of music becoming harmful in so far as its appeal to the emotions bears no fruit? I found myself resolving Saturday night, as I listened to Beethoven's Serenades—a perfect succession of young raptures—that I would no more offend you with black clothes, even if I do make a mountain of myself."[75]

That winter the Jameses' regular circle included Mrs. Elizabeth "Bessie"

Glendower Evans, widow of Glendower Evans, a lawyer and William's student during the 1870s. Bessie had energetically taken up varied social causes after her husband's death: reform schools, child labor laws, socialist movements, labor movements, and feminist issues. She also had a real interest in philosophy. She loved Alice for her warmth, wit, and intelligence. After her husband died in 1886, Bessie had become a devoted friend of both Jameses, sharing moral values with Alice and admiring William's work but lacking both Jameses' sense of humor.[76] In January Bessie begged Alice to accompany her to Egypt for six weeks. William hoped she would go, realizing how much good she would gain from the trip, but Alice would not leave her children.[77]

In February the Jameses decided that the English school was not challenging enough for Harry. They arranged to put him in day school in Munich, where he could study Latin and German and take riding lessons. If the school challenged Harry, then Alice would stay in Germany for the next year with the other three children while William returned to Harvard. Though a year in Germany recommended itself, she dreaded such a long separation. William escorted the boy, docile Harry never complaining at leaving his friends and family behind. Alice missed them both, promising to be amenable when her husband returned. Despite all their hardships during these months abroad, she loved him more than ever. "As if I would let you be changed, or ever be capable of finding rest in life apart from your side."[78]

Even this short separation exacerbated the couple's differences. Alice's esteem sank lower, and William complained she did not care for him. They exchanged letters over the picture episode, Alice apologetic. "What you write of those pictures makes the old sick feeling come back," she told William. "Let us never speak of them again. I am guilty of a deed of violence for which I can only atone by future temperateness and gentleness."[79] He interpreted one letter to imply that his presence had made life too noisy and unsettled for Alice, as she enjoyed the quiet house while he was gone. Again she wrote proclaiming her love and devotion. "Don't ever say that it is your absence that makes the quiet—it hurts my feelings as Peggy says. You will never know the way in which I miss you. . . . Each day I try to spend as you would like, and each day when confusion and hurry invade me I feel glad that it had not destroyed your precious time."[80] When William's mental health vacillated, she took the blame. "I seem to myself to have grown so hard to live with, but William darling don't despair of me for I can change with time and trying."[81]

After Harry was settled in Munich, Alice and William had one romantic excursion. They left Billy, Peggy, and Francis Tweedy in Florence and went to Siena for two days. William, however, found the town dry and gloomy. While he admired the churches, he was disappointed in the art.[82] Alice, too, found Siena less enchanting than she had two decades before, telling her sister Margaret, "Of our visit together 18 years ago I can recall very little, not even our hotel. I do remember the picture we bought and regret having changed it for that Miss Bradford's inferior one. I suppose Siena needs the sunshine, but even with it the city would seem melancholy and poor in the extreme."[83]

Before she left Florence for good Alice helped another member of the American community, pianist Jessie Donaldson Hodder, wife of William's former student Alfred Hodder. She pitied the young woman, who expected a baby soon, and would stay to assist if allowed.[84] The Hodders arranged to rent the Jameses' apartment after their lease ran out on 31 March, and Alice was there when Jessie delivered her daughter Olive on 21 April. They wrapped the baby up in Francis Tweedy's blankets, and then Alice left the apartment so that mother and baby could be alone.[85]

William's last act in Italy was to design a stone casket for his sister's ashes. The inscription came from Dante's *Paradiso*: "Ed essa da martiro e da esiglio venne a questa pace" — "And she, from martyrdom, and from exile came unto this peace."[86] Alice too found peace here, rejuvenated by her freedom from some of her household duties. "I should like to look as much like an olive tree as I can for the rest of my natural life. Billy says my hair is green! That is one step toward it," she told Bessie Evans.[87]

On 15 April William left Italy, taking Billy with him to the Cérésoles at Vevey, Switzerland, so that the boy could resume his French studies. William told Alice that the Cérésoles reversed the roles that the Jameses held in their own family: Pastor Cérésole was strong, and Madame Cérésole was sweet.[88] On 21 April Alice followed with the two younger children, stopping overnight in Milan with Bessie Evans. The next day Alice and Bessie joined William at the Pension Gottlieben at Hinter Meggen, near Lucerne. "I am myself thankful to get out of Italy. I am no longer young enough to enjoy the general decay and shabbiness, and the ever present poverty of the people," Alice told her mother.[89] When she arrived in Switzerland, the fruit trees were in bloom, the best bloom in forty years, local people claimed.

On 4 May Henry joined the Jameses, staying nearby in Lucerne. This time it was Alice who abandoned the newly arrived Henry; she decided to visit her son, still in school in Munich. She made her plans abruptly, perhaps motivated by longing for her eldest, and then made a beeline for young Harry, who was about to celebrate his fourteenth birthday — it would have been his first alone had Alice not come. Alice planned to pay for third-class train passage, but when she learned that she would have to spend the night in a hotel in Zürich to make her transfer, she paid a higher fare for a better itinerary.[90] In Munich she met Harry's primary teacher, Miss Kern, who said he had first-rate abilities but would not work on subjects that bored him. Harry was her most honest pupil. That must have made Alice glad: she had taught him not to tell lies when he was only three. He was allowed out of school for a day, so Alice took him to Count Adolf Friedrich von Schack's art gallery, where they saw paintings by Swiss symbolist painter Arnold Böcklin, and one evening they went to the theater.[91]

During her weeklong absence William entertained Henry, discovering again his younger brother's tender heart. He stayed at Lucerne's Hotel National and walked daily to Meggen, where the Jameses were quartered. One wet afternoon Henry cried along with the raindrops as the two eldest brothers remembered the death of their brother Wilkie a decade before.[92] Henry's two nephews and niece pleased him, and Alice was flattered when he observed that Peggy spoke French very well. During her brief time with him Alice realized Henry liked to talk to her, and her spirits rose.[93] Being with his family again allowed the writer to stop and assess the direction his career was taking. He mused on the pleasant thought of leaving his theatrical ventures altogether and returning to his fiction.[94]

The Jameses decided to return to America at the end of the summer. Since Harry was not ready academically to enroll in the gymnasium in Munich, there was no reason for Alice to remain abroad another year.[95] While William was more than ready to go home in June, telling Eliza Gibbens that "we are primarily and essentially a <u>nursery</u>, with adults attached, and I don't think that my truest vocation is to be an appendage to a nursery," he agreed to spend a month in London.[96]

They arranged to go alone. More than a year earlier Henry had advised them to leave the children behind if they visited London.[97] Alice's response had been a sad but definite "no." She would not leave her children, not even to see the great capital. "I thank you very much dear Harry, for your kind invitation to me and only wish I could accept it. But I shall not leave the children to the care of strangers and I am not likely to have any other guardian for them. This may strike you as weak-hearted but if my existence is to justify itself it must be through other lives, and the children need me now, every one of them. William will really be much easier in mind for knowing that they are with me."[98]

Despite her objections to indulging herself, however, a year abroad with four young ones had weakened Alice's resolve. Harry would stay at his school in Munich, and the three younger children could go to the Cérésoles. On 17 June 1893 Alice and William set foot in London, having at last "planted" their children. The couple settled into Henry's pleasant quarters at 34 De Vere Gardens, Kensington, on a spacious cul-de-sac just minutes from Kensington Gardens. William worried their visit would inconvenience his brother, but on 22 June Henry moved to 2 Wellington Crescent at Ramsgate to avoid what he told his close friend Edmund Gosse were "the interruptions & embroilments of this horrible time," the horrible time being his ongoing assaults on London's theatrical world.[99] Since 1891, beginning with a stage adaptation of his early novel *The American* and its addition of a happy ending, Henry had been writing plays. In addition to his theatrical ventures, Henry was faced with other relations who were also visiting London: Carrie James, Wilkie's widow, with her two children, and Mary Holton James, Bob's wife, with her mother and daughter. All these relatives disturbed the rhythm of his writing, so Henry decamped and left his visitors to their own devices. He told Francis Boott that if he were in Alice and William's place, he would not return to Switzerland to get the children.[100]

Henry's generosity meant that Alice, at least, had a vacation, the first of any length with her husband since their honeymoon fifteen years earlier. William made frequent trips alone, but this was Alice's first away from her offspring. They resembled "middle aged omnibus horses let loose in a pasture."[101] She awoke in the mornings to rooms full of light, with views of streets and neighboring rooftops—and no children to satisfy. William and Henry collaborated to make her visit worthwhile, Henry by sharing his quarters and William by hoping that no news of their children's illness or other disasters would waft across the Channel.

Alice's days held seldom-experienced delights. She had time to shop, visiting London dressmakers to replace the clothes she had worn for over a year now and indulging in a marathon four-hour spree at London's cooperative stores, perhaps at the city's best known, the Army and Navy Co-operative Society at 105 Victoria Street. It later became one of her favorite London stops. Victorian department stores displayed the latest fashions, including the new tailored suits that reflected women's increasing presence in the world of work. The most popular were made of white, brown, or blue duck, worn with a white linen blouse under a vest. Alice had her blue serge redesigned to resemble London fashions, adding a sleeveless jacket and braid trim everywhere, and she altered a velvet dress that had belonged to sister Alice to wear to a dinner party.[102]

While in London she met notables Sir Leslie Stephen, Viscount James Bryce and his family, publisher Alexander Macmillan's daughter Margaret and her American husband, Louis Dyer, now at Oxford, and the Henry Sidgwicks, he the past president of the British Society for Psychical Research. At the behest of the newly emboldened Alice, the Jameses almost knocked on British philosopher Shadworth Hollway Hodgson's door after 9:00 p.m. when they saw a light on in his library window, but William feared his friendly adversary might be getting ready for bed.[103]

Riding on top of London's omnibuses, sometimes with William and sometimes alone, Alice traveled about the immense city, with its rich history and occasional pea soup fog, visiting London's splendid art galleries, including the New Gallery and the National Gallery. On 13 July she saw Hampton Court on the Thames, Henry VIII's favorite palace, with its Christopher Wren staircase, clock court, Great Fountain Garden, Chapel Royal, orangeries, maze, and world's oldest tennis court.[104]

The high point of these magical weeks was her visit to the House of Commons. During the first week in July she reserved a seat to hear the "Grand Old Man," William Ewart Gladstone, the famous Liberal leader, one of the great moral forces of his age. The debate concerned the Government of Ireland Bill, or Home Rule, which Gladstone had first proposed in 1886. In his fourth and last term as prime minister, the eighty-two year old campaigned to pass the bill, which would accord the Irish a much greater degree of self-governance. Alice still kept her interest in reform movements, despite her immersion in domestic life. She thrilled to see history in the making, listening to Arthur Balfour, conservative MP and former chief secretary for Ireland, with an open mind, finding him the best speaker for the opposition. "Gladstone is the most impressive 'human' I have ever beheld or listened to," she reported to Bessie Evans. "It seemed to me that one <u>must</u> believe what he believes."[105] Home Rule passed the House of Commons but failed in the House of Lords, and Gladstone resigned the following year. Sister Alice had been a keen supporter of Irish Home Rule, and now Alice was a keen observer.

Partway through her visit she told Henry, "I am enjoying life to a degree that is little short of unprincipled. And after all it is your kindness which make[s] London such a paradise."[106] That month she realized her most cherished desires: her love of literature, her interest in politics, her fashion fancies, and even erotic moments with her husband. All this she owed to her brother-in-law, who encouraged the visit and then stepped aside to allow her the freedom to realize these desires.

When the month ended Alice returned to Switzerland, William staying two weeks longer in London before joining her. Alice's reunion with her children brought guilt feelings. Francis Tweedy was shy, reluctant to approach her and saying "'peur de maman' [afraid of Mama]." She also reproached herself that the trip had been expensive and wreaked havoc with William's need to rest and work, telling her husband of her "sickening consciousness that you did it all for me alas! the burden of [it] saddens me."[107]

Alice returned to England in mid-August, Harry in tow, William remaining with the other children in Switzerland. Though Henry was prepared to house her, she went directly to Harrow to stay with an old friend from her Dresden days, Joseph Thatcher Clarke, and his family.[108] She wouldn't tell Henry their route in order to spare him a trip to Charing

Cross, but she vowed her allegiance. She wrote to William of her new feelings for her brother-in-law. "I shall always love Harry for his kindness to me and to everybody. And the 'Brothers' could hardly have given him a serener face."[109] Before the century was over Alice's ties to Henry would grow even stronger.

9 The Will to Endure

THE JAMESES RETURNED TO CAMBRIDGE in August 1893, only to face financial losses and the necessity of consolidating their holdings. The American economy had dipped precariously during their months abroad: two-thirds of Alice's legacy had been lost.[1] She had encountered the same thing two decades earlier, when she came back from Europe to find the Gibbens family funds depleted. Fortunately, her European sojourn had allowed her to regain some of her strength, which had been drained by eleven years of childbearing and nursing, and this time she had William as a financial provider.

The depression was deep and widespread, starting in America and then spreading across the Atlantic. The Philadelphia and Reading Railroad failed in January 1893, causing financial panic. Other railroads went next: the Erie Railroad, the Northern Pacific, and finally the Atchison, Topeka and Santa Fe at the end of the year. Widespread bank failures followed these losses, and the stock market plunged. The West and the South were already in the midst of an agricultural depression, and multiple railroad and bank failures worsened conditions in those regions. Gold reserves dwindled, falling below $100 million. This large-scale depression was not over until 1897.

Alice and William had spent considerable sums abroad, dipping deeply into their savings. They brought back twenty-eight trunks, three clocks, a set of dishes, and two maids, emblems of material success. However, the depression meant they must retrench. Some Harvard professors were let go, but fortunately William kept his job at his same salary. The Jameses were still short of funds, however. This time Alice did not consider teaching, but she entertained other plans. Learning of people willing to pay high prices for Cambridge rentals, she offered 95 Irving Street to one party for $2,000 a year, but she was unable to conclude the deal.[2] William and Alice even considered the drastic step of selling their beloved house.[3]

In addition to their financial woes, Alice barely had time to unpack before she was inundated with family and social obligations. William was vexed these years with increasing responsibilities, both to Harvard and to his profession, and she felt his frustrations. When he returned to teaching that fall William suffered depression, so he made eighteen visits to a mind-curer, a Miss Clarke, to alleviate it, calling it a spell of melancholy.[4] Sometimes these mind-cures restored his ability to sleep.[5] He also contracted tonsillitis at the end of October, but the disease at least forced him to rest.[6] Despite his depression he kept his sense of wonder at the world; nothing was quite like William James's exuberant embrace of reality. On his way to Thomas Davidson's Keene Valley summer institute, Glenmore, two summers after his return, he wrote a postcard to Peggy expressing his delight in and empathy for small things: "Yesterday a beautiful hummingbird came into the library and spent two hours without resting, trying to find his way out by the skylight in the ceiling. You never saw such untiring strength. Filled with pity for his fatigue, I went into the garden and culled a beautiful rose. The moment I held it up in my hand under the skylight, the angelic bird flew down into it and rested there as in a nest—the beautifullest sight you ever saw."[7]

That fall William resumed his investigations of psychic phenomena, even though many of his American peers refused to consider parapsychology as a serious pursuit. In England, however, experiments in psychic research had more validity. In 1893 Frederick Myers asked William to take the presidency of the British Society for Psychical Research. He refused, but in November Myers warned him he would be asked again, citing Alice's approval of the society's work. "I am sure Mrs. James would agree to much in this letter—and the dear spirits are hovering around us in the Summer Land."[8] Late in 1893 William accepted.

The Jameses were besieged at home after their return. Because of Alice's warm hospitality and William's irrepressible nature, old and young alike swarmed to 95 Irving Street. William constantly protested this stream of visitors, yet he never turned anyone away. He welcomed the stimulation and the distractions visitors brought, and, despite the financial downturn, the couple entertained constantly. Alice had grown up in a large family, and while the Weymouth Webbs and the Boston Gibbenses lacked the sophistication of her present set, she loved company and entertained in style. Her Gibbens relations praised her elaborate, well-served meals.[9]

Bob was on Alice's hands again too, at least part of the time. Still unstable, still drifting, he sought answers in the afterlife. Visits to mediums let him find his parents, sister Alice, and brother Wilkie. With the mediums' help he constructed a world where deceased family members watched over him closely, assuring him of their constant love and guidance. In December 1893 Bob visited Mrs. Piper, by now a virtual member of the James-Gibbens clan, receiving revelations through her control, Dr. Phinuit. Bob's estranged wife, Mary, would reveal her inner goodness and truth, and their marital problems would be resolved. If he only waited and believed, all good things would come to him. Bob confided his money worries to Phinuit, who replied, "'Money be hanged.'" He also learned that Swedenborg was happy that Bob displayed Swedenborg's portrait on the easel in his room. Henry Sr. assured his troubled son, "'I will watch over you always.'"[10] Despite these reassurances from the dead, Alice continued to do her share by watching Bob on earth.

That holiday season William again decamped for Newport, so Alice spent her Christmas with her children, her mother, her aunt Nannie Webb, and her sister Margaret helping her make a quiet celebration. On Christmas Day she wrote to her husband, "We miss you so much that some compensating joy ought to be won for you. . . . The lack of you is like missing the air I breathe; and just how keen a want it is I think you will never imagine because you are a man and not a woman. Heaven bless you and give us all a good new Year."[11] During the holiday accusations came from absent William, though it seems Alice might have accused him. He told her that he was not missed, he was not needed. She could not tell him enough that she loved him, because no matter how many times she did, he wanted to hear it again. She chided him for saying, "I don't think I am probably very much missed."[12] Next year, she informed him, he should plan to be at home.[13]

By 1894 William and Alice could count on money in the bank from his royalties, which helped offset the previous year's losses. *The Principles of Psychology* and *The Briefer Course* were translated into many languages, solidifying William's reputation and providing a steady income stream. But the royalties, his salary, and the income from the Syracuse properties were still not enough to maintain a family of six and two large residences. To maintain their lifestyle, William also gave lectures in the summer, often to schoolteachers and sometimes to general audiences. He was gone nearly all summer, leaving Alice with the houses and the children. While he was away, he praised her to others. After his death, Sarah Hervey Porter, who knew William at Thomas Davidson's Glenmore, remembered his visit to her Keene Valley cottage when he lay on her piazza one summer night and ruminated on all Alice had been to him.[14]

Even though she knew how much she meant to William, Alice continued to pay a price for her loyalty. Sometimes she was nearly frantic trying to keep her spouse calm and steady as he worked at an increasing pace. In 1894 William was elected president of the American Psychological Association, one more duty added to his teaching, research, writing, and lecturing. In the spring of 1894 he spent another five weeks in bed, seeking help from Miss Clarke, and summer found him still weak. He attributed his poor health to "weakness in my head" not caused by fatigue.[15] Mentally, he was not completely stable.

That spring, pushed from all sides, Alice's spirits waned. In May she went to Chocorua to open the house, taking Billy and Peggy with her, writing to William of her own depression, which he called her "heart-sunk state," which he thought usually accompanied her first days alone in Chocorua.[16] William's visits to Miss Clarke helped his headaches, but nothing helped Alice.[17] During the 1890s she was prone to having sick headaches, sometimes very bad ones. Also, she was approaching the age of menopause in an era when this transition was a fearful one, a traumatic change for women.[18]

Before she left for Chocorua for the summer Alice supervised work at 95 Irving Street, painting Peggy's bedroom, installing a mantelpiece in the dining room, and papering the dining room. As a tribute to her beloved father-in-law, she wanted to have his chair re-covered. She asked William, "Do tell me if you would like to have your father's old chair, (your desk chair) recovered in green leather and made whole. The hair is starting through the cover and the rounds below are more than half out of their sockets. Grant said he should want it a couple of weeks certainly to let the paint harden ere he rubbed it down. I love the old veteran and hate to have it touched but it must be done sometime."[19]

Though they had collaborated well on such practical matters since the first days of their marriage, their romantic relationship was changing. Since their honeymoon William had been an ardent lover, despite the nineteenth century's belief that ejaculation weakened men and hindered their intellectual development.[20] Now, however, he had problems with inflammation along with difficulties making love to Alice, something new in their marriage. In May he complained, "my 'place' got hot and a little sore to touch last night, and I found more inflammation, but it is gone today."[21] In July he begged Alice "to forget my unmanliness—banish it from your attention—there will be better days, as there have been."[22] Although his failures as a lover may well have come from age and not from a lack of interest in Alice, part of her depression could have stemmed from his failure. She was accustomed to having a passionate, even if sometimes absent, lover.

By the fall of 1894 William felt better, but Alice showed little change. He told his cousin Ellen Emmet Hunter that his wife sometimes suffered from low spirits and acute depression.[23] While she retained her belief in William and his work, she occasionally doubted her own abilities, turning inward and burying her feelings. Part of that tendency toward self-immolation came from her adherence to Swedenborg, who counseled putting aside individual needs in favor of immersion within the wider human community and thus within God. The confidence that some women now found, thanks to suffragette and feminist movements, eluded Alice. She refused to let herself think of what she might have achieved on her own.

And her work, like William's, escalated. While he finally broke down and hired a stenographer-typist, he still frequently asked Alice for help.

Also, William's seminar classes sometimes met in their library, and student advisees sought him out at home. In addition, Alice supervised school and social activities for their four children. It seemed at least one of them was sick at any given time. Despite all these demands, Alice pursued her own interests. She belonged to a sewing bee and other clubs that kept her abreast of faculty doings (Grace Hopkinson Eliot was a member of at least one group), and she kept up a constant round of visiting in Cambridge. Henry worried about the current pace of her life, but she did little to slow down.

Alice saw rewards for her work in at least one arena, as she approved of the direction William's work took in the early 1890s. His reputation as a psychologist secured by the positive reception of *The Principles of Psychology* worldwide, he extended his investigations in philosophy. He persuaded Hugo Munsterberg of Freiburg im Breisgau to return to Harvard to take over the behaviorally oriented psychology lab he had started so that he could teach courses in Kant and other subjects oriented more toward philosophy than psychology. The path he took to philosophy, though, was partly through the spiritual world—a sort of Dantean descent into Hell, according to some of his peers who could not stomach his psychic research. Alice, though, applauded the move. William's refusal to rule out an afterlife suited her religious principles. In May 1894 he even taught a seminar entitled "The Character of Swedenborg," which he deemed dull, but still, in teaching the religious mystic, he acknowledged his departed father's and living wife's credos.[24]

William and Alice continued to explore the spirit world together, particularly through Mrs. Piper. In the spring of 1894 he reported on yet another sitting. "The Shalers had a very decent success with Mrs. Piper this p.m. Mrs. Shaler sat with her (looking lovely the while) with her face against Mrs. P.'s dishevelled hair; and Mrs. P. gave her a fairly copious context to a seal which had belonged to Mrs. S.'s brother, dead within the year, family as well as Christian names etc. They both agree that it is inexplicable, and are sending to have certain facts verified," he told Alice. "Meanwhile Mrs. P. says she won[']t sit again till next Fall, after the sitting which she gives to C. Norton tomorrow A.M.—So far, so good!"[25] When Charles Eliot Norton became a moral convert at a sitting, William shared his excitement with Alice.[26]

When Josiah Royce refused to help him investigate Mrs. Piper and other mediums, William was angry. Royce would not even come to Irving Street for a single hour for a free sitting.[27] Munsterberg, too, refused to have anything to do with Mrs. Piper. That May, William defended the medium to Clark University president Granville Stanley Hall, formerly a graduate student in Harvard's psychology department and a proponent of experimental psychology. William seemed willing to risk his own credibility to pursue this line of research. Hall had proposed various tests for Mrs. Piper, but William claimed the tests would fail, as she had no clairvoyant powers. He believed that she reached what he called the "subliminal reservoir." He advised Hall, "The only way to take her is on her own ground. Sit and see what names and facts the 'aura of your person' suggests to her; or bring an object closely associated with some other person (recently dead if possible), give it to her to handle and see what it brings out. Out of 27 sittings which she has just given in N.Y. to total strangers . . . she failed completely I believe in only two."[28]

But William's psychic investigations were not enough for his wife: she wanted him to accept the reality of God. In September she told him there was only one cure for his depression: he must accept a religious viewpoint. She could help him "'lay hold on immortal Life.' Not in the old sense of looking to the future, you know I don't mean that. I mean the consciousness of the Divine in which our incompleteness is forgotten. This seems to me sometimes the only vital thing in life, the only real living."[29] She had been trying to convince him of her God's existence since 1876.

Alice worried not only about her husband but about Henry, too, now that she knew him better. Both she and William were apprehensive about the writer's theatrical ventures. Only his adaptation of his novella *Daisy Miller* had been a strong financial success (and in the case of his eponymous American heroine Henry did not realize most of the profits), but he had a more than solid reputation as a fiction writer and could count on strong reviews and modest profits. He had garnered a devoted, discriminating audience. In the early 1890s, however, he decided to try his hand at writing plays, hoping for royalties and a wider audience. Alice was so kind to Henry that she never criticized his work openly, but William confessed to her privately that he feared his younger brother (whom he called the "boy") would fail: "I have no confidence in his dramatic ability."[30] Condescending to Henry — "his agonies are most characteristic" — when he heard of the failure of *Guy Domville* on the London stage, William worried he would take the debacle "tragically," the very word he had used to describe his relationship with Alice nearly twenty years before.[31] She merely continued her warm letters to her brother-in-law.

These years, while she faced menopause and changes in her own sexuality, Alice again faced the fact that her successful mate was flattered by the attentions of other women. William liked and supported women. He loved Alice deeply, and she cared for children and home; he depended on her to help him with his work. But he could pursue more than one relationship simultaneously. Championing the importance of multiple experiences and perspectives, he had no difficulty in holding seemingly contradictory ideas simultaneously, such as the ideas of loving a wife and admiring a beautiful, vibrant young woman — or more than one beautiful, vibrant young woman.

He actively mentored women's education and careers, enjoying the attention that most academics of his era received from young women students. He helped Mrs. Christine Ladd Franklin, who was at Johns Hopkins; they shared ideas and results of experiments on optics and perception. According to William, she was "the most <u>intellectual</u> woman in the country — a great mathematician etc."[32] He mentored other women students, including Mary Whitton Calkins, a teacher of psychology at Wellesley; Gertrude Stein, his most famous female student; and one of his cousins.[33]

The cousin was Rosina Hubley Emmet, daughter of Ellen Emmet Temple Hunter, sister of Minny Temple. William thought her a lovely young woman. Rosina lived with the Jameses during the fall of 1894 while she studied at Radcliffe. Alice and William argued over her visit, having a heart-to-heart talk, the conclusion being that the girl would live with them while she studied at the college.[34]

At first William was enchanted with Rosina, telling Henry she was a regular trump. "In fact were I a youngster I should aim right at her 'hand,'" though he suspected his brother Henry would not agree with his positive valuation of her.[35] By Christmas, however, her visit had worn thin, especially for Alice. Rosina was creative and cheerful, entertaining gentleman callers by analyzing their handwriting to reveal their personalities, but she was also thoughtless and unorganized.[36] The idea of a young girl was more attractive to William than the constant presence of an active, self-centered college student who was always late to breakfast.[37] After Henry got to know Rosina, he found his young cousin crude and pathetic, as William had surmised he would.[38] When Alice visited her sister Mary in Philadelphia in early June 1895, William wrote to her, "If anything has become dead prose it is that [Rosina's] presence."[39] Alice consoled herself by shopping in the City of Brotherly Love. She found a mirror that she shipped home, and William encouraged her to buy antique night tables and a table for the parlor.[40]

Their marriage survived the Rosina episode. In August 1895 Alice confessed to her husband, "You were never so dear to me as now, and that means much for long ago I thought I had exhausted my capacity for loving, and yearning over you."[41] And later that week, "I bless you in my lyings-down and rising-up and never were you so dear. What a good winter we shall have together!"[42] But one letter written by Alice soon thereafter must have revealed self-doubts and depression, a letter that was destroyed, possibly by Alice herself. William wrote in response:

> I am feeling uncommonly hearty, and anticipate good results to myself. If they would only prove good also to you! And darling, darling Alice, never give way again to such groundless melancholy. When I look back over the years that we have passed together and see into what an entirely new man I have grown, all my normality and efficiency dating from my marriage, I cannot <u>imagine</u> anything different or what sort of a thing an alternative could be. . . . And it is the most absolutely literal of truths that you <u>never</u> stood as high in my eyes as this last year has made you stand.[43]

But her melancholy was not always groundless, as evidenced when William met Pauline Goldmark in the late summer of 1895 at Keene Valley. He was fifty-three, she twenty-one and starting her senior year at Bryn Mawr. Like Alice, she was committed to social causes, though Pauline made a distinguished career of social activism. She had qualities Alice lacked: she was physically active, a mountain climber and camper, and she was an early feminist who fought for the rights of women workers. She had no encumbrances: no fiancé, no husband, no children. Though she clearly enjoyed the attentions of an older, famous man, no record remains of her feelings for William. She never married.

William met Pauline through Dickinson Sergeant Miller, an instructor at Bryn Mawr (where he met Pauline) and a philosopher. Miller had tutored the James children during the summers and became a family friend. Pauline's family had a home at Keene Valley, half a mile from Putnam Camp, and Miller came with her to hike before the Bryn Mawr term began. At first William thought that these two young people might form an alliance, but he could not help finding Pauline lovely himself. He told Alice that Pauline was "a perfect little serious rosebud of a miss Goldmark whom Miller seems very sweet upon." She was athletically inclined and could climb like a monkey. In the same letter he announced his complete happiness, a real contrast to his previous summer's depression: "I have been happy, <u>happy</u>, HAPPY!" Then he wished that his wife were there, as Keene Valley made him remember their honeymoon.[44]

While her husband hiked with Pauline, Alice experienced poor health. William thought that some of her ailments were due to an organic cause (probably a premenopausal condition), and he advised her to seek medical help.[45] But they may have also been due in part to William's admiration of this young woman. Alice thought Jane Austen was an astute reporter of reality, and, like this author, she was enough of a realist herself to know that William still attracted other women.[46]

Perhaps partially because of her husband's ongoing attraction to and for other women but probably also because of her own history, Alice sometimes experienced feelings of low self-worth, the same feelings that had plagued her in Florence in 1893. William's current enthusiasm for Pauline Goldmark probably exacerbated Alice's tendency to denigrate herself. She told him, "For when you are away I am a poor creature. I hope that I don't live <u>on</u> you, and exhaust your vital energy."[47] Alice was right: women were attracted to William. In April 1896 he confessed to his Boston artist friend Sarah Wyman Whitman, "I am reaching a dangerous epoch in my career. Beautiful women write to tell me that I have restored their belief in God and man—by my lectures, they mean, and I can see by the titillation it produces, how in[ex]haustibly varied are the snares that satan sets for us poor children of man. Vanity of <u>this</u> kind is his trump-card. But I shall be firm."[48]

Not surprisingly, the summer of 1896 found the Jameses fighting again. When he left for Buffalo and Chautauqua, where he would give lecture series, his leave-taking was a particularly stormy one. He became violent and she cried.[49] Many of their arguments revolved around money, though his involvement with other women also could have been another source of friction. To help mend their marriage they considered a trip the coming winter to Germany, where William could pursue his research and Alice could enjoy a well-deserved vacation. He left the decision in her hands, but as their finances remained tight, he thought she would decide against the trip.[50] When she claimed family duties kept her from traveling, William applauded.[51] But if they could not spend the winter in Europe, at least Alice could come to Keene Valley in September so that they could vacation there together.[52] He wanted her to bring Francis Tweedy, too, but at the last minute a death in Cambridge prevented her coming. Their neighbor and family friend, Francis James Child, died that month, and Alice felt obligated to attend his funeral.

In January 1897 William was invited to give the prestigious Gifford Lectures on religion at the University of Aberdeen for 1898–99 and 1899–1900. The endowed Lectureship on Natural Religion alternated every two years between the University of Aberdeen and Edinburgh University. This honor meant more to Alice than any of his other accolades. While he declared that "religion is the great interest of my life," though it was an impersonal and not an evangelical interest, he preferred to wait in the hopes of being asked to deliver the lectures at Edinburgh University for 1901-2 and 1902-3.[53] He thought the Edinburgh appointment carried more prestige, so he suggested that Royce be invited to do the lectures at Aberdeen in his place. William also felt that since he had spent little time investigating religious experience, other than his forays into psychic research and his considerations of religious belief as an abstract principle, he could not be ready by 1898. When the Aberdeen lectureship went to Royce, Alice fumed. She confided in Henry that William had recommended Royce without telling her. "It is hardly probable that so rare a prize will be given to an American two years running. It has made me sick, for the world will know only that the distinguished honour of giving the Gifford lectures has been bestowed for the first time on an American, Royce!! He will not refuse, but over he will go with his Infinite under his arm, and he will not even do honour to William's recommendation. . . . There is nothing now to be done but to accept cheerfully the irrevocable."[54]

At the same time that Alice coped with William's demands and tried to push him toward even more of an international reputation, her brother-in-law Bob's ongoing battle with the bottle worsened. Her Jamesian vocation continued to expand. Bob resembled her father in certain ways: he had Dr. Gibbens's charm but also his bad habits. Early in 1897 his alcoholism was often out of control. He went to England in March to see Henry but stayed only a week. Then he sought a divorce from his wife, Mary, who refused to grant him one. He consulted Alice frequently, soliciting her empathy.

Though he declined the first offer of Gifford Lectures, William accepted an invitation to give a Decoration Day speech at the dedication of the memorial designed by sculptor Augustus Saint-Gaudens for Col. Robert Shaw. Shaw had headed the first Civil War Massachusetts regiment to include African American soldiers. Garth Wilkinson had served under him in the Fifty-fourth Volunteer Infantry Regiment, and Robertson had served in the Fifty-fifth, also an African American regiment. For William, who took nothing easily, the path leading up to the day was a crooked one, full of possible pitfalls and hurdles. He exhibited mood swings and erratic behavior, and Alice spent considerable time helping him prepare. Family friend John Jay Chapman merely advised William to "get up & say Shaw did well. & sit down."[55]

By early April William had finished the speech, sending a copy over a month before the event to Shaw's widow, who declared it perfect. He included passages from letters from his brother Wilkie, who had sustained shell wounds when the Fifty-fourth Regiment attacked Fort Wagner near Charleston, South Carolina, the battle in which Shaw died.[56] William aimed the speech at a varied audience and thus diluted its content. The delivery itself would be the most important part of the task: it should "be executed like a musical composition."[57] Alice found the biblical reference for his final sentence: "'So may our ransomed country, like the city of the promise, lie foursquare under Heaven, and the ways of all the nations be lit up by its light.'"[58]

Alice worried whether William's voice could fill Boston's great Music Hall, as three thousand people were expected to attend.[59] Just a month before, she sensed that something was amiss with her husband, now at Keene Valley at Thomas Davidson's. The day after William practiced his speech before friends, Alice felt anxious.[60] After nearly twenty years she could sense his ups and downs, even when he was gone. Part of his anxiety may have come from the fact that while his two younger brothers served in the war, he had stayed at home.

In the midst of the turmoil Alice continued to foster a convivial relationship between William and Henry, a role she had assumed early in the marriage. The couple filled some of the tense time before Decoration Day reading Henry's latest novel, *The Spoils of Poynton*, the story of lost possessions and lost love. Alice read it aloud to William after he went to bed at night, lulling her husband to sleep with his brother's words as if he were a child.[61]

The night before the great day William's throat troubled him. Fearing he would lose his voice, Alice drove with him through the Back Bay in the pouring rain looking for a throat specialist. His sore throat was a symptom of his nerves, the weeks of anxiety over the impending event.[62] A laryngologist sprayed and cauterized his throat, giving him lozenges to suck on the morning of the ceremony so that he could speak clearly for three-quarters of an hour.[63]

The dedication began with a procession that Alice and all four James children watched from a Mrs. Dewey's Beacon Street house. There were seven barouches (four-wheeled carriages with two double seats inside facing each other) in the parade. William rode in one of the carriages with Saint-Gaudens through gray skies and light rain. At the Music Hall the ceremony began with music and a prayer. Then a chorus sang "Our Heroes." William gave the oration, which was followed by "The Battle Hymn of the Republic." Next, Booker T. Washington, president of Tuskegee Institute, gave a brief address.[64] The program concluded with instrumental music.[65] Thirty or forty of the surviving veterans from the Fifty-fourth and Fifty-fifth regiments were in attendance, "the patient, good old darkey citizen," William noted.[66] Though he was disparaging of his text and worried about his performance, William roused his audience. The speech praised young Shaw's courage in leading a venture that even many Bostonians had condemned, meditated on the virtues war could arouse, and concluded with a call for the country as a whole to preserve democracy through the "civic genius" of its people.

A surge of energy replaced Alice's exhaustion. That night she shared the triumph with Henry. "You will read his address and feel its beauty, but you cannot measure the full power of it unless you had been one of that great audience in Music Hall, listening with rapt attention from the first word to the last. . . . Every kind of congratulation has come to William today."[67] Henry James jubilated with, over, under, and around his brother.[68] At last Alice had a Civil War ceremony to celebrate; she need not flee in shame from this commemoration of the Union dead.

Following the ceremony, Alice enjoyed glorious summer days at Chocorua.

> Darling William, — I have been having great days. Monday I went up the mountain with Billy. We started at 9 and reached the house (under the peak) at 3 having had many resting times on the way. We went up to the very top and saw a wonderful sunset with driving clouds and all the glory of the earth beneath and above us. The wind blew so that we could not stay long on the top for I thought we should be blown away, but we came slowly down and the moon cast our shadows behind us before we reached the house. . . . I have reflected somewhat mournfully on all the lost years when I might have gone up, but I am thankful that I have "arrived" even thus late. Some time I want to go with you.[69]

Alice had something else to celebrate in 1897, the publication of William's *The Will to Believe and Other Essays in Popular Philosophy*. The book collected addresses and articles written between 1879 and 1896, mentioning radical empiricism in its preface but focusing on the potential of human will and passion to change the world for the better. While he did not abandon his position as an empiricist, one who tests ideas against experience and reality, William affirmed the possibility of religious belief and faith, suggesting it might be worthwhile to take a chance on the religious hypothesis in a universe where there might be an anthropomorphic deity. Since humanity did not know enough on an empirical basis to rule out this hypothesis, he voted to keep religious options open, all the while trying to view religion through a scientific lens.[70]

Months before the book's release William told an admirer, "I, with no creed whatever, am inwardly certain that the salvation of mankind consists in its holding to religious ideals."[71] Rejecting absolutism in both science and philosophy, he presented an ever-evolving physical and mental world with human consciousness as a given, a consciousness where a deity (who is "other" to ourselves) is "the normal object of the mind's belief."[72] He allowed for individual differences and varying philosophies, though these ordering systems must meet tests of rationality and predictability. Clearly written and logically argued, with most of its premises carefully spelled out, the book's overall tone is one of optimism. William's moral force and energy radiate from its pages.

The book also included an essay on psychic research, "What Psychical Research Has Accomplished." Explaining the inclusion of the essay in his general preface, William claimed, "Attracted to this study some years ago by my love of sportsmanlike fair play in science, I have seen enough to convince me of its great importance, and I wish to gain for it what interest I can."[73] William risked his reputation by including this final essay, as other philosophers and psychologists remained skeptical of spiritualism and psychic research. His vigorous voice attracted a wide popular audience, though some scholarly reviews were less than complimentary. British philosopher Francis Herbert Bradley respected William's argument but parted company with him on some points, including the primacy of will, which Bradley rejected.[74]

During the same year that saw his ongoing achievements in *The Will to Believe*, William acknowledged Alice's personal growth and development. "Though your hair is paler, your heart is as ruddy and your will far more trenchant and your intellect more active than you were then, and altogether your personality more significant and important."[75]

The year 1898 proved to be one of triumph and despair in nearly equal measure. The year began inauspiciously with a setback for Bob. The first week in the year, he went to England to see Henry, who greeted him kindly but saw that his younger brother was in poor shape.[76] He telegraphed Alice and William, warning them of Bob's condition. Both William and Alice were well aware of alcohol's devastating effects, and William had studied alcoholism professionally. In his 1895 notes for a lecture entitled "The Effects of Alcohol" Alice copied a quote from Charles Godfrey Leland on intoxication and the greater exhilaration one feels in a natural state: "The best excitement was that of my own bounding life-blood."[77] William used this idea again at the end of his popular *Talks to Teachers* in the section on will, where he notes the benefits of "a sweet, sound blood," a blood free of alcohol.[78]

The second week in January Alice heard a noise outside and went out to find a cabby lifting Bob from his cab and on to her front porch. The driver informed her he had found Bob in Bowdoin Square "'knocking about.'" Since Cambridge was officially dry from 1886 to 1933, Bob had gone to Boston to drink.[79] The cabby finally managed to get their name and the 95 Irving Street address from the very drunken man. William had been so nervous that day she had sent him to a club dinner, so Billy put Bob to bed upstairs. The next morning William found a sane and sober Bob in the library. After a talk with his eldest brother he went upstairs to ask Alice what she thought. She reported her response to Henry: "I was so wretched about him that I told him the whole truth; that it <u>was</u> failing, that he was much broken, and that another six months of such racking of himself could have but one end."[80]

With Bob's permission, a doctor filled out papers allowing William to send Bob to Foxboro, an inebriate asylum filled "with the very offscouring of the police court." That threat in place, William then suggested a sanatorium as a milder measure. Determined to remain positive despite her misgivings, Alice told Henry that Bob was better physically and mentally, "his eyes are as blue as the sea and all the old defiance is gone."[81] On 13 January 1898 William took Bob to a sanatorium in Dansville, New York, near Buffalo. Alice wrote supportive letters to him. During his stay he embraced Catholicism, a religion Alice disliked, but nonetheless she remained endlessly patient with him. At first he seemed to improve. On 12 February he assured her, "I have not had a thought of drink since the second day here."[82] But within a month he relapsed. Taking the money

William had given him to buy shoes, he went to the village and got re-soundingly drunk.[83]

February brought Alice better news: William learned he had been elected to the Edinburgh Gifford lectureship for 1900–1901. She was "delighted beyond measure. I dream of it o' nights," she told Henry.[84] This was the culmination of years of hard work for both Jameses. William's faith was justified, while Alice saw her skepticism defeated. Perhaps her husband was right in exhorting people to take a chance on faith.

The year went well for the children, too. Harry passed all his entrance exams and gained early admission to Harvard, where he later became editor of Harvard's student newspaper, the *Crimson*. Billy was a well-liked, athletic teenager who painted for hours on end, and Peggy was a precocious, serious girl who loved her parents. Francis Tweedy existed contentedly in his own world. Imitating his older brother Billy, he tried to paint. A busy, loving eight year old who adored animals and the outdoors, he disliked school. His name had metamorphosed from Francis Tweedy to Francis Robertson in 1893 and now to John Robertson, though this latest change was not the final one. His family continued to call him Francis. Alice coped with the deaths of friends and a happier event, her youngest sister Margaret's marriage to McGill University professor Leigh Gregor.[85]

During the summer of 1898 Alice sent her eldest, Harry, now nineteen, to England to visit his uncle Henry, accompanied by her sister Margaret. Alice was eager for Harry to come to know his famous uncle better.[86] Harry was a model young man, nearly too good to be true. George Browne, the headmaster of the Cambridge preparatory academy, Browne and Nichols, asked Alice what she had done to turn out a youth like Harry James: "'I have always wanted to find out what you did to Harry to put him ahead as you did.'"[87] Harry kept a detailed diary of his visit; from it the portrait of a very organized and occasionally self-righteous young man emerges. He had not seen his uncle since the summer of 1893, and his first impressions were negative ones. "I doubt myself how much Uncle H. cares for me. . . . I am beginning to think that he is naturally, socially rather duller and less genial than I thought. He knows it all so that I can't tell him anything (about my impressions of England etc.)." As the visit wore on, Harry understood his complicated uncle better. When Uncle Henry was kind to his "limited" cousin Rosina, Harry noted, "[Uncle Henry] treated

her most Rosinanish outpourings and questionings with perfect respect."
By the end of Harry's visit, Uncle Henry cherished his nephew.[88]

William left Cambridge at the end of June for the Adirondacks. Stopping
at the Hotel Champlain on Lake Champlain, he enclosed a poem in his
letter to Alice. William must have read it on the train, because a railroad
advertisement is on the back of the page. He did not write sentimental
love letters, but he let the poem speak for him.

> Puella Aestivalis
> Through various kinds of summer weather—
> Hot, humid, cold and dry—
> We walked and sailed and swam together,
> My summer girl and I.
> Ah me! It was a pleasant season:
> But I did not regret
> When autumn came—for this good reason
> That summer's with me yet.
> For summer sunshine round her hovers
> Through winter's frost and snow,
> And I—"cut out" a score of lovers,
> And won her, years ago.[89]

Not long after arriving at camp, William hiked Mt. Marcy carrying
an eighteen-pound pack in pursuit of Pauline Goldmark and her young
friends, her brother Charles, Waldo Adler, and a few others. He started
out that morning at seven, engaging a guide to help him carry his things,
but he let the guide carry only the girls' baggage, shouldering a heavy
load himself. Later in her life Alice could not forgive Pauline for letting
William do this. The group walked for five hours to the top of Mt. Marcy
and camped there.

Excited by the exercise, "the influences of Nature, the wholesomeness
of the people round me, especially the good Pauline, the thought of you
and the children, dear Harry on the wave, the problem of the Edinburgh
lectures, all fermented within me till it became a regular Walpurgis nacht,"
William wrote to Alice.[90] Unable to sleep, he wandered in the woods, where

he was overwhelmed by pure sensation, by the immediacy of his own experiences. This manic episode, similar to states of elevated consciousness he had felt before, was followed by a crash. The next morning he hiked up the rest of the mountain, walking over ten hours in all. He lost his jacket and arrived finally, exhausted, at a bathhouse owned by Charles Bowditch. When Alice heard of his experience she imagined disaster.[91] She was right: he had damaged his heart.

As Alice began to understand what had happened to her husband, more trouble came. She and William learned Bob had been drunk nearly constantly while at Dansville, despite his vows to reform and his letters claiming sobriety. He still wrote to Alice; she seemed to have a positive influence on him. William realized what a drain Bob was and apologized that marriage had exposed her "to such an odious infliction."[92]

All the while coping with William and Bob, Alice maintained her vital interest in world conflicts. "Today I have been quiet, almost idle," she wrote Harry. "I spent a long time over the Sunday Herald, the world has grown so intensely interesting. The Dreyfus tragedy grows more and more horrible. The story of sickness & neglect of our soldiers is worse and worse. How can Alger look these sick men in the face! But a rumor comes that Kartoum has fallen, and that is magnificent. But before this letter reaches you all these thrilling subjects will have entered new phases."[93]

Time for her political interests remained limited, though: her husband's health had become her desperate concern. Later that same year William gave a lecture at the University of California at Berkeley entitled "Philosophical Conceptions and Practical Results," which set forth his developing theories of pragmatism.[94] But when he hiked in the high Sierra, he strained his heart further. He lay awake all night on 21 November, a fierce storm pounding outside and his heart beating. By Thanksgiving he confessed to a friend that while his heart bothered him, he would not be governed by his condition.[95] He consulted three doctors, one of them Dr. James Jackson Putnam, his Keene Valley camping friend, and all three heard a heart murmur. Although William tried to conceal his poor condition, Alice saw Putnam herself: something was amiss. He told her that William had sustained heart damage, but he assured her that with proper care the slight murmur would pose no major problems. "But was ever a man born of woman harder to take care of than William!" she moaned to Henry.[96]

During the spring of 1899 William reached another critical juncture: he had one year left to prepare the Gifford Lectures, but Alice knew that he could not give the lectures unless he rested. Cambridge physician Stephen Driver assured her that William would do well with care. She realized that she would have to enforce a healthful regime, as her husband would not follow one on his own. They would go to Europe a year ahead of the lectures so that William could regain the strength to finish them. But accompanying him abroad meant Alice must leave the rest of her family behind. She had to choose, and she chose her husband and his work: she had invested so heavily in his career. The Gifford Lectures would prove to a world wracked by Darwinism, skepticism, and agnosticism that faith was still possible. She knew that William was a genius, but that wasn't enough. Genius only reveals itself under certain circumstances, and it was up to Alice to nurture this genius back to health so that he was well enough to complete his work.

Alice and William decided to leave Harry and Billy in college at Harvard, with Eliza Gibbens nearby. Both the older boys would work that summer in Washington territory's Olympic Mountains, returning for Harvard's opening, when Billy would matriculate. The two younger children would sail with them to Europe and board with the Cérésoles at Vevey. Finally, though, William convinced Alice to leave Francis Tweedy/John Robertson with his grandmother and take only Peggy abroad. They would leave her in Vevey while William took the baths at Bad Nauheim in Germany and later find an English school for her, with Henry as her resource during school holidays. These decisions were the most wrenching Alice ever made. Although Francis was too young to understand the import of his parents' leave-taking, she would miss him desperately. "William wants to leave Francis with Mother," she explained to Henry. "There are many reasons why it is advisable so I have made up my mind to do it, but I feel like a creature walking in a dream, the child has been so dependent on me."[97] Peggy would be on her own, beginning her adolescence as a virtual orphan.

Before she left, Alice and her mother took one last trip to Weymouth, traveling by three different electric cars. She was pleased to see her childhood home again, reporting her visit to Harry. "The Weymouth household is very attractive. Poor Sam is there, patient and unexpectant, just as clean and tidy as of old. Everything about him disarms criticism."[98] Next, she took Francis to Mary and Mack Salter's summer home, Hill Top, near Chocorua, and said good-bye there. Alice and Mary allowed him to have a hen, and William had given him a female Boston terrier before he left, which Francis wanted even more.[99] By now Alice was near collapse herself.

While Alice made her good-byes William further damaged his heart, again while hiking on Mt. Marcy. He reached the summit, but, coming down, he descended into the Johns Brook Valley rather than taking the Lodge trail, spending seven hours hiking instead of three. As a result he had a bad dilatation of his heart, with severe chest symptoms after the least exertion.

Upon her return to Cambridge Alice worked fifteen hours a day and ate very little but remained in good spirits, though two days before they left she had a headache.[100] Just before her departure she told Henry, "The break-up is solemn. No more Sunday suppers with the large table full of young folks—and such dear boys! I am haunted with an old trouble of mine, what you call the 'prevision of retrospect.'"[101] But she loved her husband so much that she was willing to accept anything other than losing him. As she prepared to leave she dreamed that they were old and poor, their children gone long ago. She struggled to prepare a meager meal in a dingy tenement room, trying to make it seem like home. "When you came in it did. . . . I have felt today as if I really was your wife,—sealed to you as the Mormons say."[102]

When Alice, William, and Peggy were ready to leave 95 Irving Street, Eliza Gibbens came to bid them farewell. She said good-bye at their gate and then walked slowly up the steps of her own home at number 107, her head bowed.[103] During the next two years she would know her daughter only through letters.

10 To Bad Nauheim

ONCE ABOARD THE *Graf Waldersee*, Alice caught her breath from the last month's frantic preparations and reconciliations. Below in her large outside stateroom she found a moment to write to her sons before the ship sailed. "Now Peggy wants me to go up and see the steamer leave her wharf. I am <u>thankful</u> that no dear face will be on the wharf. I have said goodbye too many times." She warned her two older boys, who were now in Tacoma, Washington, preparing for forestry camp, not to get lost in the Northwest woods. The consequences could be severe, as she well knew. She mused on what she had left behind: "the dear old empty house!"[1] But her goal was solidly fixed: to help her husband recover well enough to prepare and deliver the Gifford Lectures. Her stamina would be crucial in saving him.

Alice resembled her paternal grandfather, ambitious Boston business-man Daniel Lewis Gibbens Sr., and her maternal grandfather, successful lawyer and senator Christopher Webb, as much as anyone in her family. Like them, she was resolute and steadfast. And she knew herself: while she was not innately jovial, she seldom succumbed to her occasional de-pression.

The next months would be full of both pleasure and heartache. Any-one who has watched a loved one suffer can imagine the difficulties she endured, trying to keep an energetic, independent, brilliant man focused on his health. But though she faced real challenges abroad, she knew also that this was a rare time for her. In Cambridge and at Chocorua her time was fully accounted for: William; children; Gibbens, James, and Webb relatives; household management; entertaining; women's club duties; gardening—the list went on and on. This interlude, however, would allow her previously rare moments alone. She wrote conscientiously to her loved ones, long, newsy, affectionate epistles, but the act of writing them was a creative one. She would travel, read, widen her circle of friends, and, not least, become closer to her brother-in-law Henry.

Even before the voyage began Alice did something for herself: she had her pince-nez glasses reset in a more modern style. The new pair was a better fit, and she thought she looked better. With them she could see her fellow passengers, finding them largely unattractive, though hearing the ship's officers speaking German made her happy.[2] She was amiable throughout the voyage.[3] Peggy had brought along books to read, William Dean Howells's just published *Ragged Lady* and *Sentimental Tommy* by the author of *Peter Pan*, Sir James Barrie. Alice believed the time William would spend with Peggy during her school holidays would help form their daughter's ethical character. During the voyage William, who was supposed to be relaxing for the first time in his life, worried that he had not left enough money behind for Eliza Gibbens to pay their bills.[4] He did not know how long it would be before he could teach again, nor was he certain he could deliver the Gifford Lectures. The series paid well and would supplement lost income if only he were well enough to give them.

The trio landed at Hamburg, no one ill from the crossing. Dressed in a blue tartan cape as she strolled about the city, young Peggy attracted the glance of the Germans, who admired her sweetness. She recalled Henry James's fictional heroine Daisy Miller, who had become a nineteenth-century household word for the archetypal innocent American girl. Whenever possible Alice economized on travel, partly from habit and now partly to stretch their budget, so from Hamburg the Jameses took third-class passage to Bad Nauheim.[5] William and Alice planned to spend four or five weeks there, boarding Peggy in Switzerland with the Cérésole family. Alice realized that this arrangement, however, would not do for an entire school year. Madame and her husband were old and tired.[6] Alice and William would collect Peggy at Vevey at summer's end, and then all three would proceed to Rye, England, where they would meet Henry.

All four children placed, William and Alice could adjust to Bad Nauheim, their new home. The town was located in central Germany in the Taunus Mountains, and its salt springs were used to treat heart and nerve diseases. The spa featured a large wooded park conducive to walking, with an occasional bench for those who needed to rest. Visitors and patients could frequent the town's numerous restaurants and attend musical performances. Although Alice missed her children and mother, she was delighted to be back in Germany. William jokingly told Francis, "Your mother loves Yurup."[7] He, by contrast, did not feel at home in Germany. He had forgotten nearly all the German he once knew, which made him feel even more a foreigner.[8] He mourned his lost American wilderness: the trees, the hikes, the climate.

Dr. Theodor Schott's standard treatment for heart patients included saline baths, regular walks, some climbing, and physical resistance exercises. At first, William thought that Dr. Schott's exams were too cursory. On some days the man saw as many as 250 patients, usually for a two-minute session. He sat in front of a standing patient and listened to the heart with his stethoscope, then wrote a prescription for a specific type of bath for the next two or three days. Though William was suspicious of these instant diagnoses, he concluded that Dr. Schott could remember each patient's heart rate and detect any subtle changes.[9] Schott also counseled his patients on diet: avoid stimulants, seasoned foods, and effervescent drinks. Bad Nauheim had five different types of baths.[10] Each brought the blood to the surface of the skin by irritating the skin; the process was thought to reduce systolic and diastolic pressure. The Jameses' Florence physician, Dr. William Baldwin, was also at the resort; he had developed arterial problems in 1898.[11]

The Jameses quickly acclimated to the spa routine and to their quarters, even though they shared one bedroom, an adjustment, as they occupied separate bedrooms at 95 Irving Street. Every morning they breakfasted on their balcony, and then William took one of the baths. Afterward he walked home, where he rested for an hour. He and Alice dined at 1:00 p.m., and after lunch he rested again. At 3:30 a man came to their rooms to help him do slow resistance exercises. The couple read after these routines, Alice often reading aloud. They walked together between five and six o'clock, took supper outside at seven, and at nine walked home across the park and went to bed.

By September, on two days out of three William took the *Sprudelstrom Bad*.[12] In this twelve-minute treatment the fizzling saltwater rushed through the bath, while carbon dioxide gas bubbled to the surface. The patient's skin turned bright red afterward.[13] "But it is seductive & soothing to an incredible degree, so I suppose that 'nerves' as well as 'heart' will have the benefit. Meanwhile it is simply <u>loathsome</u>! The only fit kind of summer is one where one can lie on nature's breast under the trees," he informed Harry and Billy, perhaps envious of their summer in the wilderness.[14] He chafed at this boring sedate life, but he finally relaxed and became a more or less compliant patient, though one day he slipped past Alice's watchful eye and went to Frankfurt, where he drank three glasses of Bavarian beer, sipped coffee, and smoked a two-and-a-half-cent cigar.[15]

While William cured, Alice took occasional long walks, one to the medieval walled town of Friedberg, and she socialized with other patients.[16] She had the ability to empathize with people from nearly all backgrounds and was tolerant of their foibles and interested in their narratives. She met a young woman who entertained her with stories of her father, who had been chief engineer in India during the Mutiny, and a wealthy American mining engineer, Frank Gardner and his wife.[17] Alice spun dreams that childless Gardner might help Billy achieve a career in Gardner's profession.[18] She also took baths for her rheumatism and drank the resort's mineral waters, welcome relaxations. "I am so delightfully rested that I don't feel cross or impatient any more," she assured her sons, "and groan in spirit when I remember how often I was both at home."[19]

In August William took a day off, perhaps at Alice's behest, as he continued to protest his treatments even as he followed Dr. Schott's orders. The couple traveled to Frankfurt, where they heard Johann Strauss's Viennese orchestra and visited the Goethe museum in the writer's house.[20] Alice saw the cardboard theater where Goethe put on his puppet show as well as his life mask and a marble model of his craftsmanlike hand. She also admired an old news clipping dated from the writer's childhood that announced the "Possenspiel [Comedy] of Dr. Faustus by Marionettes." "How long the great poem must have haunted him," she mused to Harry and Billy. William bought a Zeiss field glass there, a purchase that delighted him.[21]

While he could not work on his lectures yet, William managed some reading on religious experiences, and he and Alice followed international affairs together, especially the developments in the Dreyfus case, which they found emblematic of larger French Catholic corruption and anti-Semitism. On warm August afternoons in the park Alice and William read the complete *Figaro* reports of the second Dreyfus trial, reports not easily available in America. Alice feared for Dreyfus's fate after his lawyer, Fernand-Gustave-Gaston Labori, was shot and wounded the night before he questioned the prosecution's witnesses.[22] She believed that the military court was biased against Dreyfus and Col. Georges Picquart, who had found letters showing Dreyfus had been framed.[23]

Alfred Dreyfus, a Jewish French army officer, had been tried for treason in 1894 and sentenced to life imprisonment on Devil's Island. In 1898, however, it was discovered that documents used to convict him had been forged by a Major Esterhazy. The major was court-martialed but acquitted, and his accuser was arrested in his stead. French writer Émile Zola then wrote an open letter to the French president that was published in a newspaper under the headline "J'accuse!" alleging that the French army had wrongfully arrested Dreyfus and then tried to cover up its misdeeds. In 1899 Dreyfus was court-martialed again and again found guilty, but the president of the French republic pardoned him. Finally, in 1906 a civilian court of appeals cleared Dreyfus and reversed all previous convictions.

By September William's health had improved. Less than a month after he arrived his heart, which Dr. Schott found enlarged during his initial examination, had reduced. Although he was still languid and depressed, he felt better.[24] Alice feared, with her prevision of retrospect, that this would not be their last visit to the spa, but her spouse hoped never to return. He was anxious for Rye, where he could work. Henry was ready to receive them: he only wanted an approximate date of arrival.

In mid-September 1899 Dr. Schott pronounced William's six weeks of the *Kur* a success. He was to take his last bath on 18 September and then walk hard for two days so that the doctor could observe the effect of the exercise on his heart. When he listened, Dr. Schott found that William's heart was no longer dilated.[25] William was glad to leave "this great organization of cormorants & leeches," this purgatory.[26] Dr. Schott ordered his patient to spend two weeks at a higher altitude to strengthen his heart and consolidate the gains made at Bad Nauheim. After this interlude, the Jameses would collect Peggy at Vevey and head to England.

The question of Peggy's schooling remained, a question that precipitated a family quarrel, Alice and Henry taking sides against William. Alice had attended public high school in Weymouth, and Henry had never received a consistent formal education; both wanted only the very best for Peggy. Before they sailed Alice had written to Henry for advice, and early in August he announced that he had planned Peggy's "educatrix."[27] His niece should go to his friend Mademoiselle Souvestre's school near Wimbledon, where all the best girls studied. Joseph Chamberlain's daughters had been pupils there and adored Mademoiselle.[28]

But William would not allow Alice and Henry to decide. Even now he did not always trust his fifty-six-year-old younger brother's judgment—or his wife's. "What Peggy most wants is a kind of hardening. A year with lots of lawn-tennis, etc.," he announced to Henry, who nonetheless refused to give up his niece's cause.[29] When Alice told him that William derided her desire for a gentle school for Peggy, Henry bristled: "What kind of a one—just heaven!—would he advocate? Tell him that any second-rate girls' school in the British Island would be a <u>horror</u>."[30] The final decision was postponed until the Jameses reached England.

On 20 September, a morning bright with sunlight, Alice and William left Bad Nauheim and spent the prescribed time in the Jura above Lausanne. Next, they collected Peggy at the Cérésoles, she thrilled to join them. She had been subdued and withdrawn that summer, spending much of her time alone in her room. The reduced James family trekked to Geneva and then to Paris for two days, where Alice shopped for clothing for herself and a traveling suit for Peggy, who had outgrown her dresses that summer. They were not happy with the cheap-looking, overtrimmed dresses at the Bon Marché, though, and Peggy came away with nothing but gloves.[31]

On 2 October they endured a rough Channel crossing to England. Alice and Peggy went below while William stayed on deck, delighting in the storm. From Folkestone they went by train to Rye.[32] This was Alice's first visit to Lamb House, which Henry had recently purchased. The small, peaceful town of Rye sits atop a hill just above wide, green fields leading to the English Channel, its narrow, steep, cobbled streets lined with old brick and half-timbered buildings. One house, just below the church and small cemetery, had belonged to Renaissance playwright John Fletcher. Around the corner and below Henry's house was one of England's oldest smugglers' inns, the Mermaid, whose foundations dated back to the twelfth century. Henry sometimes housed his guests there.

William had attempted to dissuade Henry from purchasing Lamb House earlier that summer. The writer wanted the security and privacy that came from homeownership, but William feared his younger brother lacked the common sense to make a sound bargain. If the ailing and aging world-renowned psychologist could control nothing else, he could at least keep family affairs in order. Since the asking price for the house was £2,000, William counseled Henry to offer £1,500 or £1,600 and outlined exactly how Henry should finance the mortgage; he even shared the details of the purchase with William Baldwin. The doctor, Henry's longtime friend, joined the chorus, warning the writer that the price was too high, the mortgage an encumbrance, the repairs possibly formidable.[33]

Trying to modulate her husband's harsh letter, Alice wrote a gentle note wishing she and William could talk this over with Henry and advising him to bargain with Mrs. Francis Bellingham, the house's current owner. She interfered, but she also offered to loan him $2,000, money recently inherited from an aunt.[34] But Henry refused Alice's offer, insisting on negotiating the purchase as he pleased. He was particularly annoyed that William had talked to Baldwin. "I <u>hate</u> its being talked of with any one but Alice," Henry informed his brother. "My joy has shrivelled under your very lucid warnings, but it will re-bloom."[35]

It had become a case of "he said" and "she said" between the Jameses. She told Henry that "William, after asking me to repeat to you what I said to him [about the house] basely went back on me. He said last night that such an object lesson would save you from matrimony."[36] William quickly apologized, and the matter was dropped without permanent damage to intrafamily relations. Alice did not want to alienate her brother-in-law: she knew that she would need Henry's help to survive the coming months. And she would need Lamb House.

Lamb House is a well-proportioned Georgian brick house perched near the summit of the town facing West Street, its front door opening onto four steps leading to the curb. The dwelling housed the mayors of

Rye for generations. A high wall, also running along the street, hides the garden next to the house. Apricots, pears, plums, and figs were at one time espaliered on the old red wall. The spacious grounds featured a garden-house, destroyed during World War II, that provided a separate study and workroom, allowing Henry privacy even when he had guests.

When they reached the house, Alice, William, and Peggy walked up the steps and into a large square entry hall, with a brass octagonal lantern overhead and a staircase with a spindled wood banister. The front parlor, on the left, done in old oak, offered a view toward the church; the oak-paneled dining room beside it opened straight into the garden. The master bedroom upstairs had sheltered King George II, who stayed in Rye when his convoy was blown ashore by a storm in 1726.[37] Henry turned it over to his guests, and it became Alice's refuge and operating center as she shepherded William back and forth to the Continent and Peggy to her schools.

While she was thankful to be with Henry, at first Alice did not like England as well as she had liked her old haunt, Germany. Perhaps too the realization that another school year was beginning and she was not at 95 Irving Street hit home. Moreover, William's health was not better; he had gotten worse since arriving in England. Though his heart symptoms had improved, his nerves played havoc with his health. Whether it was the pressure of the impending Gifford Lectures, depression resulting from weeks of inactivity and inability to work, or another deep-rooted malady, William could not resume his normal activities. He could not sleep or see well.

After a short stay in Rye, Alice, William, and Peggy departed for London. Henry had not yet sublet his flat at 34 De Vere Gardens, and he offered it to his brother and wife, who gratefully accepted. They had nowhere else to turn. William had barely begun his first Gifford Lecture, and the inaugural speech, the first of ten lectures, was advertised for Monday, 15 January, at 4:00 p.m. in Edinburgh.[38] The De Vere Gardens flat was spacious and sunny, with five large rooms and skylights. Despite these pleasant accommodations, Alice felt discouraged. She loved Germany and the spa routine, meals out and no housekeeping. Here she coped with a deteriorating spouse in an unfamiliar country. Henry was not there to support her, and William could not entertain visitors or travel.

Alice battled to maintain her steady state and was able to paint a clear picture of their situation. She wrote Billy:

> Papa has been less well than at Nauheim and just now is housed for rest and care. We are like two strange and way worn birds perching in a strange dark forest. Uncle Henry has been kindness itself and this flat is comfortable in every way, but Sunday a great London fog shut us in, so heavy and dense that even with closed windows the rooms were full of blue haze. It was awful, and nothing I have ever read prepared me for the depressing experience. Peggy who is in bed with tonsillitis just observed mournfully, "in our other troubles we have at least always had air to breathe."[39]

The decision concerning Peggy's schooling had been made, with William casting the deciding vote. She would go to a girls' school at Egham called Northlands, run by a Miss Sophie Weisse. Though the curriculum there was a full one, Alice feared that the school was "flimsy for teaching."[40] When her friend Joseph Thatcher Clarke offered to take Peggy into his home at Harrow and send her to the local day school with his own four children, William declined the offer, just as he had declined Henry's suggestion of Mademoiselle Souvestre's establishment. Peggy had hoped to go to a girls' school near her uncle Henry.[41] Six years earlier, when he visited the family in Switzerland, she had adored him, slipping her hand into his whenever she could. But now she acquiesced to the arrangement, hoping to impress her brothers when she came home.[42]

Peggy's departure was delayed a week when she came down with tonsillitis, but finally Alice heavyheartedly took her to school. Her only consolation—and her daughter's—was that Northlands was just nineteen miles away. Alice tried to put the best face on the situation. She found her daughter's roommates, two girls named Maitland, well-bred and charming, and she planned to send Peggy family photographs to adorn her corner of the room.[43] While William claimed Peggy adjusted to her school well, the girl's correspondence suggests otherwise. A letter that fall began with news designed (consciously or unconsciously) to chill a mother's heart, especially the heart of a mother opposed to sending her to Miss Weisse's in the first place. "Darling Mamma, I had a bad billous attack and oh I felt so miserable I vomited eleven times and when the bile came <u>very</u> hard blood came with it and it came hard every time except the first. At night I felt better and slept."[44] Not all was amiss, though, as Peggy (who was called "Margie" at school because there were other Peggys and Margarets) confided that she got no schoolwork done because they were nearly always outdoors. She liked playing hockey but disliked dancing class, hinting that her mother could tell Miss Weisse to remove her.[45] She and her friends played a game in which all the girls had names: Peggy was Mrs. Charlotte Bix. Their family pseudonym was Roosevelt, and Teddy was their brother.[46]

In mid-November Miss Weisse asked Alice to take Peggy for a few days. The girl complained of pains and a cough, but the headmistress could find nothing wrong: perhaps Alice could overhaul Peggy and then return her.[47] The illness was probably in part homesickness: this school was a world away from the school Peggy had attended in Cambridge. After Peggy returned to Northlands, Alice developed a severe headache and retreated to her bedroom. William rallied long enough to challenge her to regain her cheerful spirits, and within minutes the couple reconciled. The next day they took a hansom to Kensington Gardens and sat outside for an hour.[48]

William now saw the London heart specialist Dr. Bezeley Thorne, who found he had excess uric acid coupled with arterial degeneration. He put William on a strict diet: he could have no starch or sugar, but he could have meat and green vegetables. Although Alice had not eaten meat in years, she wanted to share her husband's diet.[49] Dr. Thorne prescribed a bath regimen similar to the one at Bad Nauheim, and he wanted William kept quiet, having no more than one visitor a day, if any.[50] Though the doctor was puzzled by his patient's nervous weakness, he thought that his heart was no worse.[51] While Alice claimed William was following Thorne's orders to avoid working, she undoubtedly presented the best possible scenario to others.[52] Even if compliant, William was unhappy and depressed, as he could not work for any sustained intervals. He remained grateful for his wife's help, however, praising her to his old friend Thomas Davidson, who helped introduce them twenty-three years ago: "The woman thou gavest unto me comes out strong as a nurse, and treats me much better than I deserve."[53]

Alice found time for self-indulgence here as she had in Bad Nauheim. She shopped for clothes, having a walking suit made at Harvey Nichols.[54] She read aloud to William in the evenings, including *Le jardin secret* by Marcel Prévost.[55] She also enjoyed Henry's occasional visits, although his sciatica had flared up, brought on, he thought, by long bicycle rides, so sometimes he did not stay overnight.[56]

Domestic arrangements at the flat improved. The first servant was ill tempered, but Alice found a more suitable woman to help, a nice woman who was engaged to a sailor who "'never uses no bad language, leastways afore me, and for a sailor, he is very sober,'" Alice mimicked her to Billy. The servant drank a big bottle of beer every day; perhaps her beer habit made her work tolerable.[57]

Alice had one more reason to be happy when William's friend Frederick Myers, head of the British Society for Psychical Research, brought a medium to their flat. The medium, a Mrs. Thompson, floundered at first, confusing Alice's and Mr. Myers's friends, but then to her joy she invoked a handsome Hermann, who had left the family thirteen years ago. He loved a boy named William, who had once played dominoes with him. The communication with the lost child ended with Mrs. Thompson revealing that Hermann was with another boy. Alice imagined that this companion must be Francis. In one sitting the woman reached three of Alice's four boys, one of them a ghost.[58]

No sooner had Alice adjusted to the flat than Dr. Thorne ordered William to take the baths at West Malvern, 128 miles northwest of London. Henry had gone to Malvern in the spring of 1869 and again in the winter of 1870 to take the sitz baths and walk in an effort to relieve his painful constipation and back trouble. He complained about its Spartan diet: cold mutton or chop, toast, and tea for breakfast; leg or shoulder, potatoes, rice pudding, and tea for dinner; then cold mutton or chop, toast, and tea for supper.[59] Resigned to the move, Alice prepared for Henry's tenants, the Stopford Brookes, to take the flat in the last week of November, having everything cleaned and the rugs inventoried.[60]

On 2 December 1899 she and William started for Malvern. When they reached the Westminster Arms Hotel, the weather was too cold to allow them to venture out, though they toured for an hour on their second day.

When they reached a hill overlooking the Wye valley, Alice found the views lovely. The Jameses took their meals in the coffee room, and, unlike her brother-in-law, she found the food excellent. But William did no better here: he felt as if he were in a convent, and he could not walk at all.[61]

Alice walked alone when she could. "Yesterday I went out for a walk about 5 o'clock," she told Billy.

> It was quite dark but the air was delicious, with a feeling of the sea. I walked up the hill on which the road winds in loops just as in Switzerland. The white mist made me feel as if I was walking in a dream but I kept on till suddenly, looming close at hand I saw two animal forms barring the road. I could not tell whether they were white horses or wild cattle and so portentous were they that I turned and ran down the road, never stopping till I was sure they were not leaping after me.[62]

It seemed as though these eerie beasts were projections of her current disembodied state as she floated from one strange place to another.

After less than two weeks they took the train back to London, where Henry met them, and William rested for three days at De Vere Gardens. Then they went on to Rye, where Henry met them once again at the train station and escorted them to Lamb House, Peggy joining them there for her Christmas holidays.[63] William, covered with wraps, sat in the garden on sunny days, though often rain and wind drove him in.[64] Despite his fatigue he kept in good spirits, teasing nurse Alice at times. "[She] seems really enthusiastic now that she can hold me completely under her thumb and treat me like a baby once more," he informed cousin Katharine Rodgers.[65]

While William rested, Henry, Alice, and Peggy walked. "My favorite time for walking out is this twilight hour when through the low cottage windows we can see the families gathered round their pretty fires, taking tea and bread & butter. Such a cosy custom, and so homelike," she wrote to Billy.[66] Again she was a voyeur, seeing family life from the outside, her own family scattered. Though both agreed he showed improvement, Alice and Henry held anxious consultations about William's health.[67] Henry took precious time from his work to tell them all amusing, rambling stories.[68]

William's future remained tenuous. He made no progress on the lectures during the fall and asked for a postponement of his Gifford course until the next year. The second series had been indefinitely postponed; indeed, there was no indication that he would ever be able to give any lectures. On 20 December he wrote to Harvard requesting a second year of leave with no pay.[69] Fortunately, *Talks to Teachers* continued to bring in solid royalties, so that finances were not an immediate worry.[70] The book, a collection of talks given to teachers in 1894, contains simplified versions of his contributions to conceptions of stream of consciousness, habit, association, memory, apperception, and will plus sound, practical advice on the nature of students and classroom management. William's own moral energy and sincerity radiate throughout the text, which treats his audience's work as being of the greatest importance. The book had been a great success.

Their Rye stop was brief: now Dr. Thorne ordered William to find a warmer winter climate. By New Year's Day 1900 the Jameses had been offered the use of Charles Richet's château at Costebelle near Hyères, France, a generous invitation. William had met Richet in 1889 in Paris when he attended the International Congress of Physiological Psychology. He found the Frenchman a charming, handsome, intelligent young man; William admired his work. A physiologist, psychologist, and mathematician, Richet was a Renaissance man of deep ethical convictions, a French counterpart to William James.

Before the Jameses left for France, they sought a better place for their daughter, as Peggy's present school had proved unacceptable. She had placid companions at Northlands, and she had learned German, dancing, and deportment. However, she felt like an outsider. Northlands was an Anglican school, and not only was Peggy not a member of the Church of England, she had never been baptized. In addition, the school's curriculum was not sufficiently challenging for a girl of her ability, as Alice had feared. The school's headmistress was not happy at losing a pupil, behaving uncivilly to William after Peggy withdrew, the Jameses claimed. Five years later Henry met Sophie Weisse at a wedding banquet, and she told him that she had found Peggy interesting and desirable.[71]

Alice and William decided to send Peggy to Harrow, to reside with the Clarkes and attend Hampstead High School with the Clarke children,

Rebecca, Hans, Eric, and Dora. She would have to be vaccinated for small-pox to attend, but Frederick Myers, who among his many other vocations was an English school inspector, told Alice that the teaching there was excellent.[72] The first week of the new year Alice took her daughter to London to have her teeth examined and then on to the Clarkes at Gayton Corner, Harrow.

Just after Alice's return from Harrow, the post brought good news. The Gifford Committee had unanimously agreed to reappoint William as Gifford lecturer for 1900–1901 and 1901–2.[73] Though he feared failure, William faced his task that winter: to defend experience, not philosophy, as the heart of religious life and to make his audience believe what he believed, that "altho all the special manifestations of religion may have been absurd (I mean its creeds and theories) yet the life of it as a whole is mankind's most important function," as he explained to Fanny Morse. His attempt would be his own act of religion, an act Alice had encouraged since their courtship.[74]

Henry accompanied the pair to Dover, and the next morning they crossed the Channel and took a sleeping car to Costebelle.[75] By mid-January Alice and William were installed at the Hôtel d'Albion, Costebelle-Hyères, in southeastern France. Henry missed them. "This house is sadly shrunken & solitary, in the wet storm, without you; & tea, this p.m., was doleful & spectral," he told his brother.[76]

By the end of the nineteenth century Hyères and its surroundings had gained a reputation as a winter health resort. The town clung to the southwestern slope of a steep hill, with a fertile plain toward the south and southeast covered with orange groves. Costebelle sat atop a low hill southwest of Hyères. From the balcony of their hotel bedroom Alice and William could see the hotel's graveled terrace, ornamented with palms, orange trees, and roses. Below was a sloping garden, and in the distance was the Mediter-ranean.[77] In the mornings William sat in the garden and later moved to an easy chair on their balcony to watch the sunset.[78]

Alice's spirits rose. "I am wonderfully encouraged, and as I shrank from telling you the measure of my grief, so I am doubly eager to let you know that better days are come. It seems to me that in addition to the functional disturbance of his heart, my husband has had a complete nervous breakdown which naturally has aggravated all the cardiac symptoms. As yet he can only walk five minutes at a time and people tire him—in other words he is still very weak,—but he is gaining," she told Bessie Evans.[79] William felt better, his spirits switching from despairing to aggressive.[80]

On 21 January William and Alice moved into Richet's château at Carquéranne, in Costebelle near the seashore, and she soon found a cook and a housemaid to help her. The cook, Marguerite Godineau, proved to be the best servant Alice ever had. She wanted to take the woman home with her.[81] William was particularly fond of Marguerite's fish, artichokes, and stewed lettuce.[82] The château itself was imposing, a large cream stucco edifice with a red tile roof surrounded by palm trees and huge cactus.[83] It had a billiard room, and the estate had a pony and pony cart. If he felt able, William could fish on the nearby shore. There was also a huge shed where Richet stored the flying machine he had invented, a small unpiloted helicopter. Though it was aerodynamically unsuccessful, brothers Louis and Jacques Bréguet later designed a working model under Richet's guidance called the Bréguet-Richet Gyroplane Number One.[84] To Alice's relief this machine was not on the premises. She would never have been able to prevent William from trying to fly it.

For the first three days the Jameses were alone, but then the Myers family, husband and wife and three children, joined them.[85] Myers, too, suffered from heart disease and needed a warmer climate. William had known him for over fifteen years through their joint work on psychic research. The Englishman was also a poet and essayist; his essays on Virgil were greatly admired. Despite William's professional association with Myers, both William and Henry had reservations about the Myerses, finding them socially pretentious and occasionally personally disagreeable.[86] William once called him the "fell Myers." Their joint tenancy of the château made both Jameses apprehensive. Myers's wife, Eveleen Tennant Myers, was a photographer and a loquacious, sometimes boring conversationalist. Her family came from a lesser branch of the English Tennants, but she and Frederick wanted to socialize only with prominent people. Though William admired Myers's work, in his memorial speech for the man he noted, "Myers was, I think, decidedly exclusive and intolerant by nature."[87]

As the weeks progressed, the Jameses found Frederick easier to live with than Mrs. Myers and the children. Neither Alice nor William cared for her; William did a droll imitation of her conversation. Alice thought all three of the children were liars. After they took Charles Richet's tandem bicycle and smashed it into a gate, they told their father they had punctured the tire.[88] She called the children sinister, and William said they reminded him of the queer children in Henry's famous ghost story, *The Turn of the Screw*.[89]

With the Myers entourage came Mrs. Thompson, the medium who had contacted Hermann, and her daughter Rosy. Alice often sat with Mrs. Thompson, who told her that Mrs. Gibbens had pneumonia and Peggy tonsillitis. Alice became suspicious about these trances, wondering how Myers could be certain that the woman was communing with the spirits of the dead. One evening, to Alice's disgust, Mr. and Mrs. Myers brought Mrs. Thompson to the Jameses' room, asking Alice and William to help the three sort out their differences in what had become an emotional encounter over a séance. Alice assured Henry that "to be appealed to by both women, as I am, is enough to bring me to an early grave."[90] William remarked that Henry had missed an opportunity for a tale by not witnessing this high drama between a spiritualist and an emotional, timidly conventional British couple. Both Jameses were relieved when Mrs. Thompson left the house at the end of February, the Myerses departing a few days later.[91] Characteristically ironic, Alice thought that they judged her plain New England self "a rudimentary being, strangely ignorant of the world, with an inconvenient habit of literalness."[92]

William slowly mended. Accompanied by the wind in the palm trees, he and Alice read together of Thoreau's winter walks.[93] When he arrived he could not endure a two-hour drive, but by the third week in February he could ride for two or three hours, feeling refreshed afterward. The countryside around Costebelle was beautiful, with olive groves, some of which were two thousand years old, they were told, and fields of violets and hyacinths.[94] Alice admired the little African donkeys that pulled the peasants' carts, wishing that she could send one to Francis.

One day William and Alice drove to Hyères with the handsome young civil engineer who oversaw Richet's vineyards. Another day they took a long drive to Toulon, past the old village of La Garde. Alice explained to Billy that the village signified France's dim and sometimes tortured past: "The ruined fortress on the summit, the walled village, the evil-looking old, old masonry and shabby ancientness of the houses with their tiny loop-holes of windows—it all suggested past suffering, and present hopelessness."[95]

During these weeks they again saw the Bourgets, who lived nearby. Writer Paul Bourget and his wife, Minnie, were Henry's friends, and when they visited America in late 1893 the Jameses had entertained them, though their visit had been a trying one for Alice.[96] Bourget told Alice that he wanted Jews and Protestants alike banished from his country, and he asked William why he did not become a Catholic. Alice railed against their prejudices; she could not accommodate herself to Catholicism: "There are plenty of French people who do not hesitate to say openly that the time has come for another St. Bartholomew."[97] Though she regretted Bourget's intolerance, she tried to understand him, exclaiming to Harry, "I can easily allow for prejudices and scramble round them—they are not without a certain interest to me—like boulders in a New England pasture."[98]

Alice brightened when William began to talk about the future: his hopelessness had been nearly unbearable for her. When he winked at her one March day she knew he was gaining. Mrs. Thompson prophesied that he would be wonderfully better by early April.[99] Still, William was not dramatically better; he was only slightly better, as his heart pained him when he was tired. Just as Myers had suspected in 1893, when William tried to decline the presidency of the Society for Psychical Research, Alice worried his troubles might be partly psychosomatic. "I believe that the <u>nerves</u> of the heart are misbehaving and when his general neurasthenia is overcome the heart will be relieved but the nervous disorder will linger longest there, in the weakest organ."[100] For twenty-five years she had watched William's active, darting mind sometimes affect his body negatively. But she kept her faith, faith that helped her survive these dark months.

Even during this trying time her belief never wavered. As William wrote about religion's transformative powers, this power shone through Alice. She told Bessie Evans, "You see, dear Bessie, I believe, I almost <u>feel</u> immortality, or peradventure something infinitely better, but life and immortality are surely calling to us all—and more than ever I want to listen. This is only a confession of faith, but it is my own."[101]

The interlude proved a holiday for her and a boost to William's health. As he mended, Alice schemed for a trip home the next autumn. She knew that he needed one more warm winter abroad to ensure his full recovery, but she ached to see her mother and children. Henry assured her that he would take care of his brother during her absence. The dynamics of their triangular relationship had altered: Henry now resembled a solicitous older brother rather than a younger one, working closely with Alice to save William. When in February William was gloomy, Henry gave Alice sage advice. "Alas, for the interruption of benefit—but that is the way all improvements go! It is like driving a pig to the fair: sometimes he gets round & behind you & you have to bring him back. But at last to the fair you do get him—& meanwhile, all the time, you are on the road to it. Ask William to forgive my homely simile, but that is his natural progress."[102] And when William completed the second Gifford Lecture and was ready to begin the third, Henry applauded to Alice. "May the lectures surge & swell!"[103]

William gained, but brother Bob still hovered on the horizon. Though he could not see Alice, he wrote to her. She passed on his sad accounts to Henry, who noted, "Bob's acct. of everything else is Bobbish indeed. It is hard to live up to such a brother. I pant far behind." Henry was relieved that Alice was so far away—from Bob, at least.[104]

While William grew stronger and Alice enjoyed the sunny Mediterranean climate and their beautiful château, Peggy had not fared well in Harrow. The term began late for the girl, as she was sick in bed for three weeks after her smallpox vaccination.[105] She caught up at the school fairly quickly, at least in French, German, and math. Her Latin was weak, however, as the pupils at Northlands had not studied it.[106] She had difficulty adjusting to the busy, noisy Clarke children, especially Rebecca Clarke, who was nearly Peggy's age. She was used to her three brothers, but she was not used to competing with another young woman for attention and space. While she loved her walks with Uncle Henry at Rye, she hated walking with the Clarke brood. She reported to her parents. "Dora throws some mud at Eric whereupon Eric pounds her when of course she cries, and Rebecca calls Eric a mean pig. Then Aunt Agnes by scolding and threatening silences them and we march on." She spent her evenings reading because she believed the Clarkes were happier when she stayed in her room.[107] To bolster her low spirits, William congratulated her on the "splendid manly state of mind, & great moral health" he claimed he had found in one of her letters.[108]

While her parents wintered at Carquéranne, Henry visited Peggy. Alice dreaded having him visit the Clarkes, not knowing how a bachelor uncle would react to their large, bustling household, but he weathered the test well. He was invariably courteous to Peggy's host family. Not only did he visit Peggy and invite her to Rye, he occasionally entertained the girl and her mates in London. During the time she had spent at Rye that fall she had been much impressed with Henry. She informed her mother that it would be easy to write a novel, if she could just hit upon a good story.[109] Alice was glad that Peggy and Henry had this time together. She judged that they had similar temperaments, both of them aristocratic.[110]

In March Henry met Peggy and three of the Clarke children in London. He gave them lunch and tea and took them to see Diograph war pictures, a very early form of movies. Peggy decided that she had pro-Boer sympathies.[111] England was at the time engaged in military action in southern Africa, fighting the Boers, who were of Dutch descent, over territory. Henry found his niece looking very well, though he worried she might have nightmares after seeing the pictures.[112]

That spring Henry warned his sister-in-law that Peggy had relapsed a little into what Alice called her "'nobody likes me'" attitude, but her wise mother felt that this would pass.[113] Henry did not take Peggy's moral and spiritual development too seriously. "We (father's children,) were sacrificed to that too-exclusive preoccupation: & you see in Wm & me, & above all in Bob, the funeste [French, "devastating"] consequences! Take heed in time," he admonished Alice and William.[114] The philosophy Henry James Sr. used with his children (at least the philosophy that Henry thought his father had followed, the overemphasis of the moral and spiritual to the neglect of other things) would not work for his sensitive niece.

On 2 April the Jameses left their comfortable perch at the Château Carquéranne, returning to Costebelle for a fortnight and then going on to Geneva, where they saw a nervous specialist and the Flournoys. Finally, they returned to Bad Nauheim so that William could see Dr. Schott. Both left in much better shape than when they arrived. Upon reaching Switzerland Alice and William visited a nervous specialist in Geneva who found William's heart in relatively good shape, though his nerves were weak. He advised another brief stay at Nauheim.[115] But the spa cure did not help, so the Jameses traveled to Heidelberg to consult heart specialist Dr. Erb, who thought William's nervous condition was the barrier to recovery. He advised him not to return to Nauheim. William called Dr. Erb a hoggish brute: the only doctor worth consulting was Dr. William James, M.D.[116]

By June the Jameses were back in Switzerland so that William could take electrical treatments under Dr. Widmer's supervision. He experimented with diet, taking no water with his meals and as much hot water as possible between meals to aid his digestion, weight control, and nasal congestion.[117] Alice left him briefly to frequent Geneva's shops, where she had a chance encounter with her friend Madame Flournoy. "I am trying to get myself fitted out so that Papa and you boys will like my clothes," she told Billy. "Since Papa has had so much leisure he has taken notice of my deficiencies in the way of toilette, and I assure you I am 'looking up.'"[118] Later in the summer, however, she told Harry her opinion of European fashion. "The showy clothes I see on these smart people sickens me — I should soon take to some sort of nun's garb were I to be much longer exposed to it."[119] The day after her shopping expedition a headache struck, sending her to bed for two days.[120]

It had been twelve months since Alice had seen her boys and her mother. All of them seemed well, though it was difficult to assess Francis's condition. She knew that he struggled with math, but when she suggested he study his multiplication tables, his teacher, Miss Lathrop, wondered whether he were capable of understanding them. Uncle Henry agreed that the tables must be learned, but he noted they were the only thing in life "we needn't understand."[121] William's advice to Francis was that he not become "white trash."[122] The two older boys wrote, Harry more frequently than Billy. He plodded along that year, assisting his two younger siblings and his grandmother and seeing to financial affairs. That spring he had taken a job with the new Forestry Service in Washington DC Billy had completed his freshman year at Harvard in good order, even though that winter he had contracted a bad case of the measles. Although Alice had missed this slice of her sons' lives, she would soon hear all their news: she had taken passage home for 15 September on the *Devonian*.

In August the Jameses headed toward England, stopping in Paris for an international congress and to see a magnetic healer Alice insisted might help William, who had just finished writing a Gifford Lecture on religious healthy-mindedness that included an overview of the American mind-cure movement.[123] While William had sworn off specialists and baths, Alice asked him to give this woman a chance. She believed that his sick mind played a role in his disease, so healing that mind might work better than sitz baths or electricity. She had heard of Mrs. Melton through New Yorkers Bessie Sturges and Francis Leggett and from Sara Bull, divorced wife of Norwegian violinist Ole Bull. The Bulls had been Alice's Cambridge neighbors. All these Americans were disciples of the Indian fakir Swami Vivekananda.[124]

After his session with Mrs. Melton, during which he believed he contracted boils from her laying her hands on him, William attended an international congress with Vivekananda, who commented later that the philosopher's preoccupation with his boils prevented him from concentrating on world problems.[125] William had been suspicious of Mrs. Melton all along. He told Henry that he wanted to add her "to my anthropological collection. In this latter respect I have been richly rewarded. She is a rank type, unlike anything I ever saw."[126] These sores became very painful, but despite the pain the Jameses planned to cross the Channel to retrieve Peggy, as the Clarkes planned a family vacation to Boulogne. When William and Alice learned that the Clarkes had postponed their trip, they checked in to the Hôtel du Littoral at Ostend, Belgium, and waited for William's skin irritations to subside.[127] By now the boils were so sore that he could not turn over onto his stomach.

By 12 August William could travel. They reached London that night, resting before going to Harrow to collect their daughter. William would then stay at Lamb House with Henry as nurse while Alice took Peggy to America; they would return in November. While there were advantages to leaving Peggy with Eliza Gibbens, who would teach her manners and morals, Alice wanted Peggy to continue at Harrow. She told her mother, "If I took her home to you she would lead the old inactive life and goodbye to the athletic habits which she has begun to enjoy and which will be her great safe-guard against the tendency to depression which <u>may</u> beset her. I must try to give her what I would have given much for myself."[128]

In London, however, Dr. Thorne ordered William to return to Nauheim for a third treatment, so by the fourth week in August he was installed at the Villa Luise while Alice took Peggy to Rye, where she enjoyed Henry's company and slept deeply. But William did not fare well in Nauheim, his letters echoing Peggy's letters complaining about the Clarke children. He had indigestion in the night, he was terrified at the prospect ahead, he had fallen into depression, he felt weak and seedy—a veritable litany of complaints. He announced to Alice, "I have rarely felt more weak and depressed."[129] These days he tracked his health obsessively, monitoring changes in his blood pressure, urine, and sleeping habits, using the discipline gained from his early medical training and years in the psychology lab to observe his own condition.

On 4 September he told Alice that she must go to Cambridge, "so let us consider the matter irrevocably fixed from this day on!"[130] But on 5 September Dr. Schott told William he should under no circumstances return to damp England when this round of baths ended but should seek a warm climate instead. His resolve to let Alice go home weakened: now while she was gone he could not spend the weeks with Henry. After telling her "Of course you must go," he added, "Of course it is a rather grim prospect for me."[131] On 8 September he announced how differently the next weeks would pass for them: she would enjoy her reunion while he grimly monitored his health. He longed for one more talk with her before she sailed.[132] Reconsidering her plans, she wavered.[133] William pressed her harder. When she vacillated he adjured her, "For Heaven's sake give it up."[134] Finally, on the same day, he telegraphed her not to sail.[135]

His nerves had failed him at the thought of two months without Alice. He told her baldly, "I haven't it in me to stick it out here for two months all alone."[136] On 14 September she telegraphed, telling him she would stay abroad.[137] He was ashamed to have to tell Harry that his mother would not be coming home, but he weighed his needs against those of other family members and concluded that he needed Alice most.[138] "Your mother & the boys, in spite of the pity of it, must wait till next summer," he told her.[139] He was tremendously relieved.[140] Henry knew Alice could not have left William in his time of great need and supported her decision to remain abroad, though he had equally supported her plans to go home.[141] She returned Peggy to the Clarkes and made her way to Bad Nauheim. She confessed to Harry, "You boys can never know how I long for you nor how it broke me up to give up the three weeks at home—but how I should have been haunted by the thought of Papa, longing for what I was having. It is all right now."[142]

For the most part Peggy was reconciled to returning to the Clarkes. She and Rebecca would begin fencing lessons together. Alice hoped they could work off their animosity toward one another in a physical way. She suspected that Rebecca had too much youthful energy for Alice's prematurely old daughter, comparing the girls to a gigantic puppy and an Italian greyhound trying to make friends. Peggy felt as her uncle Henry felt as a child: both thought themselves older than their mates.[143] She considered herself more mature than Rebecca. To help facilitate Peggy's relations with the Clarke children, Alice bought tickets for all the children to see *Julius Caesar* in London that fall. Peggy could spend her Christmas holiday in Rye with her beloved uncle, which would give her time away from the noisy household.

On 22 September Henry escorted Alice to Dover and waited with her for two hours until the boat started across the Channel. They walked about the town and had tea, and then Henry settled Alice in a sheltered spot on deck before leaving her.[144] She was sorry to part from her brother-in-law; they had become warm friends. Now that his older brother, William, was too helpless to exert his influence, Henry took a nearly proprietary air toward Alice and Peggy. His relationship with his sister-in-law had shifted during the time they had spent together. He found her personally appealing, referring to her as "the dear Being" and showing an interest in her clothing, telling her she looked best in "'black—and very handsome black.'"[145] If Alice were his wife, he would make sure she always had the most attractive clothing.[146] After the two James women departed Henry told Peggy they were "all the vanished poetry of my summer!"[147] He was busy, though, finishing *The Wings of the Dove* and continuing his responsibilities as a homeowner.

Things were going as well as possible at home, given the circumstances, but Alice would not find out how her mother and children fared until another four seasons had passed.

11 Mendings

ALICE ARRIVED IN BAD NAUHEIM on 23 September.[1] This time the
Jameses had better quarters, a corner sitting room with two bedrooms
on either side so that they need not be together day and night. Their stay
was brief. With Rome as their final winter destination, they stopped first
in Lucerne so that William could strengthen his heart after the baths,
Alice traveling to Geneva for more clothes. She was not certain that her
earlier purchases would be suitable for Italy, and Henry had warned her
not to buy clothes in Rome, as the dressmakers there would be "trashy &
cheaty."[2] Now she had two men who cared enough to notice her appearance, though she gave Henry most of the credit for her new look. When
she arrived in Rome she advised him, "That I have any good clothes is
chiefly due to your encouragement."[3]

Still grieving for her mother and boys, Alice was at first painfully
homesick, but since William was improving or at least feeling better, she
allowed herself to enjoy Rome.[4] By October's end they were installed in
a pension, but she found it too small and proceeded to scout the imperial
city for better quarters. The first place she saw was in an excellent quarter
of the city; it was a large, sunny room that cost four francs a day, including
wine. There were too many stairs, though; any climbing remained nearly
impossible for her husband.[5] Within days she found two southwest-facing

rooms in the Hotel Hassler on the Piazza Pincio priced at twenty-five francs a day with meals. Here William had a writing table in the larger room, with a bed screened off for privacy, and they had a bathtub. Alice loved her cozy room; its one window had a table next to it where she could read and write.

These rooms were on a quiet street not far from their friend Dr. William Baldwin, which relieved Alice of some of her responsibility for William's care. From their windows she could see the photographs in the shop windows on the Piazza di Spagna, three hundred feet below down the Spanish Steps.[6] They were so high up they could see the hills beyond Rome.[7] The first days William developed a severe head cold and slept badly until Alice gave him sulfonal. He now weighed just 64.5 kilos, about 142 pounds, nearly his weight on his wedding day.

The Jameses had not chosen Rome only for its mild winter climate. Dr. Baldwin persuaded William to try a new remedy for his heart: animal injections, which William claimed made him a new man. Alice told only a few people of this remedy, holding each to secrecy. Patients received injections of an animal extract called Roberts-Hawley. The compound included extracts from the lymphatic duct, brain, and testicles of goats; a few drops were injected under the skin twice daily.[8] Guaranteed to promote strength in body and brain, this wonder drug might even alleviate sexual impotence.[9] The Jameses' physical relationship had been an important part of their marriage, so perhaps this drug appealed to both. Supposedly, there were no side effects.[10] Dr. Baldwin recommended two daily injections for three months, with regular physical checks of the heart to regulate the dosage. Alice administered the dose, and Dr. Baldwin monitored William's heart. She also helped William with his resistance exercises, stoutly providing the resistance.[11]

That winter Harvard professor Barrett Wendell sent the Jameses his recently published *History of American Literature*, which was an outgrowth of the first course in American literature taught at Harvard. It included a chapter with an illustration of John Greenleaf Whittier, Alice's dear friend, but there were only two pages devoted to her brother-in-law, though Wendell believed Henry's work was "masterly," even if now he perhaps should not be called an American writer. Wendell gave an even briefer mention to William and his international reputation, noting that his philosophy exemplified the turn from Transcendental metaphysical abstraction to philosophical principles based on fact. The volume proposed to show what American literature had contributed to the great tradition of English literature, but Alice found it fell short of its latent promises.[12] Frequently, she read social reform texts, too, telling Billy of one of them, written by Francis Greenwood Peabody, Harvard professor and an acquaintance of the Jameses. "I got to reading Mr. Peabody's new book on *Jesus Christ and the Social Question*, and I could hardly lay it down. It is, thus far, not only interesting but beautifully written. Have you seen the dedication to his wife? Every wife will take joy in it, most of all we who care for Mrs. Peabody."[13] The popular book called for social reforms rather than a radical reformation of society.

Both Alice and William still read Henry's latest works. She championed his writing, and even William praised his brother's shorter tales. This winter they read "The Tone of Time," the tale of a woman painter commissioned to paint an imaginary man. Instead, she paints a portrait of her dead lover, who jilted her twenty years before, and plot complications lead to a nearly impossible coincidence involving her rival. The tale meditates on the consequences of lives not lived, lives that might have gone in other directions, yet it lauds protagonist Mary Tredick's strength of character. The Jameses also read the five chapters on Rome in Henry's early collection of travel essays, *Transatlantic Sketches*.

As their Roman weeks rolled by, William made limited progress. He tried treatments with the electric battery again, besides the lymph injections. At first he saw little gain. He had great hopes for the injections, but now he thought any improvement from them might be accidental. "The weather has on the whole been detestably dark and wet—the rain is streaming down at this moment and I have had three acute upsets of bowels etc.—(I am now recovering from the last) which keep me curiously devitalized and spiritless," he informed his sons.[14] But by now Alice was an adept medical assistant, able to assess her husband's moods and make needed changes in his routine.

Though he was frequently discouraged after these long months of various medical treatments, he and Alice still befriended fellow guests, including noted British anthropologist Sir James Frazer and his wife, Elisabeth Groves Frazer. Because she was deaf and could not hear dinner table conversation, Mrs. Frazer resorted to smiling continually, a mannerism that irked William.[15] Alice found them both pleasant, the only ones in their boardinghouse she liked.[16]

William and Sir James exchanged books, *The Principles of Psychology* for *The Golden Bough*, both classic texts in their respective fields. *The Golden Bough*, a pioneering work on magic and religion, explored ongoing cultural patterns, including myths of the killing of the divine king in primitive agricultural societies. William had volumes 2 and 3 of *The Golden Bough* sent to Lamb House for safekeeping. Henry had never heard of the book before.[17] Perhaps the title may have triggered the idea (consciously or unconsciously) for the title of Henry's novel *The Golden Bowl*, which he started during the summer of 1902; at first he called it "The Marriages."

William could seldom receive visitors. Henry's friend sculptor Hendrik Andersen called, but William was too weak to see him on the day he visited.[18] Alice, who found the young man very attractive, promised she would write and let him know when her husband felt well enough to entertain him.[19] Henry advised her to see Andersen's portrait busts, which Henry called "masterly" for his age.[20]

When William proposed they go window-shopping despite the steady rain, Alice knew he felt better.[21] Before leaving Rome he managed a little sightseeing, his wife taking him by tram to distant spots in the city. They got out and walked a bit and then rode the tram home. William delighted in "the old shabby streets, with their big yellow washed buildings, and rococo churches, and the tessellated pavement flowing round them like a river."[22] One day they visited the Forum. Signor Boni, a Venetian in charge of the excavations, showed them fascinating sights. Alice was impressed with the just-discovered Lapis Niger, a black marble slab supported by two lions that marked the grave of Romulus and later was part of the meeting place in front of the Senate.[23] They also saw the house of vestals and the house of Caesar, with its small rooms and mosaic floors. Yet some aspects of Roman culture still disturbed her. "He [William] revels in the picturesqueness of the streets—and so do I in my measure," she confided to Harry. "But I belong to the north and not all this beauty can repay to me the filth, cruelty and crime-tainted atmosphere of the place."[24] Occasionally, she read Tacitus, with its record of historical cruelty, to William.[25] While she held liberal and sometimes even radical opinions on some issues, she could not accommodate pagan or present Catholic practices.

Just before Christmas William and Alice saw the monument to Giordano Bruno, the Dominican priest forced to leave his order because of his unorthodox beliefs. After Bruno championed Copernican cosmology and opposed Aristotelian logic, he was arrested by the Inquisition and burned at the stake in 1600. Alice found his figure impressive and the inscription on his monument noble:

> A Bruno
> Il secolo da lui divinato
> Qui
> Dove il rogo arse.
>
> [To Bruno
> The century he foretold
> Here
> Where the faggots burned.]

The sight should remind young priests of the church's infamous past, Alice thought.[26]

She loved most of Rome's sights and its light but tried to ignore the beggars, annoyed by their pervasive whining. The old priests with their vacant faces saddened her, but the boys in training for the priesthood upset her even more. "I met a procession of little school boys out for a walk—eyes cast down upon their white shirt fronts which were to be sure, delightfully white. They were in evening dress with tail coats like microscopic waiters but their tall hats, black kid gloves and general sanctimoniousness showed me at once that they were a very select group: and so it proved," she wrote to share her prejudices with Bessie Evans. "They are of the Jesuit school, the most aristocratic establishment in Rome. Since I used to discover those dreadful white worms at the roots of the strawberry plants I have seen no more painful forms of life."[27] Her dislike of Catholicism grew so pronounced during her Roman sojourn that William teasingly wrote Billy that he feared his mother would turn Catholic: "What I am afraid of is the attractions of the Catholic Church upon her. I think at Christmas she will kiss the Pope's toe." But he, too, found the priests devoid of manliness and moral vigor.[28]

King Oak Hill House, Weymouth,
Massachusetts, Alice's birthplace.
fMS 1092.9 (4598). By permission of
Houghton Library, Harvard University.

Alice H. Gibbens, Mary Gibbens, and
Margaret Gibbens, 1862–63.
fMS 1092.9 (4598). By permission of
Houghton Library, Harvard University.

Daniel Lewis Gibbens Jr., c. 1863. *2002M-44(b). By
permission of Houghton Library, Harvard University.

opposite: Daniel Lewis Gibbens Sr., 1842. fMS 1092.9 (4598).
By permission of Houghton Library, Harvard University.

Daniel L. Gibbons
Boston 31st May 1842.

Henry James Sr., c. 1865. pfMS Am 1094, box 3.
By permission of Houghton Library, Harvard University.

opposite: William James, c. 1865. pfMS Am 1092.
By permission of Houghton Library, Harvard University.

above: Leonora Piper during a trance state. pfMS Am 1094, box 1.
By permission of Houghton Library, Harvard University.

opposite, top: 1902 sketch of the Chocorua house by D. D. L. McGrew.
pfMS AM 1092. By permission of Houghton Library, Harvard University.

opposite, bottom: 95 Irving Street, early 1890s. fMS AM 1092.
By permission of Houghton Library, Harvard University.

Sketch of the Chocorua House by D. B. L. McGrew in Sept. 1902.

above: Alice H. G. James and Francis Tweedy, 1891. fMS 1092.9 (4598).
By permission of Houghton Library, Harvard University.

opposite: Margaret Mary James, c. 1890. *2002M-44(b).
By permission of Houghton Library, Harvard University.

Pach Bros   CAMBRIDGE, MASS.

above: Alice James, 1891. fMS 1092.9 (4598).
By permission of Houghton Library, Harvard University.

opposite top: Alice H. G. James, Peggy James, William James, and Henry James at Lamb House, c. 1900. pfMS Am 1094. By permission of Houghton Library, Harvard University.

opposite bottom: Eveleen Tennant Myers's watercolor sketch of Château Carquéranne, 1900. pfMS Am 1094. By permission of Houghton Library, Harvard University.

4

Mrs. Wm. James, M. M. James
William James, H. J.

above: Peggy James, c. 1906. *2002M-44(b). By permission
of Houghton Library, Harvard University.

opposite top: William and Henry James, c. 1904–5. pfMS Am 1094.
By permission of Houghton Library, Harvard University.

opposite bottom: Alice H. G. James and William James, c. 1904–5,
photograph by Theodore Pope. pfMS Am 1092.
By permission of Houghton Library, Harvard University.

137

Saturday, May 16, 1908

Mr & Mrs Edward Underhill
"The Lodge"
Magdalene Col. ☩ P.M.
3.30

~~Merritt, Rector of~~
~~Exeter~~

The Master's Lodgings
Balliol
7.45
Invited by Dicey — declined

above: William James diary entries, Alice and
William overwriting one another. MS Am 1092.9
(4557). By permission of Houghton Library,
Harvard University.

left: Robertson James, c. 1907. fMS 1092.9 (4598).
By permission of Houghton Library, Harvard
University.

The "Bee" — 1915.
(A.H.J. Absent.)

Standing: { Miss Caroline Peabody, Mary G. Salter, Mrs. W.G. Faslow,
Mrs. John Allyne.

In Chairs: Miss Lilly Hoppin, Mrs. C.W. Eliot, Miss Caroline Parsons.

On the Ground: Mrs. John C. Cobb.   Mrs. Martha McDaniel.

above: The "Bee"—1915. (A. H. J.
Absent). Standing: Miss Caroline
Peabody, Mary G. Salter, Mrs. W.
G. Faslow, Mrs. John Allyne. In
chairs: Miss Lilly Hoppin, Mrs. C.
W. Eliot, Miss Caroline Parsons.
On the ground: Mrs. John C.
Cobb, Mrs. Martha McDonald.
fMS Am 1092.9 (4598). By
permission of Houghton Library,
Harvard University.

right: Henry James II, c. 1905.
*2002M-44(b). By permission
of Houghton Library, Harvard
University.

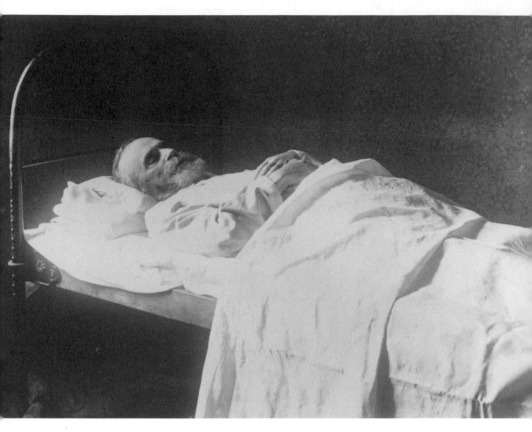

above: William James on his deathbed, August 1910.
Courtesy of Michael James.

opposite: Billy James, Alice H. G. James, and Eliza
Gibbens holding William James III, 1913.
*2002M-44(b). By permission of Houghton Library,
Harvard University.

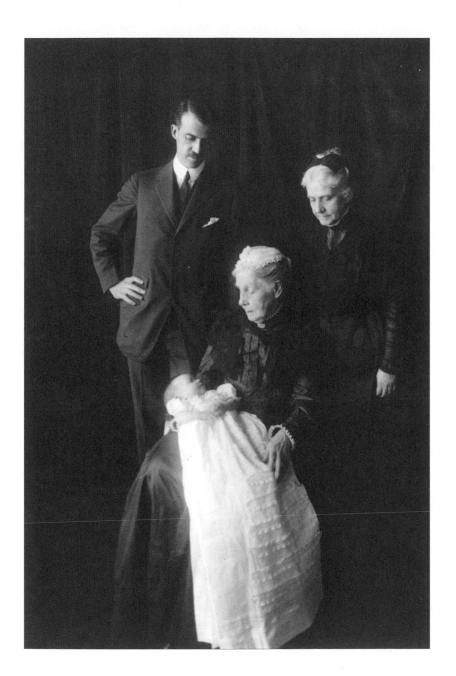

Fredericka James, c. 1917. Courtesy of Michael James.

Bruce Porter and Peggy James Porter with Robin Porter, 1918. Hookier Family, POR 209. Bancroft Library, University of California at Berkeley.

Peggy James Porter, Aleck James, and Alice H. G. James
with Sandy, Dublin, New Hampshire, 1922. Courtesy of
Michael James.

Alice's views, though intolerant and inconsistent with her earlier support of the Chicago strikers, many of them Catholic, fit social reform movements that held sway at the end of the nineteenth century, some of them advocated by Francis Peabody. Although liberal theology was usually nondenominational and nonsectarian, anti-Catholicism still existed because the Catholic Church was seen as a medieval institution and because its members might place allegiance to the pope above allegiance to their country. Nativism, antipopery, and anti-Semitism were an inescapable part of America's Gilded Age.[29]

In December they moved again, to the Hotel Primavera, where their rooms captured more sunshine. William worked on the Gifford Lectures with enthusiasm, full of ideas.[30] One morning they took a long drive on the Campagna and then lunched in town, he taking a long nap that afternoon.[31] While she was healthier and happier in Rome, Alice thought constantly of her children. She sent a report of Peggy's progress at Harrow to Bessie Evans, sharing her hope that Peggy would have the formal education Alice lacked. "Ah me, Bessie dear, this is not philosophy but a flagrant piece of natural egotism. However, each bird must use its own voice if it proves to be only a chirp, and have you not always listened kindly to my tales of the children!" Twenty years earlier Alice had longed to have the courage to join George Herbert Palmer's philosophy course at the Radcliffe Annex, but "it seemed to me then that I had no right to take the time for anything so delightful."[32] In the meanwhile, however, she had learned more philosophy than most people learn in a lifetime through her immersion in William's work.

That fall, while her mother and father traveled to Rome, Peggy contracted the mumps. Uncle Henry sympathized with her, vividly recalling his own case of mumps when he was nine or ten. He told Peggy he remembered eating hasty pudding and had hated seeing how he looked.[33] The week before Christmas he met his recovered niece at the train station in Harrow, advising her to be ready with her box labeled and a first-class ticket, which he would refund.[34] Uncle and niece spent a quiet holiday at Lamb House, Peggy reading Sir Walter Scott's *Redgauntlet*, *The Antiquary*, *The Pirate*, and *Old Mortality* during her ten days there.[35] The thirteen-year-old girl, whom her father thought engaged in "rapid, elderly, and unnecessary conversation about all things" when she was just eleven, was a suitable companion for her uncle.[36] While she did not like some of her uncle's neighbors, notably the "big-beaked & black-browed girls" who stared at her, she was happy to be with Henry.[37] Perhaps more reluctant than he would admit to have his brother take his place with Peggy, William called her a cold intellectualist.[38]

One afternoon during the first week in January Henry met Peggy and the three eldest Clarke children at Baker Street, escorting them to the Hippodrome, then to tea, and finally to Madame Tussaud's Wax Museum to see the murderers, a place he did not ordinarily frequent.[39] Peggy found the London circus, where she saw clowns, acrobats, and performing elephants and seals, splendid. She loved the Cinderella pantomime. Two days before her school term started she went with Henry to Westminster Abbey, "which I suppose you know is a very fine Cathedral where a great many of the kings and queens of England are buried," she lectured Francis. She updated her brother on Queen Victoria's health and the possibility that the Prince of Wales, the queen's successor, would be crowned in the coronation chair she had seen there.[40]

No sooner was Peggy back in school than Uncle Henry took her out again, this time for Queen Victoria's funeral procession. He wanted her to reach London early so that they could shop for a black hat, a necessity for this historic event.[41] She watched the great entourage as it crossed London, with foreign kings and emperors from Germany, Greece, Portugal, Russia, and other countries in the vanguard.[42] When William heard of Henry's putting Peggy in mourning, he felt well enough to satirize his brother to his son Billy: "Are you aweer that your Sister, by the orders of her Uncle, is in complete mourning for her Majesty? Half mo[u]rning begins April 7th & will end on June 7. I hope that you & Tweedy are in mourning too. I am all black inside."[43]

With Peggy safe in England and her husband gradually gaining, Alice's life seemed nearly orderly again. William had new insights into his material, and Henry was quick to applaud him to Alice: "Wm's cerebral boom—advancing lectures & ever crowded life—all give me a taste of the shining web & flashing shuttle on the loom of Existence."[44] Alice's nearly halcyon Roman days were interrupted, though, when the Myers family arrived to disturb her peace.[45] William had written to Frederick Myers about the success of the lymph injections. Now much worse than ever, the ailing man risked the trip for a last gamble on the Roberts-Hawley compound.

Their visit was a short-lived one, for just five days after his arrival Myers contracted pneumonia. He died on 17 January, confirmed in his belief that he was bound for immortal life after spending much of his career investigating what he called the "Subliminal Self," with a focus on life after death.[46] When William wrote a memorial essay on him later, he thought Myers's greatest contribution to psychology was his insistence that we have a self wider than we can yet understand through current empirical research.[47] After his death Eveleen Myers clung pathetically to William, talking endlessly of her husband. She wanted nothing of Alice, who mused that Mr. Myers might be in heaven taking care of Queen Victoria.[48]

After this sad episode William was exhausted, though by February he felt stronger. Although the lymph injections had been delayed at customs and Dr. Baldwin had ended his daily visits, William suffered no ill effects without the treatment. Alice was tired of Baldwin; now she thought he was "queer." While she was sad that they would soon leave Rome, William longed for Lamb House, its garden, and Henry.[49]

Just before they left, William invested in art. This time Alice did not quarrel with him over the cost. It was a good time to buy from the dealers, who had few sales that winter because people had been frightened away by Rome's November floods and subsequent cases of typhoid. William bought several pictures, including an 1835 Swiss landscape by a German painter, paying half the amount asked.[50]

During Alice's last week in Rome she made a day rail trip with Cambridge friends, Theodora Sedgwick and Edith White Norton, traveling to Albano and then hiring a carriage to see the sights.[51] She was awed by Lake Nemi but was disappointed when her friends would not climb down with her to the bottom of the crater to see the ruins of the temple of Nemi from a closer vantage point. It was a "haunted place."[52] She may have thought of Sir James Frazer, who in *The Golden Bough* discussed the meanings of the ancient bloody temple rites that took place there: whoever could kill the priest of Diana's temple became his successor.

These two long years were nearly over. The first Gifford Lecture was scheduled for 15 May, and final passage for home had been taken for 31

August.[53] Alice and William left Rome the first week in March, traveling to Perugia, Assisi, and Florence, then stopping briefly at Geneva, where he walked and rested, able to write in the morning. Upon reaching England Alice went straight to Harrow to fetch Peggy while William took the train to Rye and then walked alone up the hill to Lamb House. Henry was brokenhearted that he had not been at the station to receive his brother: he had expected him half an hour later.[54]

The weeks in Rye before the lectures were nearly idyllic. Alice, Peggy, William, and Henry fell into easy rhythms with one another. Henry spent mornings in the garden room dictating to his secretary, Mary Weld; William revised and refined his lectures; Alice read, wrote, or mended; and Peggy went window-shopping in Rye. In the afternoons Alice, Peggy, and Henry took long walks with Henry's dog, Nick. Peggy imitated her uncle shouting at Nick when he chased sheep or chickens: "Oh! oh! oh! oh! oh! you little brute! you little brute! you beast! oh! oh! oh!"[55] By now she was utterly content in Henry's presence. "'There are others who love me more, but there is no one to whom I feel so like as I do to Uncle Henry.'"[56]

One afternoon when William felt better, all four went to Brede Place, where Stephen Crane had lived briefly. It was currently unoccupied, but the farmer's wife who worked as caretaker let them in to see the oak-paneled rooms with their large fireplaces. Another day the group went to Hastings, where Uncle Henry bought Peggy old editions of *Oliver Twist* and *The Old Curiosity Shop*. Since Billy was considering a medical career, Peggy copied an inscription she saw on a brass plate. It reflected all that Alice and William had learned from doctors and their cures over the past two years:

> Isaac Letsum Doctor
> When folks is ill they comes to I.
> I physics, bleeds and sweats 'um.
> If after that they choose to die
> What's that to I, I lets um.[57]

When William and Alice left for Edinburgh, Peggy returned to Harrow.

The Gifford Lectures began on the day appointed; they were successful beyond Alice's dreams. Though Henry was doomed, as he put it, to miss all the lectures, Harry came from America to hear his father.[58] Miss McLarm, the niece of Lord Gifford, who had endowed the lecture series, told Alice she had never seen such a large audience. Forty people at best usually attended a given Gifford Lecture, while three hundred had come to hear William. After months in seclusion he grew nervous before speaking, yet all went well. By the fourth lecture he was tired, but after that he took digitalis between lectures. He delivered ten in all for the first series.

In these lectures William looked at religious experience through what he called a psychological, empirical lens, attempting to study religion scientifically. Considering religious belief as it impacts individuals rather than institutions (many of which codify religious practice and thus detract from its positive benefits), he reviewed many personal accounts of saints, religious leaders, and mystics of various denominational backgrounds, giving vivid testimony to the emotions engendered by their beliefs and conversion experiences. These intense experiences usually result in states of heightened energy and satisfaction with oneself and the universe, these states being the "fruits" of the faith-state. If religious belief is viewed pragmatically, in terms of its results, it is a positive influence in human life. Though theological creeds and philosophies of religion change over time, empirically speaking, such saintly qualities recur and are "indispensable to the world's welfare."[59]

During these exalted religious states believers sense themselves in touch with forces greater than their own that impel them to higher actions, higher mental states. William hypothesized that these powers come initially from the believers' subconscious minds, an area of consciousness he termed "subliminal" and "transmarginal." Religious belief arises in that part of our minds most nearly related to this subconscious region. A higher subconscious power within our own minds moves us to a union with outside forces that he called a "MORE," forces traditionally called "God" or other names given to deities. Religions hypothesize this force as external, but from a psychological point of view it is enough to affirm that there are powers within our minds we do not fully comprehend that somehow break through to our conscious mind. At the end of the lectures, however, he moved beyond his initial scientific-psychological point of view to affirm his belief in other worlds beyond our conscious, sensible one, worlds that intersect ours at some point. Though it is impossible to warrant any ultimate truth or idealism about religion through philosophy or science, it is possible to believe that such other worlds exist because they relate to our only absolute realities, which are our inner states. Suggesting but not defending polytheism, ultimately William believed that the world might need to embrace religious pluralism.

Throughout the lectures he entertained the idea that religious belief, which cannot be verified empirically, has proven to be a powerful tool for promoting the best moral life possible. He could see the results of this belief in his own wife, whom he had always considered to be one of the most moral people he knew.

Between lectures, though William could not accept many invitations due to his health, he, Alice, Peggy, and sometimes Harry did a little sightseeing, a welcomed time for the four after their long separation. Peggy arrived on 1 June to join her parents during their last two weeks in Edinburgh, her ordeal with Rebecca Clarke nearly over.[60] They visited Queen Mary's Craig Millar Castle and then toured the Castle of Edinburgh, seeing the room where James VI of Scotland was born and the chapel where Queen Margaret had worshiped. The next day the little group saw a procession, while a band played a minor-key tune to the words "Up with the shoesters of bonny Selkirk and down with the Earl of Hume." The following day they went to a fair.

Other day trips included steamer passage to Loch Katrina, a mountain lake with small islands, and then to Loch Lomond, where they had tea. On 19 June the Americans toured Holyrood Palace, where Queen Mary had lived with Lord Henry Stuart Darnley, her second husband, and they visited the home of John Knox and his St. Giles Cathedral.[61] After her weeks of immersion in Catholicism, Alice must have been satisfied to see this visible monument to Protestantism.

Alice was not finished helping William heal, though. When the Gifford Lectures concluded, Alice and William agreed that he needed one more stay at Bad Nauheim to consolidate his gains, even though her heart ached so to see Francis that it seemed a farce to retrace her steps. Peggy returned to the Clarkes when the other three Jameses left for Germany, Harry accompanying his parents to the spa and then touring with the Curtises through France the remaining weeks. At the end of the summer all four would return to 95 Irving Street.[62]

Alice knew it was time to go home. Eliza Gibbens's tawny silk sewing bag, which Alice had used in all the strange bedrooms she had frequented over the last two years, had finally worn out.[63]

12 A Form of Use

LATE-SUMMER CAMBRIDGE SWELTERED AS Alice struggled to unpack the gatherings of two years abroad: clothes, a little furniture, even underclothing for Billy.[1] She had sprained her ankle at Rye just two days before the voyage, and her searing headaches returned.[2] For twenty-six months she had known her mother and two of her sons only through letters, avoiding the daily household stress that had exhausted her before. Once installed at 95 Irving Street, however, she could no longer avoid the complexities of her own life. Before leaving for home Alice had reflected on what she had learned over the past two years, discovering she could maintain her positive outlook by keeping busy, having more to do than she could accomplish but keeping her own inner balance.[3]

By now she had assimilated the best of both her parents' personal traits. She had inherited her father's courage and sense of adventure without his tendency toward substance abuse, and she possessed her mother's deep convictions without her extreme timidity. She must retrain for the daily duties that shimmered on her near horizon, and while she knew she would have to work harder in Cambridge, she welcomed entering her own zone of creativity and production, vowing to meet these challenges.[4] Alice was still beautiful despite her years and cares. In a 1902 photograph her face is smooth and unlined, her hair, pulled from her high, smooth brow, completely gray. Her deep-set dark eyes look as lovely as they had when she was sixteen years old.

William found it difficult to readjust, so Alice endured his temper that fall as she resumed her other duties. "I am getting better steadily, but my temper, under even the smallest provocation, is still liable to be orful. Ask my poor wife!" he quipped to their financial advisor, Henry Lee Higginson.[5] William's health and nerves remained precarious, and when he was tired he left for quiet retreats, as he had done all their married life. He resumed his interest in Pauline Goldmark, though in a more subdued manner. He wrote to her soon after his return, asking her to remember their hikes and wishing he were able to accompany her again.[6]

William required Alice's constant vigilance to keep him from canceling the gains he had made abroad. But with her prodding he managed to complete writing the second course of Edinburgh lectures. That fall Alice traveled to Newport for Edmund Tweedy's funeral when William was unable to make the trip.[7] In addition to honoring her husband's family, she also may have relished a chance to escape her obligations and enjoy her own company again, even if only briefly.

The first weeks and months back in Cambridge, while William focused on his work and health, Alice knit together a group that had lost the habit of daily family life: an aging mother, a Harvard law student, a busy Harvard junior, an adolescent daughter who must readapt to American culture, and a ten-year-old son who scarcely knew her. The house itself also demanded immediate attention. There were leaks in the roof, and the parlor wallpaper and the stair carpet needed replacing.[8] She began the necessary renovations and looked for reliable servants, she and her mother going first to an agency where none of the "haughty" domestics would even look at her.[9]

Now Eliza Gibbens lived at 107 Irving Street a good part of the year, except for occasional long visits to her other two daughters. Mary Gibbens Salter and her husband, Mack, were in Chicago, he working for the Society for Ethical Culture. And Eliza's daughter Margaret had flown to Montreal with her professor-husband, Leigh Gregor. Alice must be her mother's primary companion and mainstay.

To his eternal credit, at least in Alice's accounting, her eldest son, Harry, now in his second year of law studies at Harvard after a year spent in

Washington DC, editing the Forestry Service's journal, needed virtually no guidance. A serious and darkly handsome young man, he took care of financial matters in his parents' absence and was learning to manage the family's Syracuse rental properties, all without complaint. She relied on his advice and support.

Billy was not there to greet his parents when they arrived at 95 Irving Street during the fall of 1901. Since he had behaved reasonably well during their absence, they allowed him to spend the summer on the Hawaiian island of Molokai at his friend Charley Hartwell's family ranch.[10] A tall, handsome boy, Billy was popular with his classmates, even though he was a little shy, as Alice had been at his age. He considered forestry and landscape design, but he had not yet found a vocation. While Billy was an active participant—sometimes too active, his parents thought—in Harvard's social life (he was a member of Delta Kappa Epsilon, also known as "the Dickey") and athletic activities (Harvard crew), he kept up his marks.

As much as Peggy had longed for home, like her mother she had to readjust. She was seasick during most of the voyage, the stewardess commenting how much she had vomited.[11] She returned with a British accent and a cool demeanor—"manlier," William thought.[12] Harry and Billy were too old to tease her, but she and Francis fought often. Peggy's schedule filled quickly: she attended dancing school, riding lessons, and parties. Alice tried to guide her daughter as smoothly as possible through these adolescent rites of passage. Eager to atone for the emotional privation the girl endured while her mother concentrated solely on her father, she relished being part of Peggy's life again. That Christmas Mary Weld, Henry's secretary, sent her a Japanese doll, a small gift from her Rye friends and a reminder of the life she had lived away from Irving Street.

Alice helped Peggy readjust to family life and Cambridge, but she had little sense of what had happened to Francis. He was now a handsome boy of ten. Because school was a struggle for him, he disliked it. Suddenly, he had two parents who took an interest in his studies. William assumed that the boy would matriculate at Harvard like his older brothers, and he brooked no excuses if Francis performed poorly. Perhaps William's patience had worn thin with this last child. Perhaps, also, both parents' guilt at leaving Francis made them determined to guide him in the direction they viewed best.

On 1 April 1902 Alice and William sailed back to Europe for the second round of Gifford Lectures. She hoped to go by way of Geneva (to buy clothes, he suspected), but he vetoed the idea.[13] They remained abroad nearly three months, taking with them the manuscript of *The Varieties of Religious Experience*, dedicated to E.P.G.—Eliza Putnam Gibbens. William imagined that all Europe would wonder who she was.[14] The book was a testimonial to the influence Alice and her mother had on his willingness to consider the religious option. Though she sometimes neglected her own needs, Alice led the balanced, healthy-minded life that William advocated.

In England they visited Stratford-on-Avon and Torquay, visiting the Edwin Godkins.[15] Before going to Edinburgh they stopped at Rye to see Henry. The Salters joined them in Scotland for the lectures. While his nerves were bad before the series began, again William delivered them to great acclaim.[16] By 19 June they were home.[17]

The fall of 1902 found Alice as she had been the previous fall: she still had headaches, and she still needed servants. Typically, she employed a cook and two serving maids full time, bringing in occasional help for heavy cleaning, sewing, and large dinner parties. She complained frequently of problems training and keeping domestic help. During her two years in Europe she saw a cadre of well-trained servants, the result of generations of a core servant class. In the pensions she frequented someone else trained and oversaw servants. Now she worried that her own standards for household management had been too low, and she vowed to improve service for her guests. However, there was no equivalent class in America. Servants immigrated from Europe to America to rise in social class, not to remain servants forever. Moreover, there were other, easier jobs for young women in factories, offices, and shops, jobs with regular days off and defined tasks. That meant that either Alice had to train Americans to rise to the European standards she wished to emulate or she must rely on upwardly mobile immigrants. They were available: in 1900 60 percent of servants were immigrants, the majority of them Irish.[18]

"The servant problem," as magazines and middle-class to upper-middle-class women deemed it, reflected wider social issues. Earlier in the nineteenth century families hired serving girls from nearby farms to help when needed. If these girls lived with the families, they usually ate with them and attended their church, accepted as household members. In Weymouth the Webb women had hired such help, Alice and her sisters working alongside the girls. The lines demarcating servants from employers were loosely drawn.[19]

As the century wore on and the Eastern seaboard became increasingly urbanized and industrialized, this system changed. Now upper-middle-class and sometimes middle-class housewives hired cooks and maids as live-in help. In a democratic country struggling to widen the franchise, ironically, some households became more rigidly stratified. Servants were no longer considered part of the family but instead were segregated as lower-class individuals who could not socialize with family members. Domestics often complained of the isolation they experienced; they had little opportunity to develop their own social network. However, their constant presence allowed women to maintain well-ordered, well-appointed homes and to entertain formally, boosting the family's social status at the expense of their servants' physical and mental well-being. Whereas before hired help performed specific tasks, including dairying, gardening, harvesting, canning, and weaving, now domestics were expected to work all the time at a variety of tasks.

Operating under verbal contracts, mistresses and servants usually had a probationary week to discover whether they suited one another. Domestics were allowed two half-days off a week, typically Thursday and Sunday, but were expected to work seven or eight hours before taking their leave. The average working day ran eleven to twelve hours, many servants working from 5:00 a.m. until late at night. The James household kept this kind of schedule; it was not unusual for dinner parties to end after 10:00 p.m. Alice entertained nearly ceaselessly, giving lunches, teas, and dinners.[20] Strenuous working conditions at her home and elsewhere resulted in a high turnover rate: in 1900 the average length of service was less than one and a half years.[21]

Alice's problems mirrored this general state of affairs. Before she sailed back to America in 1901 she tried to bring her Carquéranne servant, Marguerite Godineau, with her. The woman never responded to Alice's letter, though, partly to her relief, as she was not sure how easily Marguerite would adjust. Upon her return Alice employed European immigrants. This international experiment was time-consuming and not always satisfactory for employer or employee. She hired a German girl, Bridget, but the boys disliked her. No record remains of how Alice's children treated servants, though when Billy wanted to bring home a Swiss maid he encountered during his time abroad, Alice encouraged him. Given her second son's reported interest in women during his subsequent married life, coupled with Alice's warning not to fall in love with this maid, it is possible, though, that Billy viewed the Swiss girl as more than a servant.[22]

In September 1902 Alice hired another German maid, whom she considered "refined."[23] But by early November, after Alice spent five weeks training her, Gretchen (or Greta) gave notice, though she returned at the end of November. The current cook also left at this time. Next Alice hired an English cook, whom she disliked but who was respectable and an improvement over German servants, she believed.[24] This cook soon left, so Alice tried to hire a French cook she had heard praised.[25] Finally, in December she engaged a Scotch-Irish woman, Rebecca Dundas.[26] Alice found her "a first-class woman in the kitchen, a really good cook." Harry advised his mother to have William marry Rebecca in order to keep her: "In Utah a man always marries the cook if she is valuable."[27] While Alice would not let William become a polygamist to keep a servant, she did pay her $5.50 a week, a relatively high wage, as the average weekly wage for servants on the East Coast was $3.60.[28] Rebecca remained with the Jameses for years.

Alice did not expect gratitude, but she did expect high-quality service from these women, viewing herself as a sort of domestic manager and in effect mimicking a supervisory role in the public sphere. Despite her demands, she made sincere efforts to be a good and honest employer, even taking her servants to the dentist at her own expense.[29] Like good supervisors in every field, sometimes she worked alongside her help, even making the beds when one of the servants was sick.[30] When workmen delivered 150 loads of loam to Irving Street one summer, Alice stayed outside with them and invited them to a four o'clock tea with cake and doughnuts.[31] She found domestic work interesting and failed to understand her servants' general lack of interest in their work.[32] She was never deliberately cruel to them, but she did subscribe to her social circle's classed, gendered, and racist system. She was unable to see connections between slavery and servitude, a disjunction she suppressed because of her determination to maintain her family's social prestige.

As Alice struggled to get her household in order, William returned to his teaching, causing other stresses for Alice, as he conducted part of his duties at 95 Irving Street. William held an office hour at the house at 6:00 p.m. each evening, and William's graduate seminar, Philosophy 3, met at their home. He also occasionally invited his class, usually ten or fifteen students, to Sunday afternoon tea.[33] And after special campus lectures the whole class sometimes trooped to 95 Irving Street to meet the speaker and drink beer.[34] Henry shared with Alice his own opinion about William's ongoing involvement in the education of Harvard students: "I pray indeed for the near day when he shall sink classes & pupils to the bottom of the sea."[35] He realized what a burden it had become for both Jameses.

In general, Alice saw improvement in William's mental state: he was less depressed, his writing easier. Finished with his investigations of religious experience, William turned back to his study of metaphysics, sharing his evolving ideas with his wife, interrupting her as she supervised a Miss Farrell who was mending the upstairs carpet. He had found a sentence from Robert Louis Stevenson that struck him: "'You can make no one understand that his bargain is anything more than a bargain, whereas in point of fact it is a link in the policy of mankind.'" The maxim came from Stevenson's *Lay Morals* and concerned the lack of a moral work ethic in a materialistic society. Alice agreed it was splendid.[36]

Bob remained an ongoing concern for Alice, a sort of diffuse worry humming beneath her other responsibilities. In November he came to town and drank heavily, then returned to Concord.[37]

Alice's workload lessened when Billy left that fall. He had completed all the requirements for his degree, and he decided to spend a year abroad preparing for medical studies. She was not certain this was the best vocation for him, nor was Uncle Henry. Just two months after Billy left for Geneva to study anatomy Henry wondered whether a nineteen year old could be sure of a medical calling, but the Jameses agreed to let Billy test these waters.[38]

Though popular Billy was gone, 95 Irving Street remained a haven for young people. Alice usually thrived on the activity, but William occasionally despaired at the constant interruptions. One morning he took his towels and underclothes to the bathroom to bathe, leaving them inside while he stepped out to get something. When he returned he found the door locked. He was so annoyed at missing his morning bath that he pounded on the door, shouting, "'Who's there?'" thinking that Francis had taken his father's turn in the bathtub. But instead of Francis, William heard one of Peggy's houseguests, Mary Thayer. Suddenly remembering that he was naked, William plunged into absent Peggy's room and locked himself in her closet. When Alice told Harry the story he laughed heartily over his father's desperation and made her promise to tell Billy.[39]

Peggy presented Alice with some challenges. Alice had not had the luxury of participating in formal teenage rites of passage, but she had a gift for divining how best to help Peggy survive these years. The ancient sacrificial rites described in Sir James Frazer's *Golden Bough* were scarcely as intimidating as coming-out rituals of the Edwardian age. Though Peggy did not have the sort of elaborate, expensive debut ball that was featured in Edith Wharton's fiction, Alice might have held a tea for her at home, as did a number of Boston Brahmin families.[40] At these teas, normally held in the late afternoon, mothers officially presented their "buds" (debutantes) to society. Hostesses offered light refreshments and often decorated their parlors with white roses, the unofficial flower for these young women as symbols of their coming of age. The ultimate goal of these rites, of course, was a proper marriage. Usually only women attended these teas, but after their tea ceremony eligible girls could attend formal dances and parties, where they would meet young men.[41]

Peggy, at age fifteen, was still in the early stages of this process, which would continue for years. She had thick, dark hair, bright button eyes, a slight but firm mouth, and a straight nose that broadened at its base, very like Alice's elegant nose. When she took Peggy to her first dancing class, Alice thought Peggy looked beautiful. At first the girl handled social pressure gracefully, announcing to her mother, "'I'm neither pretty nor clever but I feel in my bones that I'm not a pill.'" Alice reported her remark to Billy, adding, "But what a hollow show it is. A most unreal proceeding."[42]

At dancing school, reserved Peggy's favorite partner was a young man who reminded her of Uncle Henry, whom she still considered her special

property. The bond she had formed with him in England remained amaz-
ingly strong: he had become Peggy's touchstone for important decisions.
When in doubt, she tried to do what he would do.[43] Henry asked Alice to
"tell Peggy with my tender love that I feel that I am listening here in the
wind of winter nights, to the far-off strains of the Boston fiddles to which
she is beginning to dance. But I wish I could see as well as hear it."[44] He
would be with his niece as a physical, loving presence if he could, telling
her, "I wish I could have taken you to your Whitney Dance instead of the
German maid. I would have straightened out your pigtail & fluffed your
dress & buttoned on your gloves with eager hands."[45]

Peggy might have done better living with Uncle Henry, as she seemed
too much like him and too much like her aunt Alice to succeed at these
games. She felt uncomfortable with courting customs. Despite her mother's
careful guidance, Peggy did not navigate these social waters easily. At first
she seemed to adapt to parties, dances, and suppers. During these years
Alice made sure that Peggy had adequate physical exercises, giving her
horseback riding lessons with cross-saddle training and skating lessons to
counterpoint her evenings spent socializing with her peers.[46] She also continued her piano lessons, learning Mendelssohn's "Wedding March."[47]

Alice continued to work with Francis, and it took all her patience to
keep him on task. Although he still disliked his Cambridge school, his
participation in school activities helped him endure his days there. During
the fall of 1902 he enthusiastically took up football, though he hated his
dance lessons.[48] When Peggy told him that she didn't want to smell like
her afternoon tea when she went out to a party that night, Francis glumly
observed, "My partners always smelt of fish."[49] He was happiest during
the summers at Chocorua, where he was surrounded by animals, farm
hands, and, for the most part, genial relatives.

Francis (and Alice) had a most unpleasant Christmas holiday the second
winter after her return. Dr. Eliot needed to sew up the boy's herniated
navel ("Francis's button") the day after Christmas. Assisted by a nurse
trained in administering ether, Dr. Eliot performed the surgery at the James
home. Alice dreaded the ordeal both for Francis and for herself.[50] Francis
said he was going to be dissected.[51] The operation went well, although
the boy's language as he emerged from the anesthetic was unrepeatable.
He was cynical, sarcastic, and profane. After his stitches were removed

a week later Dr. Eliot declared the wound had healed perfectly. Now Alice's task was to keep him quiet so as not to open it again. She kept the nurse a few extra days and then took over Francis's care herself.[52] As she prepared to put him to bed she told Billy that she prayed, "Let us hope that in the sight of Providence 'small service is true service'—or there'll be no place for me some day."[53]

A handwritten letter from Francis to Billy tells of the ordeal.

Dear Bill:

How are you getting along with your bones.

I wish it was spring don't you? the reason I wish it was, because I want it nearer summer than it is.

I am mighty glad I have had this opperation because I will be a great deal stronger and I won't be haveing to think about it when I play football etc.

The good thing about staying in bed is that you get read to and get ice cream and grap[e] fruit and other such stuff. We have read three book since I have been in bed.

Peggy is learning to skate at the Rink this winter.

I am sorry I could not send you a better preasant than that Calendar for Chirstmas.

All our wood has come down from Chocorua.

I got eight dollars for Christmas which is going to be spent (for a certain thing) up in Chocorua.

It is not going to be a Rabbit.

Excuse the writing and the paper since I am in bed.

After I am all well I am going to sleep in your little old room.

From your loving Francis
Jan. 8 1903
Cambridge[54]

By mid-January the boy, thin but in good spirits, could go out to the garden. He recovered enough to resume the pranks he played on his family, his sense of humor remarkably like his father's. On 17 January Alice's dinner guests entered the dining room to find a yellow sheet that Francis had pinned on the wall. It said:

<u>Reply Calmly</u>
Even when the other person seems to be in the wrong.[55]

William had written this message to Francis, but Alice remarked that it applied to everyone in the family except Harry.

It took the entire winter for the boy's strength to return. Alice was anxious to get her youngest to Chocorua for the summer.[56]

During her brother's surgery and recovery Peggy's activities continued. The girl's wardrobe became a near obsession with Alice. Perhaps she believed that the appropriate window dressing would help her daughter negotiate formal events more easily or at least would give her needed confidence to succeed at the endless rounds of social events designed to help young people meet potential mates. Alice altered a pink dress for her daughter for one party; she thought Peggy looked like a rose in her gown. She had another of her Parisian gowns, buff with velvet forget-me-nots on the shoulders and a silk petticoat underneath, made over for her daughter.[57] Peggy did not enjoy herself as much as her mother had hoped she would. One evening when she came home she looked white and spent. She had had a headache all week, so Alice took her upstairs to bed and gave her supper in her room. Although Dr. Driver gave her something for headaches, there seemed no easy remedy for them.[58] Weeks later, Peggy was again sick, this time with grippe.[59]

On 29 March 1903 Alice documented what she believed was Peggy's first nervous breakdown. Though she was careful to keep the news from others, she shared her fears with Billy. "I do not tell Papa (least of all Peggy) what I see. We talk about 'grippe' but the poor child has had her first nervous breakdown, and I have a . . . feeling that it won't be the last." Although this was a blow, Alice was determined to prevent her sixteen year old from becoming another sister Alice. She wanted to keep Peggy from an obsession with her own illness, so she made her dress and attend a tea given at Harvard.[60] The next morning, though, Peggy was back in bed. She was languid and weak for days after this episode, only attending school sporadically that spring.[61] Alice saw no salvation in the ongoing social rounds for the girl, who was at best amused by them and at worst depressed.

Careful not to force Peggy into early romantic relationships, Alice hoped that she would acquire the formal education that Alice never had. The German Club women encouraged her to send her daughter to college, so she weighed the idea that Peggy deserved an education as much as her brothers, but she put off the decision for the time.[62] In *Talks to Teachers*, in the chapter "Psychology and the Teaching Art," William had already declared his enthusiasm for coeducation.[63] Realizing that her daughter was happiest with books, like her uncle Henry, Alice resolved to let her try college.[64] She thought it might help her find a meaningful profession, possibly in landscape design, as the girl loved flowers.[65]

During this nearly frantic winter Alice squeezed in time for her own interests. Though never as manic as William, she possessed great stamina. She went to musical performances, she heard lectures, she viewed pictures, and she entertained her various women's groups. Just after Francis's operation she heard her brother-in-law Leigh Gregor speak to Boston's Alliance française on three Canadian authors.[66] The next week she and her mother heard a reading of Tennyson's poem "Enoch Arden," accompanied by Richard Strauss's music.[67] She attended symphony concerts in Boston, and in March she and Harry took the train to Concord to hear a lecture on Lord Falkland, the seventeenth-century British writer and King Charles loyalist who was killed by Cromwell's forces.[68] Another afternoon Alice and Eliza viewed a Turner and Corot exhibit at Copley Square.[69]

Alice also continued her work for her husband from behind the scenes, constantly active in her own network. While these associations kept her in touch with Cambridge politics, she also had the chance to learn, as these groups often included an educational component. She held a meeting of her Mothers Club and invited a speaker, John Brooks, to speak on England's Great Coal Strike.[70] Brooks supported the strikers, the laboring men.[71]

After publication of *The Varieties of Religious Experience* William's reputation grew even larger. He was overwhelmed by letters from admirers and from those seeking answers for their spiritual malaise or psychological distresses. Alice complained to Billy of William's "raft of letters, answers to all the daft people who write to him."[72] But she reveled in his fame, despite its inconveniences. When in January 1903 William was invited to give an address at the centenary celebration of Emerson's birth, Alice thought he would have been sorry if he had refused, even though he declared he was no expert on Emerson.[73] It is not clear today who would have regretted his absence at the occasion, because William had decisively refused the opportunity when first asked.[74] At some point, though, he gave in and agreed to speak.

Alice still wielded influence with her husband. Sometimes she overwhelmed him: he realized that she would never give up until she reached her desired ends. This agitated and excited him. He carefully detailed her method, informing her, "Haven't I been noticing how often of late you have smilingly and easily averted the arousal of the slumbering demon of contradiction in me, by seeming to agree with the opposite of what you favored, and thus knocking out all my interest in following it—inimitable & tactful wife!"[75]

Though she remained a devoted wife and mother, in her fifties Alice developed some unappealing qualities. When that winter the Jameses attended a reception at the home of Hugo Munsterberg, a man whom Alice now disliked because he threatened William's position at Harvard, she could scarcely hide her feelings. William told Billy, "Don't get engaged to an oriental jewess—with fleas—your mother's prejudices are too strong. We went to a big reception at the Munsterberg's last night, and you could see the faint dry film of ice all over her being through the evening. It would not melt."[76]

Alice had other personal prejudices, other people she could not tolerate. In the case of the Charles Sanders Peirces, their poverty annoyed her. When William decided to help his marginally employed friend Peirce by finagling Harvard into paying him $600 for six philosophy lectures, Alice had to house and entertain the couple, doing it reluctantly. Peirce was a brilliant but difficult man, and his wife was odd, Alice thought. Fortunately for Alice, William departed on a trip not long after their arrival, so the Peirces left Cambridge, sparing her a longer visit.[77] In later years she called him "the wretched Charles Peirce."[78]

Alice also disliked Polish philosopher Wincenty Lutoslawski, a longtime admirer of William.[79] When William arranged for him to give a series of

Lowell Lectures one fall, he invited Lutoslawski to stay at Irving Street but then confided in Peggy that he felt caught between Lutoslawski and Alice. His first lecture went extremely well, "but he and your Mar are the most fearful combine, and between them I am in a bad plight," he complained to Peggy. He went on to add that he did not like the man either: "He disgusts me with all cranks and unconventionals."[80]

Her husband's teasing manner let Alice accept his criticism of her prejudices. She accepted Cambridge's social class structure, in practice if not in principle, wherein professors, writers, and other intellectuals were superior to the working classes. Money did not determine rank; rather, intellect and professional success could advance families socially. Whereas Weymouth had been a sort of rough New World aristocracy, with genealogy the main index of social position, her present world was a meritocracy. William Dean Howells claimed that there had never been a community wherein money was less important than it was in Cambridge.[81] It had long prided itself on its literary culture. Given her father's failure, Alice would never have achieved in Weymouth the rank she now enjoyed through her connection to the Jameses. Because of her husband's prominence at Harvard, now more and more successful at defining itself as an elite institution, Alice had a well-defined position. Her relationship to Henry also enhanced her status, though she never exploited their friendship. Although William would not let her rest easy with these attitudes, her eldest son later defended her, admitting that she had damned Catholics, the Irish, and Jews but claiming there was a discrepancy between her general views and her particular judgment: "When confronted with an individual of flesh & blood, [she] melted into sweet reasonableness, charity and affection."[82]

In general, at least at this time in their lives, William tended to be more tolerant than Alice. He championed women and minority groups, helping women students and mentoring the Polish Lutoslawski, and he taught W. E. B. Du Bois, but he believed in the value of the intellectual class and its interests.[83] This idealization, however, sometimes insulated his family and others of his class from unwanted immigrants, suffragists, African Americans, and the lower classes in general. In a talk at Radcliffe in 1907 entitled "The Social Value of the College Bred," the speech that allowed Alice to recognize her vocation, William claimed that some individuals had greater worth than others and that the test of a good education was to learn to recognize this human value. He believed that strong and talented people had so much to give to the human race that we must allow them a leadership role. These leaders in turn were obligated to use their talents to aid the advancement of the human race. Humanity can only progress if these geniuses show the way.[84] Alice continued to believe that her husband was such a genius.

Alice grew more conservative as she aged in other ways. While William remained an anti-imperialist and a Democrat in principle, neither of the Jameses was an active social radical or reformer. In 1903 Alice supported President Eliot's position on the growing labor union movement. A workingman protested what he perceived as Eliot's antilabor stance, wishing Harvard's leader "'hard work and long hours.'" Alice shared Eliot's answer with Billy: "The President said he had rejoiced in both all his life."[85] Her support of him was inconsistent with her earlier support of the Haymarket Square strikers.

During the spring of 1903 Alice spent a long, rainy morning at her mother's house sewing. Peggy lay on the sofa while Grandma read aloud to the little group. The tale that Eliza Gibbens read was Henry's "The Beast in the Jungle," in his just-published collection, *The Better Sort*. Alice loved the story. She told Billy what she thought of Henry's art, deprecating her own intellect: "I am beginning to love his 'later manner' and see, or rather feel, what I have long suspected, that the lack, the want is in me, not in these works of Art."[86]

In this carefully set and crafted tale protagonist John Marcher believes that he has a remarkable destiny, but he does not know what it might be. He is a completely self-absorbed man, waiting passively for fate to overtake him. During a country weekend he becomes reacquainted with May Bartram at the great English country house Weatherend. She remembers him and their first meeting in Naples much more clearly than he does. And she remembers, though he does not, that he told her of his strange predicament during a boat crossing to Sorrento. He is astounded to realize there is a living being who knows his secret. As their friendship progresses he takes comfort from her as he awaits his unknown fate, but he does not reciprocate or even recognize the love she feels for him. Described as a sphinx and a lily, she dies before Marcher understands her feelings for him. It is only at her graveside that he realizes they might have loved one another. It is loving and being loved that he has missed: his life has been a jungle, with a great beast lurking in it, but he avoids any final leap of enlightenment or self-knowledge by flinging himself on May Bartram's tomb. "Beast's" central theme of a life turning in upon itself did not reflect Alice's fate, but she had abandoned her own pursuits to help others, and, like many of Henry's characters, she sometimes reflected on missed opportunities.

That spring Henry announced great news: it was his turn to visit them. He planned to spend six months in America. Once Alice learned that he was considering the trip she started planning how she would welcome him to her large, noisy household. She vowed to make the visit a pleasant one. "Papa says he wouldn't stand this house a week," she wrote to Billy. "It's a hard saying and may be true, but I'll not believe it till it's proven. We will install him up-stairs with bed-room, sitting-room and bath-room to himself. He shall have his breakfast upstairs by himself, and how can he help liking to be among us a little when we all love him."[87] Alice tried to enlist Billy in her plan to make Henry welcome, suggesting he encourage Henry's trip when he visited Lamb House.

Her imagination teemed with ideas, one of them that William and Henry would go around the world together after Henry completed his American tour. William particularly wanted to see "Burmah."[88] Anticipating her husband's retirement the next spring, Alice also schemed for the brothers to see the American South or West after Harvard's spring term ended. Henry professed to like all her plans, though what he wanted most was to see Chocorua.[89] As eager as she was for his visit, though, Alice worried he would never care for her.[90] Though they were close friends by now, she had not overcome her feelings of inferiority next to her famous brother-in-law.

As she planned for Henry's coming Alice kept her focus on her children. Around this time she began referring to Francis as Alexander Robertson in her letters, though she frequently slipped after that and called him Francis. The previous fall William had announced the official name change.[91] This name stuck. Later, Alexander dropped the Robertson and was known as Aleck.

Spring found Aleck happier, fortunately for Alice, because as he recovered from his operation Peggy continued to show nervous symptoms. Despite all his absences from Browne and Nichols, the same prep school his brothers had attended, Aleck received an A+ in Latin. Better, he had been invited to join a bird club, in which an older boy taught him how to record the birds he saw. The school allowed him to drop his hated science class and study birds with Mr. Ralph Hoffman instead. He was so happy that he stopped teasing his sister.[92] By the end of March she was thrilled to tell Billy, "Francis lives in a highest heaven of his own where only birds do congregate."[93] Now he vowed to never kill another bird.[94] He identified forty-two different kinds of birds, including the rare woodcock.[95] In May Alice allowed the boy to bring two of the three other Cambridge bird club members to Chocorua.[96] There Aleck had fifteen hens and a cock that crowed cheerfully each morning.[97] The youngest James had inherited his father's sense of humor and his mother's love for chickens. Henry rejoiced to Alice at his nephew's ornithological turn: "[It] seems quite to give feathers and wings and elated song to one's hopes for him."[98]

As she prepared for Chocorua William rewarded her faith and her endless patience at the Emerson celebration, which took place on 31 May 1903. He gave the speech to warm public accolades. Though she did not feel as satisfied as she had at the Shaw oration or during the Edinburgh victory, Alice reveled in her afternoon at the Concord church: "It was a most beautiful thing from beginning to end, and Daddy's brief address the best of them all,—'A living thing' as Mrs. Higginson said," she told Billy. There was a dinner afterward and more speeches, and the Jameses returned to Cambridge at midnight. Emerson's complete works were at Chocorua, so that summer her entire family could read him.[99]

Another gratifying moment came when William was awarded an honorary doctorate. The Harvard Corporation had wished to confer the doctor of laws degree upon him in 1902 but mistakenly believed he would not return in time for commencement. President Eliot assured Alice then that the attempt would be made again the next year.[100] Wearing the only red gown, his Edinburgh robe, on the commencement platform, William received the honor in June 1903.[101] Alice declared his speech the best, and she thought he received the greatest applause when Eliot called William's name, adding "Psychologist and Master of Style." William confided afterward he feared Eliot would have gone on to call him "'Talker to teachers,

Experiencer of religion, willer to believe.' . . . Papa spoke up right loyally for the strangers and the lonely men who really mean so much to their college," she proudly told Billy.[102] Her brother-in-law Henry agreed with her assessment of William's speeches. "Each is perfect—& I can scarce say which I prefer."[103]

When the family moved to Chocorua for the summer, Alice had a much easier time with Peggy and Aleck. Aleck had his birds, and Peggy improved when she was removed from the artificialities of Cambridge's social world. At Chocorua she was surrounded by loving relatives and had no need to try to impress her peers.

Alice and William left the farm briefly to visit Sarah Whitman. William remained intrigued by her, and Alice seemed to have accepted her husband's warmth toward other women as part of his expansive, open nature, though her own destruction of many of her letters to William leaves the possibility open that his behavior sometimes wounded her. When they returned to New Hampshire, William reported that Alice had a headache from the strain of the visit.[104] Overall, though, the summer proved a good one. The Jameses bought more land, the old place that belonged to William Ralph Emerson, for $780. It was a beautiful site and made their rural empire secure. Alice charged Billy never to sell the Chocorua properties.[105]

Henry arrived in America on the *Kaiser William II* on 30 August 1904, Harry meeting him at the dock in Hoboken, New Jersey. He took his uncle's extra luggage on to Boston while Henry went directly to Deal Beach in New Jersey to the home of George Harvey, the president of the Harper & Brothers New York publishing firm. He spent a few days there, Mark Twain entertaining them all on the piazza, before coming to Boston and then on to Chocorua.[106] Harry traveled with his uncle to New Hampshire, where Alice eagerly awaited his arrival. William detailed her preparations for this all-important visit, telling cousin Ellen Emmet Hunter, "Alice, thinking nothing good enough for Henry, has been for a week repainting, scrubbing, sweeping, dusting, shaking, beating and polishing the house, turning everything upside down, & inside out till she is almost sick with fatigue and all the rest of us with discomfort."[107]

Henry found Chocorua much more beautiful than he had imagined. While he railed at the lack of any advanced cultural systems (no parsons, no squires), he thought the landscape was lovely. "The great boulders in the woods, the pulpit-stones, the couchant and rampant beasts, the isolated cliffs and lichened cathedrals, had all, seen, as one passed, through their drizzle of forest light, a special New Hampshire beauty." He found nature in a quantity that he had not encountered in years. He decided it was the summer people from urban areas who might be the making of this beautiful but currently impoverished land, much as moneyed Europeans were with Switzerland and Scotland. In 1907, when he published the record of his travels, *The American Scene*, he gave accolades to this rural world that Alice and William loved.[108]

Though his New Hampshire stay was brief, Henry used Alice as a touchstone throughout his tour of the United States, which extended to a year. She took care of his mail and his baggage, scheduled his occasional visits to his dentist in Boston—anything to make his trip easier. His letters to her provide a running commentary on his firsthand impressions of his homeland, a country he had not seen for twenty-two years. Many places he saw for the first time as he traveled by train to Florida (with stops in New York, Philadelphia, Washington, the Biltmore House near Asheville, North Carolina, and Charleston, South Carolina) and then to Chicago and on to the West. How could she have resisted his appeals for help when he began his letters with phrases like "I hurl myself on you for an angelic service in addition to those you have deluged me with"?[109]

Through Henry's eyes Alice saw distant reaches of her country she had never visited. He reported on Florida: Palm Beach had a southern intensity and charm but overall "the huge human mob [was] awful, as yet, for bareness (with a fearful flaccid fatness) of type."[110] In Chicago he described "the visual ugliness of it all, & the fatigue of the good kind but too boresome people."[111] The American Southwest had "unspeakable alkali deserts"; San Diego was "a really beautiful & comfortable garden by the sea"; while in San Francisco he was "so handsomely treated & flowered—huge nosegays & boxes of such carnations!"[112] As William had suspected, Henry found the American landscape beautiful but most of its inhabitants less than desirable, though he regaled the Irving Street Jameses with the tale of his San Francisco friend Bruce Porter's experience with ghosts in Berkeley. Porter would later play an important role in Alice's life.[113]

She was sorry to see her brother-in-law return to England. Before he left she was touched to learn that he planned to leave Lamb House to her Harry.[114] With his characteristic thoughtfulness Henry wrote to Alice from the *Ivernia* on his way home to Rye: "And I failed at the last to do what I most intensely meant—viz: to leave a particular affectionate farewell to your mother."[115]

Peggy finished her secondary schooling and was accepted at Bryn Mawr for the fall of 1905, fulfilling Alice's and the German Club's desire for education for women. But Alice decided to postpone Peggy's matriculation for a year and have her finish the coming-out process instead. No clues remain concerning this decision, though perhaps in line with her sense of their social position and her husband's international reputation Alice felt that Peggy should undergo this ritual. It continued for months. She attended as many as three social events a day and was pressured to think of nothing but being popular. The round of dances, teas, parties, and suppers proved an exhausting experience for Alice, who had only come out in Weymouth to leave it for Europe. Like her aunt Alice before her, Peggy adjusted poorly to what her father called "the puberty-ordeals of savage tribes."[116] That winter she collapsed, repeating the previous year's nervous prostration. She never wholly accommodated herself to the ritualized and sometimes cruel process.

In August 1905, following a head cold, Alice had one of the worst headaches she ever endured. She had been feeling so well that this change in her health surprised her. Dr. Cogswell gave her an eighth gram of morphine and a trace of atropine to ease her pain, and she planned to visit Franz Pfaff, a "chemico-physiological" Boston doctor, for a thorough examination.[117] In the meantime she experienced relief from the morphine, which causes a relaxed, drowsy state.[118] Candidly, William confessed that he felt worse after nursing her, evidence that the relationship revolved around his need for her.[119] Alice kept him focused, and when she was unable to help him, he suffered. While she relished his affection, his energy, and his work, she could not expect him to take care of her.

The headache allowed her another rare chance to focus on herself, and the morphine gave her an excuse to rest. It can cause nausea, muscle weakness, and respiratory depression, however, and Alice experienced some of these side effects.[120] After hearing of her illness Henry admonished her: "I can't help telling you that you have, even if the odious visitation <u>has</u> been outlived, my tenderest sympathy in the whole business—for the moral of it is that <u>you need an Easier Life</u>, that you need it quite direfully, and that you will perish utterly and leave us blankly bereft if we do not succeed, among us all, in seeing that you absolutely get it."[121]

The year after Henry's return to England Alice at last had an opportunity to see more of the vast land he described when William was offered a temporary position at Stanford to lecture and help build the philosophy department. Harvard agreed to let him go for the spring semester of 1906, and Alice joined him in February after he had a chance to settle in to his work. William negotiated a high salary, $5,000 for the semester, allowing him funds for Alice's fare. This would be her first time in California in nearly half a century. At that time, matters at Irving Street were under control. Harry had finished law school and had a job with a Boston firm, and Billy was abroad studying art, having given up the idea of a medical career. While her mother continued to worry about Peggy, William believed his daughter had returned to the serious young woman she had been, freeing Alice to join him at Stanford. Aleck was stable enough to do without his mother temporarily.

13 The Lull before the Storm

FOR MONTHS HENRY HAD LOBBIED for Alice to take a vacation, so he wholeheartedly approved of her decision to go to Stanford, praising sunny, flowery California. "It will be so much money in my pocket, or balm to my heart, to know that the leaden load of Quincy St. is for a time lifted off you."[1] Alice and William considered bringing Peggy, though William had reservations. If she came, he suggested that Alice come first, Peggy following later with her cousin Mary Webb after Peggy's coming out was officially concluded so that he and Alice could be alone.[2] His physical need for her was as strong as ever. He hoped for another "honeymoon picnic time."[3]

William went first. On New Year's Day, 1906, he left for his lucrative semester-long residency. As usual, leaving Alice made him feel closer to her. From the Grand Canyon's South Rim, where he visited a Hopi lodge, he reflected on their marriage. "Never have you seemed as near and dear to me as in the past six months," he told his wife. "It is a good thing, little as you think of 'friendship', to have friendship grow deeper and deeper—after 27 years of matrimony! Isn't it?"[4] The previous summer he had written in his diary when she joined him briefly at Glenmore, Thomas Davidson's summer institute, "Alice ultra sweet," perhaps a comment on their physical relationship.[5] The marriage was more than either imagined it could be when they first met: it was a genuine love story.

After he left, Peggy's activities again escalated. Henry sympathized with her mother from a safe distance. "[Peggy's] imperfect joy in 'going out' . . . [is] confirmatory of everything one has felt about her essential inner 'superiority.' None of the little blatant usual, merely gregarious things will ever suffice her—& she won't be really interested but in the really interesting."[6]

Alice's worries about Bob continued. He was in Concord that winter, writing to her on stationery that included an elaborate letterhead: "LEAGUE OF THE . . . SCHOOL REPUBLIC / TO EXTEND INSTRUCTION IN MORAL AND CIVIC TRAINING IN THE SCHOOLS. / ROBERTSON JAMES, PRESIDENT / CONCORD, MASS." The self-proclaimed head of the League of the School Republic shared his recent psychic experiences with his sister-in-law. He had received a phone call from a spirit called Mud who left a one-inch circular piece of canvas sewn with silky hair like his dog's next to Bob's chair, an object mysteriously stolen from his pocket two days later. When he went to a medium, Frank Foss, for a sitting, an old man named Joe with his musical band appeared and put his arm around Bob's neck. Finally, Foss materialized a new spirit, an Indian doctor who whispered in Bob's ear, kissed his cheek, and made him strip from the waist up in order to give him an upper-body massage. He looked forward to getting a rare coin from these three spirits on his next visit to Foss.

While Bob objected to Mr. Mud's lack of refinement, he was happy with his visitors. He assured Alice, "For 3 months past I've been a totally different being mentally from what I have ever been. Full of health, cheer, joy with an ever broadening conviction or rather assurance that everything good on Earth is coming to me."[7] Bob was convinced of Foss's veracity, though William suspected fraud. Fortunately, the next winter Bob improved, turning from the séances to follow the Christian Science religion. He fasted often and took no breakfast most days.[8] His improvement meant one less worry for the Jameses.

Alice fell ill in January, ill enough that she could not write to William frequently, but she did not take morphine this time, perhaps because of the side effects.[9] She longed for her husband, but he said he felt "so impotent or idiotic" when she had her attacks that he did not regret being gone. Bereft of Alice's presence and her encouraging letters, William suffered, sleeping poorly during his first weeks away. His heart disease was well advanced by now. He was trying every possible remedy to alleviate its symptoms (more lymph injections, mind-cures, electrical treatments), but nothing halted his physical deterioration. Besides his ongoing battles with hypertension and his heart, after the first few weeks in California William developed gout, brought on by tension, he thought. First one foot would ache and then the other.[10]

Henry, on the other hand, believed his brother had gout because he had not Fletcherized enough. Fletcherizing was a dietary innovation popularized by Horace Fletcher, who advocated chewing one's food many times before swallowing it. William had sent the man's book to his brother on New Year's Day, 1904, and Henry quickly became a convert. He now reminded William of the method's virtues.[11]

When Alice arrived in San Francisco on Valentine's Day, William could not meet her at the station.[12] Whether it was from inadequate Fletcherizing, gout, or another cause, he hobbled about. As he had to hop to their dwelling on his crutches, William was unable to help her, and there was no household help. They inhabited quarters on a university residential street, 15 Salvation Row, with a sitting room, a den, two bedrooms, a little kitchen, a bathroom, good light, and a fireplace at the cost of $250 for six months. For $16 a month they had hot lunches and dinners at the boardinghouse across the street.[13] The Jameses had the second floor, and another philosopher, Miss Lillien Martin, had the first floor.[14]

They were only an hour and a quarter train ride from San Francisco, but the drawback to the location, according to William, was the university's distance from civilization: young professors, the majority of the faculty, were not paid well enough to travel back east or to Europe during their summer holidays.[15] On the other hand, Stanford paid its few star professors very well. Two hundred and seventy-five students enrolled in William's course, validating President David Starr Jordan's decision to hire him.

Alice soon discovered that Stanford was worlds apart from Harvard. In comparison to Harvard, founded in 1636, Stanford was a newcomer in the world of higher education. Endowed in 1885 as Leland Stanford Junior University, in honor of California governor and railroad magnate Leland Stanford's deceased son, the school's first classes met in 1891. Mrs. Stanford decreed there would be no commercial district near the university, so the town of Palo Alto was a mile from campus. In 1906 it had fifteen thousand citizens. Tuition was free for the institution's fifteen hundred students of both sexes. Alice decided that she approved of this co-ed education. "The girls and boys are just as nice together as they can be—equally free to come and go at all hours—and never abusing this liberty," she explained to Bessie Evans.[16]

Although Alice did not feel well during her first days, she soon recovered, and a week after her arrival she entertained visitors.[17] Her days were repetitions of her Bad Nauheim days, though this time William was occupied with classes, lectures, and meetings rather than health cures, leaving Alice on her own during the day. She attended a lecture series on the Acts of the Apostles given by a Dr. Hodges, and she also wanted to attend a course on English translations of Greek playwrights. On 25 February she attended one of her husband's talks, what she called his "peace speech," "The Moral Equivalent of War," judged by many of his era as his best. William declared himself opposed to war but not to the virtues it engendered: intrepidity, hardiness, unselfishness, and obedience to higher principles. He envisioned an early equivalent of a Civilian Conservation Corps, proposing that America's "gilded youths," the young men only, be drafted to physically build the nation: "to coal and iron mines, to freight trains, to fishing fleets in December, to dish-washing, clothes-washing, and window-washing, to road-building and tunnel-making, to foundries and stoke-holes, and to the frames of skyscrapers."[18]

Besides attending lectures, Alice had time to read and write.[19] Though she still suffered an occasional headache, she declared to Harry, "An island of the Pacific couldn't be more peaceful. No decisions, no obligations, no spiritualists . . . nothing in short to disturb us or make us afraid."[20] She had some daily chores, as faculty wives did most of their own cleaning and cooking, but she had nowhere near the responsibilities she faced in Cambridge. A male Japanese student cooked and served dinner at their boardinghouse, part of a work-study plan wherein students worked to cover their boarding expenses. At meals he bowed formally when he served, and Alice wanted to bow back.[21] Claiming he wanted to write "an analytic biologico-psychological account" of his wife, William told Peggy that while Alice directed him under the guise of obeying him, she was happy and growing fat with this easier life. "'Her face is smooth as a young girl's, and her voice, which lays down the law, communicating valuable information and advice to all, in a steady stream, is like clarified butter of a firm consistency.'"[22] Soon after his helpmate's arrival William's health improved.

Alice and William took time for sightseeing during their stay in California. During Stanford's spring break they visited Santa Barbara and then traveled to Los Angeles on 28 March, where they spent five days with Alice's childhood friend from Mountain View, Katharine Putnam Hooker.[23] Alice had not seen Kate since her honeymoon. Now she lived in a luxurious home with a two-acre walled Italian-style garden. She took them touring in her motorcar through southern California. The Jameses also traveled to San Francisco when William attended the Association of American Colleges meeting. Alice thought San Francisco had a low "moral tone," and its buildings were "<u>vile</u>," but she found the Chinese shopkeepers quiet, even dignified. While she saw this new world with a more open mind, some of the West's easier ways provoked her, particularly contract marriage. Since marriages between Anglos and Chinese were illegal in 1906, sometimes lawyers drew up marriage contracts, but Alice could not accept the practice.[24]

During one of their trips the Jameses visited Mountain View, which was not far from Stanford. Alice was able to locate the site of Daniel Gibbens's former ranch.[25] Her life had come full circle; she experienced a measure of the happiness she had enjoyed here as a child.

The only thing marring Alice's idyll was news from Bessie Evans regarding her old Florence friend, Jessie Donaldson Hodder, who had given birth to her baby in Alice's Florence apartment. In 1895 Jessie's husband, Alfred, took a teaching position at Bryn Mawr. She and the baby followed him, and in 1897 she had a second child. In 1898 Hodder left the college, sending Jessie and the two children to Switzerland. She thought he would follow, but he never came: he had fallen in love with Mary Gwinn, an English professor at Bryn Mawr. In 1904 he married Gwinn, claiming he had never been married to Donaldson.[26] Alice had counseled Jessie to go to Boston, where she introduced her to Bessie Evans. Bessie, then connected with the Massachusetts reformatory system, found a job for Jessie in the system.

In 1906, with Bessie's help, Jessie decided to sue Hodder, claiming she was married to him and that he committed bigamy when he married

Mary Gwinn. Alice was named as a witness in the trial. After learning this news Alice wrote a note to Jessie from California, wishing her justice and happiness.[27] Alfred Hodder died in New York City, though, before the proceedings began, so Alice was spared testifying at what might have become an embarrassing trial.[28]

Alice's California holiday rudely terminated at 5:20 a.m. on 18 April, several weeks before the semester officially ended, when the great San Francisco earthquake shook the Stanford campus. She had been in bed half-awake when the house began to move "as a terrier might shake a rat."[29] Declaring he was neither frightened nor nauseated, William ran in from his bedroom. Their downstairs neighbor rushed up to tell them to leave the house immediately. As they dressed an aftershock struck. Their chimneys collapsed, bricks filled their sitting room, and large cracks streaked their walls. Lillien Martin's heavy furniture literally danced across her rooms.

The trio ran to Stanford's quad, where they saw that the church spire had fallen and two of the dormitories had been damaged. Many of the university's other buildings were partially or totally destroyed. When Alice heard them fall after the first shock, she thought she heard thunder. Two floors of Roble Hall, the girls' dormitory, caved in, and in the men's dormitory, Encina Hall, some students were hurt. While William went back to clear out their house, Alice and Lillien Martin remained in the quad to watch rescuers pull the young men out of Encina. One student was dead when he was pulled from the rubble. Alice made coffee and buttered toast, serving it on the porch to William, Lillien, and Lillien's assistant, Mrs. Gabel.

William claimed that neither he nor Alice was afraid. He later personified the earthquake: "The perception of it as a living agent was irresistible. It had an overpowering dramatic convincingness."[30] The couple's subsequent reactions to the cataclysmic natural event typified their differences. After her initial shock was over, Alice bustled about to help others. After his initial delight at this seismic experience subsided, William rushed to San Francisco to be closer to the center of the action. Alice telegraphed her family with the message that local authorities had asked all residents to send: "'All well after earthquake.'" She also sent a letter that day to her family, assuring them that she and William were safe.

William decided to take Lillien Martin into the city, as she was frantic about her sister, who lived there. Also, he wanted a closer view of the quake's aftereffects. At Palo Alto they boarded the last train into the city, where they encountered a literal inferno. Fires had broken out everywhere. Since many of San Francisco's water mains had been damaged, firefighters could not contain the blazes. After a day in the city the pair caught the last train away that night.[31] Alice paced the floor awaiting William, and he noted that she seemed angry when he returned.[32] Henry commented how characteristic it was of his older brother to rush heroically into the inferno, but he worried about his sister-in-law having been left alone.[33] William, though, had been fascinated by everything he saw in the crumbling city, especially people who nailed roller-skates to the corners of their kitchen table and loaded their household goods on it as they left their homes behind.[34]

The Jameses slept outside that night; everyone had been warned not to go back into their houses. The day after the earthquake Alice busied herself feeding hungry people. That morning she and William walked to Palo Alto and stood in line for bread, one of the only items available. Fortunately, she had bought extra food just before the quake. Though chimneys were down, she prepared light meals on her oil stove.

The quake engendered tremendous damage and social upheaval. There were multiple aftershocks, and throughout the Bay Area general chaos reigned. At San Jose the insane asylum collapsed, killing hundreds while hundreds of other patients wandered off. In San Francisco soldiers caught a man carrying a woman's hand, its fingers covered with rings. They ordered the man to dig his own grave and then shot him on the spot, one story claimed.[35] Alice and William tried to find rainbows in the midst of all the destruction. She remarked on their driver and his wife, who housed five homeless people: "It's the golden side of democracy."[36]

The golden side for Alice and William was the closure of Stanford University—there were scarcely any buildings left standing, so the university declared the term over. William had no regrets at leaving his post, and Alice was glad to return to her family. Later assessments of the Great Earthquake revealed the scope of its damage. The death toll was more than three thousand, and the cost came to $500 million in 1906 dollars. The shock was felt from Coos Bay, Oregon, to Los Angeles and east to the middle of Nevada, approximately 375,000 square miles in all.

At Palo Alto Alice packed four trunks marked "Boston." The Jameses left Stanford on 26 April, friends driving them to Oakland. That night she wrote in her diary, "'A beautiful morning on this old country road we took with father fifty years ago.'"[37] The next morning they took the Oakland Ferry to San Francisco, where they boarded a Pullman car on the Southern Pacific for home via Denver.[38]

On her last afternoon another aftershock shook the house. Alice ran halfway downstairs immediately, so accustomed had she grown to the earthquake drill. Her last thought at leaving Stanford was her long-lost Hermann, whom Billy had mentioned in a letter to his mother. "How I crave the sound of his voice," she confessed to Billy.[39] Neither time nor distance nor even the earth cracking open could erase her loss.

William and Alice returned in time for the Harvard graduation ceremonies. Alice resumed her juggling act, keeping most of her balls in the air most of the time. Two of her children had left her nest, but three remained, one of them an adopted nephew. Weeks after her return, Alice fell ill again, this time with kidney problems.[40] By June she had recovered from the ailment, though she remained in Cambridge while William went to Chocorua. Perhaps the illness affected her ability to juggle, because that summer she dropped a ball in the form of her sister Mary's adopted boy, Jack Salter.

Mary Sherwin Gibbens Salter had borne one child, Eliza Webb Salter, on 20 January 1888. On 2 December 1889, less than two years later, the little girl died from diphtheria. Mary grieved deeply, and the Salters had no more children. Mary's husband, Mack, was a man of deep principles who believed in seeing them translated into ethical actions. Along with Felix Adler, he founded and then led the Ethical Culture Society, and he helped start what eventually became the American Civil Liberties Union. From 1894 until 1915 Mack also played a leading role in the Indian Rights Association. The latter group was comprised of liberals who hoped to assimilate Native Americans into white Protestant culture. One way they accomplished this goal was by encouraging members to adopt Native American children, weaning them from what they viewed as a heathen, godless culture. The principle was the same one that Alice held when she sometimes disparaged Jews and Catholics: humankind was divided into groups strung along a racial chain that privileged white Anglo-Saxon Protestants of Western European origin. Even if Alice approved of the Indian Rights Association in theory, she was not pleased when the Salters decided to adopt a Native American child and raise him to follow their own religious and ideological truths.

For Mary Gibbens Salter there was another motive: she wanted a child and would do anything to get one. During the spring of 1900 she and her husband contemplated such an adoption. When the Jameses heard of this plan, both were alarmed. William expressed their objections to his mother-in-law, as Alice felt too timid to write. Both hoped the letter might arrive in time to change the Salters' mind. The Salters were both near fifty. Moreover, a child would drain both time and finances from the social causes that the Salters energetically espoused. Insisting that he was "absolutely objective," William thought such an adoption would be "worse than annexing the Philippine Islands."[41] Whether or not he equated the assimilationist policies of the Indian Rights Association with imperialism is not clear from the record. If the adoption were already fact, however, he begged Eliza Gibbens, who had her own qualms about this project, to say nothing of their fears.

But any objections came too late. In June 1900 the Salters provisionally adopted a two-year-old boy, a ward of the state.[42] The boy was Frank Gray, described by his descendants as a Micmac–St. Francis Abenaki–St. Regis Mohawk. The boy's mother, Mary "Mamie" Gray, was the granddaughter of Lewis Annance, a famous nineteenth-century Maine guide who had been educated at Dartmouth and was a close friend of historian Francis Parkman.[43] Several Annance women worked for the Salter and James families at Silver Lake and Chocorua, so the Salters knew Frank Gray's family and the child. Mary Gray began working as a domestic at age ten. Because she and her husband were very poor, they were persuaded to let the Salters adopt their son. The adoption was finalized on 19 August 1901, and Frank Gray's name changed to John "Jack" Randall Salter.[44] Mary was thrilled: she had a child again.

At first the Jameses welcomed Jack with open arms. The Salters lived in Chicago during the year but spent their summers at their home, Hill Top. Alice vowed to help her sister, telling Eliza Gibbens that if Mary and Mack went to Europe the next summer, 1901, she would care for the baby at Hill Top.[45] In March 1901 Mary sent Alice a picture of her handsome boy.[46] A year after the Salters brought him home William announced, "Jack is simply <u>great</u>. He calls himself my uncle."[47] He began calling the boy Uncle Jack.

By 1906, however, it was clear the adoption had not gone well: Jack had emotional and behavioral problems. That summer Alice cared for him while the Salters spent a year in Europe. The boy stayed at 95 Irving Street, spending some time at 107 Irving Street with Eliza Gibbens. Although Alice made sure Jack wrote to his parents and tried to do what she felt was right, the boy wearied her. She could not apply her general moral principles to this particular case.

Alice shared her worries with Billy: "It's a warm June Sunday after days of rain. The house is quiet as the day, and while Jack is over at mother's I make haste to write to you. He has led us a weary dance but Miss Clarke is now treating him and he certainly seems a better boy. She says it is a case of obsession and I believe she is right. I lock him into his bedroom at night to keep him from roaming about the house at 5 in the morning and gorging himself in the pantry on cake and sauce. And yet he always has this innocent look of surprise up to the very moment of conviction."[48]

When Alice accused the child of deceiving her and his parents, Jack admitted to the fault. Later he told Aleck he liked being deceptive, though what the word meant to an eight-year-old boy is difficult to say. Alice sent him to the mind-cure specialist, Miss Clarke, which helped a bit, but she concluded that her sister and brother-in-law had made a terrible mistake. She believed Jack would have done better in a working-class family, revealing again the class prejudice that was now her worst feature.[49] Writing to Billy, Henry minced no words about what he thought of the Salters leaving her with the child: "Their having on their hands & backs the burden of that wretched small child of the Salter's adoption effects me as almost too horrid to be borne. Where <u>are</u> the Salters (with their seemingly so fatal mistake!) and why this incubus?"[50]

At the end of June Alice pronounced Jack cured by Miss Clarke, but still she found him uninteresting. She did not want the Salters to know that the boy troubled her because she feared cutting short their trip, but she tried to send him to a school in Canada for the summer. William empathized with Alice, realizing how much trouble Jack had caused. He even wondered whether the child might have inherited some of his bad mannerisms.[51] In desperation, Alice sent Jack to Weymouth to her Webb relatives for July.[52] Peggy and Alice visited Weymouth in August to see Jack at cousin Rebekah Webb's home. "Jack looked hearty and smiling as ever but alas! his smile has no meaning for me." She told Billy she would leave him there another month.[53]

That summer Alice read Upton Sinclair's *The Jungle* and was horrified at the conditions in Chicago meat-packing plants and stockyards, wishing she could distribute books to immigrants to warn them away from Chicago.[54] She had manifested sympathy for working-class people most of her life—in the abstract, at least. But her charity did not always extend to those close to home. William was more tolerant, and he had encouraged Jack to develop as an artist, but he never assumed his daily care.

As William had predicted, the Salters were too old to cope with a child, nor did they realize how difficult it would be to assimilate him. Although Jack was only two when he was adopted, he arrived with his own personality traits and memories. After the Salters returned from their year abroad, they left the boy in Weymouth indefinitely with Rebekah Webb, as Mary Salter planned to go south with Eliza Gibbens after Christmas for a needed change.[55] Mary's disappointment must have been severe, and the damage the family did to the adopted child was irreparable.

The next summer the Salters tried harder to help Jack, and Alice found the boy much improved. Mary tutored him in writing, and Mack coached him in arithmetic. Trying to bond with the boy, Mack made Jack play ball with him, but he was nearly hopeless as a parent. "It is a pathetic picture, Mack's tall grave form opposite the small Jack bestowing the same conscientious care on the passing of the ball that he would give to an ethical lecture," Alice explained to Billy. However, Mary was happy that summer running a household with a child.[56] As he grew older and learned about his own heritage, Jack resented his adoptive family. In 1913, when he was fifteen, he ran away from the Salters, and while he visited them from time to time he never lived with them again. Much later he attended the Chicago Art Institute on funds from William James's estate. John Randall Salter became a successful artist and a college professor at Northern Arizona University, never changing his name back to his own Frank Gray.[57]

Though Alice's 1906 summer with Jack did not go well, seeing fifteen-year-old Aleck improve rewarded her. The boy's situation was a complex one. If genes can account for certain behaviors as well as for certain physical traits, then Aleck's passions for art and the outdoors could have been inherited from his father. While William was never a cruel parent, he was determined to mold his youngest son into a scholar or at least into a successful student who could matriculate at Harvard. William's own adolescence and young manhood had led him to erratic pursuits, fits and starts of widely varied interests, so it is ironic that he did not allow Aleck such digressions. The boy must have had what today are called learning disabilities, and if he had been allowed to learn in alternate ways rather than being force-fed, he might have achieved some success at school. Alice tried an easier approach with him, but it was not enough, and at the time there were no medications or alternative programs available. As the case stood, Aleck was doomed to failure. He was the most loving of the four surviving children, and he fashioned a contented life as an adult, but his days at Irving Street caused consternation for his parents and himself.

The spring Alice and William returned from Stanford Aleck passed all his exams at Browne and Nichols. Maybe a winter on his own had helped Francis/Alexander/Aleck/Friese relax. (Alice still slipped sometimes and called the boy Francis, and the family frequently called him Friese or Frese.) While his passion for birding waned, he remained a very active young man who grew handsomer as he advanced into the teen years. His voice as well as his body was changing; by the end of 1906 he was taller than Harry.[58] That summer his parents sent him to a camp Billy recommended where he would study Latin and French two hours a day. He was glad to go.[59] While a tutor had helped him during other summers, as Aleck came closer to taking college entrance examinations (which then included a test in Latin) Alice and William felt he needed the intensive preparation this camp would provide. When the boy returned that fall he seemed more mature.[60]

Despite summer camp, in September Aleck had difficulty concentrating. Though he was popular with other boys, he was miserable at school.[61] Alice and William differed in their approaches to the problem. She feared Aleck's teachers hectored him too much, as the boy had a constant wary look.[62] Sometimes she felt her son was in the right, that some of the teachers failed to understand him: "He [Mr. Nichols] and Francis never will understand each other," she explained to Billy, "though I think Francis is the more comprehending of the two."[63] William, however, thought Aleck had been babied at home, and though he undoubtedly meant well as he coached his son, their drawn-out sessions usually resulted in exhaustion for both.[64] "At this moment loving Dad with a U.S. History in one hand and the President's message in the other is explaining to him the 'Alien & Sedition' laws and the conflict of state with federal authority—as applied to the Japanese in California. Poor Francis has to hand in a written paper tomorrow on this fascinating theme," she told Billy.[65] A month later she mused to him again, "Tomorrow will be Hummy's birthday, 23 years old. I wonder if our little measures of the days and years count there."[66] Perhaps this thought gave her patience with her living son Aleck as she sat across the library table from him while he struggled with his Latin.

Though Uncle Henry was too kind to tease the boy, he indulged himself with a laugh at his nephew's spelling: "I think his spelling transcends the bounds of comedy! (His friend who 'feighnted' with laughter!)"[67] Then he put it more gently: "[Aleck's] letters a rare treat, as always, as to ingenuous expression & orthography."[68] Bachelor Henry wisely believed that his youngest nephew's withdrawn behavior was an adolescent phase: "Aleck's 'taciturnity' is a logical feature of growth!"[69]

Although Aleck was ill during the winter of 1907 with influenza and earache, Alice never let him fall into depression. Along with Prentice Mulford, one of whose books her father had read on the *Manhattan* when he sailed to Liverpool all those years before, she believed that the right mental attitude could cure depression and suicidal tendencies. With the arrival of spring Aleck's spirits improved. Not only had he received an A for his paper on Cromwell, he was named the manager of the Browne and Nichols baseball team. He ordered uniforms, scheduled games, and, to the teachers' and students' delight, found a wonderful coach, Fred Grant, a law student who played for the Boston Americans (which later became the Boston Red Sox), where he earned $2,500 a year.[70]

During his spring vacation of 1907, after spending a week camping on Mt. Monadnock with two friends, Aleck rebelled against academic life: he would become an artist. He consulted Billy, who still studied art in Paris, about the advisability of spending at least one year in college, but he would prefer to finish high school and then begin his chosen profession. Aleck too had been reading Mulford, and he described his decision as a conversion experience. "'I don't know how it happened, partly the smell of the paint, but it's as if a thunder burst had struck me and I <u>know</u> what I want.'"[71] Billy supported his brother's choice, writing to his mother from Paris (that same day copying a little Degas head that American artist Mary Cassatt had loaned him): "If Aleck's to be a painter in heaven's name have him begin young!" He added that he felt no jealousy that his younger brother might paint.[72] After Aleck's spring vacation, Alice, still determined to at least have him graduate from a secondary school even if he became an artist later, hired two tutors to prepare him for his exams, though to no avail: he received two E's and an F.[73] That summer he went to Mr. Spooner's Maine camp with his mandolin and his dog, Rylie.[74]

Alice had more time for Aleck that fall after Peggy matriculated at Bryn Mawr College near Philadelphia. Uncle Henry applauded his niece's choice of colleges, and he confided in Billy that he hoped she would "stick."[75] Henry had given a lecture, "A Question of Our Speech," there during his American tour and had been impressed with the college's president, M. Carey Thomas. Bryn Mawr, endowed by Dr. Joseph Taylor, was committed to women's education. The first trustees were all Quakers, though the college was open to women of all religious backgrounds.[76]

Alice felt Peggy was ready. She was not the twelve-year-old child who had been left behind in England, where she was lonely and homesick. No longer plagued by nervous depression and in better general physical condition, she was a mature and bright young woman. Alice informed Billy that his sister had "grown <u>wise</u> and she says it is due to Rector [Mrs. Piper's latest control] and his wonderful talk to her. At any rate she is very different from the nervous child of last winter."[77]

The first week in October Alice traveled with Peggy to Bryn Mawr, spending four days helping her daughter settle in. She helped her move twice during those first few days. At first Peggy was housed in unsuitable rooms in Rockefeller Hall but then was invited to room with a senior, Esther Williams, in East Pembroke. Her move disappointed her freshman roommate, Mary Worthington, a sweet, fair-complexioned girl and the niece of President Thomas, so Thomas decided to let Mary and Peggy room together in West Pembroke. That fall Peggy studied philosophy, biology, and English and took required physical education classes.[78] Alice had not lost her daughter completely. Upon Alice's return from Philadelphia she went to Mrs. Piper's séance, where Rector talked to her about Peggy.[79]

Peggy confided in Henry that she was homesick. He agreed that leaving the rich atmosphere of 95 Irving Street was a loss, but he reminded his niece that she could develop her interests without giving up her home. He envied her the formal education his father had denied him when he was young. "No one took any interest whatever in his development, except to neglect or stunt it where it might have been helped — & any that he was ever to have he picked up wholly by himself."[80]

Some of the young woman's experiences were typical only of a daughter of a famous man. Peggy learned that her nickname at Bryn Mawr was "Jimmy Psych" (the nickname used by students for *The Briefer Course*) and that her father had written to the dean announcing that his daughter was sweet but boring. When Peggy complained, William advised her to "'cultivate repose and dullness.'"[81]

Distance did not lessen Alice's ingrained habit of worrying. By November she feared that college work was too much for Peggy. She planned a gala Christmas holiday for her, with a new gown and a dinner for her friends on 22 December.[82] Peggy relaxed at home, though when she attended the funeral of Ralph Waldo Emerson's granddaughter Florence, she had a minor breakdown. News of the death had shocked her, but worse came when she went to the funeral in Concord. "She came back rather silent but after Papa had gone up to the attic (where he sleeps erewhiles in a hurricane) she ran into my room and broke down completely with the most pitiful terror of death," Alice recounted to Billy. "She refused to even try to sleep for when she shut her eyes, she saw 'that poor waxen face with its wonderful smile' and she kept sobbing out 'it is so unjust, so unjust.' She said 'I have a terrible fear on me — I don't know of what.' So she slept in my room — or rather lay silent there all night long for she never closed her eyes though I had given her a good dose of bromide."[83] Peggy's heightened sensitivity sometimes caused her depressed moods, her mother believed.

When Peggy returned to Philadelphia after Christmas, another student stalked her, coming continually to her suite. This young woman, Ethel, drank, smoked, and read bad books, Peggy claimed. Mary Worthington thought she and Peggy should help the girl.[84] Alice, however, did not inhabit a morally ambiguous universe. "That poor wretch who has taken to so haunting Peggy ought to be taken out of college at once." She cautioned Billy to silence, however, because if the story were known, it might be a setback for women's colleges.[85]

At the end of March, accompanied by Mary Worthington, Peggy came back to Irving Street to rest, her nerves frayed. Dr. Emma Call ordered her to bed at nine each night, cautioning her to avoid all athletic endeavors. In early April Peggy returned to Philadelphia to complete her freshman year.[86] Despite her daughter's difficulties, Alice retained her commitment to women's education. Peggy repaid her mother's faith when she gave a dinner speech toward the semester's end.[87]

During the summer between Peggy's two years at Bryn Mawr, the two women temporarily lost their self-restraint and reserve, Alice reporting the curious incident to Billy. Although William had experimented for years with mind-altering substances, including inhaling ether and taking various new drugs, the women in his family never considered expanding their conscious minds. Even in the early twentieth century respectable women were constrained from expressing their emotions.

For years Peggy had gathered edible mushrooms on the Irving Street lawn. That July she brought a crop to her mother and her two seamstresses, Mrs. Kreidel and Miss Farland. Alice, Mrs. Kreidel, and Peggy sampled the mushrooms. An hour and a half later Alice felt weak, and her face turned bright red. She couldn't see well and could scarcely hold her needle. Next, Mrs. Kreidel felt her hands go numb. Alert enough to realize that the mushrooms were hallucinogenic, Alice rushed downstairs to get vinegar and water for all three. While they could hardly talk, the women couldn't stop laughing.

Peggy went into her room and sat by the window, refusing the vinegar: "'No vinegar for me, thank you—I am happy. I am <u>right</u> for the first time in my life. I know I am drunk but it's the only fit condition to be in and I only wish I had eaten <u>all</u> the mushrooms. Vomit, did you say? No indeed, nothing shall deprive me of this blessed mushroom.'" Then Peggy took off her dress and started dancing around, laughing all the while, convinced that she would never again take the universe seriously. Finally, Alice persuaded her to drink the hot water and vomit up the mushrooms. The girl prayed in between her hysterical laughter, repeating a line from one of her favorite hymns, "'O love of God, all love excelling Joy of Heaven to Earth come down.'" Every time she starting to sing the word "joy" she laughed so hard she had to stop. Not even black coffee sobered them. By early evening Miss Farland had escorted Mrs. Kreidel to the cars, while Alice and Peggy went to sleep, tired and with aching heads.[88] The experience drew mother and daughter closer.

Peggy's second college year was much easier. The day before she returned she told her mother entertaining stories of college life until nearly midnight.[89] Alice did not believe, though, that college would make her girl either emotionally or financially independent. While Bryn Mawr had been a positive experience, Alice feared the girl's long-term prognosis for a mentally and physically healthy life was not a good one. She had been sick at times that summer, and Alice feared that she would never be able to take care of herself.[90]

Peggy was not quite as homesick her sophomore year, though by November she confessed that she missed her parents immensely.[91] Her class had dwindled over the summer: there were seventy-eight members instead of ninety-five, perhaps because a college education was a new thing for women, and not all of them had the stamina to continue. Her studies were demanding. She went to Dr. Laguna's lectures on ethics, reading Plato's *Republic*, Joseph Butler's *Fifteen Sermons*, Cicero's *De finibus bonorum et malorum*, and John Stuart Mill's *Utilitarianism*. She also took a psychology class that included a two-and-a-half-hour lab on Friday afternoons. In addition, she studied French literature and German, with another course in English literature with a Miss Donnelly.[92]

Peggy adjusted well to Bryn Mawr's activities; she was not just a grind. On weekdays she played hockey and on Sunday mornings went to church. She belonged to a sewing circle, and she went to dinners at the Deanery, Lantern Night, a suffragette meeting, parties, and hockey games. She took part in a performance, playing the part of Jack Worthing ("Ernest") in Oscar Wilde's *The Importance of Being Earnest*.[93]

According to school reports, Peggy had emerged by spring as a leader in her class and one of the nicest students enrolled. One of Alice's dreams had come true: to have her only girl gain the education she had missed herself. She remained anxious about Peggy's nerves, though she thought her steady roommate, who planned to be a doctor, calmed her daughter. Peggy also formed an intense friendship with Marianne Moore, who would become one of America's most famous modernist poets.[94] Peggy, a dark and intense young woman who also happened to be William James's daughter and Henry James's niece, fascinated Moore.[95]

William finally resigned from Harvard on 22 January, after thirty-five years, to accolades and the gift of a silver loving cup from his students, Alice present for this last lecture.[96] Harvard awarded him a generous yearly pension of $2,600. Along with his royalties and the Syracuse rent payments, the Jameses could live well. During their time in Cambridge they had seen many changes: the faculty and the student body had tripled since 1878, and the campus had added impressive buildings, including the Fogg Museum and Memorial Hall. Under Eliot's leadership Harvard had become a major modern university.[97]

William continued many of his professional activities, however, all the while trying to write about his evolving ideas so convincingly that the world would accept his views. He was sixty-five years old and had serious health problems, yet he refused to slow down. After his last semester ended he began organizing his lectures on pragmatism for the book that was so important to him, shifting from his previous focus on radical empiricism.[98] He also started the Oxford lectures that later became *A Pluralistic Universe*.[99] Alice and Henry pleaded with him to go slower, to pace himself, she noting the ongoing stream of visitors. "At present he consorts chiefly with the insane! They are interesting beyond a doubt," she told Billy.[100] But they were also siphoning her husband's energy. On 28 April she complained to Billy of the people who visited William each morning: "And <u>he sees them all</u>." She thought she could direct his hours better by keeping people away, but William would not let her plan his mornings.[101]

That spring Alice maintained her own sanity through vigorous physical activity, tending to the concrete world as she had done all her married life. Some days she woke at 6:00 a.m. and went directly to her garden, planting, digging, and weeding—earthy pursuits that allowed her to maintain her mental balance.[102]

She needed to keep balanced, as sweeping social changes for women sometimes made her question her roles. The feminist movement grew stronger with the dawn of this new century, and Alice was well aware that these women presented new models for her sex. When a Vassar professor came to a dinner party at Irving Street, Alice, who regretted her own lack of a formal education, disliked her despite the woman's degrees. She found herself increasingly alienated from a world on the edge of modernity, claiming that her species (devoted wife and mother) was becoming extinct, and "I don't know how to commune with the new order," she told the absent Billy.[103]

Alice had valued friends with successful careers, however, including Connecticut architect Theodate Pope.[104] She and William sometimes visited Pope at her country estate, Hill-Stead House, and by 1906 Pope came frequently to Boston for sittings with Mrs. Piper, often staying at 95 Irving Street and assisting with the investigations of Mrs. Piper's work. Trained by Richard Hodgson, Australian-born psychic researcher, she sometimes took notes at the séances for William when he had trouble reading the automatic writing Mrs. Piper produced.[105] On one visit, Pope found William in a very nervous state, constantly in motion, running to light the fire in the sitting room during dinner or leaving the sitting room to run upstairs to light the fire in Pope's bedroom so that she would not be cold that night. One evening, while Alice and Theodate chatted happily, he made the two women come into his library and talk while he corrected proof.[106] Age had not diminished his restless behavior.[107]

The spring of 1907 saw the publication of *Pragmatism*. Alice did not have a chance to examine the finished book closely until the next winter, however, during a trip to Montreal to visit her youngest sister, Margaret. Constant interruptions in the Gregor household made progress with the book slow, but studying it was a way to keep closer to her husband. She wanted William to explain it to her orally so that she could read it again and offer more helpful criticism, "be more comprehending as to 'points' and objections."[108] Though William believed that truths were relative and could evolve, Alice felt differently. She believed in moral and religious absolutes; her truth was spelled with a capital *T*.

Though the book sold well, the initial reviews of *Pragmatism* were not positive, at least those from the academic community, but Alice defended her husband's views because she felt in her heart that his "Truth" would prevail over other philosophies and belief systems of the day. Josiah Royce told one of Alice's friends, a Mrs. Davis, that "'Pragmatism is Believe what you like, Change as often as you choose, and the other fellow is always wrong.'" Alice brushed aside such cynical assessments. Her husband's philosophy was like her brother-in-law's fiction: its day would come. "It will take a generation or may be 15 years to establish itself and you must so wisely live as to see the great day, you and I together."[109] Henry, too, lauded his brother's work, telling Alice that "I find Pragmatism, tell him, <u>overwhelmingly</u> the Philosophy for the Artist & the Novelist—if it had been cooked up for <u>their</u> direct & particular behoof it couldn't suit me more down to the ground."[110]

The book was destined to make a major contribution to intellectual history. While Charles Peirce conceptualized pragmatism initially, William developed and refined the concept, which was, among other things, for him an attempt to think clearly. He considered rationalism, which is monistic and absolutist, and empiricism, which is pluralistic and materialistic, but proposed pragmatism and the pragmatic method as a method of settling these metaphysical questions: trace the consequences of each belief system and then judge its usefulness (or truth) by its outcomes. He claimed that there are no objective, overall, absolute truths, as rationalists would have it. Our knowledge of the world is incomplete, so we create individual systems, truths, beliefs, and concepts based on our experiences, hypotheses that lead us toward reality. We modify these hypotheses as new facts arise, so that there is an ongoing interaction between experienced reality and our intellectual formulations of it. Though his ideas later became adapted as a practical substitute for philosophy, he stressed pragmatism's interest in interrogating what we mean by truth itself. Throughout the book William also considered temperament, the tough-minded and the tender-minded, the two temperaments influencing which philosophy we espouse. The tough-minded can tolerate philosophies that change and evolve pragmatically, whereas the tender-minded need fixed, absolutist philosophies that allow them to cope with an empirical world.

Pragmatism holds that the world is not finished and that individuals, through their actions, can make a difference in its outcome. British philosopher Frederick Canning Schiller called this "humanism," the belief that humans can create truth from the world's sensible flux.[111] Thus, the difference between pragmatism and rationalism is not just a theoretical difference but concerns the very nature of the universe and our behavior within it. There is a live possibility that our ideals, put into action, might create a better universe. William himself believed in pluralism, in a universe both challenging and capable of being changed. This made him one of the tough-minded, someone who needs no absolute, overarching systems that hold reality in place. In his last lecture he considered religion, which also must be evaluated pragmatically. If religion's hypotheses work well, then those hypotheses must be true. He avowed that his own pragmatism was not atheism.

Bob already understood pragmatism, though he thought William should have added a chapter titled "Common Sense." "I find on rereading your great work on the meaning of truth that you are nearer to it than appears owing to the verbosity which seems to curse all prophets and professors. I could have told you very simply all about it long ere pragmatism was launched. Where there is no knower nothing can be known." He recommended that William edit the book and reissue it with a dedication to Robertson James: he claimed that the new edition would sell well in the underworld.[112]

Though Bob might have said it better, William James insisted again and again in *Pragmatism* that there was no one way to theorize the universe. There could be no unified definition of reality, no single interpretation of the universe, because truth and truths kept shifting. Truths become true through our ideas and our perceptions, they are not imposed upon us from without. William announced in *Pragmatism*, "The world is full of partial stories that run parallel to one another, beginning and ending at odd times. They mutually interlace and interfere at points, but we can not unify them completely in our minds."[113] Bob and William led parallel lives: Bob had embraced pluralism wholeheartedly, following Christian Scientists, Catholics, Swedenborgians, and spiritualists in his own quest for truth, while William theorized pluralism. But neither Alice nor William had been able to help Bob overcome his dependencies and depressions—that was a truth.

Although Alice sometimes feared her species might become extinct, her outwardly conventional life was made up of a variety of interesting stories, points where her life intersected with the lives of others.[114] While many events were beyond her control, she scripted her own life as she influenced those around her. She had adapted to the complex world of the Jameses while holding on to her own moral and religious convictions. She lived what William wrote about, lectured about, inquired about: the need to be constantly in touch with the world as we experience it. The last years of his life she battled for him to stay alive in this world to write his truths.

14 Summer's End

IN DECEMBER 1907 BILLY, who showed promise as an artist and who had returned from Paris, painted his mother several hours a day while she sat with her eternal sewing.[1] He represents her as beautifully serene, even though her duties still entailed considerable exasperation.

Both Aleck and William were sick during the winter of 1908, Aleck with tonsillitis and William with grippe. They were housebound and keeping one another company after Alice left for Montreal.[2] Peggy, too, became ill. That spring Alice left suddenly for Philadelphia when she learned her daughter was in the infirmary with colitis, returning in time to sail for England with William in the *Ivernia*.[3] They rented the Chocorua house, planning to spend nearly six months abroad. Frederick Schiller, an advocate of pragmatism, had invited William to give the 1908 Hibbert Lectures at Manchester College, a Unitarian school in Oxford but at the time not part of Oxford University.

They arrived in Liverpool on 30 April. From there they took the train to Chester, going next to Leamington for a day, finally reaching Oxford on 3 May.[4] Alice's days were filled with social engagements and sightseeing in the beautiful spring countryside, which was cold at first. While William took a great deal of medication, he was able to give his talks; hundreds came to hear him, with many others turned away.

These lectures, titled "On the Present Situation in Philosophy" and later published in 1909 as *A Pluralistic Universe*, considered the reigning Oxford school of philosophy, absolutism, and attempted to refute it in favor of William's own loosely defined "radical empiricism." He asserted that the absolutist "logic of identity," used to argue for a universal monism wherein everything was subsumed under an idealistic absolute, was ultimately untenable. While absolutism could lead to a sense of peace and harmony that might be desirable for humans, its supposedly rational premises did not hold up under closer examination.

William also examined Hegel's dialectical method, concluding that his conception of negation had great use in reconciling worldly empirical contradictions, but his insistence on one incontrovertible eternal truth made him dogmatic and absolutist.[5] William proposed that philosophers consider Gustav Fechner instead of Hegel.[6] Fechner, through a process of analogical reasoning, postulated a higher, totalized consciousness that might be called "God." Our individual consciousness eventually becomes part of more inclusive forms of consciousness. William then critiqued intellectualism: its logic does not allow us to understand reality, which is nonrational. After a prolonged struggle, he found his own antidote to intellectualism in the ideas of French mathematician and philosopher Henri Bergson.[7] Bergson believed that intellectual knowledge was inadequate to explain reality; we must return to the experiential world to arrive at an understanding of the world. We must abandon logos as the way to truth, William counsels.

William briefly proposed radical empiricism as a way of understanding an ever-changing reality: our conceptual systems are fixed, but his method considers experience as continuous and overlapping. Further, he suggested that our subconscious mind might be at the margin of another central self, a sort of finite superhuman consciousness. The existence of split personalities, mediums, automatic writing, and so on suggests that there may be a superior consciousness available to us, as Fechner theorized. In the end, William posited an incomplete, pluralistic universe.

William was feted throughout Oxford. Since women were excluded from certain events, occasionally Alice was left to her own devices. While William lunched one day, she read Edward Edwards's *The Life of Raleigh* in her room, munching on a Bath bun. She recommended the book to her mother and also told her of the lovely walk she had taken along river footpaths to the Bertrand Russells' home in Bagley.[8] By now Alice's and William's lives were completely intertwined. She helped him keep track of social engagements by writing them in his diary, he then crossing out some of her entries and she his, in effect overwriting one another. On 2 June she wrote, "Tea at Westbury with Miss Marsett 4.30." Next to this entry William noted, "revoked."[9]

In June, the lectures over, the Jameses removed to the Swan Inn in Bibury, Gloucestershire, where their rooms needed a coal fire to offset the gray, cold, rainy weather. The inn itself sat beside a fishing stream. Bibury was the loveliest place in the world; masses of cream white roses blanketed the gray walls and mossy slate roofs of the village cottages. "If I were in disgrace with fortune and men's eyes," she wrote to Billy, "I should hide myself in such a place as this."[10]

Alice also enjoyed seeing ordinary English women. One day she saw an attractive woman standing at her gate, the wife of Mayor Knollys' groom. The woman invited Alice to see her view from her sitting room, which she found homey. "We agreed that we should like to know her history for her speech was as beautiful as her face."[11] On another outing in the Cotswold country Alice saw forty-two "Mothers" taking tea at a hotel. They had driven through the rain from Burford for their outing. Though they were poor, they were quiet, decent, and cheerful, all virtues to Alice. Their meal consisted of a ham, a joint, boiled beef, two kinds of cake, bread and butter, and tea.[12] They were the English working-class equivalent of Alice's Cambridge clubs.

Besides relishing these working-class women, Alice appreciated the English nobility, perhaps more than she liked to admit. She was struck by Henry's friend Lady Ottoline Morrell, telling Billy, "She looks like a Flemish saint of ages ago." The two women got along well. Alice noticed the woman's liberalism: though she was the Duke of Portland's sole sister, she had married a commoner, a pacifist member of Parliament, Philip Morrell.[13] Perhaps the woman's liberal politics made it easier for Alice to admire her rank and title.

Although her husband inveighed against "exclusive worship of the bitch-Goddess SUCCESS," noting to H. G. Wells the cash value by which he feared Americans exclusively measured their lives, Alice's acquisitiveness sometimes took over.[14] Her escalating urge to shop might have represented a reaction to the relative poverty she had endured as a girl, among other things. She loved buying furniture and beautiful household objects, finding a Sheffield china workbasket, a wedding gift for Billy's friend Charley Hartwell. She feared the Hartwells would not appreciate the basket's quality, but she thought it might look beautiful on her sideboard.[15] When Henry saw the basket, he cried, "<u>Why</u> didn't you get me one.'"[16] Thorstein Veblen, in his *Theory of the Leisure Class*, published less than a decade before, explained that such conspicuous consumption marks upper-class and upper-middle-class status: "The consumption of expensive goods is meritorious, and the goods which contain an appreciable element of cost in excess of what goes to give them serviceability for their ostensible mechanical purpose are honorific. The marks of superfluous costliness in the goods are therefore marks of worth."[17] That summer Alice and Henry made sure they were so worthy.

During their months abroad William wrote often to Pauline Goldmark, who was touring Europe. As Pauline traveled from Greece to Italy, William longed to accompany her. She was the touchstone for his lost youth, his relationship to her tinged with nostalgia and a touch of impossible romance: "'How I wish I might have been with you there for 24 hours!'" But he could no longer match her energy, so she would do best to forget him.[18] Alice may or may not have known of these letters.

Toward the end of June Peggy joined them, all she would have of a college education finished. Next, Harry arrived for a brief holiday, returning to America on 14 July, entrusted with the precious Sheffield china. Alice, Harry, and Peggy went sightseeing for a week, arriving at Lamb House on the Fourth of July. Then Alice and her daughter went together to see the cathedrals at York, Lincoln, and Ely.

Alice found Ely's cathedrals more interesting than the one in Lincoln, telling Billy, "Tucked away under their shadow were the most beautiful bits, old arches where the sunlight fell through flickering leaves on gray stone and flecks of pink or white, the little star-like flowers which live and bloom on the seams and holes of the old walls."[19] At Lincoln they took rooms at the White Hart Inn near the cathedral. She was disappointed in their hotel, however. It was expensive, but the food was miserable.[20]

When Alice and group arrived, Henry left Lamb House briefly, but he planned to meet them in London to see *Cyrano de Bergerac* and then return to Rye. Alice left Peggy and William at Lamb House, going to Harrow to visit the Clarkes. Henry missed her, Peggy told her mother. "He almost wept when he came in to me and said you weren't expected to come till Friday and were to start off in a few days for the Continent again."[21]

On 31 July Alice and Peggy traveled to Switzerland, leaving William with Henry to socialize with Rye friends.[22] Alice made the trip to Geneva in good order. With the help of a porter she negotiated the customhouse with her baggage marked as hand luggage, thus incurring no extra charges. Over years of travel she had learned many tricks to avoid customs charges. Normally honest and forthright, she unhesitatingly lied to customs agents in order to bring her purchases back to America duty-free. Harry wrote jokingly to Peggy: "Bill and I are reducing expenses and trying to save up $1000 to bail her [Alice] out. Tell her that under the new regulations she doesn't have any opportunity to sit down cosily with a much flattered 'Colonel' and make out a declaration which 'suits him.' She must write out her declaration in loneliness on the voyage and hand it in to the ship's-purser. Later it is produced on the dock to confound her." Harry warned Peggy to try to restrain their mother. "If the thought of these things seems to check her career at all, tell her that Bill and I don't want to stop her, but that we should like her to select. Thus if she wants to let herself go on dresses for you and herself we will cheerfully save up for the customs at this end. But if on the other hand she's buying more night-tables, we shall desert her with them on the dock. That is a passion whose further indulgences does us no good. We condemn it."[23] Alice survived the customs officers, though she complained of the French shoving and pushing.[24]

In Switzerland the two women visited the Flournoys, and Peggy spent time with the Bryn Mawr girls who were in Geneva that month. She proved to be very popular with the group. "It's the 'James' charm coming out," Alice explained to William. She declared Peggy a wonderful, cultivated companion but thought her daughter lacked vitality, as the girl herself admitted.[25]

Following the Swiss sojourn, Alice planned a trip to the Low Countries with William, gathering information from Peggy's Bryn Mawr friends. She and Peggy would meet William in Rotterdam, and then all three could sightsee. She wanted to take a canal trip between Rotterdam and

Amsterdam, stopping at The Hague. After Antwerp, Ghent, and Bruges they would go to Ostend and from there return to England.[26] William left Rye on 20 August, lunching with Pauline Goldmark and her brother Charles in London and then taking Pauline to a Franco-English exhibition. On 21 August he crossed the Channel and met Alice and Peggy at the Hôtel Guillaume, going from there to Brussels.[27] They toured the city, seeing paintings by Peter Paul Rubens and the school where Charlotte Brontë once taught, immortalized in her novel *Villette*. From Brussels they traveled by train to Antwerp. They also visited Delft, Haarlem, and The Hague, where they toured the old prison.[28] Amsterdam proved to have an impressive gallery as well as a zoological garden and an aquarium, though the boat ride there was very windy and rainy.[29] Returning via Paris, they visited bankers, making more than one shopping trip to the Bon Marché.[30]

After their return to England Alice and Peggy went to Rye while William stayed in London to meet Aleck, on his way to Oxford to work with a tutor. When the trio left England on 6 October William described their leavetaking to Henry: "I forgot to say that when the train moved, it found both Alice & Peggy bitterly weeping at being borne away so fast from you. I was firm as a rock, and ere long they followed my example."[31] Peggy was sick all the way home.[32]

Francis Tweedy Alexander Robertson James arrived in England on 6 September, a month before his parents and sister left, so that his family could help him settle in Oxford. The previous spring he had failed his exams again, French and algebra.[33] He had headed to Spooner's summer camp in Maine while his parents were abroad, but in a last-ditch attempt to enroll their son in Harvard the Jameses decided to send him to England that fall to be tutored by Arthur Lionel Smith, who had an excellent reputation of preparing students for the rigorous college examinations. Alice had consulted Smith in May while she was in Oxford.[34] While William had recommended patience with students who were poor test-takers in his *Talks to Teachers*, he seemed to have forgotten his own advice: "Be patient, then, and sympathetic with the type of mind that cuts a poor figure in examinations. It may, in the long examination which life sets us, come out in the end in better shape than the glib and ready reproducer, its passions being deeper, its purposes more worthy, its combining power less commonplace, and its total mental output consequently more important."[35]

Aleck agreed to go.[36] He could spend his holidays in Rye, benefiting from Henry's company, Alice believed. She worried as she left her youngest son behind, but William was determined to follow their plan. As she sailed from England she confided to Henry, "A very homesick letter from Aleck troubles me a bit, but William says it is inevitable."[37]

Henry bought Aleck a dictionary and suggested he enjoy Oxford's fall beauties. He kept close contact with his nephew throughout the fall, sending encouraging messages at least weekly. Planning a November visit, he urged Aleck to write if he needed anything at all. Henry thought perhaps some of Aleck's difficulties at adjusting came both from homesickness and from British behaviors and attitudes, so unlike the American easy ways, as he told his nephew: "I guess the Smith queernesses & apparent deficiencies are only differences of <u>form</u> from what you've been used to, & that you would find them under stress, as English people mostly are, kind & faithful & helpful."[38]

At the end of 1908 Henry told Peggy that Aleck had been an acceptable replacement for her at Christmas, though he felt deprived of his niece's company. He was enthusiastic about Aleck: an exceptionally handsome young man, he made a delightful companion and was a social success. Henry's Rye friend Mrs. Dacre Vincent introduced the young American to her brother Charles Hotham, who took tea with Aleck at Lamb House and then invited him to visit him in Essex. Aleck also charmed Mrs. Ford Maddox Ford's daughter Esmé Stephenson, who took him to the annual subscription ball at a monastery. For the occasion Henry loaned his nephew his evening dress, though the writer's white waistcoat was too large. Henry found Aleck genial, gentle, tactful, appreciative, and animated; he thought the boy would marry in England.[39]

While Aleck was not as homesick when he returned to Oxford after his Christmas holiday, he made no progress with his work. Smith made him study alone in his room, giving him no specific directions or tutoring. To his close friend and Rye neighbor Fanny Prothero Henry confided, "I have been scandalized to learn that though he is now in his 4th month there & being paid for at a fancy figure, he hasn't yet had an hour's tuition from Smith, or from any delegate of Smith, & hasn't either a decent bed to sleep in, but just pigs in as on the cheap."[40]

Aleck spelled out his situation: if nothing else, his parents were getting little value for their money. At Alice's behest, Bessie Evans saw him that winter while she was in England, bringing him a violin from home.[41] Aleck told her he wanted to leave. But despite her son's complaints, Alice wanted him to stay the course. She consulted friends who knew Smith's work, telling Henry, "Roger [Merriman] knew him for 2 years intimately and loves and reveres him. But he says his outside is rough and that he had been there almost a year before Smith gave the slightest sign of caring about him."[42] Uncle Henry concluded that Aleck should continue the program until the Easter holiday and then return to Lamb House, where he could be tutored in French and perhaps also German. He was just the surrogate parent that Alice wanted for her distant and confused son. In the end, however, William decided to leave his son with Smith through the winter. He wanted Aleck to confront the tutor, having him open up to Smith to enlist the man's sympathies. He found his son too reticent, too closed: he only communicated with his mother. He, too, wanted Aleck to stay the course.[43]

Somehow Aleck prevailed. On 11 March William cabled him to return home, though he lay awake two nights after debating the decision.[44] Aleck would be allowed to paint for a year. Smith released him to Henry and Lamb House on 15 March 1909. First Aleck visited Charlie Hotham in Essex and then went to Rye. He booked passage for America on the *Bohemian* for 3 April.[45]

Alice still believed in her son's abilities, but she did not always agree with her husband's wish to send Aleck to Harvard, as she had a broader view of what education meant. She shared her concerns with Henry. "He may take Harvard as a special student, or not take it at all, but he must get an education, the power to work, and a horizon, a knowledge of far countries of the mind. I may never see it, but the child is very gifted and ways must be kept open till he knows his own needs more justly."[46]

At least that was the resolution in the spring of 1909, but by June Aleck was back in Cambridge, being tutored for the college entrance examinations (which he failed five times in all).[47] William announced that the boy was working hard and kept in good spirits and that he had given up the idea of a painting career, at least for the time.[48] Alice, still in Cambridge, told William, who had gone to Chocorua, "Oh dont you hope Aleck will pass his exams."[49] The day he took the exams, 14 June, William hoped, "He crosses the bar on a flood of knowledge too deep for sound or foam, but able to float him."[50] But despite his mother's hopes and his father's optimism, Aleck passed only German. After a ten-day break William consigned him to Boston's Stone School, which prepared young men for the Harvard entrance examinations.[51] "How long, oh lord, how long?" William moaned to Henry.[52]

Henry still wanted Aleck to have at least a year at Harvard. At one point during the grueling months of exam preparation someone (perhaps Aleck himself) suggested that he go out west to join a friend at a lumber camp, leaving studies behind, but his uncle feared that if he did that, he would repeat Wilkie's and Bob's mistake of going west to Wisconsin for work and then marrying and settling there. Henry believed that his younger brothers should have had better opportunities, including a chance for more education. And he did not want to see Aleck returning home married, as Wilkie and Bob had done. "My heart sinks to see <u>our</u> (poor dear Father's & Mother's) confused lights & poorer resources repeating themselves in the new generation. Doesn't William feel that?" he asked Alice.[53] But in the end Henry, frequently the more practical of the two oldest James brothers, could only pray for his nephew.[54]

Though William was still determined to have his last son matriculate at Harvard, artist Abbott Hendersen Thayer rescued Aleck. The artist met him during the summer of 1907 in Dublin, New Hampshire, through Thayer's son Gerald.[55] Thayer urged William to let Aleck study art with him at Boston's Museum School. "'How inconceivable it looks to me to believe in persisting in trying to make an animal eat what some inner sense objects to.... To me you are doing for Aleck the same thing as if one were to lash the magnetic needle, nail or cement it, fast in an approved northerly direction! For better or for worse the needle does not consent to settle north till it has done its swinging.'"[56] The family finally agreed—or William was finally persuaded. In November 1909 Aleck began art school.[57]

After her summer abroad Alice faced the failing health of both William and Henry. During the winter of 1909 Henry told them of his bad heart, and William suggested he try Dr. James MacKenzie in London.[58] Henry quickly cabled back, "Stopt fletcherizing — practically well!"[59] William's heart bothered him intermittently, though he still had little trouble walking.[60] By late April he wanted to go back to Bad Nauheim—anything to help him feel better.[61] He occasionally lost his temper, and Alice still suffered from headaches.[62]

The summer of 1909 seemed remarkably like other summers, though it was marked by a poignancy that William's summers at Chocorua and Keene Valley might soon end. While he still took an active interest in the farm affairs, looking for a mare and finding a new hired man, even taking part in the haying in July, he was not well.[63] He started the lymph injections again, although this treatment had never helped him.[64] Despite William's poor health, a strong physical bond still existed between the Jameses. William told her, "[I] long to have you in our lowly cots with no disturbing presence for a while, but our mutual selves."[65] He still desired Alice, who remained heavy despite her attempts at dieting. He confided in Henry, "Her weight seems inalterable."[66] But he told her she always looked pretty when she met him, and she still missed him when he left.[67] The Jameses tried to balance their moments of romance with the practical details of their lives, but those details again overwhelmed them. William thought it might be time to sell the Chocorua property. When opening up the house for the summer, he was discouraged to find that the water closet bowl had broken: a new one might cost $18.[68]

By the fall of 1909, despite the summer at his two loved retreats, William was no better, showing further signs of physical deterioration. Ignoring the advice of a homeopathic doctor, James Taylor, not to walk, he thought if he walked slowly enough, he could do no damage. "Taylor said I mustn't walk! 'Store up energy,' etc. Fudge!"[69] In entries in late October 1909 William noted, "'Decided symptoms of nervous prostration all day.'" Then on 25 October, "'Dreadful angina on going to bed.'" Despite his symptoms Alice could not induce him to relax. He was sleepless many nights, and he also suffered from dyspnea, a breathing difficulty caused by his angina.[70] In November he tried a Christian Science treatment.[71]

On Christmas Day, 1909, Alice hosted Robertson James and the 107 Irving Street Gibbenses for dinner. Bob's wife, Mary, had just announced she was leaving him, so Alice and William would again have Bob on their hands. Mary and Bob had lived together in Concord again after their daughter's wedding in 1907, but in the fall of 1909, when he started drinking heavily again, she left for Europe.[72] The week after Christmas Alice had just half a headache.[73]

With the new year and at work on a new book, William felt a bit better, due, he thought, to the lymph injections.[74] That January Alice planned a celebration to commemorate his work at Harvard and to unveil the portrait that friends and former students had commissioned from a successful portraitist, William's cousin Bay Emmet. At the banquet on 18 January the portrait was presented to Harvard's new president, Abbott Lawrence Lowell.[75] William called the event "an Erckmann-Chatrian feast" after the feasts in the books of French writers Émile Erckmann and Louis-Alexandre Chatrian, whose tales contain vivid and realistic descriptions of Alsatian peasant life. The event, held for twenty-two men, was an artistic achievement for Alice. All four children helped her stage the dinner. Peggy decorated three tables in the library, where the guests ate by candlelight. Billy broiled brant (small geese) he had caught in New Brunswick over the furnace fire, Aleck carried them upstairs, and Harry carved them. Several guests spoke, lauding William's long and distinguished career.[76]

After the banquet William traveled to Concord to see Bob's medium, Frank Foss. Bob had gone to some lengths to prove Foss's veracity, running checks and cross-checks on him until he was convinced he was honest, but William still suspected fraud.[77]

In February Alice entertained two of Henry's closest friends, Sir George and Margaret Frances "Fanny" Prothero.[78] Sir George edited the *Quarterly Review*, while lively Irish-born Fanny was Henry's Rye neighbor and companion, helping him with household management and nursing him through various health crises. The two women made fast friends during the couple's weeklong visit. William liked Sir George but did not appreciate Fanny as his wife did.[79] Alice adored her. Their bond came from their shared devotion to Henry; the British woman brought the latest news of the writer.[80]

Despite his poor health, William did not give up his psychic investigations, partly to satisfy his own never-quelled curiosity and partly to help Alice contact loved ones. That year the Jameses held sittings at 95 Irving Street for the renowned Italian medium Eusapia Palladino. While she deceived many noted scientists during her career, before her death Harvard professor Hugo Munsterberg unmasked her. According to Harry's version, Munsterberg caught her moving the table with her bare foot. Afterward a verse ascribed to Royce entitled "The Search for Truth" made the rounds at Harvard:

> Eeny, meeny, miney, mo
> Catch Eusapia by the toe;
> If she hollers, then we know:—
> James's doctrines are not so.[81]

The publicity William had gained from his otherworldly investigations became an embarrassment to Harry, who tried to minimize William's involvement after his death.

Mrs. Piper was also scrutinized. The medium, who lived to ninety-three, lost most of her ability to enter into trances after 1909, when psychologists G. Stanley Hall and Amy Tanner experimented on her, sometimes inflicting pain to determine whether she was really unconscious or not. Now Mrs. Piper thought perhaps she had extrasensory perception rather than contact with spirits. In 1907 William told Charles Slattery, "Mrs. Piper has supernormal knowledge in her trances; but whether it comes from 'tapping the minds' of living people, or from some common cosmic reservoir of memories, or from surviving 'spirits' of the departed, is a question impossible for <u>me</u> to answer just now to my own satisfaction."[82]

It was possible that Mrs. Piper's knowledge of the Gibbens and James families came through a network of servants.[83] In 1929 one of her two daughters, Alta Piper, wrote a book explaining her mother's methods and mentioning that in 1885 the Pipers had an Irish servant whose sister worked for a Beacon Hill family where Eliza Gibbens visited frequently. The woman (and other mediums) developed sophisticated ways of "fishing" for facts. During séances Mrs. Piper often held clients' hands against her forehead, detecting their muscular reactions to talk. Also, sometimes while the medium appeared to be in a trance sitters talked to one another freely, thinking she did not hear them.[84] She had multiple ways of extracting information from clients, all of them taking place in this world, not the next.

On 4 February 1910 the Jameses received a letter from Henry's secretary, Theodora Bosanquet, dated 23 January, telling them that Henry had been ill.[85] Though she wanted to reassure them, relaying the doctor's report that he was much better, he had been sent to bed, where he was fed every two hours.[86] Alice and William could scarcely find the news comforting: they were not aware Henry had been sick. Although Alice wanted to leave at once, on 9 February Henry cabled, "Excellent recovery."[87] Dr. Ernest Skinner, the Rye physician, returned a reassuring word that while Henry was ill, no immediate crisis required that Alice come to England.[88] She and William feared a surprise visit might startle him.[89]

It was this very dilemma, which brother most required her care more, that occupied all her waking (and sometimes sleeping) hours. The previous fall she had felt depressed and overwhelmed. Although William loved her sincerely, he could not interrupt his trajectory of health cures and writing to help her: "Darling Alice, at a distance (as well as near by) you seem to me so <u>pathetic</u>."[90]

Henry had suffered for several years from the family heart disease and was now bedridden, suffering depression in addition to gout and stomach upsets. In the fall of 1909 he had gardener George Gammon burn the accumulated drafts and proofs from his last two years of intense work: his New York Edition (a revised edition of nearly all the novels and tales he had written during his long career); the play *The High Bid*; editions of two travel books, *English Hours* and *Italian Hours*; a volume of criticism, *Views and Reviews*; and other assorted materials, including some of his correspondence.[91]

Henry conjectured that his poor health and depression were a result of Fletcherizing. Introduced to the practice by William, who had abandoned it in 1906, Henry had chomped away religiously for five years. While it had initially benefited his health, the method's final results had been disastrous. Because each morsel of food was fully digested in his mouth before he swallowed it, his stomach had no work to do. For months he had experienced severe stomach pain, which he thought was "an immediate preparation for the tomb."[92] He feared that Fletcherizing had stressed his stomach and strained his heart, but his health was better than he believed—better than William's, at least. He reassured Alice, "My heart is so normal that even during these 20 days I haven't thought—so much as <u>thought</u> of going to see [Dr.] Mackenzie as a form of consecration."[93]

Now Henry swallowed his food in small pieces rather than chewing until everything was reduced to a liquid. After just ten days his condition improved. Until he concluded that Fletcherizing caused more problems than it helped, however, he endured a miserable autumn. Even changing his chewing habits did not bring full relief, however. Despite his infatuations with various younger men over the years, Henry never found a lifelong partner. He was lonely, and the spring before he had confessed to Alice how important it was for him to see both of them yearly.[94] After Christmas he collapsed into bed, Dr. Skinner sending a trained nurse to assist him. He gradually improved, but he was by no means well.

William had gained better control of his health when the news came that Henry was ill. While he had a cold, which forced him to rest for two weeks, William felt much more comfortable and could write and read steadily on infinity, his current preoccupation. He walked only as much as necessary, took no regular morning bath, rested for fifteen minutes several times daily, took a quarter grain of nitroglycerin three or four times daily, and avoided taxing social events. Henry roundly applauded his brother's decision to rest.[95] William took vibratory massages from Dr. Taylor; Alice took them too and was grateful for their benefits.[96] In the spring William planned a trip to France to consult Dr. Alexandre Moutier, famous for his treatment of arteriosclerosis.[97]

In mid-February, the Protheros still in Cambridge, Alice and William decided to send Harry to his uncle's side, though at first Henry had wanted Billy.[98] Then they weighed whether William could make the Atlantic crossing and whether Alice should go. She was reluctant to leave her husband. Though he felt better, he was by no means a healthy man. Finally, Harry took leave from his Boston law firm and sailed on the *Saint Louis* on 19 February, arriving in England by the end of the month.[99]

Although Henry was relieved to have his nephew there, no immediate improvement followed. He told Alice, "My flares & flickers up are followed so damnably by relapses, & the drops seem so deep & disheartening that I am afraid I am rather demoralized & abject."[100] He begged them to come that spring, bringing Peggy. He wanted desperately to be well enough to work, and he did not want Harry to leave.[101] Alice assured him she and William would take care of him. If need be, they would rent the Irving Street house and stay with him through the next winter. "So you see we are all holding hands and ready to see you safely through. You can get better and you will, with a whole new kingdom to reign over."[102] And Henry wanted Alice. "I, who have no right to her, whine for her like a babe."[103]

As loyal as she was to her mercurial, demanding, loving husband, Alice resolved to be equally loyal to Henry. She loved him for his kindness to her and her children and for his great talent. Now she could repay what he had generously given them. "The Jolly Corner," published in 1907, Henry's account of Spencer Brydon, who returns to New York after years abroad to discover what he might have been had he stayed home, contains an embedded tribute to Alice. The tale's heroine, Alice Staverton, is a model of stability and love—and she lives on Irving Place. She is one of James's splendid women, strong, steadfast, self-assured, and loyal. Financially and emotionally independent, "she affronted, inscrutably, under stress, all the public concussions and ordeals." Alice Staverton was all the same as exquisite as "some pale pressed flower (a rarity to begin with)."[104] The tale ends with an affirmation that love is possible between mature adults. Alice Howe Gibbens James was also a rare flower, one that had not wilted under her withering vocation.

15 Last Things

UPON HEARING HENRY'S DISTRESSED WAILS from deep in Sussex, William decided to take passage for 29 March on a newly launched ship, the White Star Line's *Megantic*.[1] In mid-March Alice agreed that William should go first, she following in a few weeks, so the brothers could have a few days together.[2] But at the eleventh hour, responding to Henry's pleas for help and realizing that William could not go alone, she decided to accompany her husband. It may have been the closing of Henry's letter ("I dream of the companionship of Alice") that swayed her.[3] Her husband was grateful to have her along.[4]

At this same time, accompanied by his nephew, Henry visited a London doctor, William Osler, who gave him nearly a clean bill of health: his heart, arteries, lungs, and stomach were in excellent repair.[5] Henry denied that his nerves had played any role in his illness, however; he attributed everything wrong to Fletcherizing.[6] Harry returned on the *Empress*, arriving in New Brunswick on April Fool's Day just as his parents sailed from Boston. Uncle Henry would have to cope alone as best he could for ten days.

Alice felt relieved when she reached Lamb House. Now both James brothers were under her sight and under as much control as she could exert over them. Keeping her balance as she mediated between them would be less precarious now because they were both physically in her care. The brothers' decades-long, usually amicable sparring had nearly vanished, as each was genuinely concerned for the other's health. After a two-day relapse Henry felt well enough to go with Alice to an estate sale.[7]

She settled into a routine, alternating between Henry and William yet still finding precious moments alone. At 8:00 a.m. Minnie Kidd brought up hot water so that Alice could bathe and then dress. By 9:00 a.m. she was downstairs at breakfast. After her morning meal she went to Henry's oak-paneled sitting room and read Swedenborg's *Angelic Wisdom Concerning the Divine Love and the Divine Wisdom*, which she found repetitive but rewarding, recalling her father-in-law's injunction that Swedenborg was "'insipid with veracity.'"[8] The book drones on about abstractions of love and will, wisdom and understanding, degrees of spiritual and earthly existence, forms of use. She could imagine as she read that her father, Dr. Gibbens, had gone into the world of spirits after his death to review his life and prepare for heaven or hell. Perhaps she could believe he had become an angelic spirit on the way to heaven rather than an infernal spirit headed for hell. Other parts of the book were frightening, filled with the devil's creatures: crocodiles, scorpions, rats, noxious insects, even "damned dust."[9] In addition, she learned that parents could pass on their evil tendencies to their children. While she could have received nothing but good traits from Eliza Gibbens, might she have inherited some of her father's weakness?

When Henry's valet, Burgess Noakes, called, Alice went back upstairs to sit with her brother-in-law while he breakfasted in bed. Then all three lunched, William napping and Alice resting afterward. At five o'clock she walked with Henry for an hour or more. William was not strong enough to come on long walks, though he was able to work on his article on Benjamin Paul Blood, an amateur philosopher. Dinner was served at seven; Alice enjoyed the brothers' long mealtime conversations.[10] After dinner she read French plays aloud to William while they sat by an open fire in his bedroom, and finally she slipped into her bed, wearing her mother's white shawl and bed shoes.

During her stay Alice admired the deep yellow and red blooms on Lamb House's brick walls and the gardens around Rye. Though it was a cold spring, Alice told her mother, "The flowers are succeeding leaf and bud in the most beautiful and spiritual way."[11] All around her the world remade itself, even as the two brothers deteriorated.

Henry's boon companion, writer Edith Wharton, generously shipped her motorcar from France so that the three could drive about the countryside. Since William could walk only for short intervals, driving was the only way he could enjoy the English spring. The trio visited Battle Abbey and the country villages of Tenterden and Biddenden. Their rides calmed Alice. "And the sky hung low with tumbled, silver clouds making soft shadows on the far stretches of green upland. I could only think of the psalms and the green pastures and still waters that David loved," she told Billy. William rested well after their excursions, but Henry continued to experience his "fateful rhythmic depression."[12]

Now, Alice's eminent psychologist husband had time to turn his lens upon her. She "represented a type 'half way between himself and Bob [James] and half way between himself and Henry,'" he teased his son Billy. She hoped her children would recognize this view of her.[13] By now she had earned the right to be an honorary James, though whether this was boon or bane remained uncertain.

She negotiated spring and summer plans with both brothers. William thought he should return to Bad Nauheim for one more course of baths, stopping in Paris to consult Dr. Moutier. Alice was torn between staying with her brother-in-law or going with her husband, the reverse of her dilemma six weeks earlier. Henry was not interested in a long stay at Bad Nauheim; he feared it would bore him. But, on the other hand, he did not want to stay at Lamb House alone. He was loath to lose Alice.[14] She saw her way when she learned that one of William's philosopher friends, Charles Strong, son-in-law of John D. Rockefeller, would be traveling to Paris early in May. He invited William to accompany him. Strong would provide William another kind of intellectual stimulation than he enjoyed with Henry. For years the two men had debated the nature of reality.

On 5 May William and Strong crossed the Channel together, a wet, rolling voyage, and then took the train to Paris. Strong's rue de Surène apartment had only one bedroom, and he insisted on giving it to an exhausted William, taking a room in a hotel for himself. In contrast to Henry and Alice, whose presences soothed him, William found being with Strong tiring. On the second day he and Strong discussed philosophy until nearly lunchtime:

"He is the same monster of monotony and integrity that he always was, only more so."[15] And Strong was increasingly deaf to boot.[16]

The day after his arrival the patient consulted Dr. Moutier, who gave a good report of his hypertension; his diastolic reading was 150 mm, though the anginal pains returned that evening. The doctor did not think his treatment methods would work for William, so he advised him to return to Bad Nauheim. After his consultation William moved through Paris like a cyclone, albeit a weakened one. He visited Edith Wharton, lunched with Dr. Baldwin, went to a museum with Strong, visited his French translator, received various callers, met French philosopher Henri Bergson and his wife at their home, dined several times with Henry Adams, and called on his nephew Edward Holton James (his brother Bob's son, known as Ned) and his family.[17] All these activities exhausted William, erasing any gains he had made.

On 12 May, his visit nearly over, William James and Theodore Roosevelt were inducted into the French Academy as foreign associates.[18] The next day he moved to the Institut Thiers, staying with French philosopher Émile Boutroux and his wife for a few nights.[19] On 16 May Strong took him to the station, where he boarded a night train to Frankfurt.

Alice remained with Henry a month. She kept dieting, following a low-carbohydrate diet that allowed no bread but instead recommended a gluten biscuit, which she thought tasted very good.[20] Although Henry still battled depression, he and Alice visited Mary Smyth Hunter, a wealthy English socialite, at her large estate, Hill Hall, near Epping Hill north of London.[21] The writer felt better here, sitting for his portrait to Edna Huestis Swinerton, who did miniatures and historical paintings. He and Alice stayed until 1 June so that John Singer Sargent could make suggestions about Mrs. Swinerton's portrait before she finished it.[22] Alice so loved Hill Hall and its guests that William feared she had been "corrupted from her pristine Weymouth" to the Elizabethan world of Edmund Spenser's *The Faerie Queene*, his epic poem to Elizabeth I.[23] He announced to his wife, "Your wealth-worship must be greater than ever after this experience of the power for good wh[ich] wealth confers!"[24] If she needed money, though, he advised her to borrow it from her brother-in-law.[25]

Upon their return to Rye Henry dipped again, so Alice tried to cheer him. She even gave him a knitting lesson, a lesson that did not take.[26]

He decided to go home with Alice and William that summer, perhaps a permanent move, so she planned changes to the house to make it more comfortable. Burgess Noakes, Henry's valet, would come, but he would have to live out until they added another servant's room at the rear of the house.

Henry nearly gave up his room at the Reform Club in London, a decision Alice applauded to Harry. "I suspect the Club itself is not 'on the rise' and certainly anything more dreary than the moribund old men I saw crawling about there I never wish to behold. And the fee for the bedroom is 100 [pounds] a year and last year he used it hardly at all."[27] She was happy to take charge of the details of her brother-in-law's life. Practically speaking, Alice would benefit from the arrangement: Henry could bring some of his things to America free of duty, including the best of his Reform Club furniture.[28] In the end he decided to keep his room there for at least another six months.[29]

Finally, William began to fret because Alice and Henry were still in England. Although he wanted them in Bad Nauheim by 1 June, he acquiesced to a later arrival when he learned that Henry did so well under his wife's expert care. He was glad they got along and was proud when Henry declared that Alice had been a great social success.[30] When they delayed their arrival, William wrote in his diary, "Must tread wine press alone!"[31] Besides, he had his cure to occupy him — "the embalming and perfuming of my own invincibly squalid little corpus!"[32] Alice was torn between rushing to Bad Nauheim and staying longer at Rye. She was no longer a virtual bride for two brothers; she was now literally a life partner to both.

William found rooms in a villa at Bad Nauheim for all three. Henry could have the room at the front, Alice and William would have two connecting rooms on the same floor.[33] On 6 June Alice and Henry traveled to Germany through great heat. After their arrival William felt debilitated from the bath regimen, and Henry was depressed. Alice noted in her now lost daybook, "'William cannot walk and Henry cannot smile.'"[34]

Though it was hot that spring, the air was perfumed.[35] There were still concerts in the park, but Alice found Bad Nauheim less pleasing than ten years before, even though the food was excellent and their rooms were adequate.[36] When William rested or took the baths, she strolled with

Henry. In the afternoons she took both brothers driving. One evening the trio invited a young Jewish couple, Professor J. Goldstein and his wife, to dine. He was translating William's *Pluralistic Universe* into German. Alice overcame her anti-Semitism (something William claimed she had) and enjoyed them both.[37]

Again, she was privy to the brothers' conversations as they indulged in the long talks they missed during the decades they lived on opposite sides of the Atlantic. When they received the Memorial Day address that Harry gave at the unveiling of the Spanish War commemorative tablet at the Harvard Union, their reactions typified their lifelong rhetorical oppositions.[38] Alice gave them a copy, and while she went up to get her gluten biscuit, both read it. They thought it was perfect, William for its philosophy and Henry for its feeling.[39] While both agreed that it was eloquent, rhythmic, and imaginative, William thought Harry's ending was too long, while Henry thought it was too short. "Papa said to him [Henry], 'do you think it could have been condensed'—'No,' said the Uncle—'I should rather say the ending might have been more developed.'"[40]

On 23 June the trio left Bad Nauheim for Geneva, Switzerland, William and Henry longing for cooler air. The elder brother was better, the younger worse. The bath treatments had done William some good because at Bad Nauheim Dr. Theodor Groedel reported that his heart was smaller than it had been on his arrival and his nerves were steady. The change of scenery had not helped Henry, however. Struggling with depression, he tried not to burden Alice and William. "It is heartbreaking to see him in these states and the effort he makes not to give us trouble," she confessed to Billy.[41] She decided that Henry's condition was like her aunt Nannie Webb's. She had suffered from "visceral melancholy," marked by timidity, fear of solitude, and constant anxiety about the future. Henry, on the other hand, "has the habit of self-control, of a trained will, and the interests of a great brain to steady him." It was worrying about one's "insides" that marked Henry's similarity to Aunt Nannie, an anxiety that Dr. Skinner told Alice was the worst form of depression.[42] Henry confided his depression to Edmund Gosse: "But black depression—the blackness of darkness and the cruellest melancholia are my chronic enemy and curse." William and especially Alice had been lifelines. Terrified at the solitude he faced without them, Henry still planned to go home with them in August.[43]

Once in Switzerland William lost ground with the increasing altitude, while Henry gained. In Zürich all three went sightseeing.[44] When they reached Lucerne, William's breathing became labored. He claimed that the air bothered Henry but then admitted that his own breathing was worse.[45] Despite her nursing duties, Alice found time to visit the weekly pottery market.[46] William announced to Eliza Gibbens that Alice had been positively angelic during these long weeks. He debated getting her a Red Cross uniform "so as to excite less remark, as she crawls beside us, or sits with her back to the horses when we hire a cab."[47]

The three then went lower, to Geneva, where they visited William's old friend Théodore Flournoy, who had recently lost his wife. They found him depressed and in poor health.[48] Here Henry consulted a Dr. Mayor, who helped his gout; Henry recovered enough to escort Alice while she shopped for clothes.[49] William saw the physician next, as they were all impressed with his care of Henry.[50] Dr. Mayor put William to bed for a day, announcing that with good care he had years left to live.[51]

In Geneva the news came that Robertson was dead. Alice tried to hide his death from her husband, but while she and Henry were shopping, William intercepted a telegram that had gone first to Lamb House and then been forwarded abroad.[52] Bob died alone in Concord on 3 July 1910, probably from a heart attack. His body had not been discovered for two days. Peggy relayed the circumstances: "He just passed out, smiling, in his sleep, & the poor storm-tossed spirit is at rest. It was the most beautiful way to go." This death alarmed her, perhaps because she feared that her father's was imminent.[53] William took the death philosophically: "'It fills me with a new respect for Bob, and how I should like to go as quickly.'"[54] Henry recorded in his date book, "'Dark troubled sad days.'"[55]

The return trip to England went relatively well. On 11 July, the day after Alice and William's thirty-second wedding anniversary, the three left Geneva. When they arrived in Paris they took a late meal at the Hôtel du Louvre. William slept well, perhaps because the elevation was lower. Even Geneva's twelve-hundred-foot altitude had been too much for the severely ill man.[56] The first night in London William slept soundly. Henry stayed at the Reform Club, also sleeping well.[57] Their health still seesawed, though. On 14 July Alice told Harry, "But no sooner is one better than the other goes down. Uncle Henry is now descending."[58] She believed that the move to the Reform Club put Henry too far from them.[59]

On their first full day in London Dr. MacKenzie saw William at the hotel. The next day William visited his office for a more thorough exam, calling again five days later. Dr. MacKenzie, like Dr. Mayor, thought William's heart would last for years if he were only careful.[60] Alice was pleased with this London doctor, if only because he gave her hope. She told her second oldest son, "I have never seen a better man—a big, powerful gentle wise human being, and he knows how to understand his patients—at least this one."[61] While Alice refused to admit how sick William was, he knew he would not live long enough to write about his truths. In July he wrote to his old friend Flournoy, "I doubt if I ever do any more writing of a serious sort."[62]

Alice's freedom of movement remained constricted, as both William and Henry became anxious if she left for long. "Though my presence seems often to be a doubtful blessing I can not be free to go off and risk either of them missing me. I am not much of a success as a traveling companion—but I don't know why I should drag in my 'invincibly squalid little person,'" mimicking William's phrase to her mother.[63]

Learning that Theodate Pope was in London that summer, Alice invited her to their rooms, perhaps hoping to distract her husband—and herself. Accompanied by her nurse, maid, chauffeur, and Chow puppy, Miss Pope was installed nearby in Brown's Hotel. When she called, Henry and Theodate talked of the séances she had attended the past winter at 95 Irving Street with the suspect Italian medium, Eusapia Palladino. Although William could scarcely talk, he remained keenly interested in their conversation.[64] On 21 July Theodate took all three in her elegant yellow Packard to tour Chelsea, visiting Thomas Carlyle's house (where William and Henry waited in the car while Alice and Theodate went in) and other spots.[65]

American writer William Dean Howells, longtime editor of the *Atlantic Monthly*, also called on them. Howells had just lost his wife. Alice was touched at seeing him and Henry grieving, two ailing literary giants together.[66] Once again these social demands exhausted William. On Saturday night he had severe attacks of chest pain, one attack lasting more than two hours. He took three morphine tablets, which helped his chest pain but upset his stomach; he breathed with great difficulty. Back to bed he went until he felt strong enough for Alice to take him to Lamb House.[67]

When Alice, Henry, and William reached Rye on Saturday, 23 July, the weather echoed their inner distress: it was cold and wet and windy, a gale raging.[68] At first Alice and Henry thought to send William back to London to see Dr. MacKenzie, but it became apparent that it would be best to keep him absolutely quiet at Lamb House, allowing him to rest before they made the Atlantic crossing. Dr. Skinner called daily to assess William's condition.[69] He experienced great difficulty breathing, though Henry insisted that his brother's condition was a nervous one, just as William insisted that Henry's ailments were the result of melancholia. This time Henry rallied to devote himself to his brother's care, thankful for Alice's devotion. "Your Mother of course is magnificent & beyond all praise—for courage & cheer & ability & energy, & general matchless virtue; besides her appearing quite remarkably well & blooming & unassailable," he told Peggy.[70] He judged that the Bad Nauheim visit had been a terrible mistake, making William much worse.[71]

Alice made plans for their diminished life, unable to foresee a future without her husband. It was as if she could keep him alive through sheer willpower. She cast her vote with the affirmative side, as William had advised, holding on to a will to believe that he would get better. She knew there would be no more long summers at Chocorua—William could not live so far from his doctors. While pessimistic about his longevity, he told her that he wanted to expand their Cambridge home, so she planned a balcony and other improvements.[72] She wanted a larger garden.

Alice kept hope when there was none. On 31 July she reported that William's breathing, eating, and sleeping were slightly better.[73] He dozed in the garden, scarcely able to talk or even to read, she reading to him during the day as she always had done at bedtime. Edith Wharton took Henry to Windsor for two nights to see Henry's loved friend Howard Sturgis, giving Alice and William a few moments alone, the last they would ever have.[74] After visiting Sturgis Henry remained in London, awaiting his brother and sister-in-law's arrival.

In Alice's final letter to her mother before leaving Lamb House she announced that William was on his way to recovery. "Poor Mrs. Oliphant says in one of her letters that there is no happiness in life to be compared with the lifting of a great anxiety. And this joy has come to me, and I am filled with gratitude."[75] The whole world opened up for her again, yet there was still a hint of what was to come, her prevision of retrospect. Warning signs insinuated themselves into her consciousness. "It is a strangely haunted and haunting morning. The sun comes and withdraws, the bees buzz about the great bush of blossoming lavender beside the door, the wind sounds a menacing note, as of rain to come."[76] She begged her mother to meet them at Chocorua, as Eliza Gibbens had done so many times before. William noted his symptoms in his diary. "On the whole have gained strength, and breathe better, but Lord, how little!"[77]

Despite her forebodings, Alice busied herself with practical concerns. She wrote to Theodate Pope to share the names and addresses of her favorite Geneva shops: her corset woman, Madame Duby, between the rue du Rhône and the rue des Allemands; her furrier, Graupner et Nicolet, in a new building on the Entresol; and the prize-winning watchmakers Vacheron et Constantin. She assured Pope that Henry was in fine shape and William was better.[78] "It has evidently been an acute attack of neurasthenia—if the word means anything—I don't think it explains much!"[79]

On 11 August the group traveled by train to London, staying at Garlant's Hotel. On her final morning Alice visited two shops with her retail companion, Henry, before the party caught the noon steamer-train from Euston to Liverpool.[80] On 12 August they went aboard the *Empress of Britain*, a Canadian Steamship Line vessel, loyal Burgess Noakes traveling with them.[81] William had to be carried onboard. Alice prepared carefully for the trip, bringing a basket chair and arranging for the upper berth in their large stateroom to be removed. Dr. Skinner thought William would stand the voyage well, but Henry recorded in his date book that while the crossing was a smooth one, William suffered so that it was anguish to see him.[82] He told Alice, "'Ah, if I could only wake <u>there</u>!'"[83] She assumed he meant in the afterlife; she wanted desperately to believe she would not lose him forever. But he could just as easily have meant Chocorua.

Crossing the Atlantic in just six days, they steamed down the St. Lawrence River, arriving in Quebec in a terrible rainstorm. William passed a bad night at the Frontenac Hotel, which Henry pronounced horrible and vulgar, and the next day Alice struggled through customs. Harry met them and took them by train to Intervale, New Hampshire, and then returned to fishing and hunting in New Brunswick. From Intervale, near North Conway, Billy motored the group to Chocorua. William's feet became terribly swollen as fluids built up in his body, his heart failing rapidly.[84]

For the first few days William sat at the table with the family, though he could not eat. The brothers recounted their trip from Quebec through the Canadian wilderness. Henry thought the territory was desolate, with its flatness, emptiness, and monotonous fir-topped wilderness. William, though, was grateful to be at home: "'Better than anything in England, Henry. Better than anything in Europe,'" Billy recalled years later.[85] Although Chocorua was a long distance from Boston's expert doctors, Dr. George Shedd's son, also a physician, stayed at the house so that William had round-the-clock care. Alice also hired a trained nurse to help. On 25 August a heart specialist from Boston made the journey to New Hampshire and found that William still had a chance.[86]

In reality, he had no more chances. He lived only one week after his arrival at Chocorua. Although Alice telegraphed for him to come back, Harry did not arrive in time for his father's final hours. Aleck was spending the summer in Wyoming; he, too, did not reach home in time.

Henry thought that ever since the news of Bob's death came William had been hastening on his way.[87] For two days before his death he took morphine to ease his passing, and at the end he had no pain. When Alice came into his room with his milk at 2:30 p.m. on 26 August, she found him unconscious. She lifted his head from his pillow and supported him, and he died in her arms.[88] While his forehead was nearly unlined, his eyelids and sockets had fine wrinkles. His beard was grizzled and his hairline had receded. In death his face wore a look of calm repose. Alice wrote to Fanny Morse that day: "You must keep hold of my hand for dear William's sake."[89]

The autopsy revealed a swollen aorta and enlarged heart.[90] John Sumner Runnells, vice president of the Pullman Company, sent his private railroad car from Buffalo to Conway to take William's body and the family back to Boston. On Tuesday morning the family arose at 4:30 a.m. to go by hearse to the train station. Alice and Henry rode in the hearse with William's body, Eliza Gibbens and Peggy following in the Runnellses' automobile. They took the coffin first to 95 Irving Street until 4:00 p.m. and from there to the Harvard campus. William's body lay in state in Appleton Chapel, where he had attended morning services for decades.

He had once told Alice that he wanted all the trappings and ritual of a cathedral funeral when he died, so she arranged a solemn service. The Reverend George Gordon, once William's student and now minister of Boston's New Old South Church, performed the service, calling his professor a deeply religious man.[91] "'The scholar, thinker, teacher is merged at last in the human being. The man is the ultimate and everlasting value.'"[92] Appleton's organist played Alexis Chauvet's "Funeral Prelude," while six pallbearers, including Henry James, Supreme Court Justice Oliver Wendell Holmes, and William's student Ralph Barton Perry, carried the casket.[93] Among the honorary pallbearers were Harvard's president, Abbott Lawrence Lowell; William's financial advisor, Henry Lee Higginson; William's longtime friend and physician James Putnam; philosopher Charles Strong; George Dorr; and Harvard colleague George Herbert Palmer.[94] Alice had William's body cremated and then had the ashes buried in the Cambridge Cemetery on a knoll near his parents' graves; later she erected a small headstone to him. She only lost his physical body; his spirit awaited her in the afterworld with Hermann and Daniel Gibbens.

William's last breath "was gentle as a tired child's." And he went swiftly. Alice told Théodore Flournoy, "You know how quick he was when he had decided to do anything and having made up his mind to go he made no tarrying."[95]

16 The Philosopher's Widow

"NO MAN CAN KNOW HOW a wife can miss her husband," Alice informed Harvard professor Barrett Wendell six weeks after William's death.[1] In her case, however, William's international reputation allowed her a sphere of action denied to most widows of her era. Driven as she had been to ensure his success while he was alive, she was now even more driven to ensure his reputation. Alice had told William that the day when his ideas would be accepted would come. Now it became her work to hasten that date. Such service was consistent with the ethical code she had followed since childhood. "He has left me with much to do for those he loved, and many a lesson to learn myself before I can hope to have the right to die," she explained to Théodore Flournoy. "Sometimes I get a glimpse of a life so ordered, faithful & serviceable that I may follow him, though afar off."[2] She wore black every day for the rest of her life, long past the time dictated by mourning customs.

The day after William's funeral Alice and Henry returned to Chocorua. Autumn was beautiful, with "these innumerable mountains and great forests and frequent lakes, a magnificence of crimson and orange, a mixture of flames and gems," as Henry described it to Mary Smyth Hunter.[3] He decided to remain in America longer because the air was saturated with William's presence.[4] For the time he needed Alice and her children, and they needed him. Henry rallied as best he could, though he confessed to Bob's widow, Mary Holton James, "He was my best of friends in the world, as well as the greatest of brothers—and his death changes and blights everything for me. . . . We are living into what William's extinction means for us—and verily we stagger under it."[5]

Partly due to his added responsibility for Alice and her children, Henry's depression lifted. He was the only one of the four James sons left, the virtual head of this fatherless family. Less than four weeks after William's death he was able to work through the mornings, taking a drive or walking with one of Alice's children in the afternoons.[6] His health improved, and although that fall he fell ill again, he was relieved to be with Alice and her children.[7]

Alice, too, faced lonely days without William's physical presence, even though she was convinced his spirit awaited her in the afterlife. She copied out a quotation about saints that Harry claimed formed the credo she lived by after his father's death. "Why were the saints saints? because they were cheerful when it was difficult to be cheerful, and patient when it was difficult to be patient; because they pushed on when they wanted to stand still, and kept silent when they wanted to speak, and were agreeable when they wanted to be disagreeable. It was quite simple and always will be."[8] She had not always been a saint with William, but now she had no one who aroused her passions as he had. Theirs had been a deeply fulfilling marriage. To Bessie Evans she described her days: "I dust the books."[9]

Alice's first duty as widow involved replying to scores of sympathy letters. William's writing and his many lectures had earned him countless friends and admirers who shared their grief with his family. Henry helped Alice answer the letters, both using black-bordered writing paper. "My sister-in-law & I have been breasting, since my brother's death, a perfect flood of letters—as to the main mass of which however I have been able but to gape & sigh & postpone," Henry confided to Jocelyn Persse.[10]

William's death received attention around the world, from Boston to the *Times* of London to the Paris *Figaro*. Estimates of his reputation differed, but *Le Temps* called him "'the most famous American philosopher since Emerson.'" Journals quibbled over whether he should be remembered as psychologist or philosopher or something else altogether.[11]

When they left Chocorua in mid-October, Henry went to New York for ten days to Mary Cadwalader "Minnie" Jones, his close friend and divorced wife of Edith Wharton's brother, while Alice returned to a subdued 95 Irving Street.[12] She realized her husband's beliefs had never been fully articulated: he had not finished writing his last book, the introduction to philosophy (and specifically to metaphysics). He believed it would settle all the questions that pragmatism, empiricism, and the pluralistic universe had raised among philosophers who had more training in formal logic and philosophy; in it he had planned to answer charges that he had not fully defined some of his terms. His open-mindedness, his embrace of all experience, his intense scrutiny of consciousness, his belief that the world could become a better place if people would try to influence events positively, and his refusal to accept an empiricism that excluded faith—these crucial ideas must have an audience.

Just weeks after his death Alice and Harry began gathering William's letters for an edition. They wrote to his friends and colleagues, and Harry placed ads in a number of papers in America and abroad asking for the return of letters William James had written. Most people were eager to help, though not all were willing to relinquish their letters. Benjamin Blood, the American mystic about whom William wrote his last article, wanted his back.[13] Others, like Henry Adams, were happy to return them.[14] By 1913 they had assembled four volumes of letters, though it would be some time before any were published.[15]

In the meantime, Harry, along with Horace Kallen and Ralph Barton Perry, William's former students, prepared a posthumous edition of William's last work, *Some Problems of Philosophy*. Subtitled *A Beginning of an Introduction to Philosophy*, the book was dedicated to French philosopher Charles-Bernard Renouvier. Designed as a textbook for undergraduate students and based partly on the 1906 Stanford lectures, it gives a clear overview of William's pragmatic philosophy, whereby "empiricism and rationalism may join hands in a concrete view of life." Much of the book concerns the difference between precepts and concepts, concepts being abstractions derived from experience. As he worked on the book during his last months, William hoped it might secure the kind of royalties he had received from previous successful works. An appendix to the book entitled "Faith and the Right to Believe" promotes the possibility that active faith might change the world. "It [faith] may be regarded as a formative factor in the universe, if we be integral parts thereof, and co-determinants, by our behavior, of what its total character may be."[16] This belief was also Alice's.

Despite her belief, she endured dark hours that fall and winter. Eight months after William's death she mused, "I wonder sometimes that this library, full of his beloved books, does not crumble into ruins now that he has ceased to use it. Every corner of the house is strange and empty, and every morning dawns on an ever-deepening sense of loss."[17] Fanny Morse tried to reassure her of the crucial role she had played in shaping her husband's career. Alice knew she had devoted herself to serving William, even to the extent of sometimes submerging her own subjectivity. She confessed that her role as watchdog had sometimes burdened her husband, who did what he thought best without always minding the consequences. Reflecting on her protective influence on her husband, she wondered how effective she had been or whether she had gone too far in shielding William from the world that he exuberantly embraced and then theorized. "I did mean, God knows, to make my life serve him, to stand between him and all harmful things. But sometimes it oppressed him and I fell far short of the help I wanted to be to him. And how I must have failed him this last year to have let him go to the fatal Nauheim," she confided to Fanny. "And when I have been haunted by those weary days and suffering nights then the thought that I once could help him comforts me. And he used almost your very words not long ago when he told me that I had transformed his life."[18]

Fortunately, Alice had her children to distract and occupy her. On 17 May 1911, Henry still at Irving Street, Peggy had an emergency appendectomy at home.[19] She hovered in critical condition for several days and was finally pronounced out of danger, but she still needed round-the-clock care from her mother and the nurses.[20] Henry was literally interrupted midletter, as he was writing to his California friend Bruce Porter, with whom he had carried on a brief flirtation, when Peggy failed to rally after her surgery. He left Irving Street for a prearranged visit to some friends at Needham and then visited Theodate Pope and next the Connecticut Emmets. From there he went to his old Harvard law school friend George Abbot James in Nahant, Massachusetts, leaving the field clear for Alice to nurse Peggy. Eighty-seven-year-old Eliza could help Alice, "rock-like as to a foundation," as Henry put it.[21] Sometimes he had taken his breakfast with her at her smaller but graceful white house at 107 Irving Street that spring, escaping the bustle at number 95.[22]

By June Peggy was nearly recovered, so Alice moved her household to Chocorua, her first summer there without William. Henry remained in America until late July and then crossed to England on the *Mauretania*. Exactly one year after William's death, Alice told her brother-in-law, "I have been thinking of you, as I am sure you have of me, during these memorial days—but all days are to be for me henceforth memorial days. It is so changed a world that I feel surprised to still be moving about in it—but for the children."[23]

In September 1911 Billy, now a practicing artist, became engaged to the daughter of John Sumner Runnells, who had loaned his railroad car to transport William's body. Alice Runnells had known the Jameses most of her life, as her family owned a summer home at Chocorua Lake. Her grandfather John Runnells had been Tamworth's and Chocorua's Baptist minister for thirty-five years. The local townspeople revered Elder Runnells. The old town butcher once told Alice, "'There ain't a man in Tamworth will be missed like him'—*He always minded his own business.*"[24] By 1911 the minister's son, John Sumner Runnells, had become president of the Pullman Company, a powerful and very wealthy man.

Alice Runnells and Billy had been seeing one another for some time. Peggy and Alice had been friends for years, the girls' friendship allowing Billy and Alice to meet naturally.[25] Peggy admired the adult Alice, claiming she was much more of a person than she appeared to strangers.[26] Alice sometimes modeled for Billy's paintings. Though Alice had noticed Billy for two years, he had been slow to recognize her interest. Henry described her to Fanny Prothero as "very tall & goodlooking & gentle & sympathetic & intelligent & well-brought-up—& comes of a house full of money."[27] During the summer of 1911 Billy began a second canvas of Alice Runnells but was unhappy with it.[28] His relationship with her was changing, and he no longer saw her with an objective eye. Alice was delighted with the engagement, and Henry too welcomed Alice Runnells, hoping that this engagement would add new interest to his sister-in-law's life.[29] He captured the spirit of the arrangement exactly when one partner brought great wealth to the marriage: "I fondly congratulate Bill on the pleasure & pride it must be to him to have such a beautiful & distinguished captive to lead in his train & exhibit as his prize," he wrote Alice.[30]

Billy would never make his father's mark. When he finished high school at Browne and Nichols, Headmaster Browne wrote in his college recommendation, "He is not brilliant or quick; but solid, manly, clean & fine. I wish there were more such fellows in Harvard College."[31] Although Billy studied medicine for a time and was now an artist, his mother did not expect him to follow in his father's footsteps. In fact, he never developed his father's strength of character, revealing personal weaknesses as he aged.[32] But he could marry well, bringing Alice a desirable social connection. When he seemed to want to postpone the date, she applauded her future daughter-in-law's insistence on an early wedding. Writing to Alice Runnells, Alice explained her son's hesitation as a result of his own insecurities. "Billy will take every care that he may appear before you his old resolute self and henceforth he and you will be, together, safe from all his sad anxieties. They were all about himself—never about you, dear Alice."[33]

Like her aunt Alice James over forty years before, who had been too ill to attend William's wedding, Peggy was ill before this ceremony. Her tendency toward depression increased after her beloved father's death, Henry then consoling her: "You are reserved for high destinies and this evil episode a thing that will shrink like a shuffled off sticky garment—lying, when cast, in a vague heap on the floor."[34] At the eleventh hour Peggy rallied, however, and was part of the wedding, which took place on 6 January 1912.[35]

Although Alice was pleased at her son's choice of partners, she did not relish losing her children; they were all she had left of William. She reported to Billy that one of his childhood friends, Eileen Love, asked at supper, "'I miss Bill James. Why did he have to go off and get married?' To which no response was forthcoming."[36]

True to his promise to help Alice parent her children, Henry invited the newlyweds to honeymoon at Lamb House, he removing to the Reform Club to allow them privacy. They arrived in England at the end of January, and Henry sent them to Rye, housing them in Lamb House's east rooms.[37] They could stay as long as they liked. The newlyweds fit nicely into Henry's social milieu, and he enjoyed introducing this striking young couple to his friends. In all, he counted their visit a success: Alice left his cook, Joan Paddington, "ever so much better than she found her."[38]

While Billy and Alice honeymooned, the widow sought for William in the afterlife, others joining her.[39] During the spring of 1912 Theodate Pope sent Henry a paper written by someone purporting to be in communication with William. Henry told Peggy it was "a dozen typed pages of vulgar verbiage purporting to be a séance with your father, a thing inept & inane & offensive, without the faintest value, for me to 'glance at' & gossip with her about." Shocked, Henry scolded Theodate for sending the report.[40] He did not share her (and Alice's) belief that it might be possible to find William in this way.

Another cycle began when Alice welcomed her first grandchild, Alice and Billy's son, also named William, born 17 April 1913. Henry protested the name: this would be the fourth William James in the line, beginning with William of Albany. He had resented being Henry James Jr. The grandmother, however, approved the choice and found the baby handsome, a vigorous suckler and a good sleeper. Long ago, she told Henry, she and William had noticed "with our babies how curiously revealing the newborn creature is. He strikes the note of character so clearly—and then it dies away and we have the happy, slumbering, nursing, young animal."[41]

Glad to think of it as child-haunted again, Alice gave the Chocorua place to Billy's family for the next few years. Longing for a less feminine atmosphere, Alice considered moving to England to be near Henry when Aleck left home.[42] Alice's brother-in-law Leigh Gregor had died in Montreal of lung disease, so her youngest sister, Margaret, planned to return to 107 Irving Street to live with Eliza, leaving Alice free to go.[43] Always sensitive to Henry's needs, she judiciously weighed her relationship with him. She knew that he needed privacy, but she also knew how much he needed a sympathetic listener when depression struck.[44] In the end she decided not to go.

Casting about to keep busy, Alice began the improvements to the house that she and William had planned during the summer of 1910, effectively making 95 Irving Street a shrine to his memory. Henry applauded her work, as he, too, attached great value to the house. "William is there, always, as he is nowhere else, & to let go of it [the house] would be in a manner to lose part of our grasp . . . of him."[45] She installed electric lighting and remodeled the front hall, and she bought a new icebox for the kitchen.[46] Although Henry wished she did not have to work so hard, he knew the work soothed her, helping her keep her balance as she grew accustomed to a world without William. "I could wish you a more lotus-eating summer than the job of sawing planks and breaking bricks that you seem to be in for—& yet after all your lotuses have always been planks & bricks, when it hasn't been the shirt-buttons & the rent socks & the still more inward interests of your children & of all those that are yours."[47] All her life Alice had worked hard as a means of keeping depression at bay, and this time she sought the same remedy.

During the summer of 1912 Harry moved to New York to become the business manager for the Rockefeller Institute of Research, now Rockefeller University. Aleck continued to paint, relatively content and causing relatively little trouble. But Peggy presented more of a challenge. If she were to marry, then Alice must make sure it would be to someone emotionally stable enough to help Peggy conquer her depression. Uncle Henry advised Peggy, "Don't 'mind' depression (any more than you can help!) and it won't mind you."[48] Fearing her daughter might fall into the life of an invalid like her aunt Alice if she were not vigilant, Alice kept her busy paying visits to relatives and friends, including Bryn Mawr classmate Madeleine Edison, daughter of Thomas Alva Edison. Peggy's visit to the Edisons' Florida home lifted the depression that had blighted her since her father's death.

Alice also helped her daughter find solace in Swedenborg's credo. Now living in a boardinghouse in Cambridge with his daughter Mildred, widower William Dean Howells visited Alice in April 1913.[49] "I cannot tell you what a comfort it was to be with you the other day—to be with my own spiritual kind. We may not think Swedenborgianly any more, but we <u>feel</u> so. I did not make account enough of that beautiful and so noble experience of your daughter, which she gave so simply and so movingly."[50] Though extant documents contain no specific information on this experience, Alice and Peggy continued to seek spiritual consolation.

In the summer of 1913 Alice sent her daughter along with Harry to visit their uncle Henry. The pair arrived in England on 16 July, staying first in London. Henry fell ill after they arrived, taking to his bed in his flat, number 21, Carlyle Mansions, in Chelsea. On 22 July he and Peggy took the train to Rye, Harry going on to the Continent for the Rockefeller Institute. Alice did not accompany her children, though the winter before she had considered doing so.[51] She wrote to Fanny Prothero for advice and then sent Henry a cheerful letter, but she did not volunteer to visit.

Henry improved when his niece arrived. Despite his gout and heart ailment, he took long walks with her.[52] While she adored her uncle, the contrast between Henry and her departed father became occasionally painful. She confided in her "mammy," "To be quite candid, I miss any of Dad's quality in Uncle Henry—especially any spiritual or speculative turn. Speculative about people yes—but of any abstract occupations of mind I can see no glimmer."[53] For the first time her uncle seemed unreal to her. She disliked his friend Mary Cadwalader Jones, although Henry thought they were an excellent combination and urged his niece to visit Minnie in New York the next winter.[54] Peggy thought Mrs. Jones was silly.[55] Overall, she enjoyed her visit, though she found Dr. Skinner's garden party a dull affair, where ladies followed Uncle Henry about everywhere he went.[56]

That summer Peggy concluded that her uncle's poor diet was the root of his health problems: he thought he was eating well because he had given up sweets and stimulants, but in reality his diet was abysmal. Local Rye physician Dr. Des Voeux advised him to eat a wide variety of foods in small amounts, but actually he ate large quantities of the same thing, Peggy told Alice. "Every day for lunch three or four fried fish with mayonnaise sauce and potato chips, salad or some cold meat. . . . For dinner he eats fish in the same way, a good deal of meat and potato chips—very little green vegetables if any, and stewed fruit or a sweet. He is quite apt to have apple fritters!" When questioned about his unhealthy diet, Henry parroted what Dr. MacKenzie had told him: that he knew more about his own diet than the doctors and should be his own guide in matters of nutrition.[57]

On 20 September Peggy sailed home on the *Mauretania*, Henry hoping she would return next summer. In 1900 William had thought his daughter was like Henry, but now Peggy reminded Henry of her father. He praised his niece to her mother: "The beauty & interest & intelligence

& general large nobleness & sweetness of her endear to me more than I can say—we get on ideally together (she reminds me in mind & nature & tone intensely of her Father)."[58]

During her daughter's absence Alice continued searching for William. In July she heard his name, or at least heard it spelled out in Morse code.[59] When Peggy returned from England, she joined her mother in these searches. Henry was receptive when Peggy told him that a medium had sent a message for him. The woman spoke of a wheeled chair, which Henry thought meant the old armchair in his upstairs study, a chair with smoothly rolling castors, or the wheeled chair could refer to the bath chair he used in London, the first time in his life he could not walk everywhere. The medium also told Alice and Peggy that Henry repeatedly looked at his sister Alice through a plate of glass. This, he decided, referred to his deceased sister's two glazed photographs, one hung over his desk and the other near the fireplace. No matter which way he turned, her image always hung before him. Further, the medium mentioned the golden bowl given him by his friends for his seventieth birthday.[60] Still skeptical of supernatural powers, Henry conjectured that this was a case of mental telepathy, that the medium disengaged these images from the minds of the sitters, who had seen them at Lamb House. She selected these particular items from the millions of things in her sitters' consciousness. Struck by the message's accuracy, he wished a similar communication would come from William.

Besides searching for William beyond the pale, Alice and the family continued to promote his worldly reputation. Peggy wanted to transcribe the notes he had scribbled in his books and publish them as his marginalia. Henry was thrilled with the idea, more so than with hearing William's ghostly voice, if there was enough substantial material to make the project worthwhile, but Harry discouraged his sister.[61] He feared his father's jottings might reflect poorly on his published work, possibly a sign that Harry did not understand William's beliefs, which were always developing, always changing. Publishing his marginalia would present his thought in progress, in that flux he exalted.

Henry negotiated with Scribner's for "Early Letters of William James, with Notes by Henry James," a project that never saw fruition.[62] Instead, he memorialized his brother in autobiographical accounts of their youth.

He and Harry had misunderstandings over how and how much Henry would use William's letters, as Harry feared his uncle's project might detract from his and Alice's projected "William James Letters." Henry had used, quoted, and misquoted his brother to create his imaginative account of their childhood, his autobiography. As he prepared the book for publication, he told his nephew that if he called the first volume "A Small Boy and Others" he would be bound to call the second "<u>A Big Boy & Others</u>—the boy being again me, & the pre-eminent of the others your Dad."[63] Harry, who sometimes lacked the Jameses' dry humor, was not amused.

Despite the wrangling over the letters edition, Henry thrilled Alice with the first volume of the autobiography, *A Small Boy and Others*, received just before Peggy went abroad. After finishing two-thirds of the book, she praised it to him. "I cannot begin to tell you how beautiful it seems to me. I suspect you have made there an imperishable record of a child—an immortal child. And the grace,—and the tenderness—and the charm!"[64] Alice relayed the book's enthusiastic reception by old Cambridge family friends Sally Norton, Arthur Sedgwick, and John Gray: "Everybody worth counting is enchanted with the <u>Small Boy</u>."[65]

Henry struggled, in Rye and London, working some days and unable to work others, battling depression, stomach woes, gout, shingles. The family heart ailment was pursuing its now familiar course. He kept up his social engagements as best he could, but he divulged his woes to Alice and Peggy in long letters. He would not return to Irving Street or to America, despite his continued love for his brother's family. "Think of me as nearing my time-limit," he told his niece.[66]

Though still largely preoccupied with Jameses, Alice received a link to her own past at Christmas 1913. Harry gave her a cutout silhouette of her grandfather Daniel Gibbens in a long frock coat and pointed shoes. This ghostly representation of her father's family thrilled her; the Gibbenses had nearly been submerged beneath the sheer number and weight of the Jameses. Although she had been only five years old when Daniel Gibbens Sr. died, she remembered him fondly. "He was a dear old man in my childish memory and I have come to recognize qualities of mind and character that I hope may still return—as they have. Thank you with all my heart dear Harry for this splendid present. But you must never give me another!! I have no more grandfathers."[67]

In March 1914 Alice was stricken with herpes zoster, or shingles, an inflammation of the nerves with accompanying neuralgia. Henry advised she take morphine, as he should have done when he was afflicted with the disease. In 1912 and 1913 he had had a severe case, aggravated by stomach problems.[68] That same month the second volume of Henry's autobiography, *Notes of a Son and Brother*, came out. Henry made liberal use of his cousin Minny Temple's letters to John Gray. "The whole working-in of Minny was difficult & delicate—highly so; but I seem already to gather here that my evocation of her appears by her touchingness & beauty, <u>the</u> 'stroke,' or success, of the book," he boasted to Alice.[69]

A bright, vibrant young woman, Minny Temple died in 1870 of tuberculosis. Her death had been one of the tragedies of William and Henry's youth. In May 1913 Harvard Law School dean John Gray brought Alice Minny's letters to him. Gray did not want the letters to go to Minny's family, the Temples or the Emmets. When Alice asked if she might give them to Henry, Gray left that decision to her. She found them "a gallant and haunting record—almost too perfect to be broken up," she confessed to her brother-in-law, but she knew that he would make good use of them. She wished William had seen the letters.[70]

When Alice read *Notes*, she thought it even better than *A Small Boy and Others* and longed to read it aloud to William. She found Minny's portrait compelling, having the strange feeling that she had received all the rich life Minny relinquished by her early death. She confessed her feelings to Henry: "You may not understand in the least how I feel but it almost seems as if I had had all that she deserved. Were you ever haunted by a 'vicarious atonement' feeling? That some one else was going without that you might be blessed?"[71] John Gray too was pleased; he found Henry's representation of Minny wonderfully done.

Besides Henry, who was across the Atlantic and often ill, Harry was Alice's greatest ally during the years after William's death, carrying out family duties and always solicitous of his mother's welfare. In the spring of 1914, after Peggy left on a second trip for England, Alice visited Harry in New York. When she finally made up her mind to go, Peggy applauded. "I had despaired of your ever going to New York but you are like the Lord's mills, isn't it in the Bible? You get to a thing in the fullness of your own time if it is a thing worth the doing!"[72] When Alice arrived, the city seemed foreign, but nonetheless she enjoyed her visit. She took tea at the Rockefeller Institute where Harry worked; she rode on the top of a bus to see Webb relatives Mary and Louis; and she visited the Natural History Museum. She was pleased to learn that Harry was respected in New York's business circles. She even made a day trip to Milford, Pennsylvania, where Charles Peirce, nearly forgotten and poor, had died of cancer on 20 April, to pay a condolence call to his second wife, Juliette.[73]

She returned to find her tulips emerging on the south side of her porch.[74] Eliza Gibbens had given up her dream of wintering in a warmer climate, deciding to stay put at 107 Irving Street, but Alice wanted no such life. She begged Peggy, "When I get to be 86 I hope that you will cheer me on to <u>take risks</u> — not to be any older than I have to be."[75] Fighting the limitations imposed upon elderly widowed women, she loved life too much to bury herself.

When Peggy returned to England in April 1914, bringing with her a distant cousin, Margaret Payson, and a maid, England was not yet at war. Henry found a flat for the girls in London in between having teeth pulled as a palliative for his sinking health. He thought Peggy's presence would rally him, so he worked hard to expedite her stay.[76] When they arrived, the young women immediately entered London's social whirl, thanks to Henry's connections. They saw Lady Ottoline Morrell, and Peggy brightened when the woman announced she had just reread William's *Principles of Psychology*: "She said her walk and talk with him [William] five years ago was one of the big things in her life. I believe her," she told her mother.[77] But while Peggy still missed her father, this time she felt utterly at home with her uncle.

While Peggy was in London that spring, Mrs. Mary Wood took a meat cleaver hidden beneath her cloak and made three gashes in John Singer Sargent's birthday portrait of Henry, which hung in the Royal Academy. Mrs. Wood did not know the writer, but she learned the painting was valued at seven hundred pounds, so she attacked it in protest, claiming that a woman painter would never receive such a large sum. Peggy protested loudly to Alice: "Isn't this last suffragette outrage too sickening? It is simply frightful."[78] These early feminists challenged Alice's choice of traditional roles, and she had passed her opinions of them to her daughter.

Although Peggy tried to be open-minded about women's rights, attending a suffrage meeting and tea at Mrs. Prothero's, she was largely unsympathetic to the cause.[79] Just after Mrs. Wood's attack on the painting, Peggy visited Theodora Bosanquet, her uncle's secretary, and three of Theodora's friends. She applauded their willingness to work, but, she told her mother, "they had a distinctly self-sufficient attitude and tone and a consciousness of being clever that seemed a great pity to me. I fear that lots of the new women haven't yet digested their new freedom or intellectual attainments, which after all amount to what?"[80] There were some things in this changing world neither Peggy nor Alice could accept. Though both believed in higher education for women, they did not believe women must assume public roles.

Alice and Peggy were part of a larger movement of antisuffragists sometimes called "remonstrants." In America prominent women and men in Boston and New York led the movement. Elite women feared a mass electorate might diminish the privilege and access to power they enjoyed as wives and daughters of influential men.[81] Women's clubs, charity associations, temperance campaigns, and evangelical crusades provided the antisuffragists their own networks; they feared enfranchisement would end these complex feminine, personal associations. They viewed employment opportunities for women in offices and industry as evil, not as social progress.[82] Satisfied with the lives they led and unwilling to surrender their own prestige as relatives of two famous men to make their own way in the world, Alice and Peggy naturally fell into this group.

Aleck and a friend came to England that summer, giving Henry even more interest, though he found Aleck's fellow artist, Demmler, an "incubus." The summer before Henry had fretted to Alice about his nephew's friends and connections ("I wish he could see people & 'have society' of a more developed & informing type than seems to be the case"), but still he held great hopes for the young man's artistic career.[83]

In July Peggy, Margaret, Aleck, and Demmler motored through England for several days, and then Peggy went to Rye, where she met more of her uncle's friends: writer Hugh Walpole, popular Victorian novelist Mrs. Humphry Ward, drama critic Desmond MacCarthy, writer Vernon Lee, and poet Rupert Brooke.[84] Peggy had a crush on Rupert Brooke, pasting a picture of him in her scrapbook.[85] By the end of July she decided that she would marry an Englishman and settle there, having a job and writing on the side, a contradiction of her former views.[86] Perhaps she remembered her childhood idea that it would be easy to write a novel, if she could only find an idea.

While Alice's children vacationed in England, to her dismay and to Henry's the war on the Continent escalated. William's death had marked the end of an era; their insular world was on the verge of dramatic transformation. Europe was on the eve of war, England involved before America, which remained more or less isolationist until 1917. On 4 August England declared war on Germany; tension ran high among the British. Henry reassured Alice that all was well with her family. He would send her daughter and son home the moment she commanded, but at present Peggy and Aleck were held spellbound, watching history unfold before their eyes.

Despite his despair at the war, Henry admitted that the situation was thrilling. American tourists fleeing the Continent crowded London, waiting for passage home. Because of England's strong naval presence, the Atlantic was still safe. Henry rejoiced that William had not lived to see "the abyss of this collapse & of this bitterness." England sent 100,000 troops to allied France, while huge Russian forces massed at Germany's eastern border, so Henry was hopeful as to the war's outcome. But in the meantime, between the escalating war and his declining health, he was relieved to send Peggy and Aleck back to Cambridge in October. Alice considered going to Italy that year, but Henry told her such a trip was a delusion, as Italy was cut off from the rest of the world as it hung between peace and war.[87]

That fall Harry traveled to Belgium with the Rockefeller war relief effort. Henry assured Alice that her son was safe because esteemed American minister Brand Whitlock refused to leave the embassy in Belgium, even when ordered to do so by the Germans. Whitlock would do everything possible for Alice's son and his companions.[88] Harry spent twenty-five days in Belgium and another four days in northern France behind German lines. He hoped to go into Serbia later.[89] On Saturday, 20 March, Harry sailed for home on the *Lusitania*, spending a few days with his uncle before he embarked.

Harry reached home safely, but Theodate Pope, who sailed on the *Lusitania* in May 1915, was not as fortunate. On 7 May 1915 the ship was sunk by a German submarine off Queenstown, Ireland; 1,153 persons died, among them 14 Americans. The British vessel was unarmed, though the Germans protested that it carried guns and ammunitions for the Allies. At 2:45 p.m. Theodate jumped into the sea, wearing a lifebelt. She was picked up as a floating corpse by a tugboat at 5:00 p.m. that day but began breathing when a woman worked on her. At 11:00 p.m. she regained consciousness: actively warming her up had enabled her to breathe again.[90] Her maid, also in a lifebelt, was lost, however.[91] Alice sympathized with Henry's horror, but she still refused to believe that her beloved Germans, as a race, were evil.

By now Aleck was a great comfort to Alice. With William gone, the pressure on the young man to succeed lightened. Alice accepted his artistic ambitions, supporting him financially. A gentle, likeable young man who gave her little trouble, he lived with her when he was not in Dublin, New Hampshire, studying with Abbott Thayer or traveling with friends.[92] He no longer had to compete with William for Alice's attention.

During the summer of 1914, when Aleck was in London, he saw Frederika Paine, whom he had met at the Museum School in Boston in 1912, when she was only seventeen. Her father was also in London that summer, and Henry apparently met him, as he told Peggy that Frederika's father was a "feeble enough person."[93] The couple courted in London because Henry refused to let Aleck bring Frederika to Lamb House, in part because of his poor health but also because he knew Alice disapproved of the courtship. He felt the young woman monopolized his nephew's time and money, and she wanted to sail home with him, a plan that Henry disapproved. When the couple asked to announce their engagement, Alice and Henry declared that they would not acknowledge it. Michael James, Aleck and Frederika's son, claims that when Aleck brought Frederika to 95 Irving Street to meet his mother, Alice would not invite the couple to enter the house.[94] No formal announcement was made in 1914.

At least two possible reasons existed for Alice and Henry's objections. One concerned Frederika's mother, who was of questionable character. In her memoir Frederika explained her family history. Her father, Frederick H. Paine, had been a naval lieutenant and inventor of a torpedo. When he took a position in Paris, he and his beautiful wife, Marion Isabelle Myers Paine, moved to France with their young daughter, and the Paines became part of Parisian society. But suddenly Mr. Paine and Frederika left Paris, leaving her mother behind with their French maid, Marie.[95] Apparently, Mrs. Paine had abandoned her family to pursue various adulterous affairs. Frederika's oldest son, Alexander R. James, stated that his grandmother left her family to live with the marquis de Choiseul, eventually marrying him. Together the couple preyed on sculptor Auguste Rodin because they wanted his estate: Marion Paine was Rodin's mistress for seven years.[96] According to one account, she would get drunk and perform a striptease for the aged artist.[97] Finally, Marion Paine de Choiseul married a Monsieur Twombley, whom she also outlived.

Another reason for Alice's disapproval may have been Frederika's upbringing. In Paris she was often left with the maid, who spanked her regularly and took her to dance halls at night. Family lore has it that Marie encouraged the young girl to dance on the table, the maid pocketing the centimes the child earned.[98]

When Frederika returned to America with her father, they settled in Newport, where a succession of French governesses took care of the girl. Though her father wanted her to mingle with upper-class people, Frederika vowed, "I hoped that never never would I be rich and I knew that never would I envy people because they had palaces and horses and all the white gloves they wanted. There had been too many quarrels behind the scenes." Later, she remembered her father as gay, courageous, honest, and devoted, and with grace she forgave her mother.[99]

Despite her disappointment over the engagement, Alice had other matters to occupy her. By 1911 Mrs. Piper had given up trances and turned to automatic writing.[100] Alice and Peggy decided they also would try automatic writing, a method of delving into the unconscious mind or into cosmic consciousness. At Thanksgiving 1914 Peggy received a message about Aleck. The message was not from William but from another unnamed spirit. One evening in the midst of incoherent markings Peggy's hand started to draw. Alice inferred that this message concerned Aleck, who was trying to become a painter. The next morning Miss Closson, who gave Eliza Gibbens massages, helped Peggy write out the message. "'Tell Aleck from me not to delay to come directly home to you (A.H.J.) now because time is flying and he must be at work. Allow him to choose his school himself and attend to all the business connected with his Art, and allow him to choose his abiding place.'" Alice asked the unseen spirit whether Aleck might be able to paint with his older brother Billy: "'No, sorry, but not possible.'" She compared the message to dim lights seen far offshore whose warning should be heeded no matter how faint a beam they cast.[101] It expressed her wish to keep Aleck at home, away from Frederika. Not admitting that the messages might derive from her own needs and desires, she allowed the spirit world to guide her decision making.

As the war escalated, Alice, now sixty-five years old, longed to contribute to the Allied cause. After she heard Harry speak at a fundraiser for the Serbians, she decided that she should go to Serbia, accompanying a nurse's corps as housemother.[102] She insisted that she was in very good health, mentioning that when her sister Mary had diphtheria as a child, Alice slept in the same bed with her and never caught the disease. Peggy was not strong enough to travel, and Alice did not know who would take care of her daughter, but she was desperate to leave complacent Cambridge.

While she had complained little since her husband's death, Alice felt she could wait no longer to live her life. She had done her duty to her family, and now she wanted active service to enact the convictions she had held since childhood. "I am so tired—so <u>tired</u> of my empty life. I have been the most private-spirited of human creatures. I never lived at all till your father found me and then his great life, and all our joy in you children and each other and all the activities of our family life—it all filled my days and made my horizon, and it has all vanished. In going to serve a human need elsewhere I am not turning my back on anyone I love or neglecting a single duty. Dear Harry, help me!" She held off mailing her letter for a day to see whether her feelings were as strong the next morning: they were.[103]

Two days later British historian Sir George Trevelyan breakfasted with Alice Runnells, Billy, and Peggy.[104] Alice did not join them, but Peggy, guessing her mother's plans, insisted that she meet them after breakfast. When Sir George told her that she was too old and that the English forces had turned down many such offers from well-intentioned people who could add nothing to the war effort, Alice accepted the bad news gracefully. She had only wanted to be a form of use once more.[105]

On 4 June 1915, travel to England difficult, Alice and Peggy set out for California to visit Katharine Hooker, who now lived in San Francisco on Pacific Avenue. It was a wonderful summer to visit the city, as the Panama-Pacific International Exposition, one of America's most beloved world fairs, was under way when they arrived. The fair celebrated the completion of the Panama Canal and commemorated the four-hundred-year anniversary of Balboa reaching the Pacific. San Francisco competed with other cities to host the event, but in 1911 President Taft announced that the California city had won the competition. Psychologically and economically, the event was important to the earthquake-damaged city. Alice and Peggy found the fair endlessly fascinating, especially the horse that did arithmetic, made change from a cash register, and played a verse of "Nearer My God to Thee."[106]

Architect Bruce Porter, who by a great coincidence was a friend and disciple of Henry James, had designed Mrs. Hooker's striking home. Architect, writer, critic, and art promoter, Porter was a presence in the San Francisco arts community. In addition to the Robert Louis Stevenson Memorial in Portsmouth Square, he had designed the stained-glass windows in San Francisco's Swedenborgian Church. He helped organize and promote the 1913 New York Armory art exhibit and also edited a literary magazine, the *Lark*, with Frank Gellett Burgess.[107] A practicing socialist for a time, he had become an elite, refined, hypersensitive, self-made man.[108]

During his stop in San Francisco during the spring of 1905 Henry met Porter, later remembering him as his "best human recollection of California."[109] The day after Henry left the city Bruce told Kate Hooker, in whom he confided nearly everything, how intense their meeting had been and how much they had meant to one another. "We hit it off from the very first instant that he came in—the good round man in clothes that had a hint of shabbiness—with the fine head on top & the kind, sad eyes. . . . O! I'm set up! The police man on the corner knows there's something wrong with me. It's perceptible to any casual Chinaman—that I've had a romantic adventure." Porter was tempted to follow Henry to his next stop in Seattle.[110]

While Porter was in England investigating the Bacon-Shakespearean authorship controversy during the summer of 1910, the two men met again, just before Henry left with Alice and William for Chocorua.[111]

Porter had contracted the measles, but he and Henry managed a brief lunch in London before he fell ill. The two never met again, but Henry wrote at least once. Overtones of his playful erotic interest emerge in the letter Henry wrote Porter in 1911, while Peggy lay critically ill from her appendectomy, the letter that was interrupted during one of her crises. Apologizing for the lapse in their correspondence, Henry wrote, "You will even for a long, long time say nothing whatever—so far as my catching any echo of it is concerned; & with the beautiful magnanimity & the noble intelligence that you have always treated me to so abounding a measure of, will simply believe me & trust me & 'like' me still, simply take the inevitability of the whole thing from me as part of the penalty of having so calculably incalculable & so irregularly regular a <u>lover</u>."[112]

On 16 June Porter came to Katharine Hooker's home and was introduced to Peggy James and her mother. Alice found him refined. Peggy and Bruce felt comfortable together immediately because both adored Henry James. Uncle Henry rejoiced to learn that his niece was seeing his old friend.[113]

Alice and Peggy enjoyed their visit so much that they stayed in California for more than six weeks. During the visit Alice, Kate, and Porter made a trip to the Sonoma and Santa Rosa valleys, visiting a utopian community in Santa Rosa. Alice had great interest in this experiment: the communal movement had been one outgrowth of the antebellum perfectionist movement. A Universalist minister, Thomas Lake Harris, had founded a periodical to propagate Swedenborgian views, though by 1857 he claimed to have gone beyond Swedenborg in his understanding of the scripture.[114] In 1858 he had founded his own church, Church of the Good Shepherd, in New York State. He freely adapted the doctrines of Swedenborgian French social theorist Charles Fourier, who advocated reorganizing society into phalanxes, self-sufficient units that redesigned conventional living arrangements, property ownership, and marriage. William had corresponded with Harris, who claimed to have discovered eternal youth, but he confided to Henry Rankin that the man's projects seemed unwholesome.[115]

Bruce Porter, who followed some of Swedenborg's teachings, was also interested in Harris's community, so he made inquiries, and the trio visited the place where the group settled. The commune had owned rich vineyards and three hundred acres of fruit orchards. Only one old Japanese man named Kanaye Nagasaw now lived in "that house of so many sorrows." The polite caretaker gave them ice cream and answered their questions. Alice thought Henry should visit and then write about this haunting spot.

That night they stayed nearby in a little hotel in St. Helena, and the next day they drove to the top of St. Helena Mountain. The party climbed up train tracks to the abandoned Silverado Mine, where Robert Louis Stevenson had honeymooned. Sixty-six-year-old Alice experienced no difficulties with the ascent. The last day they toured through the Napa and Vallejo valleys. She shared the Sierra's natural wonders with Harry. "I shall never forget one long day through the great swirling valleys Napa, Vallejo, and many another, olive groves, fruit orchards of vast extent, the great Zinfandel vineyards, and always the encircling wall of blue mountains."[116]

Alice began to appreciate Bruce Porter during this three-day tour, and he tried to accommodate himself to her.[117] After Porter saw a copy of one of Billy's portraits in the July issue of *International Studio* magazine, he made suggestions and praised his potential, a move sure to please a fond mother.[118]

Peggy gained remarkably during their visit. She liked the Californians, young and old, and made special friends with Marian Hooker, a medical doctor and Katharine's only daughter. During the summer Peggy came to know Dr. Martin Fischer, a physiologist, and his wife, Charlotte. Fischer had been on the faculty at Berkeley and was preparing to go to the University of Cincinnati. Childless Mrs. Fischer planned to do research in the public schools, and she asked Peggy to be her assistant, also inviting Marian Hooker to participate. The two young women could find a small apartment together near the Fischers. Alice was relieved. "I feel as if my great problem was solved, i.e. how to get Peggy settled," she told her eldest son.[119] That fall Peggy went to Cincinnati, and Henry congratulated her on her noble work. While he longed to see his niece, he did not want to take her from her mission, nor did he want her coming abroad during the escalating conflict.[120] The Cincinnati work for the Fischers must not have been as satisfactory as Alice and Peggy hoped, however, because by December 1915 Peggy had gone back to California.[121] Too, her living situation with Marian Hooker had proved difficult.[122] Perhaps, also, she missed Bruce Porter. By now they were fast friends, a friendship based on their mutual love and admiration for Henry James.

Lonely in Cambridge without her daughter, in December Alice went to New York to live with Harry for the winter, an experiment she hoped might work. She was not there long, however, when Harry received a cablegram from Uncle Henry, who was at Carlyle Mansions: "'Had slight stroke this morning. No serious symptoms. Perfect care. No suffering. Wrote Peggy yesterday.'"[123]

It was hard to secure passage because the war raged on the Continent, but within thirty-six hours Alice had embarked in the middle of a winter storm, sharing a berth with a stranger in a small stateroom.[124] Desolate when the ship left the dock, she remembered what William had asked her the last week of his life: "'Promise me that you will see Henry through when he comes to the end.'" She was not sure that Henry would want her there constantly, but Alice could not break that promise.[125] She did not anticipate staying in London long because Peggy would take her place at her uncle's bedside, but it was time for her to nurse another dying James. On 4 December, just before leaving, she dashed off a quick note to Eliza.

> I am off in an hour. I seemed to be the only one who
> could make this boat. I hope I can be of use or comfort to
> Henry—Dearest love to you all.
>
> > Yr loving Alice
> > Give me a thought blessed Mother![126]

⚜17 Passages

ALICE ARRIVED IN LIVERPOOL on 13 December 1915. Her passage on the *New York* went relatively well despite the weather, which caused the roughest crossing the steward had seen in fifteen years. Though her errand was a grim one, she made friends onboard. Her roommate was a Miss Moseley, who drank strychnine instead of bromide the day before the voyage. She ended up in bed with Alice's hot-water bottle while Alice took bromide and walked on the deck.[1]

Before the voyage's end Alice became well acquainted with a number of the passengers. None of them traveled abroad for pleasure; all had serious business of one sort or another. They included Butler, an Englishman on his way back from China to join the British army; Dr. Braithwaite, who worked in Paris for the American ambulance corps; another American physician, Anderson, a specialist in antitoxins; and Miss Lowles, the manager of Lady Duff-Gordon's dress-making establishment. Alice was particularly interested in Miss Lowles, whose firm did complete makeovers for women, including hats, dresses, shoes, and even hairstyles. Alice proclaimed Lady Duff-Gordon a genius and vowed to visit the firm if she ever bought clothes again. Along the way she read Zola's account of the injustices of the Dreyfus case, *J'accuse!* in an English translation.[2]

Arriving a day late due to the weather, Alice reached London at 11:30

p.m. on 13 December. Fanny and Sir George Prothero, accompanied by Burgess Noakes, met her at Euston. From there she took a taxi to Garlant's Hotel, and by 10:00 a.m. the next morning she was at Henry's flat, where she found Theodora Bosanquet, Henry's secretary since 1907, and servants Minnie Kidd and Burgess, along with two nurses, one taking the day shift and one the night. Henry was so glad to see her that all her fears of being unwanted washed away. It was evident to Alice that she must stay there through the nights, as he wanted her near him nearly constantly.[3]

The next weeks would prove a roller-coaster ride as Henry dipped precariously in and out of consciousness, his recovery at best tenuous. He had angina, which he previously had interpreted as digestive problems. Recently, he had started taking digitalis, as William had. He had suffered a stroke, which damaged his brain and paralyzed his left side, and he had also contracted pneumonia in his right lung. Just after the first stroke he had another, lesser one. Henry had to be moved in a wheelchair through his flat. The doctor believed he would make a partial recovery, though he thought the writer would never again be able to do significant work. It would take all Alice's remaining stamina to nurse him, but she believed that the patience she had learned from nursing William would stand her in good stead. Although she had hesitated to come, fearing forcing herself upon him, she realized immediately that, far from being in his way, Henry desperately needed and wanted her soothing, embodied presence.

One of her first tasks was to take authority for Henry's various affairs, a task that, in addition to household management, included negotiating Theodora's involvement. Alice judged that Theodora had done admirably, but the woman looked weary.[4] Slowly but surely, Alice weaned Henry's amanuensis from his side, confident she was doing what was best for the ailing giant. The doctor advised keeping all visitors away, as they would tire his patient, but Alice feared that Theodora would try to countermand this order, especially in the case of Edith Wharton.[5] When she let a message from Wharton through, Alice reacted quickly and virtually banned the woman from Henry's Chelsea flat.

Theodora had been with Henry during the last months, loyal and attentive to his needs. She was a bright, independent, capable person, not eager to relinquish her authority to a sixty-seven-year-old woman she scarcely knew. At age thirty-five she would not want to change her work, or so

Alice believed, and she wanted to give Theodora some sort of settlement if Henry had not remembered her in his will.[6] Theodora represented everything Alice disliked about the women's movement. Alice's vocation had been different: her work, since she resigned her teaching post in 1878, had been unpaid but demanding. She was on firm footing now, doing the work she had done all her life, tasks that she believed were her rightful purview.

Theodora defended Alice's presence, particularly to the night nurse, who said that Alice insisted on staying up all night with Henry but lacked the physical strength to lift him.[7] Alice, on the other hand, thought Theodora disturbed Henry. The secretary sometimes had her typewriter set up in his bedroom for dictation, but Alice asked her to take the machine away, claiming that hearing its noise twelve hours a day was disturbing.[8] During this time Alice made well-intentioned efforts to be fair, just as Theodora maintained a professional demeanor toward her. When Alice took over paying the monthly bills, she claimed that Minnie Kidd had asked her if she would mind doing it instead of Theodora. Alice defended Henry's longtime secretary to Peggy: "This [turning money matters over] does not imply any dislike or mistrust of her [Theodora]. On the contrary, she had been an invaluable support to the whole household."[9]

Much later, Theodora Bosanquet told Leon Edel her impression of Alice during Henry's last days. She felt that Alice was eager to control information coming in and out of the flat. Alice knew that Theodora sent frequent posts to Edith Wharton on Henry's condition. As Alice disliked Mrs. Wharton, she resented Theodora allowing the writer to remain informed. From Theodora's perspective, recalled nearly forty years later, "Edith Wharton . . . was such a well-established and firm friend of Henry James, and so very unhappy about his condition."[10] Perhaps it was not possible for the two women to find common ground, given their very different histories. Neither seemed able to negotiate the other's differences. Long afterward, Theodora noted, "Looking back on those difficult days, I rather imagine that Mrs. James very much preferred having her dau. [Peggy] at hand rather than a secretarial assistant for whom there was so little work."[11] She regretted leaving Henry's side" "I can only regret more than ever that Mrs. William James appeared to have no use for me or my services after a short time."[12]

The day before Alice's arrival, Henry manifested Napoleonic delusions. He rambled about the Bonaparte family from his own point of view, as if he were one of them. Then he dictated letters in the style of Napoleon, his sentences clearly formed. The first letter went to Alice and William. They were to decorate apartments in the Louvre, keeping him informed of their progress. The work "is, you will see, of a great scope, a majesty unsurpassed by any work of the kind yet undertaken in France." He signed this first dictation "Napoleone." Also addressed to his "Brother and Sister," the second letter offered great opportunities in a minor capital of the republic. He exhorted them to take this chance; their failure would be judged severely. "Don't leave me a sorry figure in consequence but present me rather as your fond but not too infatuated relation, able and ready to back you up, your faithful Brother and Brother-in-law, Henry James."[13] His feverish imagination led him to elevate Alice and William to royal status, a status consistent with their importance in his life.

In the days and weeks that followed his delusions took the form of travel. Henry himself called this a "geographical muddle." Sometimes he thought he was staying on the coast of Ireland in strange rooms.[14] Just after Alice's arrival he believed that he was in California in rooms that looked like his Chelsea quarters.[15] One day he found himself in Cork, where his rooms also resembled his flat, and later talked of California and its lack of a past—"It stands like a shabby beggar hat in hand, asking for a few pennies.'"[16] Often he thought he was traveling in foreign cities. At times he believed he was on a ship, perhaps because he sometimes reclined on a lounge near the window with a view of the Thames. When he called Burgess one day and Alice said he was out, Henry commented, "'How extraordinary that Burgess should be leaving the ship to do errands!'"[17] It was painful for Alice to think that he might outlive his brain, as she knew that a life of inactivity could do nothing but frustrate him. Despite his ramblings during these weeks, however, Peggy claimed that he had coherent moments, though when he said things like "'Now I must rest from my sensibilities and discriminations,' the nurses thought he was delirious when he was talking naturally."[18]

Two days after her arrival Alice's patient held steady, and at first she anticipated a long illness. She adjured Harry and Peggy to stay in New York for now. The following days were relatively peaceful. Alice sat and talked with Henry when he wanted her, religiously keeping visitors and messages away. He loved having her there.[19] He began to regain movement on his left side, first in his left fingers and next in his left foot. When his appetite returned, he ate fish and mashed potatoes for dinner. His spirits rose, and one evening he asked the night nurse if people his age ever recovered. The nurse replied that she knew a lady over eighty who recovered so well that she knit socks for the soldiers.[20]

On 19 December Dr. Des Voeux found another small clot on Henry's lung, but his heart remained strong, and the doctor hoped that there would not be another attack of pneumonia.[21] Henry continued to progress the week before Christmas, eating a baked apple and a piece of cake and drinking orange juice. Still unable to move, he had to be lifted day and night.[22] Despite his progress and though she had thought a week earlier that he might have a long convalescence, by 21 December Alice feared he might die soon. He had pleurisy, he ran a temperature of 101°, and he was weaker. She sat with her patient during the days, holding his hand with her right hand and keeping pressure on his shoulder with her left. She sat frequently with him until late at night.[23] He did not want to be alone, and he craved these healing physical touches.

On Christmas Day Henry was wheeled into his dining room, where he sat for two hours shifting restlessly and asking to be moved, taking a bit of milk and egg for his Christmas feast. He paid attention when Alice announced that Peggy was on her way: he thought her visit would help him most.[24] After the holiday Dr. Des Voeux started Henry on a weekly shot of digitalis for his heart and thought that he would continue to regain the use of his left side.[25] The doctor also prescribed bromide and valerian to counteract his nervousness, as Henry was exhausting the nurses, Burgess, and Minnie Kidd.

At this holiday season Alice found London dark and somber, its climate oppressive, a white, wet fog hiding the views of the Thames and the arched bridge. "Everything is a soft grey blur outside through which I lately caught sight of the sun very small and tight and red."[26] Despite the weather she took forty-five-minute walks to keep up her own health and spirits. "The bridge, the shafts of light and waving wreaths of smoke from opposite chimneys, the scow barges always gliding past make a perpetual picture. Endless Turners," she informed Harry.[27] On 1 January Henry's name appeared on the New Year's Honours List. He had been awarded the Order of Merit. A letter from Lord Stamfordham dated 28 December, with messages from the king, had come to Henry announcing the honor, and on 9 January Alice asked Theodora to write a response, though she believed the response should have come sooner. "Mrs. James is a bit worried & puzzled by this kind of English etiquette & prefers, I think, to forget it," Theodora noted in her diary.[28]

Peggy arrived during the first week in January, and on 11 January, William's birthday, Alice again feared the end was near, mourning the passing of a man so noble. "He has done good to all men, all the days of his life, a lonely being with all the sad insights into other hearts," she wrote Billy.[29] That afternoon Henry's temperature rose, and he was chilled. After three hot-water bottles, warm covers, and two spoonfuls of brandy in his milk, the chills passed, and he fell asleep. By evening, however, he had a fever of 102°, and the doctor was called back. Henry claimed he had pain in his chest. The doctor thought he would live another three or four weeks at most, but again he rallied. By Wednesday morning his temperature had dropped, and his mind was clearer: he recognized his night nurse, and his vacant look disappeared. He asked Alice what had happened to him. He feared his leg would be operated on, so she reassured him that there would be no surgery. He told Minnie Kidd he wanted to go to Rye as soon as he could be transported so that he would have more room for his family.[30]

While he lived past William's birthday, after this episode Henry's mind deteriorated further, though he still struggled to understand the extent of his illness. At first he conceptualized it as a long tunnel with a blue light at the end.[31] Later he explained his state as the result of a blow to the head so severe that he was fortunate not to have sustained more damage.[32] If he could only see William for four minutes, he could ask his brother to explain what had happened to him.[33]

Henry slept enough now that Alice could pursue her own activities. On Sundays she went to St. Ethelburga's, a high Anglican church, because she liked the preacher, overcoming her decades-old prejudice against candles and incense and genuflections to hear him. This was for her soul.[34] For her material being Alice managed to find time for shopping. Just three weeks before Henry's death she had a prevision of retrospect that Peggy would need mourning clothes, so the two women found a tailor shop and ordered a black suit. The shop owner also carried furniture, and Alice found four early Victorian mirrors that might work for Alice and Billy, who had bought the lot next to her on Irving Street and planned to build a house there. The man asked ten pounds for all four.[35] In another shop she found cups and saucers with gilt edges that she wanted for Harry.[36]

Alice and Peggy also participated in war relief efforts. Peggy worked mornings at the Serbian relief center, and Alice rolled bandages in Miss Emily Sargent's apartment in the afternoon.[37] The two American women admired the courage these women evinced in facing what was happening to their husbands and sons, most of them serving in the British forces. Sir Ian Hamilton's nephew was in a German prison, and every week his mother sent him a package of bread, chocolate, and cigarettes. A German officer took the chocolate and cigarettes and gave only the bread to the British soldier.[38]

Alice continued her walks. One afternoon she saw a home she coveted, full of exquisite paintings and with a lovely garden, the home of a man who had gone down on the *Lusitania*. In another, hypothetically constructed life, she would find a partner to buy this house with her and live on the embankment of the Thames.[39] In her imagination she defined herself differently: no family, only herself and a partner in this handsome home.

When Harry arrived in early February, Uncle Henry did not recognize him. Although it seemed strange to consider the disposal of Henry's things while he still lived, Alice wanted to make some arrangements while Harry was with her. On 9 February Harry sailed for France, having helped Alice sort out Henry's legal affairs and the immediate matter of paying bills. She considered which of the furniture to bring home after his death. Much of it she didn't want, though she wanted some pieces because they reminded her so of Henry. Some of the pieces Alice shipped were over one hundred years old; they came into the States duty-free.[40]

During his last days Alice's patient entered equilibrium. He dozed most of the day, still struggling to comprehend his condition and wondering whether people knew he was seriously ill. He lost considerable weight, and his face had fallen, his left eye nearly closed. He had difficulty completing his sentences. Half the time he confused Alice with his mother. In one breath he would call her name and in the next cry, "'Take your poor old boy to your heart.'"[41] Sometimes he wanted his glasses and paper, imagining he was writing, and other times his hand merely moved over the counterpane.[42]

Sometimes Henry asked for Alice's sons, his family feeling growing stronger at the end, or so Alice believed. One day he asked Burgess to go to Rye and get Lamb House ready because his nephews were coming to visit. "'I should like to arrange to live quietly with Albert,'" by whom Alice assumed he meant Aleck. He told her he did mean Aleck. Next he asked about Billy, wishing that one or the other had "connections" in England. When Alice told him that he was their connection with England, Henry said he was also their connection with the future. "'Tell them <u>to follow, to be faithful</u>—<u>to take me seriously</u>.'"[43] He asked for William repeatedly, telling Alice how much he wanted his older brother—"'he is the one person in all Rome I want to see.'"[44] During these days Alice never found Henry angry. "It is as if the very essence of his gentle spirit shone out through the ruined brain," she told Billy.[45]

During his last conscious moments Henry asked Alice to stay with him. His last days he slept steadily and deeply, not even waking for meals. Toward midnight on Saturday, 26 February, he waked and rambled to the nurse, all his ramblings about William. At 1:30 a.m. on Sunday morning he took a cup of Benger's Food, a nutritional supplement mixed with milk that was easy to digest. At 3:25 a.m. he had a small convulsion, so the nurse woke Alice. She found him feverish and trembling, murmuring a few words. Then he fell asleep, sleeping all day Sunday. When the doctor came that evening he believed Henry might rally, but there was no hope. By Monday morning he was unconscious, breathing only with great difficulty. On Monday, 28 February, at 6:00 p.m., his sister-in-law at his side, seventy-two-year-old Henry James took three sighing breaths and was still.[46]

Alice had satisfied her charge, helping this second James brother leave this world. She believed that Henry, too, was now on the other side. She wrote to Barrett Wendell, "All the hardships of the way are over now. His was a beautiful going, with the light of the great and blessed country foreshadowed in his face. He somehow made death seem less final."[47]

Peggy took his loss hard, developing a bad cough. Henry had asked to be cremated, but before the cremation Alice planned a service for him at Chelsea Old Church, Reverend Farmer officiating. She placed a notice in the *Times* and in the *Telegraph* requesting no flowers, but nonetheless many floral tributes arrived. Henry had many friends and a warm following among the British. Before his December illness he had spent many hours with wounded soldiers in London hospitals, like Walt Whitman, he thought. The American Academy sent flowers, and the American Embassy and the Society of Dramatists sent wreaths; nearly twenty wreaths in all came. Henry's body lay in state in the front room among his books and the laurel wreaths. She described him to Harry, who could not be there: "His vanished youth has come back with an expression of wisdom and of grandeur." John Singer Sargent advised having a death mask made; he knew an Austrian who was an expert at making masks. When it was done, Alice pronounced it a thing of beauty.[48] Before the funeral she invited Theodora Bosanquet to see Henry's face one last time before the coffin was closed.[49]

At the service, held the Friday after Henry's death, Alice and Peggy followed the coffin into the church. A boys' choir sang hymns, Reverend Farmer read part of the Anglican burial service, and Archdean Bevan read another part. Edmund Gosse gave the funeral address, mentioning Henry's devotion to England during the war and his beautiful life and art. The ceremony concluded with a rendition of the funeral march from Beethoven's Piano Sonata No. 12. After the service Rudyard Kipling was overheard saying to his wife, "'It is the most touchingly beautiful service I have ever heard.'"[50] Many of Henry's friends' servants attended the service, one old man on crutches coming by bus to Chelsea. Another old man cried through the entire service.[51] Mourners filled the church, including the great actress Ellen Terry and Charles Dickens's daughter. Then, accompanied by Emily Sargent, Violet Ormond, and Bailey Saunders, who insisted they might need his help, Alice and Peggy went to Golders Green and waited an hour while Henry's body was cremated. Alice brought his ashes back to Cheyne Walk in a copper vase.[52]

The weeks after the service Alice and Peggy kept constantly busy. They planned to stay in London for two months, and then three, and then finally remove to Lamb House for an indeterminate time before returning home. As she had done after William's death, Alice began answering the large pile of letters that arrived, with Peggy as her assistant.[53] Archdean Bevan offered to let the family place a memorial tablet in the Chelsea Old Church churchyard, an offer Alice gratefully accepted, asking her sons to supply the wording.[54]

Two years earlier Henry had taken a seven-year lease on the Carlyle Mansions flat, so Alice hoped to sublet it for the next five years. She also had to make plans for Lamb House. While she did not want to sell it, as she hoped her children might someday use it, she wanted to find a suitable tenant. She began sorting out Henry's literary affairs, which were now her own, as she had inherited his copyrights. Edmund Gosse advised Alice to keep back the unfinished "Middle Years," the third volume of the autobiography, as it would be worth more later. He also suggested she write to Scribner's to tell them that Henry had not finished his novel "The Ivory Tower" and ask whether the estate owed the publishing firm money from the advance paid for it. Gosse warned her against giving away the three fragments left (the third was another barely started novel, "The Sense of the Past").[55]

As she sorted out Henry's literary remains Alice also arranged to dispose of his textile remains. With Peggy's and Minnie Kidd's help, Alice sorted out his clothing. She kept his new mesh and silk underwear for her three sons as well as some of his better jackets. The remainder of the garments went to Burgess Noakes; Minnie Kidd's brother; the porter, William; Lamb House gardener George Gammon; and Henry's former servant Smith. Alice found things for Gammon's father and for someone she called "the poor little half-clad new boy."[56] As she grieved for Henry she was glad to have this responsibility for the great man's estate. Writing to Billy, she laughed at her efforts: "How Papa and Uncle Henry would smile to see my laggard pen toiling through the piles of letters, and trying to fathom the difference between a 'Venerable,' a Reverend and a very Reverend."[57]

According to the terms of Henry's will, Alice inherited all of his property, with the exception of Lamb House. After her death the property would pass to her children. Harry inherited Lamb House and all its contents, and Peggy got her uncle's insurance. Other gifts went to other nieces and nephews, with the omission of Bob's son, Ned James. Because of Ned's antiroyalist views and because he had published a libelous antiwar tract,

Henry, who had become a British citizen in 1915 to show his devotion to England during the war, left Ned out of his will.[58] The repaired Sargent portrait went to the National Portrait Gallery. Lucy Clifford, Jocelyn Persse, and Hugh Walpole each received one hundred pounds, and the servants received bequests.[59] Alice did not know Persse. He had been Henry's theater and dinner companion for years, a supportive, loving young man. Alice thought Walpole had abandoned Henry during his illness. He sent a note and called once, and then Alice heard no more from Henry's adored younger novelist. Longtime friend Lucy Clifford, on the other hand, remained devoted throughout Henry's illness.[60] There was no bequest to Theodora Bosanquet.

Now that Henry's apartment no longer had to be guarded against visitors, Alice and Peggy embarked on a round of visiting and being called upon. As energetic as Alice remained at age sixty-seven, she wished for additional energy so that she could enjoy more of the social events she could only have dreamed of as a young woman in Weymouth. She enjoyed a temporary infatuation with upper-class British life and manners consistent with the elitism she had developed in Cambridge, though now she realized that she loved her own country best.[61] "What a test it is of high breeding, the power of putting others at ease," she said of Lady Lyttelton. In mid-April Alice and Peggy took tea with her in her private rooms at Chelsea Hospital, Alice raving over the room's proportions, its white marble mantel, the life-size portraits of Charles II and his queen, and the Vandyke painting of Charles I and his family.

Now that she was no longer needed as nurse and house manager, Alice's shopping escalated. She admired an old Hepplewhite bureau with the original handles and velvet lining, and she coveted a 1770 twelve-foot-wide sideboard and a bookcase with old glass doors that could be disassembled for packing. These items were expensive but could be shipped duty-free because they were over one hundred years old. She thought Billy might want them.[62]

The third week in April Alice and Peggy left the Cheyne Walk flat for Banwell Abbey in Somerset. They stayed there at the home of Sir George Gilbert and Lady Mary Henrietta Howard Murray until 1 May. A professor of Greek, George Murray was known for his edition of Euripides. He was also an internationalist who later promoted the League of Nations. In April 1907 the Jameses had hosted the Murrays in Cambridge when

Murray gave six lectures on Greek poetry at Harvard. Murray, now a captain in the British military, was away from home on duty. The couple had four children who danced while their mother played the piano for guests after lunch. Alice found the children charming, but their daily dance recitals soon became monotonous.[63]

Some days the women traveled around Somerset, taking along a thermos of tea and returning to Banwell Abbey at seven. They saw the old church and graveyard at Cliveden and then the house of eighteenth-century religious writer Hannah More, Barley Wood. Driving through the English countryside, Alice fell in love with the espaliered fruit trees and the box-bordered gardens, their walls hung with wallflowers, arabis, and ivy. On one trip they visited Nealsey Court. There Daniel Defoe had met Alexander Selkirk, whose story had inspired Defoe to write *Robinson Crusoe*. And she could not help herself: Alice found more bargains. Because of the war prices were low in rural areas. This time she admired the old oak refectory tables, in fashion now again for dining room tables. One was priced at just twelve pounds.[64]

After the two women returned to London Peggy went to the Isle of Wight for a visit. In mid-May Alice left London for Rye to put Lamb House in order. She arranged to have the roof and gutters cleaned and the chimneys swept. The parlor's oak floor had extensive water damage from the hot-water pipes Henry had installed beneath it, but Alice repaired that too. She had everything repainted and repapered. The windows were reset so that no rain could leak in, and the upper hall cracks were replastered. For the most part she left the house as it was when Henry had been alive, though she wanted to take books, a few pictures, and certain pieces of furniture home. She also took down the brass chandelier and dismantled it, numbering its pieces and wrapping each piece separately. She left Henry's grandmother's old blue china and the tea room's Chinese scroll.[65] She wanted to leave most of Henry's French library at Lamb House, though she left that to Harry to decide. Surely, her children someday would return to this beloved home. Her positive outlook returning, she again laughed at her own efforts, this time to Billy: "I think if their great spirits take note at all of us here below Papa and Uncle Henry would smile over my activities in this place."[66]

In May it was hard to find passage home, as the war still raged. The gardener, George Gammon, had been drafted into service, though Alice remarked to Billy, "He does not seem destined by nature to fight anything more formidable than snails."[67] On 17 June, Billy's thirty-fourth birthday, Alice and Peggy were still in Rye. Peggy missed her uncle even more here. During the day the pair often walked to Camber for tea with Henry's friends Alice Dew-Smith and Mrs. Lloyd, returning for supper and then reading in the study. Alice loved small Rye. As she went about town she heard many accolades for her late brother-in-law. She felt weak, though, her walks tiring her more than they had in the past.

Finally, the first week in August 1916 Alice and Peggy sailed for home, their packing and sorting out finished. Alice gave Percy Lubbock Henry's watch.[68] The Carlyle Mansions flat had been let, the tenant due on 11 August. The last three nights the two women stayed with Emily Sargent while Alice finished her work in Henry's rooms.[69] His loss was a great personal blow because she told Billy she had long believed that "he is himself bigger than his greatest work."[70] She made final arrangements for a marble slab in Chelsea Old Church's More's Chapel before she went. It read:

IN MEMORY OF
HENRY JAMES O.M.
NOVELIST

Born in New York 1843. Died in
Chelsea 1916. Lover & Inter-
preter of the fine amenities,
of brave decisions & generous
loyalties, a resident of this
parish who renounced a
cherished citizenship to give
his allegiance to England in
the 1st year of the Great War.

Alice had been away for nearly eight months. Along with her purchases and some of Henry's possessions, she took one more thing. An expert at evading customs, Alice smuggled Henry's ashes onboard. She buried them in the Cambridge Cemetery near William, his parents, his sister, Alice, and Hermann.

18 Living Option

IT WAS AS IF TWO LIGHTNING BOLTS had torn through Alice. Who was she after years of immersion in the James clan? William had demanded far more of her than Henry had. She collaborated in his life and work, steadying him so that he could work productively and providing constant emotional and intellectual companionship. Pragmatism, which became literally a household word, has again been taken up by some professional philosophers as a subject for study, and William's work on radical empiricism, never finished and never completely assimilated, raises questions concerning the relationship between the knower and the known that are still debated in epistemological studies.[1] Henry was who he was: a sensitive man, a great writer, someone with many friends, a man who loved any number of young men passionately, but a lonely man, one who needed Alice so much at the end that her presence was a healing balm. He gave her his books, and he loved her children, yet he too made demands. She cared for him selflessly in 1910 and 1911 and then again in 1916.

Less than two years before she died Alice reflected on her life with William and Henry. She thought of what she had done and what she should have done not for herself but for them. She confessed her thoughts to her oldest friend, Katharine Hooker:

Perhaps some of our failures <u>had to be</u>, and out of failure is born for some of us mercy, pity, sympathy and what Swedenborg would call the knowledge of, and longing to extinguish our "selfhood." . . . You say truly that no second chance, no new beginning can let us do for those we love, what once we might have done—and didn't—but what if our failure was of deeper value to them? I am saying these things to you as I say them to myself—"Accept, renounce and keep a good word to the future."[2]

She had learned the same thing from a Japanese shopkeeper in San Francisco who once told Alice he had attained Nirvana. She was struck by his worn patience and deep faith. When she told the man that Nirvana equaled pessimism, he informed her, "The nirvana we strive for is the extinction of <u>self</u>."[3]

At times Alice had nearly extinguished herself during her years of caring for others: her union with the Jameses proved to be no basement bargain. The dreams Alice had for her four children were not fully realized, perhaps because there was no way to re-create the extraordinary circumstances and the convoluted family dynamics that led to William's and Henry's achievements, but they became her dearest friends at the end of her life. But despite all she had given to the Jameses, the Gibbenses, and her children, something of her own subjectivity remained. The self-narrative she had created as a child remained alive as now she reenvisioned herself as a moral reformer. In her old age Alice participated in the same kinds of causes that had captured her imagination as a child. In spite of her feelings of grief and inadequacy (or perhaps because of them) her horizons widened. The determination that had allowed her to survive personal tragedy at a young age now came to her aid. She traveled, she nourished friendships old and new, and, most important, she found the energy for more education and an active involvement in the Sacco and Vanzetti case. As her husband had advocated in *Pragmatism*, she used her ideas about truth and reality to try to change the world.

While Alice remained in England winding up Henry's affairs, Aleck formalized his engagement with Frederika Paine. Aleck and Frederika were alike in many ways: both had been abandoned by their parents for a time at a young age, both studied art, both were happy spirits. Even their spelling was alike. Aleck did not want to marry a woman like Billy's wife, a wealthy, sickly woman with family encumbrances. He wanted someone who loved him, who supported his ambitions for art, who had no interest in the name "James." He needed to break from Irving Street, where he had been a misfit. While he had adapted socially to the Cambridge and British Brahmins, their life was not the life for him. As a child and adolescent he had escaped the James stronghold whenever possible for the outdoors. He had no desire to remain in this circumscribed world.

Aleck made a red chalk drawing of William for Alice that spring, his gift to his mother before leaving her.[4] He adored her, so the decision cannot have been an easy one.[5] Although he was ill that winter with chills and fever, his painting went well: an art museum bought some of his drawings.[6] He was dividing his time between the Museum School in Boston and Dublin, New Hampshire, where he studied with Abbott Thayer.[7] During the spring of 1916 Alice heard little from Aleck, so she frequently asked Billy for a word on his well-being and health.[8]

Finally, in late April or early May Aleck asked her consent to announce his engagement. Alice gave that consent, though she could not be there when the young couple made the announcement, as it was still impossible to take passage home. She asked Billy and his wife, Alice, to represent her and be as cordial as possible to Frederika and Aleck. "I mean to obey Beechnut's rule 'When you consent, consent cordially,'" she explained to Billy.[9] Finally, in June both Frederika and Aleck wrote her "beautiful letters." Alice had hopes for their future: "I have an ever-increasing faith in the young ones," she told Billy.[10] While she claimed no responsibility for the outcome, she tried her best to ensure the success of the marriage.[11]

The couple married in 1916 and moved to Dublin, where they made do without servants. In May 1917 the two young people visited 95 Irving Street, Alice pronouncing their visit brief but successful.[12] Still, in July Alice told Billy she was fortunate to have his wife, Alice, as a daughter-in-law, but she made no mention of Frederika.[13] Freddie was an unwanted intruder into the set Alice had cultivated. A year after the marriage she blamed herself for Aleck's choice of mates, believing that if William had lived her son would never have married Frederika. She thought she had spoiled her youngest son, so he found a mate who would not be a good partner. She shared Peggy's views of Frederika with Billy: "Peggy says that already Aleck is conscious of her quality."[14]

Harry, too, married the year after Henry's death. This time Alice approved of the bride, Olivia Cutting, who came from a distinguished Long Island family. Her father, William Bayard Cutting, was a renowned New York lawyer, and her mother, Olivia Murray Cutting, an active philanthropist. However, like Alice Runnells, who was a semi-invalid most of her life, Olivia Cutting revealed herself less than an ideal mate. Reportedly, Harry learned that she was a lesbian shortly after they were married.[15]

Alice was no longer the best judge of character, at least with her sons' wives, because Frederika and Aleck achieved the happiest marriage. She continued to weave narratives of success for her family, as she had done for William, but she had lost touch with what success meant. During her last years she regained her youthful idealism, but during the first months of double widowhood success meant wealth, power, and good breeding.

On 3 May 1917, not long before Harry's wedding, Alice suffered a tremendous blow. Born on 8 June 1828, Eliza Gibbens was nearly eighty-eight years old. Still gentle and kind, still living at 107 Irving Street with her youngest daughter, Margaret, Eliza had been under the care of doctors and nurses for months, ill since early November 1916. Her last Thanksgiving she told her daughter, "'The doctors help us into life—I wish they would help us out.'"[16] Alice spent most of the winter tending her mother.[17] During her last two weeks Eliza grew weaker and weaker. "She has earned the right to die, and when she is gone—ah, the difference to me," Alice told Harry.[18] The night before her death, Alice and Peggy with her, Eliza lost consciousness. Alice felt that Eliza's death would be even harder for her sisters to bear, but still it was a great blow. Again to Harry she exclaimed, "It feels as if the rooftree was crashing in."[19] Once recovered from the horror of her husband's death, Eliza had anchored Alice for decades. When Theodate Pope's mother died in 1920, Alice told her what mothers meant: "As long as one's mother is here it is as if a stout defence, a rampart saved us from all unkind forces. It is the protective attitude which survives in mothers long after its use has been outgrown."[20]

One more momentous event occurred in 1917. History keeps its secrets as to what Alice thought of her only girl's marriage to Bruce Porter, but, given Bruce's age and Peggy's propensity for depression, she must have been apprehensive about the match. And Peggy, Alice's closest companion since William's death, was moving an entire continent away. In one year Alice lost the two women she loved the most: her mother and her daughter. Henry, at least, would have rejoiced—if he had not been puzzled, that is. Peggy was thirty years old and Bruce fifty-two; she was Henry James's virginal niece who never had a serious boyfriend, and he was one of Henry James's loved and probably bisexual younger men. Their shared devotion to Henry had taken them to another plane. Alice found Peggy beautifully happy, so she decided that this was the right thing.[21]

There were elements of predestination about the union, or at least Bruce liked to think so. Bruce's brother Robert had attended Harvard while Peggy was a little girl. He used to watch a delightful eight-year-old girl walking to school, and someone told him she was William James's daughter. And when Peggy was eighteen she kept a book of verses that she liked. Among them were all of Bruce Porter's poems, which she had found in the poetry magazine he coedited, the *Lark*, and copied into her book. When Bruce told Kate Hooker he was engaged to Peggy, he said he knew the moment they met that he loved her. "I knew, two years ago, how much I cared and put the strange emotion aside as an injustice to her youth—put it as far away as the years that divided us. On her return—I still sought to see her in company—or not at all—and then—it was of no use whatever—and since Monday we are quite sure it is right." He believed that nothing would ever break the couple's inner bond.[22]

On 6 October 1917 Peggy and Bruce married in the Swedenborgian Church at the edge of the Harvard campus. Peggy wore a white walking suit, and Alice and writer Witter Bynner witnessed the marriage certificate.[23] After honeymooning in New England the couple left for San Francisco, their permanent home. Aleck and Frederika moved west that year to Santa Barbara, so half of Alice's children were now a continent away.

During that same year Alice lost, at least temporarily, one more of her children. As soon as America entered the war Billy wanted to join up, but Alice opposed his going. "I want to say now the result of long searching that you boys must not <u>fight</u>. If you want to serve it ought to be in some other way."[24] A few weeks after receiving his mother's well-intentioned advice, Billy enlisted, even though he was beyond the age limit. He asked to serve in the ranks. Again, this time more forcefully, Alice begged him not to serve. His wife and two sons needed him more. "I pray that you may be rejected, that all the heavenly influences may save and protect you," she wrote to him from Asticon, Maine, where she visited Charles Eliot and his wife along with three other Bee club members from Cambridge.[25]

Billy ended up in the Military Aeronautics Division and was in Paris at one point. Alice worried constantly when she did not hear from him or know where he was stationed. She heard from her son and from his wife so seldom that she feared she had offended them.[26] While Alice had written to Billy every week since he left for France, she had only one letter from him. Billy spent the last six months of the war in Paris as a civilian attaché in the air force, sketching war materials.[27]

After Alice visited Harry for ten days in January 1918, he, too, decided to enlist.[28] That winter he signed on as a private with the 342nd Machine Battalion of the Eighty-ninth Division of the American Expeditionary Force after he was unable to obtain a quick commission as an officer. While Alice mourned, she applauded his courage.[29] Captain Sellers was surprised when Henry James, thirty-nine years old and a successful lawyer who spoke French and German, was assigned to his unit as a private. He offered to send Harry to the Fourth Officers Training Camp, but Harry refused because he wanted to see action. On 1 November 1918 Harry was commissioned a second lieutenant in the infantry, but the war ended before he saw active duty. He stayed on in Europe, first as assistant secretary to the American Commission charged with negotiating the peace and then as the American member of the Inter-Allied Danube River Commission.[30]

Alice missed her sons terribly, confessing to Billy, "After little Hummy died I seemed to be a part of the great army of mothers, the Rachels mourning for their children and now I belong to the older army of mothers whose sons are in France."[31] She prayed often, badly, she thought, but the act comforted her. "When I wake in the night and think of you, a lonely sentry, or trying to sleep in noisy barracks I could not bear it but for the blessedness of prayer," she wailed to Harry, though she questioned her own faith, announcing that it was time for her to "lay hold on a real religion."[32]

Though her own chickens had hatched and flown, in 1918 Alice realized a dream. She had one remaining passion: for chickens. Her satisfaction in something so quotidian set her apart from the other Cambridge matrons, redeeming her to some degree from the elitism she had espoused. While she claimed she had her henhouse built and furnished with hens to keep Burgess Noakes busy (he was now in America in her service), she longed for them. She went to city hall that spring and badgered reluctant officials into giving her a permit: "'Mrs. James is authorized to keep twelve hens but no rooster.'" After the coop was erected she told Harry, "'I have eight hens of the sweetest nature, and it makes the place cheerful to hear an occasional cluck in the back yard.'"[33] In July 1918 one hen hatched eleven chicks, and Burgess gave eggs to Billy's wife and her two sons.[34] At a meeting at 95 Irving Street to benefit the Mental Hygiene Association, a sick hen, temporarily housed in the cellar, screeched loudly during ex-president Eliot's speech. Afterward Alice observed, "'You can't be yourself and accomplish anything in this world without being publicly betrayed.'"[35]

During the summer of 1918 Alice traveled to San Francisco to be with Peggy during the last two months of her first pregnancy. She hesitated, fearing she might be in the way, but she knew Peggy's record of poor health and depression. She could not stay away, and she had Kate Hooker as a resource if she became burdensome. So far her daughter's marriage seemed a happy one. In March 1918, when Bruce knew that Peggy was pregnant, he told her, "Body & soul, we are man & wife—mortal in the flesh open to every human vicissitude—but immortal in our good honest love for each other—& to go on & on forever—hand in hand heart to heart—learning how to bear the ever increasing light & warmth of the final & perfect love."[36] Cambridge gossip had it that "Peggy James has married & reformed a fascinating rake and appears happy!" he later told Katharine Hooker.[37]

The couple bought a home at 944 Chestnut Street on Russian Hill, less than a block from the cable car line. Sitting up from the street, the gracefully proportioned house was lovely, featuring a sleeping porch in the back to take advantage of the sea breezes. Behind was a large garden Bruce could landscape. From it the Porters could see the bay, the blue water, the sailing boats, and Alcatraz. It was one of the few older homes that had survived the fires that followed the 1906 earthquake.[38]

When the current tenants were slow to vacate the building, the Porters rented a home on Union Street, Alice with them most of the time. The last weeks of Peggy's pregnancy went smoothly, and Alice managed to keep busy despite her fears of being in the way. Occasionally, Aleck visited her from Santa Barbara. She sewed for the Red Cross and did Peggy's mending.[39] Still, she worried about intruding.[40] Everything in this world except her daughter seemed strange. At night she lay awake hearing the cry of the foghorn and the clatter of the cable cars plunging down the steep street. She described their sound to Billy: "It wakes me sometimes as by an explosion, so thunderous is the descent."[41]

At 9:45 p.m. on 6 August the baby was born. He weighed over seven pounds. Peggy labored eighteen hours, but the doctors gave her ether so that she felt no pain. Peggy named him Robert Bruce, after Bruce's brother Robert and after her husband, planning to call him Robin.[42] Bruce Porter was thrilled with his wife and his son, blood relatives of Henry James. Alice too felt grateful for this new life. "It's a mystery of the depths, the coming and ebbing of life," she explained to Billy.[43]

The house at 944 Chestnut Street was not ready for occupancy by mid-September, when the lease on the Union Street house expired. Peggy, Bruce, and Robin went to Bruce's mother, while Alice boarded out with Minnie Kidd and Joan Paddington, Henry's former servants, who now worked for her.[44] She debated remaining until January, helping Peggy with Robin and also spending time in Santa Barbara with Aleck, Frederika, and their first child.[45] The war was over, but Alice was in no hurry to return to her large, empty house or to the cold Cambridge winters.

That September Alice enrolled in a Red Cross nursing certification class at the YMCA. At last she had the opportunity for an education. She was proud of her work and even prouder of her exam marks. She received a 90 in hygiene and an 82 in first aid. However, she could not take hospital nursing because the course was only available for women young enough to go to the battlefront.[46] Alice continued to follow her moral imperative to serve others, recalling that William used to call her "a form of use." She told Billy, "I can only pray that I may be led by a plain path to some form of use."[47]

Alice wanted to help influenza victims but was told that, since she was not a trained nurse, she could only take care of the sick under a doctor's instructions. Besides, she told herself, she did not want to carry the disease germs into the Hooker household. Then she considered learning Braille to help the blind. She feared she was becoming like her aunt Nannie, weak and worrying, "the native hue of resolution so sicklied o'er."[48] (While she claimed to know little of Shakespeare, she frequently used his phrases as tags to illustrate her mental states.) She considered going to France to work as a "searcher" in the hospitals there, since she was forbidden to go as a nurse, though she realized that this was a vain hope.[49]

In her spare time Alice continued her program of self-education, reading Harry Emerson Fosdick's inspirational book *The Meaning of Prayer*; Mrs. Humphry Ward's *Recollections*, which included a tribute to Henry; John Ruskin's *Modern Painters*, perhaps even the copy her father had given her as a child; and, consistent with her humanitarian interests, *The Autobiography of Kropotkin: Memoirs of a Revolutionist*, telling Billy he would love the book and its author.[50]

Though he may or may not have been aware of her interest in revolutionary movements, Harry knew how important it was for Alice to keep busy doing work she considered useful. He would see more of her when he returned from the war, but in the meantime he was grateful for Peggy's care of Alice, who did not like to think she needed any care. "The great thing will be to give her some sense of being helpful in the world; but whether anything will give it to her is another question," he explained to his sister. "It's pretty difficult seeing that she's bound to despise everything she does as insignificant and [she is] temperamentally averse to seeing its importance as others see it. Old age hath still its honors & its toils, but one must accept it that the toils are different from the toils of middle life, & their difficulty may lie partly in accepting the difference."[51]

During her San Francisco visit Alice became a grandmother again. She was not there when Aleck's son Alexander Robertson James was born on 10 December 1918. While she longed to help, she knew the couple would not want her. "I should so gladly be of use to her & Aleck when their baby comes, but they would not want me—how could she?"[52] Early in January Alice went to Santa Barbara to see her grandson. The baby was beautiful, with wide-set eyes and an impressive face. She was content with what she saw: the marriage was a success, and she predicted to Billy that it would continue so. "Frederika makes a good and reassuring little mother who bids fair to do well by the child and I am celebrating all my thankfulness by taking her in as one of us and resolving to faithfully obey your good rule of not criticizing."[53] That month the flu epidemic raged in Santa

Barbara, and Frederika was allowed no visitors outside of family. The schools closed, and when Alice returned to San Francisco everyone wore masks to keep from breathing airborne germs.[54]

John Dewey, one of William's colleagues and an important American philosopher and educator, invited Alice to accompany him and his wife to Japan and China that January.[55] Mary Salter was excited. She felt that the trip would do her sister great good and urged her to accept the invitation.[56] At first Alice planned to go, but then she found reasons to change her mind.[57] Peggy was without a nurse that winter, and Alice was reluctant to leave until her daughter found the right servant. That servant would not be available until 1 March, long after the Deweys had sailed for the Orient.[58]

When Alice returned to Cambridge in March 1919, she had massages, rested, and resumed her reading program, starting with Lytton Strachey's *Eminent Victorians*.[59] Alice resumed her renovations at 95 Irving Street, having the maids' and Burgess's rooms painted and papered. That summer Irving Street itself was being repaired with cut stones, gravel, and tar.[60] Alice spent time with Olivia; Harry was still in Europe and would not return to the States until July. Billy and his wife had finished building their house next door. Though they were not always there, when they were in residence Alice had the interest of two grandsons, William and John Sumner. She continued her Cambridge community activities, and she also had the company of her sister Margaret and her eighteen-year-old daughter, Rosamund, who had developed a nervous condition, at 107 Irving Street. Alice's other sister, Mary, who now lived in Philadelphia, was ill. Diagnosed with heart problems, she had been hospitalized for complete rest.[61]

While family legend claims that Peggy underwent another spell of depression after Alice returned to Cambridge, no one specifies an underlying cause. James family history is replete with cases of depression, and Peggy had inherited the family weakness. She conceived again during the summer of 1919, but this pregnancy gave her nausea, so much so that she was hospitalized in July.[62] Her doctor, Dr. Wakefield, saved mother and unborn child, and the baby was born on 15 November, but the little girl died less than four weeks later.[63] Peggy grieved over the loss of her baby. Just before her third child was born she told her mother, "I somehow don't want to have another baby without you and feel as if I could have borne it about my little girl much better with you here."[64] Family legend also claims that Bruce took Peggy hiking in the mountains to overcome her sorrow, pronouncing this the California cure. That may be true; physical activity was part of William James's cure for his own depression.

Alice did not go to Peggy that fall. Her work sorting out William's manuscripts and papers was not finished, and the editions of Henry's and William's letters had not yet seen print. She continued writing to correspondents to retrieve the originals or copies of William's letters. She was also involved with the publication of Henry's letters. Harry was the main force behind that edition. Since the writer's reputation had ebbed after his death, both Alice and Harry wanted Henry's letters to affirm his genius. She devoted many hours to the project. This raking over her past, William's past, Henry's past caused her anguish. "All these letters, Henry's and William's have at times fairly rent and torn me," she moaned to Kate Hooker.[65]

Percy Lubbock was preparing the edition of Henry's letters. Max Beerbohm had suggested either Edmund Gosse or Edith Wharton as editors, but Alice was opposed to Wharton, despite the fact that Edith and Henry had been close friends and literary confidants for years and that before his death Henry had specified to his agent, J. B. Pinker, that he did not want Gosse as editor.[66] Percy Lubbock approached Theodora Bosanquet on the possibility of his editing Henry's papers before approaching the family. A protégé of Arthur C. Benson, the young man had been a librarian at Magdalene College from 1906 to 1908 and Henry's friend, and he knew Edith Wharton, though the Jameses were not aware of their friendship. Harry was impressed with the obituary he had written for the *Quarterly Review*, and during the weeks after Henry's death Alice had liked him.[67]

By the summer of 1916 Lubbock had been chosen, with Edmund Gosse as literary consultant. Gosse had advised Alice during Henry's last weeks concerning the writer's works-in-progress, and he was a seasoned writer, an editor, and librarian to the House of Lords; he knew nearly everyone Henry knew. He hired Theodora Bosanquet to copy the letters gathered in England. Alice went over Henry's letters to family members, the letters available in America. Peggy then copied letters or parts of letters that would be included, mailing her copies to Lubbock. Because of the war and the irregularities in mails and communication, however, some letters were lost forever.

It took Lubbock three years to assemble and edit the letters. He and Harry agreed the edition would begin in 1869, starting with Henry's first adult trip to Europe. Alice, Harry, Peggy, and Billy all read through the edition before it went to press, anxious to present the best image of Henry but also wanting to avoid libel charges. They knew how cleverly and maliciously he had gossiped. The book presented him as "the fictional lawgiver, as well as the gregarious expatriate."[68] Many of the funny but gossipy letters were omitted as well as salutations in some of the loving letters to younger men, this at Gosse's insistence.[69] The letters should be socially sanitized yet revealing as literature and literary history. When Harry read the type-copy of Lubbock's two-volume edition on his way back from Europe in 1919, he was impressed. "'The book makes a deeper and bigger impression on careful reading. . . . It will, I rather think, make Uncle Henry count very much more than he did already.'"[70] In Lubbock's brief but eloquent introduction he described Henry as writer, artist, and accomplished, even brilliant, correspondent. The style of the letters seemed to interest Lubbock more than the man.

When the edition was published, Alice was not happy with it. "Percy Lubbock repeated far too much. I wish that we had done the letters with paid help so that the final yes was ours," she told Harry.[71] Lubbock made too many apologies for Henry's dictated letters. Worse was his treatment of Edith Wharton, who Alice thought occupied too prominent a position. "His staging of Mrs. Wharton is excessive but as someone said there was not a touch of real affection for the woman in the whole exhibit."[72]

When the letters came out early in 1920, Alice sent copies to selected friends, among them the Protheros. Sir George Prothero told Alice, "The book is unspeakably precious to us, for never was there a finer illustration of 'He, being dead, yet speaketh;' but coming from you, who were so much to him, it has a double value."[73] Most recipients were delighted to receive the books.

A few others were not so pleased, including Edith Wharton. The letter that she sent to Alice no longer exists, but Alice sent a copy of it (or the original) to Peggy, who reacted strongly: "[Wharton's letter was] disgusting—deliberately insulting and cold. I am very sorry you sent her the book. She is a minx and not in the least a lady."[74] The family's dislike of Wharton had solidified when she tried to raise a large sum of money to give Henry for his seventieth birthday, a gesture they resented, as they found it patronizing. If anyone gave Henry money, it should be his family, Alice and her children believed.

Harry consoled Alice that no edition could have been perfect: on the whole, Lubbock's had been very good, and future generations would shed further light on Uncle Henry.[75] Harry believed his uncle's oeuvre would stand the test of time. But Alice was upset, even more so as further impressions came in. She was unhappy with Lubbock's work, thinking Peggy should do another, better edition. She was annoyed with the responses to Henry's love letters. She told Harry, "People are putting a vile interpretation on those silly letters to young men.—Poor dear Uncle Henry."[76] Her puritanical Weymouth upbringing did not allow her to see anything other than kind affection in those letters, and perhaps she also respected Henry's privacy.

The edition of William's letters, also released in 1920 by the Atlantic Monthly Press but later in the year, was more tightly controlled by the James family. Harry edited both volumes, pleasing Alice greatly with its dedication:

> To my Mother,
> gallant and devoted ally
> of my Father's most arduous
> and happy years,
> this collection of his letters
> is dedicated.

This collection too was sanitized, though this time not for homoerotic interests or gossip but for the epistolary arguments William and Alice had had, their judgments on other philosophers and Harvard professors, his constant irreverence, and probably his occasional interest in other women. Alice and Harry worked hard to present William as a psychologist-philosopher-genius whose work was original and enduring.

According to Harry, Alice starting examining and organizing William's letters in 1911, eventually destroying some. He claims that her children told her she must decide which ones to keep.[77] It is impossible to know how she made her decisions, but she may have felt that ordinary, daily letters did not present William at his best. And as they often quarreled by mail during his frequent absences, she also may have preferred to keep their marital differences private. Harry believed that she destroyed many of the early letters, written before their marriage, and he himself destroyed others later, letters that "would be liable to misinterpretation if not accompanied by explanations that I couldn't find the time to compile." He claimed that he preserved all significant letters, though of course he used his own judgment on what "significant" meant. And he destroyed all but two bundles of his mother's letters, selected at random because her correspondence was "bulky and has not seemed to me to possess the special interest that attaches more or less to all of my father's letters."[78]

Alice worked closely with Harry, answering questions and helping with notes. She had an extensive knowledge of William's work (and his library), and she wanted the edition to be as accurate as possible. "The reference you copy as 'Hall's paper Donaldson' is evidently a reference in Vol. X 1885 page 577, under the heading *Research to Motor Sensations on the Skin* by Prof. G. Stanley Hall & Dr. D. D. Donaldson. It is considerably marked by W.J." To be sure the record was straight, she looked up Donaldson in *Who's Who*, sending Harry the reference.[79] Another query concerned a book on demoniacal possession under the possible name "Nevins."[80]

Harry remained hypersensitive about giving offense to no one. When he found a reference in a letter to Henry dated 17 October 1867 to a Reverend Foote of "Stone Chapel Notoriety," he debated including this phrase. Reverend Foote was the father of a family friend, Dorothea Foote Merriman, and he was still living in 1920. Harry asked Alice to inquire of President Eliot or his wife if they thought this sentence might hurt Foote's feelings. Another sentence about Foote being "hand in glove with the Bootts in Italy" would also have to go if Foote's name were blanked out in the first sentence. Or, Harry mused, he could leave out the phrase "Stone Chapel Notoriety."

Harry realized that his editing practices would raise questions later. He told Alice, "I hate such omissions, somebody is always wondering what lies behind them."[81] Of course, he was right: it is impossible not to conjecture what was omitted about William, given the destruction of his letters and this heavy-handed editing. Looking for a manuscript page to include as an example of his father's handwriting, Harry rejected any on psychic research because he felt the papers had overemphasized that aspect of William's career.[82] He was suspicious of his father's psychic research, which he called "spiritistic."[83] Although Harry often lacked his father's sense of humor, he finally chose a postcard to Henry Adams as the example: one of William's "insufficiently intelligent" students who had to write about a "hydraulic ram" in an exam wrote instead about a "hydraulic goat." The family history of destroying the past continued, with Alice in full agreement with Harry's editorial practices, letter by name by footnote. She praised her son's final version to Bessie Evans: "I feel that he has done the work well and I can read his pages with no sense of discrepancy—his father thought Harry knew how to write."[84]

In August and September 1920 some of William's letters appeared in the *Atlantic Monthly*. Editor Mark Howe was eager to have the book and persuaded Harry to let him release certain letters before the final edition was ready. After the two-volume edition appeared the response was generally enthusiastic and laudatory. Charles Eliot praised the edition and Harry's writing. Over the tea table he announced, "'It's a splendid case of heredity—I who knew the 3 generations, Mr. James, William James and now your son.'"[85] This was success for Alice: she had raised a son who might follow William and Henry. The *Yale Review* asked essayist John Jay Chapman to write a notice of the book, but he sent Alice what he would really like to publish, a poem about William.

> Leave your logical obsessions,—
> Problems, purposes outgrown;
> Enter on the new possessions
> That your griefs have made your own.
> Many a man has had a Mission
> That consumed him in his youth:
> Was it ever more than Vision,
> Was it ever less than Truth?
> Silence! for the bells are ringing.
> Peace!—the heavens speak for you;
> And the fire that you were swinging
> Burns your silver censer through.[86]

Peggy planned to visit Alice during the summer of 1920, but she claimed the doctors did not want Robin in Cambridge's hot, humid summer, recommending she go in the fall instead. Alice confided to Harry, "I am rather broken up by the Peggy episode — but I can go to see her one of these days on a fruit-steamer via Panama."[87] "One would think I lived in the tropics," she told Kate Hooker.[88] In the end Peggy did come home that summer, leaving Robin behind. She was pregnant again. When she returned to San Francisco on 2 July, it was not without regret. The day before she left Cambridge she shared her guilt with Bruce. Alice's health was failing, so when Peggy said good-bye, it might be for the last time. "I am the one she wants the most now. Somehow our marriage hasn't divided Mama and me a bit."[89] While she loved her husband, she missed her rich life with her parents and Uncle Henry. Bruce had a protective and sometimes controlling attitude toward his wife, who had had considerable independence as a young woman.

Nearly ten years after her father's death Peggy told her mother she still missed William; the ache was worse. "I am trying not to show any missing of you and the others, because Bruce thinks I appear a bit unsettled since my return, and I don't want him to know of my being homesick. If I didn't appreciate life in Irving St. and Chocorua enough when I had it, I am making up for it now. The past seems to rise and call me with great protecting arms. But I am happy really, here and now, and I think this Katzenjammer is due to physical fatigue."[90]

Peggy nearly died during her third pregnancy and almost lost another baby because of a morphine overdose.[91] A substitute nurse gave her a half-grain of morphine, but fortunately the regular nurse, Mrs. Holmes, discovered the mistake. Peggy went by ambulance to Dr. Wakefield's hospital, where she took three grains of Calamite to make her vomit. If Mrs. Holmes had not discovered the error, it would have killed Peggy, because she had eaten little for eighteen days previous to taking the morphine.[92]

That fall Alice asked her daughter a question. Whatever that question was, Peggy was unhappy at its content and then angry at her mother. In November Alice acknowledged her propensity for meddling in her children's affairs. Billy told his mother that she was a bad in-law, and she admitted to the charge, but she also told Bruce she would never be able to disassociate herself completely from her daughter's life. "Some day,

320 ✦ LIVING OPTION

when Robin grows up you will understand how incredible it is to find your child <u>grown up</u>, making his experiences inevitably for himself and reconcile yourself to standing by without a rescuing hand."[93]

Despite their temporary quarrel, Alice was there on 23 May 1921 at 7:10 a.m. when Peggy delivered a healthy baby girl, named Katharine Barber after William James of Albany's third wife, Peggy's great-grandmother.[94] Anxious during the entire pregnancy for the mother and unborn child, Alice was relieved when her granddaughter was born. The beautiful little girl had a head of dark hair. This time Peggy not only nursed her baby, she had milk to spare for a premature infant whose mother could not nurse her child. The dependable Mrs. Holmes was with Peggy to ensure there was no repeat of last fall's near catastrophe. Alice befriended the woman, widow of an itinerant preacher. The couple had traveled together, he giving funeral sermons. He made coffins for the deceased, and she made the linings. "I should like to look back on such a life of service," Alice told Harry, too modest to admit that she had lived such a life.[95]

Alice was tired now. Harry warned Peggy, "The bottom fact is that old age has weakened her inhibitions, as it frequently does. She's more of a 'motor' than ever. She discharges and re-acts to everything that impinges on her attention."[96] That spring she had attacks of aphasia (difficulty in using language due to a brain lesion), which slowed her down. After she arrived in San Francisco, she missed a luncheon with Dr. Philip King Brown because of an attack. While Alice was humiliated, Dr. Brown advised her that she must rest. She protested to her oldest son. "In short, <u>I</u> am to have the sort of care which your father did not have."[97]

She wandered through the Chinese quarter and visited her Webb cousins in Berkeley. Some days she sat in the beautiful garden that Bruce had created, reading Wilfred Blunt's *My Diaries*.[98] One evening she accompanied Bruce to a Jewish Passover dinner, where unleavened bread was served. Alice was surprised to find herself in harmony with the group and happy to see they did not pretend to be Christian.[99] "I greatly respected them," she told Harry. "Wouldn't loving Dad have smiled at me, especially when Mr. Koshland made a slow wink at me!! It was just to show that I understood him! But don't tell this to the others—I would not make fun of my kind hosts."[100] Some of the prejudices that had marked her middle years had abated.

A portrait Billy painted of Alice in 1921 shows her dark, luminous, sad eyes, windows onto this world and the next. As an act of letting go, she wrote to Horace Kallen on 12 January 1921, one day after the anniversary of William's birthday. Each year since William's death Kallen had sent her a dozen red roses on 11 January to commemorate what his revered teacher had meant to him. From an Orthodox Jewish background, Kallen had rejected Judaism. In 1905 he had enrolled at Harvard as a graduate student. William had promoted his career, naming Kallen to edit his last, unfinished work, *Some Problems in Philosophy*. Now Alice needed no more reminders of what William meant to her: "And for me—all my days are anniversaries—and I keep them alone."[101]

During her last years, despite her aphasia and developing heart problems, Alice returned to the radical social causes that had engaged her as a girl. At the start of the twentieth century's third decade, political progressivism had taken hold. The progressives supported working-class movements, including trade unions. Thanks to Bessie Evans and also to her own political idealism that finally trumped her infatuation with wealth and privilege, Alice became involved with the Sacco and Vanzetti case. On 15 April 1920 in South Braintree, just a short distance from Weymouth, two men shot and mortally wounded a paymaster and a guard who were carrying a shoe factory's payroll. Three weeks later the police arrested two Italian immigrants, Nicola Sacco and Bartolomeo Vanzetti. Sacco was a shoemaker and Vanzetti a fish peddler, but both were also anarchists and labor agitators. The police also charged Vanzetti with an attempted robbery that had taken place in Bridgewater. During the summer of 1920 Vanzetti was convicted of this second crime and sentenced to ten to fifteen years in prison. On 14 July 1921 both were found guilty of robbery and murder.

Following the sentencing a long legal battle began to overturn what many viewed as an unjust conviction. There was little concrete evidence to convict the men other than the fact that both had guns on them when the police arrested them and that they lied to the police in initial questioning, possibly because they feared their anarchist convictions might jeopardize them. It was very difficult for the men to find justice: Judge Webster Thayer and the twelve-man jury were all Anglo-American businessmen. The fervor of patriotism sweeping the country after World War I translated to near-xenophobia toward anyone not stamped with a white middle-class Protestant mold. Furthermore, new fears of anarchism, aroused in 1901 after President William McKinley's assassination by an anarchist, swept the country following the Russian Revolution.[102] In 1919 sentiment against the Reds led to deportation of certain known anarchists to Soviet Russia. Alice had the courage to support these avowed anarchists, despite the tide of public opinion.

Longtime friend Elizabeth Glendower Evans had spent most of her life espousing liberal causes, winning international respect as an organizer and agitator. In 1907 she had gone south to study child labor conditions, and in 1908 she had traveled to England to study with socialists. Unlike Alice, she supported women's suffrage. She had been the American delegate to the 1915 International Women's Congress in The Hague. Most recently she had walked the picket line in the second Lawrence, Massachusetts, mill workers strike. In 1920 she was named national director for the American Civil Liberties Union; that same year she met Nicola Sacco and Bartolomeo Vanzetti.[103] She believed passionately in their innocence and became their personal friend, and she convinced Alice of her views.

Alice's Harry was right about her prejudices: while she clung to their general shape, in particular cases she transcended them to do what seemed to her to be the right thing. The Sacco-Vanzetti incident by all rights should have aroused her prejudices: both men were Italian and Catholic. In addition, they were working-class men, and while she did not dislike the lower classes on principle, she was so entrenched in her Cambridge-Boston-London-Rye world that she had little contact with such people other than as servants. But she forgave the accused men their "pagan practices" and their lower-class origins because she felt that they had been wrongfully accused. It had been her husband's belief, held as early as 1868, that the foundation of moral goodness lay in "a sympathy with men."[104] Alice judged that these men deserved her sympathy.

She read reports of the Sacco-Vanzetti trial aloud to Bruce, and she sent Bessie a check for $10 for the two men to divide, for tobacco or any other comfort. She believed in their innocence and longed for a day when the country would see social renewal.[105] This aging yet still committed woman even visited the men in prison, her luminous presence inspiring them as she had once inspired her students at Irene Sanger's school. Nicola Sacco reported to Mrs. Evans, "I begin to read aloud from the day you and Mrs. William James came to see me."[106]

In 1921 Alice attended the first hearing for a new trial with Bessie Evans, both women searched by the police for concealed weapons. She went to at least one more hearing, on 29 October, taking her old friend Helen Bigelow Merriman along. It was so hot in the courtroom that the two women left early; the heat bothered Mrs. Merriman tremendously, though seventy-two-year-old Alice seemed unconscious of it. She was pleased with Vanzetti's lawyer's performance, hoping that Sacco's man would do as well. She sent Bessie another check, this time for $25. After seeing both the defendants in person she told Bessie she was even more convinced of their innocence: "As Mrs. Merriman said, we both felt as if could we talk to the judge or jury our conviction of the innocence of those men would be theirs—two <u>good</u> faces!"[107] She offered to go with Bessie to the next hearing, if there would be one. The last May of her life, even though she was bedridden, she asked Peggy to take her again to the Dedham jail to see the convicted men. Harry advised Peggy to say that she could not bear such a visit, as it would be the only way to dissuade their mother from jeopardizing her own health by visiting these men.[108]

But despite all efforts, both men received the death penalty. After numerous passionate and lengthy appeals, Sacco and Vanzetti were executed in 1927.[109]

With the birth of Aleck's second son, Danny, Alice had one more tie to bind her to this world. In 1920 the young couple moved from Santa Barbara back to Dublin, where they lived in an old brick farmhouse.[110] By 1921 Alice had mended her bridges with Frederika to the extent that her daughter-in-law was willing to have the baby at 95 Irving Street. While the couple had a peaceful place, conducive to Aleck's painting, their living conditions were primitive: they had a well and an outhouse and no electricity. Irving Street was a more comfortable and a safer place to give birth.

At the end of November Aleck and Frederika spent the night with Alice, the next day visiting local Dr. Swain, whom Frederika liked. He advised that Alice's quiet house in Cambridge would be right for the birth and that Frederika and Aleck should come a month before her due date, which was

7 March, so that Frederika could rest.[111] Daniel James was born in mid-March, an eight- and-a-half-pound baby. Alice thought he was splendid. Frederika slept in the brown room, and the nurse and the baby were in a room on the other side of the entry. Alice placed a buzzer in Frederika's room so that she could summon Miss Ferguson as needed.[112] Frederika, though, still felt uncomfortable with her formidable mother-in-law, later remembering her as a dark presence coming in to her room.[113]

While keeping close watch on her family and on important political events, Alice kept an eye on the other world; pursuit of William's spirit remained her passion. Alice followed developments in spiritual research closely. During the spring of 1920 she heard a lecture by British researcher Sir Oliver Lodge. While some points did not convince her, she found him benign and tolerant.[114] In 1920 she read William McDougal's presidential address in the Society for Psychical Research's journal, *Proceedings*. He claimed that our souls continue to evolve spiritually, that people can re-mold themselves into something vital and worthy.[115] Not only was Alice searching for her ghosts, she hoped through her explorations to develop her soul. Alice believed she had begun this transformation through her ongoing education and her involvement with Sacco and Vanzetti, among her other pursuits. Weary of her house, she wanted to rent it to people without children who would care for William's books.[116] She was ready to loosen the ties that tethered her to the earth, but loosening those ties entailed forays to the other side.

Alice and Peggy still shared a belief that they could find William. In the spring of 1920, after Peggy had lost her baby and while she debated whether to go to Cambridge, she practiced automatic writing with the help of a Mrs. Lewis. One evening Peggy received six pages of information from someone, generalities about keeping in good spirits, taking care of her child, news that her mother would be coming, but no substantive facts. Mrs. Lewis did not think these messages came from William, Peggy told her mother. "She said she thought it was extremely unlikely that Dad came through me because he was a great teacher and would naturally be giving the big impersonal thing but I should probably have my own guidance in the matter."[117]

During the summer of 1922 Peggy again visited Alice, leaving Bruce and the children behind. She was not only drawn back to the world of her childhood, but, like Persephone, she was drawn to the world of the dead, where Alice sometimes dwelled. A Mrs. Johnston came to hold a séance in the library, where William's spirit would be strongest. As she knew these attempts to reach him were crucially important to her mother, Peggy was determined to see the séance through.[118]

However, Peggy upset Bruce when she told him of their attempt to reach William in heaven or wherever he might be. He asked her to choose: if she persisted in trying to reach William, he and the children would have to participate in séances, too. And he, at least, did not think her father would have approved of her activities. William would have been happy seeing Peggy's happiness: he would not have wanted "all this fluency in trite words." Bruce made his wife's choice crystal clear: "Your duty to your Mother is kind truth. Your duty to your husband & your children is first—and is unencumbered happiness of heart & mind." It was as though Bruce Porter and Alice James waged a battle for Peggy; her soul lay in the balance scales. If she really dealt with heaven, then he would follow her. But if she communicated neither with heaven nor hell, then she must return (in body *and* in spirit) to her family. "Now ponder this choice—because it is absolutely up to you. I refuse to play on any half-hearted conviction. It is a dedication or a repudiation. You have got to say which." If she remained loyal to Alice, then Peggy abandoned Bruce and the children.

Bruce thought Alice caused some of his wife's depression, calling her daughter "Poor Peggy," though unreliable Aunt Margie was the source of this last remark. Middle-aged Bruce summoned the energy to help raise their children, but he could not shoulder Alice's troubles.[119] He had his own convictions, a blend of Unitarianism and Swedenborgianism, but these convictions did not include a belief in psychic communications. Most of all, he wanted Peggy to reenact the same sacrifices her mother had made to the Jameses, giving up her own life for her family.[120] Bruce Porter won this battle, at least outwardly, as Peggy left 95 Irving Street that summer and returned to California, leaving Alice alone with her ghosts.

In the end those ghosts sustained her. Even before her last summer with Peggy, Alice grew reconciled to what was to come. On 10 May 1922, the forty-fourth anniversary of her engagement to William, she had told Harry, "I ought to go on my way gratefully, for I have had my turn."[121]

That spring she ate and slept well, napping each day. Her spirits remained strong.[122] With Aleck's help, that summer Alice bought a new automobile, an Essex.[123] She continued to battle with the Irving Street house. Mice had chewed through wool packing around the lead pipe beneath the kitchen sink and greasy water overflowed, making a terrible mess. The plumber wrapped the new pipe in tin to prevent the mice from doing more damage.[124]

Early in July, with Dr. Taylor's approval, Peggy and Alice traveled to Dublin to visit Aleck. He was in the midst of renovations, having a man plaster the ceiling of the sitting room, paint, hang wallpaper, and fix the floor.[125] The visit went well: Alice found the family happy, Aleck's studio plastered, Danny weaned—and, always her passion, "a brisk sale of broilers [chickens] by Miss Venable," the family's part-time nurse.[126] Alice was sorry to leave the rural quiet for Cambridge, but she planned to spend next winter in Dublin, those fences mended at last. Aleck and Frederika discussed plans for altering their house to make it more comfortable for her.[127] Alice now called her first grandson Sandy, "my unearned increment."[128]

When Peggy left in mid-July, Alice was sorry to see her leave, but it was at last time for Alice to be selfish. She had fought to become who she was, an independent, intelligent, ethical, and passionate woman who had led a fascinating life. She consoled herself with the thought that she could read more when she was alone, informing Harry, "It is time I read Shakespeare—as I have never done—save by fractions."[129] She also read biographies, essays, and, again, Prentice Mulford's work.

Even as she enjoyed her own pursuits, Alice's physical being failed. She talked (or whispered) to herself more and more, a way of focusing her activity.[130] Though Dr. Taylor ordered her to stay in bed because her heart was so weak and her circulation so impaired, she defied orders more than once. One day Minnie Kidd could not find her anywhere on the lower three floors of 95 Irving Street. While she looked for Alice in the library, the ailing woman slipped into her bedroom carrying a load of family papers she had fetched from the attic on a tea tray.[131] In solitude she winnowed through the remnants of her past, destroying letters and papers so that certain chapters of her story—and William's and her father's—would never be told.[132]

Less than a month from her death Harry marveled at her self-control; she had reached Nirvana. "The wonderful and beautiful thing is Mama's serenity of mind."[133] But by the end of August her conditioned had worsened: she had pain in her feet that kept her from sleeping at nights. Dr. Taylor gave her small doses of morphine to relieve her distress. While she could still write, her vision was affected so that she could not read, and objects over twenty feet away looked blurred. She remained in good spirits nearly to the end, turning over favorite memories and enjoying having someone read aloud to her.

Her last days she endured more pain, so much so that sometimes she cried out. Billy's wife, Alice, gave her laudanum when the pain intensified.[134] On 12 September Alice wrote her last letter to her daughter, her once firm, rounded handwriting weak and wavering. Though she was sad to leave her family, she was not afraid. "I have a queer feeling that my time is short here, and you know that I believe that life and death are all part of the heavenly order, and so I have believed in death, never as a punishment but as part of the journey. Now that I have come to the end of the road it feels lonely to be going away from you all but my love will never leave you. So when you read this believe that all is well with me, and all [of] you must promise to survive and endure."[135] After receiving this letter Peggy came from San Francisco. At the end Alice lost consciousness. Peggy wrote to Bruce of her mother's last days: "She is wrapped in such serenity and peace. It's been a blessed life and she goes much loved and mourned and having done her gallant best."[136] Alice died at home on a Saturday morning, 30 September.

On 7 October 1922 Alice's obituary appeared in the *Cambridge Chronicle*, "Widow of Prof. James." In the obituary her birthdate was listed as 1840, not 1849. She was cited for providing the family home that "during the life of Professor James was the center of much intellectual activity, where the students coming in touch with Professor James at the college, as well as men and women of scholarly attainments, were always welcome." Her funeral was held in Harvard's Appleton Chapel the Tuesday after her death, the Reverend Samuel Crothers of the First Parish Church holding the service. She was buried in the Cambridge Cemetery, her name engraved on the tombstone with William's. Next to her is a smaller tombstone with the inscription:

HERMAN
3rd Son of
William and Alice James
Jan 31 1884—July 1886[137]

Just one hundred yards from the James family plot lies the grave of Rufus
Ellis, who had counseled Daniel Lewis Gibbens and married Alice and William. His epitaph reads: "GONE, INTO THE WORLD OF LIGHT."

Alice left a detailed will, made three years before her death. Harry was
her executor. The first clause named bequests of $1,000 to Henry's former
servants, Minnie Kidd, Burgess Noakes, and Joan Paddington Anderson.
William's library went to Harry, and various itemized household goods
were given to her four children. She left annuities of $600 a year to her
sisters. The rest of her estate was divided into four shares, one for each of
her children, though Harry administered Peggy's share. Witnesses were
John Singer Sargent's sisters Emily Sargent and Reine Ormond and Henry's
architect, Edward H. Warren.[138]

Alice died a wealthy widow, her personal assets valued at $255,691.63 and
her real estate at $25,000, which was only the property at 95 Irving Street.
It did not include the land in Keene Valley or the farm at Chocorua. She
owned shares in such diverse concerns as the Montana Power Company;
U.S. Smelting, Refining & Mining; Hayes Wheel Company; New York
Telephone Company; Bell Telephone of Canada; Great Britain & Ireland
War Bonds; General Electric Company; Seamless Rubber Realty Associates; American Sugar Refining Company; United Fruit Company; and
Quaker Oats. She held the copyrights to William's and Henry's work, the
combined rights valued at over $26,000. She also owned a one-thousand-
dollar mortgage on the house that belonged to the deceased Charles Peirce
and his wife, Juliette. Finally, she owned "about a dozen hens," valued
at $15.[139]

In front of 95 Irving Street once stood a stone engraved with the number
"1876." Forty years after Alice's death her grandson John Runnells James,
Billy's second son, announced that he had solved the mystery of the number:
it was the year that Alice Howe Gibbens met William James.[140]

Appendix 1: Alice Howe Gibbens Genealogy

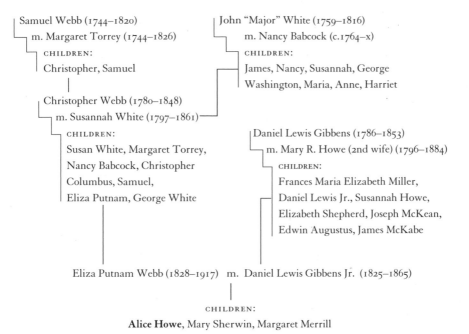

Samuel Webb (1744–1820)
m. Margaret Torrey (1744–1826)
CHILDREN:
Christopher, Samuel

John "Major" White (1759–1816)
m. Nancy Babcock (c.1764–x)
CHILDREN:
James, Nancy, Susannah, George
Washington, Maria, Anne, Harriet

Christopher Webb (1780–1848)
m. Susannah White (1797–1861)
CHILDREN:
Susan White, Margaret Torrey,
Nancy Babcock, Christopher
Columbus, Samuel,
Eliza Putnam, George White

Daniel Lewis Gibbens (1786–1853)
m. Mary R. Howe (2nd wife) (1796–1884)
CHILDREN:
Frances Maria Elizabeth Miller,
Daniel Lewis Jr., Susannah Howe,
Elizabeth Shepherd, Joseph McKean,
Edwin Augustus, James McKabe

Eliza Putnam Webb (1828–1917) m. Daniel Lewis Gibbens Jr. (1825–1865)

CHILDREN:

Alice Howe, Mary Sherwin, Margaret Merrill

Appendix 2: William James Genealogy

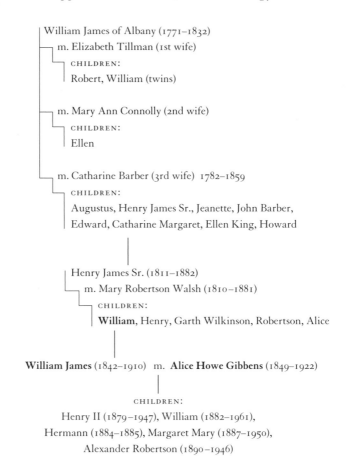

William James of Albany (1771–1832)

m. Elizabeth Tillman (1st wife)

CHILDREN:

Robert, William (twins)

m. Mary Ann Connolly (2nd wife)

CHILDREN:

Ellen

m. Catharine Barber (3rd wife) 1782–1859

CHILDREN:

Augustus, Henry James Sr., Jeanette, John Barber, Edward, Catharine Margaret, Ellen King, Howard

Henry James Sr. (1811–1882)

m. Mary Robertson Walsh (1810–1881)

CHILDREN:

William, Henry, Garth Wilkinson, Robertson, Alice

William James (1842–1910) m. **Alice Howe Gibbens** (1849–1922)

CHILDREN:

Henry II (1879–1947), William (1882–1961),
Hermann (1884–1885), Margaret Mary (1887–1950),
Alexander Robertson (1890–1946)

NOTES

ABBREVIATIONS

Proper Names

AHGJ	Alice Howe Gibbens James
AJ	Alice James
ARJ	Alexander Robertson James
DLG	Daniel Lewis Gibbens
EPG	Eliza Putnam Gibbens
FRM	Frances R. Morse
HJ	Henry James
HJ II	Henry James II (called HJ III by some scholars in order to distinguish him from his uncle Henry James, the novelist, and his grandfather, Henry James Sr.)
HJ Sr.	Henry James Sr.
JGW	John Greenleaf Whittier
MMJ	Margaret Mary James (Mrs. Bruce Porter)
RJ	Robertson James
WJ	William James
WJ Jr.	William James Jr.

Archival Abbreviations

ALS	autographed letter signed
B	Bancroft Library, University of California at Berkeley
H	Houghton Library, Harvard College Library, Harvard University

H bMS Am 1092.9–1092.11	James, William, 1842–1910, Papers
H bMS Am 1938	James, William, 1842–1910, Papers
H MS Am 1095.2	James Family Additional Papers, 1858–1947
H MS Am 2538	James Family Additional Papers, 1859–1922
H fMS 1092.9	Alice Howe Gibbens James Family Photos
H pfMS Am 1094	Henry James Photos
H *2002M-44(b)	Margaret Mary James (Mrs. Bruce Porter) Collection
H bMS Eng 1080	Letters to Margaret James Porter

M	Rare Books and Special Collections Division, McGill University Library
S	Schlesinger Library, Radcliffe College
TLS	typed letter signed

1. Robert Richardson, *William James: In the Maelstrom of American Modernism* (Boston: Houghton Mifflin, 2006), 268. Richardson has a persuasive account of Alice's important role in facilitating William's work.

2. ALS, AHGJ to HJ, 11 November 1907, William James Papers, 1842–1910, H bMS Am 1092.11 (47). William gave this lecture more than once, beginning as early as 1905. I am grateful to the Houghton Library, Harvard College, for permission to quote from the James Family Papers. I also thank Bay James for her generous permission to use James family material deposited in archives and collections.

1. STIRRINGS

1. Information on Weymouth comes from *History of Weymouth, Massachusetts*, vol. 1, *Historical* (Weymouth MA: Weymouth Historical Society, 1923). I am grateful to Debra Sullivan, Philip Lawson Smith, and Bill Tormey of the Weymouth Historical Society for their invaluable and generous help. Information on the Gibbens family comes from Henry James II's unpublished memoir of his mother, "Alice Howe Gibbens, 1849–1922," courtesy of Michael James.

2. Information on nineteenth-century rural medical practices is taken from "Medicine," in *The Reader's Companion to American History*, n.d., 15 January 2004, http://college.hmco.com/history/readerscomp/rcah/htmal/ah_058700 _medicine.htm.

3. ALS, AHGJ to WJ Jr., 4 January 1907, James Family Additional Papers, 1859–1922 (bulk), 1859–1986 (inclusive), H MS Am 2538. Gift of the late William James III through the agency of Roberta A. Sheehan and of Michael James.

4. Richard D. Pierce, ed., *The Records of the First Church in Boston, 1630–1868*, Publications of the Colonial Society of Massachusetts (Boston: Colonial Society of Massachusetts, 1961), 40:568. The First Church of Boston, now located at the corner of Berkeley and Marlborough streets in the Back Bay but at the time on Chauncey Place, was actually a Congregational Unitarian Church. Between 1805 and 1825 Congregational churches divided into Trinitarian or Unitarian bodies, the First Church becoming "Congregational Unitarian." I am grateful to Dr. Harold F. Worthley, librarian at the Congregational Library, Boston, for information on First Church.

5. Sydney E. Ahlstrom, *A Religious History of the American People* (New Haven CT: Yale University Press, 1972), 387.

6. Edmund Soper Hunt, *Reminiscences: Weymouth Ways and Weymouth People* (Boston: Privately printed, 1907), 91; Weymouth Town Records, Tufts Library, Weymouth, Massachusetts, 11 September 1826.

7. Henry James II's memoir of his mother makes it clear that this separation was not only for economic reasons. See sec. 2, "Alice Howe Gibbens, 1849–1922."

8. Caption for daguerreotype, H bMS Am 1092.9 (4597.1).

9. See www.maritimeheritage.org/ships/ss.html. If the Gibbenses sailed on the *Northern Light*, that ship's last run from New York to Nicaragua was in February 1856, which would help date their voyage.

10. John Haskell Kemble, *The Panama Route: 1848–1869* (Berkeley: University of California Press, 1943), 162.

11. See Sim Moak, *The Last of the Mill Creeks and Early Life in Northern California* (Chico CA, 1923), 3–6, for a description of this area.

12. For further information on the ill-fated Walker rebellion see Amy S. Greenberg, "A Gray-Eyed Man: Character, Appearance, and Filibustering," *Journal of the Early Republic* 20, no. 4 (2000): 674. This skirmish may have been the battle near Virgin Bay, one of the towns on the Vanderbilt transit route. The battle took place in August 1855, and sixty Legitimists died. See Roger Bruns and Bryan Kennedy, "El Presidente Gringo," *American History Illustrated* 24, no. 10 (1989): 20.

13. See Kemble, *The Panama Route*, app. A, for a list of the Vanderbilt ships and the years they sailed the Nicaragua routes.

14. ALS, AHGJ to Aunt Nannie [Nancy Babcock Webb Jackson], 23 December 1892, H bMS Am 1092.11 (63).

15. "Alice Howe Gibbens, 1849–1922," 14.

16. Information on the Santa Clara Ranches during this period comes from Clyde Arbuckle, *Santa Clara County Ranches* (San Jose CA: Harlan-Young Press, 1968).

17. Alice's daughter Margaret "Peggy" James Porter learned this from a friend named Janet Peck who inherited the property through Dr. Murphy's estate. "Alice Howe Gibbens, 1849–1922," 16–17.

18. Details on the California years come from "Alice Howe Gibbens, 1849–1922."

19. HJ II, "Notes," H *2002M-44(b), box 1, folder 6.

20. ALS, DLG to AHGJ and sisters, 28 July 1859, H bMS Am 1938 (287).

21. Grandmother Gibbens to Alice and Mary Gibbens, n.d. [ca. late 1850s], H bMS Am 1938 (286).

22. Bertram Wyatt-Brown, "Conscience and Career," in Laurence B. Goodheart and Hugh Hawkins, eds., *The Abolitionists: Means, Ends, and Motivations*, 3rd ed. (Lexington MA: D. C. Heath & Co., 1995), 96–97.

23. Linda Simon, *Genuine Reality: A Life of William James* (New York: Harcourt, Brace & Co., 1998), 151–52.

24. John Brown, "Speech to the Court (1859)," in Goodheart and Hawkins, *The Abolitionists*, 66.

25. Hunt, *Reminiscences*, 69–72.

26. Goodheart and Hawkins, *The Abolitionists*, xx, xxi, 69, 115. Antinomianism can be loosely defined as a religiously motivated desire for the end of the rule of law, which would be replaced by an age of spiritualism.

27. John L. Thomas, "Romantic Reform in America, 1815–1865," in Goodheart and Hawkins, *The Abolitionists*, 80–81.

28. F. O. Matthiessen, *American Renaissance: Art and Expression in the Age of Emerson and Whitman* (London: Oxford University Press, 1941), viii.

29. Ahlstrom, *Religious History*, 483–88.

30. Details on his time as ship's doctor are from his unpublished diary, "Daniel Lewis Gibbens Journal of a voyage N.Y. to Liverpool and return (Nov. 7, 1859 to Feb. 15—1860) as ship's surgeon on the 'Manhattan' of the Liverpool line," H MS Am 2538.

31. ALS, Rufus Ellis to DLG, 31 December 1861, H bMS Am 1938 (285).

32. ALS, DLG to AHGJ, 28 November 1862, H bMS Am 1938 (287).

33. ALS, George Foster Shepley to DLG, 1 March 1864, H bMS Am 1938 (291).

34. Album notes on photograph, H bMS Am 1092.9 (4597).

35. ALS, DLG to AHGJ, 11 May 1865, H bMS Am 1938 (287).

36. *Boston Herald*, 25 November 1865, 4.

37. Appendix A, "The Strange Death of Daniel Gibbens," in R. W. B. Lewis, *The Jameses: A Family Narrative* (New York: Farrar, Straus and Giroux, 1991), 590.

38. Newspaper clippings included with ALS, DLG to AHGJ, 10 November 1865, H bMS Am 1938 (287).

39. ALS, DLG to AHGJ, 2 July [1865], H bMS Am 1938 (287).

40. ALS, DLG to AHGJ, 9 June 1865, H bMS Am 1938 (287).

41. ALS, DLG to AHGJ, 13 August 1865, H bMS Am 1938 (287).

42. ALS, DLG to AHGJ, 2, 4 July 1865, H bMS Am 1938 (287).

43. ALS, DLG to AHGJ, 9 June 1865, H bMS Am 1938 (287).

44. ALS, DLG to AHGJ, 14 July 1865, H bMS Am 1938 (287).

45. ALS, DLG to AHGJ, 13 August [1865], H bMS Am 1938 (287).

46. ALS, DLG to AHGJ, 10 November 1865, H bMS Am 1938 (287).

47. "Alice Howe Gibbens, 1849–1922," 20, 22.

48. ALS, DLG to AHGJ, 10 June 1865, H bMS Am 1938 (287).

49. "Alice Howe Gibbens, 1849–1922," 22.

50. 20 August 1865, "Alice Howe Gibbens, 1849–1922," 23.

51. "Alice Howe Gibbens, 1849–1922," 23.

52. ALS, EPG to AHGJ, 13 August [c. 1865–67], H bMS Am 1092.11 (64).

53. Samuel Atkins Eliot, *A History of Cambridge Massachusetts (1630–1913), Together with Biographies of Cambridge People* (Cambridge MA: Cambridge Tribune, 1913), 59–60.

54. Samuel Eliot Morison, *Three Centuries of Harvard, 1636–1936* (Cambridge MA: Harvard University Press, 1936), 250.

55. S. B. Sutton, *Cambridge Reconsidered: 3½ Centuries on the Charles* (Cambridge MA: MIT Press, 1976), 2.

56. "Alice Howe Gibbens, 1849–1922," 22.

57. MS, HJ II, "Notes on the Death of Daniel Lewis Gibbens," March 1938, H bMS Am 1938 (289).

58. *Boston Herald*, 2 December 1865, 2.

59. Details of Gibbens's last days come from ALS, J. F. Bailey to AHGJ, 27 December 1865, H bMS Am 1938 (284).

60. ALS, J. Bailey to Gibbens, 1865, H bMS Am 1938 (284). The envelope for this letter is addressed to "Mrs. D. L. Gibbens, Weymouth, Mass.," but the salutation is to Alice. Other details of Dr. Gibbens's last days come from "Alice Howe Gibbens, 1849–1922" and from Appendix A, "The Strange Death of Daniel Gibbens," in Lewis, *The Jameses*, 590–92. Lewis concludes that although Henry James II decided that his grandfather had not been guilty of wrongdoing, Gibbens must have played a role in the widespread fraud that characterized the Civil War's end.

61. Gay Wilson Allen, *William James: A Biography* (New York: Viking Press, 1967), 217–18. Allen's biography contains information about Alice Howe Gibbens available nowhere else, as he had access to her diaries, which disappeared after the 1960s.

62. Paula Cope of the North Weymouth Cemetery Association kindly researched their records: there are no Gibbenses (or Gibbonses or Gibbinses) buried there (30 June 2003).

63. ALS, J. Bailey to AHGJ, 1865, H bMS Am 1938 (284).

64. New England Historic Genealogical Society, Norfolk County Records, Administration #7,952, p. 186.

65. HJ II, "Notes on the Death of Daniel Lewis Gibbens," 20, H bMS Am 1938 (289).

66. *Weymouth Weekly Gazette*, 2 May 1867.

67. *Weymouth Weekly Gazette*, 6 December 1867.

68. *Weymouth Weekly Gazette*, 17 January 1868, 13 March 1868.

69. *Weymouth Weekly Gazette*, 10 July 1868.

2. NEW VENTURES

1. Information on the years abroad comes from "Alice Howe Gibbens, 1849–1922," 27–33.

2. Patrick K. O'Brien, *The Economic Effects of the American Civil War* (Atlantic Highlands NJ: Humanities Press International, 1988), 17, 18, 52.

3. Pro-Quest, *New York Times Historical Edition*, July 1868.

4. Alice's sister Margaret mentioned this journalist and her article, but I have not been able to locate it. "Alice Howe Gibbens, 1849–1922," 28.

5. ALS, WJ to AHGJ, 30 July [18]85, H bMS Am 1092.9 (1400). In 1885 William recalled Alice's "delightful recital" of the trip to Giessen, mentioning Eckstein's name.

6. AHGJ to EPG, 31 May 1900, quoted in "Alice Howe Gibbens, 1849–1922," 30–31.

7. "II. Heidelberg," in Samuel Clemens, *A Tramp Abroad* (New York: Harper Brothers, 1880).

8. ALS, EPG to Deborah Webb, 30 August 1869, H bMS Am 1938 (262).

9. ALS, EPG to Deborah Webb, 30 August 1869, H bMS Am 1938 (262).

10. Clara Thies' family owned the house at 20 Quincy Street, first renting it and then selling it to Henry James Sr. in 1870. See Alfred Habegger, *The Father: A Life of Henry James, Sr.* (New York: Farrar, Straus and Giroux, 1994), 448.

11. "Alice Howe Gibbens, 1849–1922," 4.

12. WJ to AJ, 23 November 1873, in Ignas K. Skrupskelis and Elizabeth M. Berkeley, eds., *The Correspondence of William James*, 12 vols. (Charlottesville: University of Virginia Press, 1992–2005), 4:459. Hereafter cited as *Correspondence*.

13. Henry James, *Italian Hours* (Boston: Houghton Mifflin, 1909), 422.

14. *Baker's Biographical Dictionary of Musicians*, 8th ed. (New York: Schirmer Books, 1992), s.v. "Vannuccini, Luigi."

15. AHGJ to Margaret Gibbens, 30 March 1893 [or 1892], H bMS Am 1092.11 (24).

16. Information on Alice's Boston years (1873–78) comes from "Alice Howe Gibbens, 1849–1922," sec. 5.

17. Robert S. Cox, *Body and Soul: A Sympathetic History of American Spiritualism* (Charlottesville: University of Virginia Press, 2003), 12–16.

18. George Trobridge, *Swedenborg: Life and Teaching*, rev. Richard F. Tafel Sr. and Richard F. Tafel Jr. (New York: Swedenborg Foundation, 1992), 68.

19. Trobridge, *Swedenborg*, 58.

20. Trobridge, *Swedenborg*, 92–93.

21. Eugene Taylor, Ph.D., lecturer at Harvard's School of Psychiatry, has written extensively and persuasively concerning William James's debt to Swedenborg. See *William James: Consciousness Beyond the Margin* (Princeton NJ: Princeton University Press, 2001) and many other essays by Dr. Taylor.

22. I am indebted to Sheldon M. Novick, scholar in residence at Vermont Law School, for information on these Boston neighborhoods in the 1870s.

23. Boston directories, conversation with Peter Drummey, librarian, Massachusetts Historical Society.

24. See Megan Marshall, *The Peabody Sisters* (Boston: Houghton Mifflin, 2005) for a discussion of private schools run by women during this period.

25. By 1870 there were 123,980 women teachers to 78,709 men, according to Anna C. Brackett, *The Education of American Girls, Considered in a Series of Essays* (New York: G. P. Putnam's Sons, 1879), 89. There is no information as to how these numbers were ascertained.

26. Averil Evans McClelland, *The Education of Women in the United States* (New York: Garland, 1992), 123–24.

27. McClelland, *The Education of Women*, 125.

28. Simon, *Genuine Reality*, 154, 407n29.

29. ALS, JGW to AHGJ, 27 March 1876, H bMS Am 1092.9 (4351).

30. Information on the Radical Club comes from Mrs. John (Mary E.) Sargent, ed., *Sketches and Reminiscences of the Radical Club of Chestnut Street, Boston* (Boston: James R. Osgood & Co., 1880).

31. Ahlstrom, *Religious History*, 764–65.

32. Background on the Radical Club comes from Habegger, *The Father*, 458–59.

33. Sargent, *Sketches*, 384–85.

34. ALS, JGW to AHGJ, 26 March 1875, H bMS Am 1092.9 (4346).

35. Lewis, *The Jameses*, 273; ALS, JGW to AHGJ, 24 October 1874, H bMS Am 1092.9 (4343).

36. ALS, JGW to AHGJ, 15 October 1875, H bMS Am 1092.9 (4348).

37. ALS, JGW to AHGJ, 20 March 1877, H bMS Am 1092.9 (4353).

38. ALS, JGW to AHGJ, 20 March 1875, H bMS Am 1092.9 (4345); JGW to AHGJ, n.d., H bMS Am 1092.9 (4350).

39. JGW to AHGJ, [27 March 1876], H bMS Am 1092.9 (4351).

40. ALS, JGW to AHGJ, 17 February 1875, H bMS Am 1092.9 (4344). The poem in its second part reads:

Two faces bowed before the Throne
veiled in their golden hair,
Four white wings lessened swiftly
down the dark abyss of air.
The way was strange, the flight was
long, at last the angels came
Where swung the lost and nether
world, red-wrapped in penal flame.
There Pity dropped a tender tear, and
Love, too strong for fear,

Took heart from God's almightiness

and smiled a smile of cheer.

And lo! that tearful Pity quenched the

flame whereon it fell,

And, with the sunshine of that smile

hope entered into hell!

41. ALS, JGW to AHGJ, 1 June 1875, H bMS Am 1092.9 (4347); ALS, JGW to AHGJ, 17 March 1877, H bMS Am 1092.9 (4352).

42. ALS, JGW to AHGJ, n.d., H MS Am 1095.2 (36).

3. HE LOVES ME, HE LOVES ME NOT

1. Lewis, *The Jameses*, 270–74.

2. Habegger, *The Father*, 277–79, 333–34.

3. Sargent, *Sketches*, 210–11.

4. Thomas Davidson (1840–1900) was a professor and talented linguist. He lectured on sociology in New York, forming a special class for young Jewish men and women. "Alice Howe Gibbens, 1849–1922," 34.

5. Simon mentions that William went alone to a Radical Club meeting and then went again, asking Thomas Davidson to introduce him to Alice (*Genuine Reality*, 154).

6. Lewis, *The Jameses*, 270.

7. WJ to RJ, 14 November 1869, *Correspondence*, 4:389–90.

8. William James of Albany's net worth was estimated at $1.2 million. In his complicated will Henry James Sr., who had disappointed his father by his irresponsible youthful behavior, received a lifetime annuity of $1,250 but no portion of the trust. The will was contested, and by 1837 Henry Sr. knew that he would inherit his share of the fortune (Habegger, *The Father*, 109–12, 141–42). See also Habegger, *The Father*, for an account of Henry James Sr.'s life and his influence on his children. Sheldon M. Novick in *Henry James: The Young Master* (New York: Random House, 1996) gives another account of HJ Sr.'s inheritance and income: his family had comfortable financial circumstances, but they were not wealthy, as former estimates suggest.

9. See Jane Maher, *Biography of Broken Fortunes: Wilkie and Bob, Brothers of William, Henry and Alice James* (Hamden CT: Archon Books, 1986).

10. Simon, *Genuine Reality*, 86–92. Simon notes that Henry Sr.'s willingness to allow William to attend the Lawrence Scientific School may have been a way to keep his son from enlisting.

11. WJ to Alice James, 25 December 1866, *Correspondence*, 4:149.

12. Ralph Barton Perry, *The Thought and Character of William James* (1948; reprint, Nashville: Vanderbilt University Press, 1996), 105.

13. WJ to Thomas Wren Ward, [7] January 1868, *Correspondence*, 4:250.

14. For an account of Alice James and her early relations with William see Jean Strouse, *Alice James: A Biography* (Boston: Houghton Mifflin, 1980), 52–55.

15. WJ to AJ, [30 January 1867], *Correspondence*, 4:151.

16. WJ to AJ, 16 March 1868, *Correspondence*, 4:264.

17. "Reproductions of William James Drawings," H *2002M-44(b).

18. ALS, HJ to HJ II, 3 October 1913, H bMS Am 1094 (1403).

19. WJ to AJ, 14 May 1868, *Correspondence*, 4:295.

20. Allen, *William James*, 148.

21. WJ to Thomas Wren Ward, 24 May 1868, *Correspondence*, 4:305, 309.

22. WJ to Catherine Havens, 24 February 1869, *Correspondence*, 4:368.

23. WJ to Catherine Havens, 29 August 1868, *Correspondence*, 4:334.

24. ALS, Catherine Havens to AHGJ, 30 July 1913, 6 September 1913, H bMS Am 1092.10 (323).

25. Allen, *William James*, 163.

26. Allen, *William James*, 155.

27. Simon, *Genuine Reality*, 121n. Simon has the most complete account of the McLean records for that time, but she found no proof that William James had been a patient there in the winter of either 1870 or 1871.

28. WJ to Henry Bowditch, 24 January 1869, in Henry James II, ed., *The Letters of William James*, 2 vols. (Boston: Atlantic Monthly Press, 1920), 1:150.

29. HJ to WJ, 30 November [1869], *Correspondence*, 1:126.

30. WJ to HJ, 27 December 1869, *Correspondence*, 1:132.

31. WJ to HJ, 19 January 1870, *Correspondence*, 1:140.

32. Mary Temple to WJ, [15 January 1870], *Correspondence*, 4:401.

33. William James, *The Varieties of Religious Experience: A Study in Human Nature* (Cambridge MA: Harvard University Press, 1985), 134.

34. WJ to HJ, 7 May 1870, in James II, *The Letters*, 1:158. Charles Barnard Renouvier (1815–1903) formulated an idealistic philosophical system based on Kant. He believed in the validity of personal experience, with the corollary belief that liberty is humanity's fundamental characteristic. He also believed in a finite God and thought that even atheism was better than believing in a deity with infinite power.

35. James II, *The Letters*, 1:147.

36. Catharine Walsh (c. 1812–89) lived with the Jameses for many years, traveling with the family and helping her sister Mary raise the five children. In 1853 she married a sea captain, Charles H. Marshall, but the marriage was short-lived, and she returned to the James household. She remained with

Henry James Sr. and her niece Alice after Mary's death, leaving the James household early in 1883 after HJ Sr.'s death.

37. WJ to RJ, 1 August 1871, *Correspondence*, 4:421.

38. WJ to Henry P. Bowditch, 8 April 1871, *Correspondence*, 4:418.

39. Allen, *William James*, 174–75.

40. Perry, *The Thought and Character of William James*, 125.

41. Morison, *Three Centuries of Harvard*, 334, 336, 343, 389.

42. Eliot, *A History of Cambridge*, 194–95.

43. See Louis Menand, *The Metaphysical Club: A Story of Ideas in America* (New York: Farrar, Straus and Giroux, 2001), for a history and analysis of this group. Charles Sanders Peirce (1839–1914) was a major influence on WJ's work, particularly on pragmatism, which began with Peirce's 1878 article "How to Make Our Ideas Clear." He did statistical work for the United States Coast Guard until 1887, although his bent was toward philosophy. He lectured at Harvard on logic and on the philosophy of science and wrote voluminously on his ideas. In the later years of his life his reputation declined, though WJ tried to secure funding and recognition for him. His original thinking in phenomenology and semiology has now been recognized, and his work continues to generate discussion and application.

44. See Daniel Bjork, *William James: The Center of His Vision* (Washington, D.C.: American Psychological Association, 1997), 86–90 for an overview of James within the Metaphysical Club and within wider philosophical debates of the early 1870s.

45. WJ to RJ, 20 December 1872, *Correspondence*, 4:432.

46. WJ to RJ, 20 April 1873, *Correspondence*, 4:434.

47. WJ to HJ, 14 July [1873], *Correspondence*, 1:216.

48. Transcript of ALS, Mary Robertson Walsh James to HJ, 12 September [1873], Leon Edel Papers, container 40, "Transcripts of Various Correspondents," Rare Books and Special Collections Division, McGill University Library. I am grateful to the Rare Books and Special Collections Division for permission to quote from letters and papers in the Leon Edel Papers. Researchers should note that the collection has been recataloged, so the numbers used herein have changed.

49. Allen, *William James*, 182–83.

50. WJ to HJ, 25 May 1873, *Correspondence*, 1:208; WJ to HJ, 25 August [1873], *Correspondence*, 1:218.

51. WJ to Mary Robertson Walsh James, 6 November [1873], *Correspondence*, 4:452; WJ to Garth W. James, 16 November 1873, *Correspondence*, 4:455.

52. WJ to AJ, 23 November 1873, *Correspondence*, 4:459.

53. WJ to Garth W. James, 16 November 1873, *Correspondence*, 4:454.

54. WJ to RJ, 8 December [1873], *Correspondence*, 4:465.

55. WJ to HJ Sr., 30 November 1873, *Correspondence*, 4:462.

56. WJ to Catherine Havens, 5 December 1873, *Correspondence*, 4:463.

57. WJ to AJ, 17 December 1873, *Correspondence*, 4:471–72.

58. WJ to RJ, 26 April 1874, *Correspondence*, 4:489.

59. I am grateful to Pierre Walker for this information, which comes from Mary Walsh James's and Henry James Sr.'s 1873–74 letters to Henry James. Both parents thought his battle with depression remained a severe one. See Professor Walker's Web site (www.dearhenryjames.org/) for transcriptions of these letters.

60. Allen, *William James*, 192.

61. WJ to RJ, 4 July 1874, *Correspondence*, 4:497.

62. WJ to Catherine Havens, 20 February 1875, *Correspondence*, 4:507.

63. WJ to Catherine Havens, 13 July 1875, *Correspondence*, 4:517.

64. WJ to HJ, 14 November 1875, *Correspondence*, 1:243.

65. Ignas K. Skrupskelis, "William James," in *American National Biography*, ed. John A. Garraty and Mark C. Carnes (New York: Oxford University Press, 1999), 11:842. Richardson notes that this was the first graduate psychology course in America (*William James*, 179).

66. Perry, *The Thought and Character of William James*, 142.

67. Simon, *Genuine Reality*, 145. The books were on physiology, psychology, and physics.

68. WJ to HJ, 22 January 1876, *Correspondence*, 1:251. This may have been the incident that led to William's asking Thomas Davidson to introduce him to his future wife.

69. "Alice Howe Gibbens, 1849–1922," 34–35.

70. WJ to AHGJ, [14 March 1876], H bMS Am 1092.9 (1160). In this brief thank-you note WJ mentions that he liked the verses about "the young person with the patent costume" best. WJ may have used the word "patent" in the sense of "to make patent or open to sight or notice." If so, he may mean the two stanzas about the pretty young feminist who eschewed bustles and corsets to wear a plain, loose, comfortable garment. "This pretty little pigeon" had no particular religious ideas of her own but thought that "the true religion / Demanded ease of body before the mind could soar." Alice's copy of the poem is in the Houghton Library; she signed her name on the first page "A. H. Gibbens" and annotated it in the margins with the names of those individuals whom she recognized. "The Kindergarten mother clucked in answer to this brother, / And her curls kept bobbing quaintly from the queer head-dress she wore" is "Miss Peabody," and "an ancient Concord bookworm" is "Alcott," for example. The annotations suggest that Alice was quite familiar with most

of the group's members, though it is not certain that she sent the annotated copy to William.

71. William Dean Howells (1837–1920), important American writer and long-time editor of the *Atlantic Monthly*. HJ and Howells met in Cambridge in 1866, and they became close literary friends. In 1910 Howells joined Edith Wharton in recommending HJ for the Nobel Prize.

72. WJ to Catherine Havens, 22 February 1876, *Correspondence*, 4:533–35. The Howells novel may have been *A Foregone Conclusion*, published in 1875.

73. See Allen, *William James*, 214–20, for information on their courtship. Allen had access to Alice's diaries, since destroyed.

74. Photograph, H fMS 1092.9 (4598).

75. AHGJ to WJ Jr., 2 November 1900, H MS Am 2538.

76. ALS, JGW to AHGJ, 27 March 1876, H bMS Am 1092.9 (4351).

77. Edmund Tweedy (died 1901) and his wife, Mary Temple Tweedy (died 1891), were the guardians of HJ and WJ's Temple cousins. WJ to RJ, 11 June [1876], *Correspondence*, 4:537–38.

78. Simon, *Genuine Reality*, 156–57.

79. WJ to AHGJ, [September 1876], *Correspondence*, 4:543.

80. WJ to RJ, 7 May 1876, *Correspondence*, 4:536.

81. Linda Anderson, ed., *Alice James: Her Life in Letters* (Bristol, England: Thoemmes Press, 1996), 92n102.

82. WJ to AHGJ, [September 1876], *Correspondence*, 4:545.

83. AHGJ to WJ, [26 June 1898], *Correspondence*, 8:380. Alice recalled these feelings about him much later. Allen, *William James*, 219.

84. WJ to Thomas Wren Ward, 30 December 1876, *Correspondence*, 4:551–52. At the end of 1876 James told his friend Tom Ward he feared breaking down.

85. WJ to AHGJ, [September 1876], *Correspondence*, 4:546.

86. WJ to AHGJ, [9 October 1876], *Correspondence*, 4:547.

87. WJ to AHGJ, 12 November 1876, *Correspondence*, 4:548–49.

88. WJ to Thomas Ward, 30 December 1876, *Correspondence*, 4:552.

89. Karen Lystra, *Searching the Heart: Women, Men and Romantic Love in Nineteenth-Century America* (New York: Oxford University Press, 1989), 4.

90. Lystra, *Searching the Heart*, 14.

91. Lystra, *Searching the Heart*, 157–58.

92. WJ to AHGJ, 15 March 1877, *Correspondence*, 4:554. He wrote this letter after one of Child's Chaucer lectures, so possibly both of them attended this one.

93. ALS, Mary Robertson Walsh James to AHGJ, [March 1877], H bMS Am 1092.9 (4318).

94. Francis James Child (1825–96) was a James family friend for many years. He was an authority on English and Scottish ballads.

95. ALS, JGW to AHGJ, 17 March 1877, H bMS Am 1092.9 (4352).

96. ALS, JGW to AHGJ, 30 March 1877, H bMS Am 1092.9 (4353).

97. WJ to AHGJ, 23 April [1877], *Correspondence*, 4:558.

98. WJ to AHGJ, 15 April 1877, *Correspondence*, 4:557.

99. WJ to AHGJ, [3 May 1877], *Correspondence*, 4:562.

100. WJ to AHGJ, 30 April [1877], H bMS Am 1092.9 (1173), including his photograph.

101. WJ to AHGJ, 23 May [1877], *Correspondence*, 4:563.

102. WJ to AHGJ, [29 May 1877], *Correspondence*, 4:565.

103. WJ to AHGJ, 2 June [1877], *Correspondence*, 4:569.

104. WJ to AHGJ, 2 June [1877], *Correspondence*, 4:569.

105. WJ to AHGJ, 7 June 1877, *Correspondence*, 4:570–71.

106. AHGJ's photo album contains miniatures of Judge and Madame Papineau. Courtesy of Henry James IV.

107. Henry James II claims that Alice believed she "could serve him [WJ] best by sending him away." "Alice Howe Gibbens, 1849–1922," 35.

108. WJ to AHGJ, [July 1877], *Correspondence*, 4:574–75.

109. WJ to AHGJ, 15 September [19]07, *Correspondence*, 11:447.

110. WJ to RJ, 15 September 1877, *Correspondence*, 4:586.

111. WJ to AHGJ, 24 September 1877, *Correspondence*, 4:586.

112. See Trobridge, *Swedenborg*, chap. 7, "The New Theology," for an overview of Swedenborg's teachings on charity.

113. WJ to Catherine Havens, 22 December 1877, *Correspondence*, 4:588.

114. WJ to AHGJ, 24 February 1878, *Correspondence*, 5:3.

4. ALICE IN JAMESLAND

1. HJ to AHGJ, 7 June [18]78, in Susan E. Gunter, ed., *Dear Munificent Friends: Henry James's Letters to Four Women* (Ann Arbor: University of Michigan Press, 1999), 22.

2. ALS, RJ to AHGJ, 18 May 1878, H bMS Am 1095 (42).

3. ALS, Garth W. James to AHGJ, 26 May 1878, H bMS Am 1095 (16).

4. See Strouse, *Alice James*, 181–85, on sister Alice's reaction to William's marriage.

5. Strouse, *Alice James*, 183.

6. WJ to Frances Rollins Morse, 26 May [1878], *Correspondence*, 5:13.

7. ALS, Katharine Putnam Hooker to Minnie Putnam, 23 June 1878, 9 June 1878, BANC MSS 77/1, box 1, folder 14, Hooker Family Papers, Bancroft Library, University of California at Berkeley. I am grateful to the Bancroft Library for permission to cite from this collection.

8. ALS, Katharine Putnam Hooker to Minnie Putnam, 23 June 1878, B BANC MSS 77/1, box 1, folder 14.

9. Elizabeth Glendower Evans, "William James and His Wife," in Linda Simon, ed., *William James Remembered* (Lincoln: University of Nebraska Press, 1996), 62.

10. ALS, Katharine Putnam Hooker to Minnie Putnam, 9 June 1878, B BANC MSS 77/1, box 1, folder 14.

11. ALS, AHGJ to JGW, [June 1878], Mss. 106, Whittier, box 4, folder 10, Phillips Library, Peabody Essex Museum. I am grateful to the Peabody Essex Museum for permission to cite from this letter.

12. WJ to AHGJ, 11 January [1883], *Correspondence*, 5:385.

13. WJ to AHGJ, [2 July 1878], *Correspondence*, 5:16.

14. Some of the information on Saratoga Springs and Keene Valley comes from Bjork, *William James*, 91–93, and from Simon, *Genuine Reality*, 164–65.

15. WJ to AHGJ, 29 August 1884, *Correspondence*, 5:521.

16. WJ to AHGJ, 23 June 1898, *Correspondence*, 8:378.

17. WJ to AHGJ, 22 June [18]95, *Correspondence*, 8:46.

18. Beede Hotel letterhead, H bMS Am 1092.9 (1424).

19. I am indebted to my colleague folklorist Dr. David Stanley for this list and for geographical information on Keene Valley.

20. WJ to AHGJ, [3 July 1878], *Correspondence*, 5:17.

21. WJ to AHGJ, [28 August 1879], *Correspondence*, 5:59.

22. WJ to AHGJ, [11 September 1885], *Correspondence*, 6:77.

23. WJ to AHGJ, 17 September 1885, *Correspondence*, 6:80.

24. William James, *Essays in Philosophy* (Cambridge MA: Harvard University Press, 1978), 62. One page in the middle of the manuscript of this essay is in Alice's hand (H bMS Am 1092.9 [4464]).

25. WJ to RJ, 9 July 1878, *Correspondence*, 5:18.

26. Allen, *William James*, 222. This remark is open to interpretation, as Childs may have meant that Alice was taking dictation rather than actually helping write the book.

27. WJ to Francis James Child, 16 August [1878], *Correspondence*, 5:20.

28. ALS, Katharine Putnam Hooker to Minnie Putnam, 13 September 1878, B BANC MSS 77/1, box 1, folder 14; WJ to Francis James Child, 16 August [1878], *Correspondence*, 5:20.

29. AHGJ and WJ to Francis James Child, 16 August [1878], *Correspondence*, 5:20.

30. WJ to Arthur George Sedgwick, 20 September 1878, *Correspondence*, 5:22.

31. WJ to Frances Rollins Morse, 26 December [1878], *Correspondence*, 5:29–30.

32. William James, *Manuscript Lectures* (Cambridge MA: Harvard University Press, 1988), 37.

33. Katharine Peabody Loring (1849–1943) was with sister Alice when she died. She printed four copies of Alice's diary in 1894. Their relationship began

on 17 December 1873, according to a letter Loring wrote to Fanny Morse in 1892 after Alice's death: "Nineteen years ago today, you did the greatest service to me that any one ever did: you invited me to lunch with you to meet Alice, & from the moment of that festivity is dated the great happiness of my life. It is an anniversary which we always kept unknown to any: but I feel that now it would be a joy to thank you for it." ALS, Frances R. Morse Papers 1627, carton 1, folder: To FRM from friends 1911, Schlesinger Library, Radcliffe College. I am grateful to the Schlesinger Library for permission to cite from this collection.

34. ALS, AJ to Frances R. Morse, 25 November [18]78, H bMS Am 1094 (1508). Frances Rollins Morse (1850–1928) was a prominent American social worker and sister Alice's close friend. She founded the Simmons School of Social Work.

35. See Kay Redfield Jamison, *Touched with Fire: Manic-Depressive Illness and the Artistic Temperament* (New York: Simon & Schuster, 1994), 207–16, claims that there is a tendency toward manic depression in the James family. It is important to remember, though, that while this tendency may have occurred in family members, Alice Howe Gibbens James provided a stable center that helped ameliorate this tendency in her husband. Most commentators agree that he improved markedly after his marriage, which, combined with his growing professional success, allowed him to develop a positive narrative of himself.

36. See Pat Jalland, *Women, Marriage, and Politics, 1860–1914* (Oxford: Clarendon Press, 1986), for a discussion of fathers' involvement at home. See also Gunter, *Dear Munificent Friends*, 5–8, for a brief overview of their roles.

37. WJ to Henry Holt, [June 1878], *Correspondence*, 5:14; Henry Holt to WJ, 8 June [18]78, *Correspondence*, 5:14–15.

38. WJ, "Manuscripts," H bMS Am 1092.9 (4397), folder 1.

39. Thomas Huxley (1825–95) was a British biologist who advocated Darwin's theory of evolution, and William Kingdon Clifford (1845–79) was a mathematician who also wrote about philosophy, arguing that it was immoral to believe things for which there was no factual evidence.

40. William James, "Are We Automata?" in *Essays in Psychology* (Cambridge MA: Harvard University Press, 1983), 44, 61.

41. William James, *Essays in Radical Empiricism* (Cambridge MA: Harvard University Press, 1976), 139.

42. ALS, JGW to AHGJ, 26 May [1879], H bMS Am 1092.9 (4356).

43. Julia Ward Howe, ed., *Sex and Education: A Reply to Dr. E. H. Clarke's "Sex in Education"* (Boston: Roberts Brothers, 1874; reprint, New York: Arno Press, 1972), 56.

44. Allen, *William James*, 228.

45. Allen, *William James*, 229.

46. WJ to AHGJ, [24 August 1879], *Correspondence*, 5:57; WJ to AHGJ [28 August 1879], *Correspondence*, 5:58.

47. H bMS Am 1092.9, folder 235.

48. U.S. Census, Household Record, Boston, Suffolk County, Massachusetts, 1880. Sometime in the late 1870s Eliza Gibbens and her three daughters moved to Cambridge, renting quarters at 11 Quincy Street, the Andrew Preston Peabody house, just across the street from Henry Sr. and sister Alice. There she was joined by other members of her extended family. Around 1882 she bought a home at 18 Garden Street and lived there with her two younger daughters and various Webb family members. Alice lived with her periodically during William's extended absences. After his return from England in 1883, William and Alice lived with Eliza until the summer, when they moved to rented quarters at 15 Appian Way. Alice and William did not have a permanent home until their move to 95 Irving Street in 1889.

49. See Michael A. La Sorte, "Nineteenth Century Family Planning Practices," *Journal of Psychohistory* 4, no. 2 (1976): 163–83, for a detailed discussion of birth control methods available in the nineteenth century.

50. ALS, AJ to Frances Rollins Morse, 7 October [18]79, S, Morse Papers 1627, carton 1, folder: To FRM from "AJ."

51. WJ to Frances Rollins Morse, 25 December 1879, *Correspondence*, 5:70.

52. Bernard Wishy, *The Child and the Republic: The Dawn of Modern American Child Nurture* (Philadelphia: University of Pennsylvania Press, 1968), 105.

53. WJ to AHGJ, [24 December 1879], *Correspondence*, 5:68.

54. WJ to AHGJ, [24 December 1879], *Correspondence*, 5:68.

55. The work by Luc de Clapiers de Vauvenargues was published in English as *Reflections and Conseils*. Vauvenargues was an eighteenth-century French soldier and moralist remembered mostly for his *Introduction à la connaissance de l'esprit humain*. Alice liked the title "Conseils and Reflections" for a selection of William's writing. ALS, AHGJ to HJ II, n.d. [c. 1919–20], H MS Am 2538.

56. WJ to Granville Stanley Hall, 16 January 1880, *Correspondence*, 5:82.

57. WJ to Josiah Royce, 3 February 1880, *Correspondence*, 5:83. The Royces were philosopher Josiah Royce (1855–1916) and his wife, translator Katharine Head Royce (b. 1858). Royce was taking William's place at Harvard during William's stay abroad. He had grown up in a mining camp in remote Grass Valley, California. An exceptionally talented student, by age twenty-three he had earned a doctorate from Johns Hopkins. He taught first at Berkeley and then came to Harvard as a half-year sabbatical replacement for WJ in the fall of 1882, becoming a full professor in Harvard's philosophy department

by 1892. He was the leading American proponent of the Absolute, a kind of idealistic monism whereby all reality exists in the thought of one single overarching consciousness. He and WJ argued their philosophical beliefs for decades, though they remained firm friends.

58. Allen, *William James*, 230, 233.

59. "Alice Howe Gibbens, 1849–1922," 3.

60. WJ to AHGJ, 13 June [1880], *Correspondence*, 5:101.

61. WJ to AHGJ, 4 July [18]80, *Correspondence*, 5:113.

62. WJ to AHGJ, 10 July [18]80, *Correspondence*, 5:118.

63. WJ to AHGJ, 31 July [1880], *Correspondence*, 5:128.

64. ALS, HJ Sr. to AHGJ, 22 July [1880], H bMS Am 1092.9 (4176).

65. WJ to AHGJ, 20 [August 1880], *Correspondence*, 5:135.

66. Allen, *William James*, 237.

67. William lectured at Johns Hopkins in February 1878; his lecture was entitled "The Senses and the Brain and Their Relation to Thought." He was invited to return again in 1879 to give twenty lectures, a general course on psychology. This would be a temporary appointment, however, and he pressed Gilman for more regular employment, but the two were never able to come to terms acceptable to both. Gilman could promise him lecture series and courses, but he could not guarantee WJ a permanent position for a variety of reasons, among them the university's preference for European scholars.

68. William James, "Great Men and Their Environment," in *The Will to Believe and Other Essays in Popular Philosophy* (Cambridge MA: Harvard University Press, 1979), 170.

69. Thomas Davidson to WJ, 24 December 1881, *Correspondence*, 5:191.

70. Ahlstrom, *Religious History*, 792–93.

71. HJ to AHGJ, 6 August [1881], Gunter, *Dear Munificent Friends*, 24.

72. Allen, *William James*, 239.

73. WJ to AHGJ, [27 June 1882], *Correspondence*, 5:219.

74. Janet Tarolli, "First Ladies in Medicine at Michigan," *Medicine at Michigan* 2 (Fall 2000), www.medicineatmichigan.org/2000/fall/women.

75. Lewis, *The Jameses*, 348.

76. HJ Sr. to WJ, 7 November [1882], *Correspondence*, 5:292.

77. WJ to AHGJ, 3 October 1882, *Correspondence*, 5:263–64.

78. See Deborah Dwork, "The Child Model (or the Model Child?) of the Late Nineteenth Century in Urban America," *Clio Medica* 12, no. 3 (1977): 117.

79. WJ to AHGJ, [26] October [1882], *Correspondence*, 5:282. George Herbert Palmer (1842–1933) was William's colleague in Harvard's philosophy department. Aligned with Hegel, he wrote a book on Kant but never developed as an original philosopher. He performed well as an administrator and teacher.

80. ALS, HJ to AHGJ, 16 October [1882], H bMS Am 1094 (1611). Throughout her life Alice entertained and supported William's colleagues and friends in addition to running the household. Earlier in this letter HJ refers to them as "the ghastly Royce couple" and "a couple of dreadful plasters."

81. 131 Mt. Vernon Street is now across from a fire station, but when the Jameses lived there it was located up the hill, toward Louisburg Square. The street was renumbered in the twentieth century.

82. Eliot, *A History of Cambridge*, 119.

83. AHGJ to WJ, 3 December 1882, *Correspondence*, 5:316.

84. AHGJ to WJ, 30 November [1882], *Correspondence*, 5:312.

85. AHGJ to WJ, 11 December 1882, *Correspondence*, 5:323.

86. AHGJ to WJ, 13 December [1882], *Correspondence*, 5:325.

87. AHGJ to WJ, 6 December [1882], *Correspondence*, 5:321.

88. ALS, AHGJ to WJ, 1 December 1882, H bMS Am 1092.9 (271).

89. AHGJ to WJ, 13 December [1882], *Correspondence*, 5:325.

90. AHGJ to WJ, 13 December [1882], *Correspondence*, 5:325.

91. ALS, AHGJ to WJ, 1 December 1882, H bMS Am 1092.9 (271).

92. AHGJ to WJ, 6 December [1882], *Correspondence*, 5:321.

93. AHGJ to WJ, 11 December 1882, *Correspondence*, 5:324.

94. AHGJ to WJ, [17 December 1882], *Correspondence*, 5:334–35.

95. AHGJ to WJ, [17 December 1882], *Correspondence*, 5:336.

96. AHGJ to WJ, 18 December 1882, *Correspondence*, 5:336–37.

97. AHGJ to WJ, 6 December [1882], *Correspondence*, 5:320–21.

98. AHGJ to WJ, 21 December 1882, *Correspondence*, 5:345.

99. AHGJ to WJ, 21 December 1882, *Correspondence*, 5:344.

100. AHGJ to WJ, 27 December [1882], *Correspondence*, 5:359.

101. AHGJ to WJ, 25 December 1882, *Correspondence*, 5:354–55.

102. AHGJ to WJ, 1 January 1883, *Correspondence*, 5:370.

103. AHGJ to WJ, 21 December [1882], *Correspondence*, 5:344.

104. AHGJ to WJ, 22 December [1882], *Correspondence*, 5:347.

105. AHGJ to WJ, 31 December 1882, *Correspondence*, 5:365.

106. AHGJ to WJ, 21 December 1882, *Correspondence*, 5:344.

107. See Sheldon M. Novick, *Henry James: The Mature Master* (New York: Random House, 2007), 39–41, for a thorough account of the family dynamics involved in settling HJ Sr.'s will. Wilkie had been left out of the will, perhaps at Aunt Kate's behest, because the family had invested heavily in his and Bob's failed Florida ventures. In addition, Wilkie had married into a wealthy Milwaukee family, and his heirs would be assured money from that source, while sister Alice had no means of her own. She protested the will's terms, William proposed a settlement whereby Wilkie would receive a reduced

share, and Henry finally decided that the estate should be evenly split, as sister Alice wanted.

108. Habegger describes Alice James's suffering during her father's illness: "For James's daughter, the task of managing the dying man was flatout intolerable" (*The Father*, 499). See also Strouse, *Alice James*, chap. 12, "Gains and Losses."

109. ALS, AHGJ to WJ, 14 January 1883, H bMS Am 1092.9 (290).

110. AHGJ to WJ, 22 December [1882], *Correspondence*, 5:348.

111. AHGJ to WJ, 22 December 1882, *Correspondence*, 5:347.

112. AHGJ to WJ, 27 December [1882], *Correspondence*, 5:360.

113. AHGJ to WJ, 31 December 1882, *Correspondence*, 5:366.

114. AHGJ to WJ, 27 January [1883], *Correspondence*, 5:407.

115. AHGJ to WJ, 1 January 1883, *Correspondence*, 5:371.

116. AHGJ to WJ, 31 December 1882, *Correspondence*, 5:366.

117. Denis Hollier et al., eds., *A New History of French Literature* (Cambridge MA: Harvard University Press, 1989).

118. ALS, AHGJ to HJ, 27 April 1914, H bMS Am 1092.11 (55).

119. AHGJ to WJ, 27 January [1883], *Correspondence*, 5:407.

120. ALS, AHGJ to WJ, 14 January 1883, H bMS Am 1092.9 (290).

121. AHGJ to WJ, 27 January [1883], *Correspondence*, 5:408; AHGJ to WJ, 27 December [1882], *Correspondence*, 5:361.

122. ALS, AHGJ to WJ, 3 January [1883], H bMS Am 1092.9 (286).

123. WJ to AHGJ, 21 February [1883], *Correspondence*, 5:425.

124. AHGJ to WJ, 13 December [1882], *Correspondence*, 5:325.

125. AHGJ to WJ, 22 December [1882], *Correspondence*, 5:347–48.

126. AHGJ to WJ, 22 December [1882], *Correspondence*, 5:348.

127. WJ to HJ II, [January 1883], *Correspondence*, 5:368.

128. AHGJ to WJ, 6 January 1883, *Correspondence*, 5:382.

129. AHGJ to WJ, 6 January 1883, *Correspondence*, 5:381.

130. AHGJ to WJ, 1 January 1883, *Correspondence*, 5:371.

131. HJ to WJ, 11 January [1883], *Correspondence*, 1:349.

132. On 20 December 1882 William told Henry, "I have been lapped in comfort here in your quarters—I feel in fact too much at home & wish it were more foreign" (*Correspondence*, 1:337).

133. WJ to HJ, 6 February 1883, *Correspondence*, 1:362.

134. HJ to WJ, 11 February [1883], *Correspondence*, 1:364.

135. AHGJ to WJ, 11 January [18]83, *Correspondence*, 5:389.

136. TLS, WJ to AHGJ, 8 January [18]83, H bMS Am 1092.9 (1331). William acquired a typewriter (which he sometimes called a "caligraph") in Paris in November 1882, so some of his letters during this period are typed rather than handwritten.

137. ALS, WJ to AHGJ, 3 February 1883, H bMS Am 1092.9 (1343).

138. TLS, WJ to AHGJ, 23 January [18]83, H bMS 1092.9 (1338); TLS, WJ to AHGJ, 8 January [18]83, H bMS Am 1092.9 (1331); TLS, WJ to AHGJ, 3 February 1883, H bMS Am 1092.9 (1343).

139. WJ to AHGJ, 5 January [1883], *Correspondence*, 5:377.

140. WJ to AHGJ, 13 February 1883, *Correspondence*, 5:416.

141. TLS, WJ to AHGJ, 3 February 1883, H bMS Am 1092.9 (1343).

142. WJ to AHGJ, 13 February 1883, *Correspondence*, 5:416.

143. WJ, to AHGJ, 15 March [1883], *Correspondence*, 5:440–41.

144. WJ to AHGJ, 19 December [1882], *Correspondence*, 5:339.

145. Henry James, "The Impressions of a Cousin," in *Watch and Ward, Longstaff's Marriage, Eugene Pickering, and Other Tales* (London: Macmillan, 1923), 366.

146. James, "The Impressions of a Cousin," 412.

147. James, "The Impressions of a Cousin," 373.

148. James, "The Impressions of a Cousin," 401.

149. WJ to HJ, 9 May [18]96, *Correspondence*, 2:39.

150. WJ to AHGJ, 13 February 1883, *Correspondence*, 5:416.

5. THE GRIEF CHILD

1. Lewis, *The Jameses*, 370–72.

2. HJ to WJ, 20 February [1884], *Correspondence*, 1:375n.

3. HJ to WJ, 25 January [1884], *Correspondence*, 1:373.

4. Allen, *William James*, 272.

5. HJ to WJ, 20 February [1884], *Correspondence*, 1:374.

6. Allen, *William James*, 272. Allen notes that William and Hagen had been friends.

7. HJ to WJ, 26 March [1884], *Correspondence*, 1:378.

8. HJ to WJ, 21 April [1884], *Correspondence*, 1:379.

9. Quoted in "Alice Howe Gibbens, 1849–1922," 47. Frequently, the baby's name is spelled "Herman," yet in his memoir Henry James II spells it "Hermann." I have decided to honor his usage because he was meticulous about details. However, the name on the family tombstone is "Herman."

10. WJ to HJ, 18 October [18]84, *Correspondence*, 1:385.

11. WJ to AJ, 7 December [1884], *Correspondence*, 5:540.

12. AJ to AHGJ, February 1884, in Anderson, *Alice James*, 112.

13. William James Jr., "In Space and Time and Memory," typescript, c. 1940, H *2002M-44(b), box 1, folder "Jameses."

14. WJ to Thomas Davidson, 30 March 1884, *Correspondence*, 5:498.

15. WJ to AHGJ, 11 September [18]84, *Correspondence*, 5:524.

16. WJ to Kitty Prince, 25 June [1884], *Correspondence*, 5:502.

17. Simon, *Genuine Reality*, 188.

18. ALS, WJ to AHGJ, [23 July 1884], H bMS Am 1092.9 (1361).

19. ALS, WJ to AHGJ, 29 August 1884, H bMS Am 1092.9 (1378).

20. Calendared, WJ to AHGJ, 13 August [1884], *Correspondence*, 5:570.

21. Habegger, *The Father*, 504.

22. ALS, WJ to AHGJ, 17 August [1884], H bMS Am 1092.9 (1373).

23. ALS, WJ to AHGJ, 29 August 1884, H bMS Am 1092.9 (1378).

24. ALS, WJ to AHGJ, 13 August [1884], H bMS Am 1092.9 (1370).

25. Maher, *Biography of Broken Fortunes*, 170–73.

26. *Funk & Wagnall's New World Encyclopedia* (New York: World Almanac Education Group, 2002), s.v. "diphtheria."

27. ALS, WJ to AHGJ, 29 December 1884, H bMS Am 1092.9 (1386).

28. Maher, *Biography of Broken Fortunes*, 173.

29. WJ to AJ, 9 March 1885, *Correspondence*, 6:19; WJ to Kitty Prince, 10 March [18]85, *Correspondence*, 6:20.

30. William Bridgwater and Elizabeth J. Sherwood, eds., *The Columbia Encyclopedia* (New York: Columbia University Press, 1950), s.v. "scarlet fever."

31. WJ to AJ, 20 March 1885, *Correspondence*, 6:21; WJ to Kitty Prince, 21 March [1885], *Correspondence*, 6:23.

32. WJ to Elizabeth Ellery Sedgwick Child, 27 March [1885], *Correspondence*, 6:24.

33. WJ to HJ, 1 April [18]85, *Correspondence*, 2:12.

34. WJ to HJ, 26 April [1885], *Correspondence*, 2:16.

35. WJ to Catharine Walsh, 28 June [18]85, *Correspondence*, 6:41.

36. *Funk & Wagnall's New World Encyclopedia*, s.v. "whooping cough."

37. WJ to AHGJ, [16 June 1885], *Correspondence*, 6:33.

38. ALS, WJ to AHGJ, 27 June 1885, H bMS Am 1092.9 (1396).

39. WJ to AHGJ, 22 June [18]85, *Correspondence*, 6:36.

40. WJ to AHGJ, 24 June [18]85, *Correspondence*, 6:38; WJ to AHGJ, 26 June [1885], *Correspondence*, 6:40; WJ to AHGJ, 24 June [18]85, *Correspondence*, 6:38.

41. WJ to AHGJ, 26 June [1885], *Correspondence*, 6:40.

42. WJ to Kitty Prince, 1 July [18]85, *Correspondence*, 6:43.

43. WJ to Catharine Walsh, 11 July [18]85, *Correspondence*, 6:43.

44. WJ to Katharine James Prince, 12 July [18]85, *Correspondence*, 6:44.

45. WJ to AHGJ, 30 July [18]85, *Correspondence*, 6:46.

46. WJ to AHGJ, 30 July [18]85, *Correspondence*, 6:46.

47. William James, *Principles of Psychology*, 2 vols. (Cambridge MA: Harvard University Press, 1981), 2:939.

48. Bernhard Lang, introduction to *Heaven and Its Wonders and Hell: Drawn from Things Heard & Seen* by Emanuel Swedenborg (West Chester PA: Swedenborg Foundation, 2000), 18.

49. HJ to WJ, 24 July [1885], *Correspondence*, 2:23.

50. AHGJ to WJ, 28 May 1905, *Correspondence*, 11:51.

51. WJ to AJ, 16 August [18]85, *Correspondence*, 6:67.

52. "Alice Howe Gibbens, 1849–1922," 47–48.

53. WJ to AHGJ, 28 August [18]85, *Correspondence*, 6:69–70.

54. WJ to AHGJ, [30 August 1885], *Correspondence*, 6:71–72.

55. AHGJ to WJ, September 1885, quoted in "Alice Howe Gibbens, 1849–1922," 48.

56. William MacKintire Salter (1853–1931) was a leader of the Ethical Culture Society and wrote books on philosophy, including *Ethical Religion* and *First Steps in Philosophy*.

57. WJ to AHGJ, [11 September 1885], *Correspondence*, 6:77.

58. WJ to AHGJ, 2 [3] August [18]85, *Correspondence*, 6:52; WJ to AHGJ, 3 August [1885], *Correspondence*, 6:53–54.

59. ALS, WJ to AHGJ, 7 August [18]85, H bMS Am 1092.9 (1408).

60. WJ to AJ, 24 December [18]85, *Correspondence*, 6:94.

61. "Alice Howe Gibbens, 1849–1922," 5.

62. ALS, WJ to AHGJ, 26 December [18]85, H bMS Am 1092.9 (1431).

63. Henry Adams (1838–1918), descendant of two American presidents, was an historian, writer, and statesman. He and HJ first met in 1870 in London, when he introduced HJ to important people. His wife, Marian "Clover" Hooper Adams (1843–85), was a New England socialite, correspondent, and photographer. HJ met her in Newport in the late 1860s and admired her intellectual grace. He also was disturbed by her suicide.

64. ALS, Ellen Gurney to AHGJ [1879], H bMS Am 1092.9 (4306).

65. ALS, Ellen Gurney to AHGJ, n.d., H bMS Am 1092.9 (4307).

66. ALS, Ellen Gurney to AHGJ, n.d., H bMS Am 1092.9 (4309).

67. ALS, Ellen Gurney to AHGJ, n.d., H bMS Am 1092.9 (4309).

68. WJ to AJ, 8 April 1886, *Correspondence*, 6:129.

69. Allen, *William James*, 285.

70. WJ to AJ, 16 August [18]85, *Correspondence*, 6:66–67.

6. NEW DIRECTIONS

1. William James, "Review of *Planchette*, by Epes Sargent," in *Essays in Psychical Research* (Cambridge MA: Harvard University Press, 1986), 2.

2. WJ to Catherine Havens, 14 June 1874, *Correspondence*, 4:496.

3. See Deborah Blum, *Ghost Hunters: William James and the Search for Scientific Proof of Life after Death* (New York: Penguin, 2006) for an account of the nineteenth century's preoccupation with spiritualist matters.

4. Allen, *William James*, 282.

5. Bjork, *William James*, 211.

6. Robert A. McDermott, introduction to James, *Essays in Psychical Research*, xiv.

7. Photograph, H pfMS Am 1094, box 1 of 3.

8. WJ to AHGJ, 24 December [18]85, *Correspondence*, 6:92.

9. There are two differing accounts of the connection between Mrs. Piper and the James and Gibbens households. Mrs. Piper claimed her maid had a friend who worked at 95 Irving Street, but her daughter, Alta Piper, later said her mother had a maid whose sister worked in a Boston home where Eliza Gibbens visited often. See James, *Essays on Psychical Research*, 397.

10. Simon, *Genuine Reality*, 199–200.

11. Recorded conversation with Elizabeth Glendower Evans in 1886. See Elizabeth Glendower Evans, "William James and His Wife," in Simon, *William James Remembered*, 62.

12. ALS, AHGJ to Elizabeth Glendower Evans, 5 December n.d., Elizabeth Glendower Evans Papers, Series II, Correspondence, Schlesinger Library, Radcliffe College.

13. James, *Essays in Psychical Research*, 88.

14. James, *Essays in Psychical Research*, 439–40.

15. WJ to AJ, 15 June [1885], *Correspondence*, 6:33.

16. Horace M. Kallen, *Philosophical Review*, January 1937–38, quoted in "Alice Howe Gibbens, 1849–1922," 45–46.

17. Bjork, *William James*, 210–11.

18. Allen, *William James*, 283.

19. James, *Principles of Psychology*, 1:372. He adds an extended explanation of the phenomenon from a Sidney Dean who had collected numerous examples of automatic writing.

20. William James, "The Confidences of a 'Psychical Researcher'" (1909), in *Essays in Psychical Research*, 372.

21. Alfred Russel Wallace to WJ, [13 December] 1886, *Correspondence*, 6:185.

22. Simon, *Genuine Reality*, 201–2.

23. William James, "Address of the President before the Society for Psychical Research," in *Essays in Psychical Research*, 131.

24. WJ to AJ, 8 July [18]86, *Correspondence*, 6:149. The Fourth of July was a Sunday.

25. WJ to AJ, 27 September [18]86, *Correspondence*, 6:168.

26. Quoted in "Alice Howe Gibbens, 1849–1922," 48.

27. WJ to AHGJ, 1 August [18]86, *Correspondence*, 6:152.

28. WJ to HJ, 17 September [1886], *Correspondence*, 2:51 and 51n.

29. Allen, *William James*, 286.

30. ALS, AHGJ to Margaret Gibbens, 15 September 1886, H MS Am 2538.

31. HJ to WJ, 13 November 1886, *Correspondence*, 2:52–53 and 53n.

32. ALS, AHGJ to Margaret Gibbens, 15 September 1886, H MS Am 2538.

33. WJ to Grace Norton, 11 October [18]86, *Correspondence*, 6:173–74.

34. AJ to AHGJ, 8 December 1886, Anderson, *Alice James*, 162; ALS, AJ to AHGJ, 7 November [1886], H bMS Am 1094 (1454).

35. AJ to AHGJ, 8 December 1886, Anderson, *Alice James*, 157.

36. "Alice Howe Gibbens, 1849–1922," 48–49.

37. Christina Hardyment, *Dream Babies: Child Care from Locke to Spock* (London: Jonathan Cape, 1983), 90.

38. Quoted in "Alice Howe Gibbens, 1849–1922," 48–49.

39. AJ to AHGJ, 3 April 1887, Anderson, *Alice James*, 161.

40. AJ to WJ, 24 April 1887, Anderson, *Alice James*, 164.

41. AJ to AHGJ and WJ, 20 November [1887], Anderson, *Alice James*, 175–76.

42. HJ to WJ, 7 April [1887], *Correspondence*, 2:61.

43. WJ to Henry Pickering Bowditch, 26 March [18]87, *Correspondence*, 6:213.

44. WJ to EPG, 26 March [1887], *Correspondence*, 6:213.

45. See Strouse, *Alice James*, chaps. 15, 16, and 17, for an account of Alice James's England years.

46. HJ to WJ, 1 October 1887, *Correspondence*, 2:70–71.

47. AJ to AHGJ, fourteen letters, 1884–90, H bMS Am 1094 (1451–64).

48. See John T. Bethell, *Harvard Observed: An Illustrated History of the University in the Twentieth Century* (Cambridge MA: Harvard University Press, 1998), for a brief profile of Charles Eliot. Morison, *Three Centuries of Harvard*, also includes an extensive discussion of Eliot's presidency and the reforms he enacted, many of them under protest. For a time unpopular partly due to the changes he made, at the end of his forty-year tenure he was well respected by almost all Harvard constituencies.

49. ALS, AHGJ to AJ, 6 April 1887, H bMS Am 1092.11 (25).

50. ALS, AHGJ to AJ, [December 1887], H bMS Am 1092.11 (26).

51. Elizabeth Palmer Peabody (1804–94) was an important Transcendental writer and educational reformer, one of the three sisters featured in Megan Marshall's *The Peabody Sisters* (Boston: Houghton Mifflin, 2005).

52. ALS, AHGJ to AJ, 7 April [1886], H bMS Am 1092.11 (25).

53. WJ to HJ, 12 April [18]87, *Correspondence*, 2:62.

54. WJ to AJ, [3] July 1887, *Correspondence*, 6:237.

55. WJ to AHGJ, [28 June 1887], *Correspondence*, 6:235.

56. WJ to AJ, [3] July 1887, *Correspondence*, 6:236.

57. WJ to AHGJ, 17 August [18]87, *Correspondence*, 6:247.

58. ALS, AHGJ to WJ, 2 September 1887, H MS Am 2538.

59. ALS, AHGJ to WJ, 6 September [1887], H MS Am 2538.

60. "Alice Howe Gibbens, 1849–1922," 51; Allen, *William James*, 293.

61. "Alice Howe Gibbens, 1849–1922," 52.

62. Quoted in "Alice Howe Gibbens, 1849–1922," 59.

63. "Alice Howe Gibbens, 1849–1922," 50.

64. ALS, AHGJ to WJ, 2 September 1887, H MS Am 2538. The Merrimans were probably Daniel Merriman (1838–1912), a clergyman, and his wife, artist Helen Bigelow Merriman (1844–1933). They had a summer place at Intervale, New Hampshire, near Chocorua.

65. WJ to AJ, 13 February 1874, *Correspondence*, 4:484.

66. WJ to AHGJ, 10 October [18]87, *Correspondence*, 6:269.

67. WJ to AHGJ, 12 October [18]87, *Correspondence*, 6:270.

68. ALS, WJ to AHGJ, 5 October [1887], H bMS Am 1092.9 (1484).

69. WJ to AHGJ, 7 October [18]87, *Correspondence*, 6:265; WJ to AHGJ, 10 October [18]87, *Correspondence*, 6:269.

70. ALS, WJ to AHGJ, 4 October [18]87, H bMS Am 1092.9 (1483).

71. ALS, WJ to AHGJ, 17 October [18]87, H bMS Am 1092.9 (1495).

72. ALS, WJ to AHGJ, 19 October [18]87, H bMS Am 1092.9 (1497).

73. ALS, WJ to AHGJ, 21 October [18]87, H bMS Am 1092.9 (1499).

74. WJ to AHGJ, 16 October [18]87, *Correspondence*, 6:277.

75. ALS, WJ to AHGJ, 20 October [18]87, H bMS Am 1092.9 (1498).

76. I am grateful to Susan Cottler, professor of history at Westminster College, for her clear explanation of the Haymarket Square Riot. The information comes from her lectures on American history and from the Haymarket Affair Digital Collection of the Chicago Historical Society.

77. Ahlstrom, *Religious History*, 853; Professor S. Cottler.

78. WJ to HJ, 9 May 1886, *Correspondence*, 2:40.

79. WJ to HJ, 9 May 1886, *Correspondence*, 2:40n12; WJ to William MacKintire Salter, 15 November 1887, *Correspondence*, 6:290.

80. WJ to Edwin Godkin, [21 November 1887], *Correspondence*, 6:290–91.

81. ALS, AJ to Frances R. Morse, 28 December [1887], H bMS Am 1094 (1512).

82. AJ to AHGJ, 3 December 1887, Anderson, *Alice James*, 176–77.

83. Sutton, *Cambridge Reconsidered*, 55, 65.

84. Eliot, *A History of Cambridge*, 117, 119, 120, 126, 151, 288–89, 297.

85. Caption on photograph, H bMS Am 1092.9 (4597).

86. WJ to Theodora Sedgwick, 24 January [18]88, *Correspondence*, 6:302. Maria Theodora Sedgwick (1851–1916) was Arthur Sedgwick's sister. She first knew WJ and HJ in Newport in 1860.

87. WJ to AHGJ, 31 January [1888], *Correspondence*, 6:305, 306.

88. AJ to AHGJ, 7 March 1886, Anderson, *Alice James*, 139–40. Mrs. Gurney was probably Kate Sara Sibley Gurney, wife of British aesthetician and psychic

researcher Edmund Gurney (1847–88), and Mrs. Pollock was Lady Georgina Harriet Deffell, wife of British jurist and philosophical writer Sir Frederick Pollock (1845–1937).

89. AJ to AHGJ, 5 May 1889, Anderson, *Alice James*, 234.

90. WJ to AHGJ, 5 February [18]88, *Correspondence*, 6:308–9.

91. WJ to AHGJ, 9 February [18]88, *Correspondence*, 6:315.

92. WJ to AHGJ, 2 May [1888], *Correspondence*, 6:398.

93. WJ to AHGJ, 3 February [1888], *Correspondence*, 6:307; WJ to AHGJ, 4 February [18]88, *Correspondence*, 6:307.

94. WJ to AHGJ, 5 February [18]88, *Correspondence*, 6:309.

95. WJ to AHGJ, 7 February [18]88, *Correspondence*, 6:312.

96. WJ to AHGJ, 7 February [18]88, *Correspondence*, 6:312–13.

97. WJ to AHGJ, 15 February [18]88, *Correspondence*, 6:320.

98. WJ to AHGJ, 22 February [18]88, *Correspondence*, 6:326.

99. WJ to AHGJ, 2 March [18]88, *Correspondence*, 6:336.

100. WJ to AHGJ, 4 March [1888], *Correspondence*, 6:339, 338.

101. AHGJ to WJ, 9 March [18]88, quoted in "Alice Howe Gibbens, 1849–1922," 44.

102. WJ to AHGJ, 7 March [18]88, *Correspondence*, 6:342–43.

103. WJ to AHGJ, 13 May [1888], *Correspondence*, 6:408.

104. WJ to AHGJ, 3 May [18]88, *Correspondence*, 6:399.

105. WJ to AHGJ, 24 April [18]88, *Correspondence*, 6:388–89.

106. WJ to HJ, 11 July [18]88, *Correspondence*, 2:89.

107. WJ to AHGJ, 12 September [18]88, *Correspondence*, 6:436.

108. WJ to AHGJ, 16 September [18]88, *Correspondence*, 6:437.

109. ALS, WJ to AHGJ, 2 October [18]88, H bMS Am 1092.9 (1643).

110. WJ to AHGJ, 23 September [18]88, *Correspondence*, 6:443.

111. AJ to AHGJ, 10–11 December 1888, Anderson, *Alice James*, 214–15.

112. ALS, WJ to AHGJ, 8 October [18]88, H bMS Am 1092.9 (1646).

7. 95 IRVING STREET AND BEYOND

1. WJ to Henry Lee Higginson, 14 March [18]89, *Correspondence*, 6:468.

2. James Turner, *The Liberal Education of Charles Eliot Norton* (Baltimore MD: Johns Hopkins University Press, 1999), 332. Charles Eliot Norton (1827–1908) was a professor, prolific writer, editor, and cofounder of the *Nation*. He published a number of HJ's early works and introduced him to other writers.

3. Sutton, *Cambridge Reconsidered*, 69–70.

4. Eliot, *A History of Cambridge*, 97.

5. Eliot, *A History of Cambridge*, 151.

6. Anna Robeson Burr, ed., *Alice James: Her Brothers, Her Journal* (New York: Dodd, Mead and Company, 1934), 112.

7. WJ to AHGJ, 16 May [18]89, *Correspondence*, 6:474.

8. WJ to AHGJ, 18 May [1889], *Correspondence*, 6:475.

9. WJ to AHGJ, 24 May [18]89, *Correspondence*, 6:484.

10. WJ to AHGJ, 26 May [1889], *Correspondence*, 6:485.

11. HJ II's unpublished notes on his parents' letters, 1897, H bMS Am 1092.9 (2487).

12. WJ to AHGJ, 4 July [18]89, *Correspondence*, 6:499.

13. WJ to AHGJ, 7 August [18]89, *Correspondence*, 6:523.

14. WJ to AHGJ, [2 August 1889], *Correspondence*, 6:521.

15. WJ to HJ, 30 August [18]89, *Correspondence*, 2:121.

16. Sally Zimmerman, Preservation Planner, "William James House, Landmark Designation Study Report, Cambridge Historical Commission, 11 December 2000."

17. Burr, *Alice James*, 121.

18. This figure is probably low, as current historical currency tables do not factor in the high prices of homes in areas like Cambridge.

19. James, *Essays in Psychical Research*, 83.

20. James, *Essays in Psychical Research*, 83–84.

21. WJ to AHGJ, 7 October [18]89, *Correspondence*, 6:534–35.

22. WJ to AHGJ, 7 October [18]89, *Correspondence*, 6:535.

23. WJ to AHGJ, 20 October [18]89, *Correspondence*, 6:539–40.

24. ALS, WJ to AHGJ, 31 October 1889, H bMS Am 1092.9 (1706).

25. Quoted in "Alice Howe Gibbens, 1849–1922," 55.

26. Information on the Irving Street house comes from Allen, *William James*, and from a personal interview with Greta Peterson, August 2004. I am grateful to Mrs. Peterson for sharing her experience of living at 95 Irving Street.

27. William McKinley Runyan, "History in the Making: What Will Become of William James's House and Legacy?" *History of Psychology* 3, no. 3 (2000): 288–93; and Kathleen Howley, "Getting to the Heart of William James's Former Home," *Daily Globe*, 28 February 1999.

28. WJ to AHGJ, [28 May 1890], *Correspondence*, 7:43.

29. Visual artist Sarah Wyman Whitman (1842–1904) was a well-known figure in Boston society, a designer of book covers and stained glass as well as a writer, teacher, and public personality. Sarah Orne Jewett's *Strangers and Wayfarers* is dedicated to her.

30. Simon, *William James Remembered*, 230.

31. WJ to AHGJ, 7 July 1890, *Correspondence*, 7:50–51. Sarah Bernhardt (1844–1923) was sometimes called the world's most famous actress.

32. ALS, WJ to AHGJ, 19 July [18]90, H bMS Am 1092.9 (1737).

33. William James, "The Principles of Psychology," manuscript, n.d., H bMS Am 1092.9 (4412).

34. ALS, AHGJ to HJ, 22 June 1890, H bMS Am 1092.11 (27).

35. ALS, AHGJ to HJ, 22 June 1890, H bMS Am 1092.11 (27).

36. HJ to AHGJ, 9 July 1890, Gunter, *Dear Munificent Friends*, 27–28.

37. HJ to WJ, 14 February [1889], *Correspondence*, 2:105.

38. WJ to HJ, 22 August [18]90, *Correspondence*, 2:147.

39. WJ to AHGJ, 13 July [18]90, *Correspondence*, 7:57–58.

40. WJ to AHGJ, 25 July [1890], *Correspondence*, 7:72.

41. WJ to AHGJ, 3 September 1890, *Correspondence*, 7:91.

42. For an example drawn from the animal world see his description of frogs' mating habits. Sexual acts, which in higher species depend upon the fulfillment of certain circumstances and feelings, in lower species come instinctively from lower centers of the body: "They [frogs and toads] show consequently a machine-like obedience to the present incitement of sense, and an almost total exclusion of the power of choice. Copulation occurs *per fas aut nefas*, occasionally between males, often with dead females, in puddles exposed on the highway, and the male may be cut in two without letting go his hold. Every spring an immense sacrifice of batrachian life takes place from these causes alone" (James, *Principles of Psychology*, 1:34–35).

43. James, *Principles of Psychology*, 2:1023.

44. WJ to HJ, 22 December [1890], *Correspondence*, 2:162.

45. HJ to AHGJ, 23 March [1891], Gunter, *Dear Munificent Friends*, 29; HJ to WJ, 12 February [1891], *Correspondence*, 2:173.

46. HJ to AHGJ, 23 March [1891], Gunter, *Dear Munificent Friends*, 28.

47. See Lewis, *The Jameses*, 625–26. Allen also has a summary of the controversy: "He [Alexander Robertson James] would grow up, like his uncle Robertson ('Bob') feeling neglected—not entirely as a result of the confusion of names, but that was no doubt one factor" (*William James*, 330).

48. WJ to Alice James, 23 August 1891, *Correspondence*, 7:193.

49. WJ to James Mark Baldwin, 7 March 1891, *Correspondence*, 7:144.

50. WJ to AHGJ, 12 September [18]91, *Correspondence*, 7:199.

51. WJ to AHGJ, 28 January [18]92, *Correspondence*, 7:236.

52. William Wilberforce Baldwin (1850–1910) was a noted American physician who lived in Italy. HJ toured Italy with him in 1890, and he later became friends with Alice and William. Strouse, *Alice James*, 301, 305.

53. "Note," Dickinson Miller to HJ II, [24 August 1917], H bMS Am 1092.10 (122).

54. WJ to AJ [1 October 1891], *Correspondence*, 7:206.

55. AJ to WJ et al., 5 March 1892, *Correspondence*, 7:246.

56. ALS, AHGJ to HJ, 22 March 1892, H bMS Am 1092.11 (28).

57. ALS, AHGJ to HJ, 11 April 1892, H bMS Am 1092.11 (29).

58. ALS, AHGJ to HJ, 22 March 1892, H bMS Am 1092.11 (28).

59. WJ to HJ, 1 April [18]92, *Correspondence*, 2:219.

60. ALS, AHGJ to HJ, 11 April 1892, H bMS Am 1092.11 (29).

8. ON SABBATICAL

1. ALS, AHGJ to EPG, 29 May 1892, H bMS Am 1092.11 (1).

2. ALS, AHGJ to EPG, 29 May 1892, H bMS Am 1092.11 (1).

3. See Armi Varila, *The Swedenborgian Background of William James' Philosophy* (Helsinki: Suomalainen Tieddeaktemia, 1977), for a discussion of the relationship of WJ's philosophy to the ideas of Swedenborg and Henry James Sr. The quote is on p. 43.

4. ALS, AHGJ to EPG, 8 June 1892, H bMS Am 1092.11 (2).

5. WJ to HJ, 23 June [18]92, *Correspondence*, 2:222.

6. WJ to HJ, 23 June [18]92, *Correspondence*, 2:222.

7. ALS, AHGJ to HJ, 21 June 1892, H bMS Am 1092.11 (30).

8. ALS, AHGJ to EPG, 16 June 1892, H bMS Am 1092.11 (3).

9. Hugo Munsterberg (1863–1916), a pioneer in applied psychology, came to Harvard at WJ's invitation for a three-year term as chair of the psychology lab. In 1897 WJ and Charles Eliot invited him back, and by 1898 he was president of the American Psychological Association. When the First World War broke out in Europe, he was torn between his loyalty to his native Germany and to his adopted country, sometimes attracting criticism when he defended his homeland.

10. ALS, AHGJ to HJ, 21 June 1892, H bMS Am 1092.11 (30).

11. Barry Schwartz, "The Tyranny of Choice," *Scientific American* 290 (April 2004): 70–71.

12. WJ to Charles Ritter, 13 June 1892, *Correspondence*, 7:274.

13. WJ to AHGJ, 20[?] June [18]92, *Correspondence*, 7:278.

14. WJ to AHGJ, 21 June [18]92, *Correspondence*, 7:279.

15. WJ to AHGJ, [19 June 1892], *Correspondence*, 7:277.

16. WJ to Josiah Royce, 22 June [18]92, *Correspondence*, 7:283.

17. ALS, AHGJ to Mary Gibbens Salter, 25 June 1892, H bMS Am 1092.11 (59).

18. ALS, AHGJ to EPG, 27 June 1892, H bMS Am 1092.11 (4).

19. WJ to AHGJ, [30 June 1892], *Correspondence*, 7:288.

20. WJ to Carl Stumpf, 24 June [18]92, *Correspondence*, 7:286.

21. ALS, AHGJ to HJ, 30 June 1892, H bMS Am 1092.11 (31).

22. WJ to HJ, 10 July [18]92, *Correspondence*, 2:222.

23. "Alice Howe Gibbens, 1849–1922," 58.

24. ALS, AHGJ to EPG, 15 July 1892, H bMS Am 1092.11 (5).

25. WJ to Grace Ashburner, 13 July 1892, *Correspondence*, 7:296. Grace

Ashburner (1814–93) was the aunt of Arthur Sedgwick and a Cambridge friend.

26. WJ to HJ, [14 July 1892], *Correspondence*, 2:223.

27. Dr. J. Stainback Wilson, "Diet and Drinks of Nursing Women," cited in Harvey Green and Mary-Ellen Perry, *The Light of the Home: An Intimate View of the Lives of Women in Victorian America* (New York: Pantheon Books, 1983), 38.

28. ALS, AHGJ to Mary Salter, 20 July [1892], H bMS Am 1092.11 (60).

29. WJ to AHGJ, 18 August [18]92, *Correspondence*, 7:314.

30. ALS, AHGJ to Mary Salter, 20 July [1892], H bMS Am 1092.11 (60).

31. ALS, AHGJ to Mary Salter, 20 July [1892], H bMS Am 1092.11 (60).

32. WJ to AHGJ, [18 July 1892], *Correspondence*, 7:302–3.

33. In a letter to Henry James II dated 27 July 1892 William tells his son, "Your post-card does the highest credit to your considerateness; patience; heroism; and magnanimity of character. Your mother wept when she read it" (*Correspondence*, 7:306). This same letter shares news of Billy's woes.

34. WJ to MMJ, 18 August [1892], *Correspondence*, 7:315. Theodore Flournoy (1854–1920) was a psychology professor at the University of Geneva who investigated spiritual phenomena. His 1901 book *From India to the Planet Mars* enjoyed fame with psychic researchers. He believed in the soul's survival but did not think we can communicate with the dead. He claimed that telepathy, telekinesis, and clairvoyance were real.

35. WJ to HJ, 17 July [18]92, *Correspondence*, 2:224.

36. Frederic William Henry Myers (1843–1901) was a British writer, psychic researcher, and WJ's longtime colleague. Myers and his family also knew HJ socially.

37. WJ to AHGJ, [1 August 1892], *Correspondence*, 7:307.

38. Bostonian Isabella Stewart (Mrs. John L.) Gardner (1840–1924) was an art collector who amassed a great collection during her years abroad, now housed at the Fenway Museum. She and HJ were good friends and frequent correspondents. Ariana Randolph Curtis (1833–1922) was an American socialite and playwright. Her husband, Daniel Sargent Curtis (1825–1908), was a wealthy American playwright who had expatriated to Venice in 1878 after serving three months in jail for hitting a judge. Leon Edel, *Henry James: The Middle Years, 1882–1895* (New York: Avon Books, 1962), 324–28.

39. Allen, *William James*, 348.

40. HJ to Isabella Stewart Gardner, 29 July 1892, Henry James, *Letters*, vol. 3, 1883–1895, ed. Leon Edel (Cambridge MA: Belknap Press, 1980), 391.

41. See HJ's letter to WJ of 25 April 1876 for an account of his meeting Henrietta Reubell in Paris in Henry James, *Letters*, vol. 2, 1875–1883, ed. Leon Edel

(Cambridge MA: Belknap Press, 1975), 41–42. Reubell is thought to have been the model for Miss Barrace in James's 1903 novel, *The Ambassadors*.

42. See *The Complete Notebooks of Henry James*, ed. Leon Edel and Lyall Powers (New York: Oxford University Press, 1987), 70, for a discussion of this proposed tale.

43. Steve Jobe suggests that Henry may have been at the Hôtel Richemont from 29 July to 10 August, as extant letters he wrote from the hotel to Francis Boott are written on those dates, with other letters dated in between. See Steven H. Jobe and Susan E. Gunter, *A Calendar of the Letters of Henry James and a Biographical Register of Henry James's Correspondents* (Lincoln: University of Nebraska Press, 1999), 3 April 2004, http://jamescalendar.unl.edu. Gay Wilson Allen, who had access to at least one of AHGJ's diaries, claimed that HJ returned to London on 15 August (*William James*, 348). Other information concerning this meeting between Alice and Henry comes from Allen's accounts (*William James*, 347–48).

44. HJ to Charles Eliot Norton, 4 July 1882, Percy Lubbock, ed., *The Letters of Henry James*, 2 vols. (New York: Charles Scribner's Sons, 1920), 1:195.

45. ALS, AHGJ to EPG, 13 August 1892, H bMS Am 1092.11 (6).

46. James, *Principles*, 1:273.

47. ALS, AHGJ to EPG, 13 August 1892, H bMS Am 1092.11 (6).

48. HJ to Grace Norton, 23 August [1892], James, *Letters*, 3:394.

49. HJ to WJ, 2 September [1892], *Correspondence*, 2:230.

50. ALS, AHGJ to EPG, 13 August 1892, H bMS Am 1092.11 (6).

51. ALS, HJ to AHGJ, 17 October [1892], H bMS Am 1094 (1618).

52. James Jackson Putnam, "William James," *Atlantic Monthly*, December 1910, n.p.

53. Allen, *William James*, 350; WJ to Josiah Royce, 18 December [18]92, *Correspondence*, 7:350.

54. WJ to Mary Gibbens Salter, 26 December [18]92, *Correspondence*, 7:355.

55. Simon, *Genuine Reality*, 247.

56. Leon Edel's notebook on William Wilberforce Baldwin, M, Edel Papers, container 27.

57. ALS, AHGJ to Elizabeth Glendower Evans, 6 April [1893], S, Evans Papers, Series II, accession nos. 54-2, 55–76.

58. WJ to Ellen Hunter, 9 October 1892, *Correspondence*, 7:325; WJ to Grace Ashburner, 19 October [18]92, *Correspondence*, 7:327.

59. ALS, AHGJ to HJ, 4 November 1892, H bMS Am 1092.11 (32).

60. ALS, AHGJ to Aunt Nannie [Gibbens], 23 December 1892, H bMS Am 1092.11 (63).

61. ALS, HJ to AHGJ, 7 November [1892], H bMS Am 1094 (1619).

62. wj to AHGJ, 2 November [18]92, *Correspondence*, 7:331.

63. wj to Grace Ashburner, 5 January [18]93, *Correspondence*, 7:365.

64. Simon, *Genuine Reality*, 249; hj II to Elizabeth Glendower Evans, 25 May 1931, S, Evans Papers, Series III.

65. wj to Josiah Royce, 18 December [18]92, *Correspondence*, 7:352.

66. wj to AHGJ, [7 December 1892], *Correspondence*, 7:347.

67. wj to EPG, 9 May [18]93, *Correspondence*, 7:418.

68. ALS, AHGJ to Aunt Nannie [Webb], 23 December 1892, H bMS Am 1092.11 (63).

69. ALS, AHGJ to Aunt Nannie [Webb], 23 December 1892, H bMS Am 1092.11 (63).

70. ALS, AHGJ to EPG, 25 December 1892, H bMS Am 1092.11 (7).

71. wj to Francis Boott, 30 January [18]93, *Correspondence*, 7:375. Elizabeth Boott (1846–88) was a painter and a close friend of hj and wj. Her father, widower Frank Boott (1813–1904), dilettante, composer, and musician, frequently visited 95 Irving Street after his daughter's untimely death. American Francis Loring (1838–1905) spent years painting in Europe.

72. wj to Margaret Gibbens Gregor, 3 January 1893, *Correspondence*, 7:363.

73. wj to Margaret Gibbens Gregor, 3 January 1893, *Correspondence*, 7:363.

74. Allen, *William James*, 354.

75. AHGJ to wj, 28 February [1893], *Correspondence*, 7:387–88.

76. "Memories," Dickinson Miller, S, Evans Papers, Series II, accession no. 54-2, 55–76.

77. wj to Elizabeth Sedgwick Child, 6 January 1893, *Correspondence*, 7:366–67.

78. AHGJ to wj, 28 February [1893], *Correspondence*, 7:388.

79. ALS, AHGJ to wj, [c. February 1893], H bMS Am 1092.9 (295).

80. AHGJ to wj, 28 February [1893], *Correspondence*, 7:387.

81. ALS, AHGJ to wj, 4 March 1893, H bMS Am 1092.9 (301).

82. wj to hj, 31 March [18]93, *Correspondence*, 2:265.

83. ALS, AHGJ to Margaret Gibbens, 30 March 1893, H bMS Am 1092.11 (24).

84. ALS, AHGJ to Elizabeth Glendower Evans, 6 April [1893], S, Evans Papers, Series II, accession no. 54-2, 55–76.

85. Allen, *William James*, 358; ALS, AHGJ to EPG, 26 April 1893, H bMS Am 1092.11 (8).

86. wj to hj II, 10 March 1893, *Correspondence*, 7:396.

87. ALS, AHGJ to Elizabeth G. Evans, 6 April [1893], S, Evans Papers, Series II, accession no. 54-2, 55–76.

88. wj to AHGJ, 19 April 1893, *Correspondence*, 7:408.

89. ALS, AHGJ to EPG, 26 April 1893, H bMS Am 1092.11 (8).

90. wj to EPG, 9 [8] May [18]93, *Correspondence*, 7:417.

91. ALS, AHGJ to EPG, 9 May 1893, H bMS Am 1092.11 (9). The German artist was Arnold Bocklin (1827–1901). One of his most famous paintings was *The Isle of the Dead* (1880).

92. WJ to AHGJ, [11 May 1893], *Correspondence*, 7:420.

93. ALS, AHGJ to EPG, 9 May 1893, H bMS Am 1092.11 (9).

94. *The Complete Notebooks of Henry James*, 77.

95. WJ to Carl Stumpf, 24 April [1893], *Correspondence*, 7:410.

96. WJ to EPG, 9 [8] May [18]93, *Correspondence*, 7:418.

97. HJ to AHGJ, 15 February [1892], Gunter, *Dear Munificent Friends*, 30.

98. ALS, AHGJ to HJ, 11 April 1892, H bMS Am 1092.11 (29).

99. HJ to Edmund Gosse, [23 June 1893], Rayburn S. Moore, ed., *Selected Letters of Henry James to Edmund Gosse: A Literary Friendship* (Baton Rouge: Louisiana State University Press, 1988), 96. Sir Edmund Gosse (1849–1938) was a man of letters. He and HJ met in 1879 at a London luncheon and became close friends, HJ writing him nearly four hundred intimate letters. He was one of HJ's sponsors when he applied for British citizenship in 1915.

100. HJ to Francis Boott, 14 July [1893], James, *Letters*, 3:418.

101. WJ to Francois Pillon, 17 June [1893], *Correspondence*, 7:429.

102. ALS, AHGJ to EPG, 18 June [1893], H bMS Am 1092.11 (11); ALS, AHGJ to EPG, 2 July 1893, H bMS Am 1092.11 (12).

103. WJ to S. Hodgson, 23 June [18]93, *Correspondence*, 7:430–31. Shadworth Holloway Hodgson (1832–1912) had been president of the Aristotelian Society and a follower of Kant. Sir Leslie Stephen (1832–1904) was the general editor of the *Dictionary of National Biography*; his second wife was Julia Jackson Duckworth Stephen (1846–95). The Stephens were the parents of writer Virginia Woolf.

104. See WJ's letters to HJ during the month he and Alice spent in London for details of this visit (*Correspondence*, 2:269–72).

105. ALS, AHGJ to Elizabeth Glendower Evans, 8 July [1893], S, Evans Papers, Series II, accession no. 54-2, 55–76.

106. ALS, AHGJ to HJ, 26 June [1893], H bMS Am 1092.11 (33).

107. AHGJ to WJ, 17 July [1893], *Correspondence*, 7:441.

108. Alice met Clarke in 1868 in Germany and had kept in touch with him since then. Joseph Thatcher Clarke (died 1920) was an historian who wrote on ancient architecture and methods of teaching history.

109. AHGJ to WJ, 17 July [1893], *Correspondence*, 7:441. Alice might be referring to the Brothers of Common Life, once a Catholic religious community. This group was established in Utrecht in the late fourteenth century. Devout men could live in this community without taking monastic vows. Thomas à Kempis lived there during its early years. The majority of members were laymen,

attending religious services in the morning. The more educated members copied manuscripts, but all had to earn their living in some way. The order flourished in the fifteenth century and influenced a revival of religion in the Netherlands and northern Germany. All its houses were gone by the middle of the seventeenth century.

9. THE WILL TO ENDURE

1. WJ to HJ, 17 December [18]93, *Correspondence*, 2:292. Also described in Simon, *Genuine Reality*, 252.

2. WJ to HJ, 1 October 1893, *Correspondence*, 2:284; WJ to HJ, 29 October 1893, *Correspondence*, 2:286–87.

3. WJ to HJ, 17 December [18]93, *Correspondence*, 2:292.

4. WJ to Frederic Myers, 17 December [18]93, *Correspondence*, 7:474.

5. WJ to AHGJ, 17 May 1894, *Correspondence*, 7:501.

6. WJ to Katharine Rodgers, 30 October [18]93, *Correspondence*, 7:466.

7. WJ to MMJ, 19 [18] June 1895, *Correspondence*, 8:44.

8. Frederic Myers to WJ, 16 November [18]93, *Correspondence*, 7:468.

9. ALS, Aunt Holly to Mary Gibbens Salter, 31 January [18]99, H bMS Am 1938 (292).

10. Notes on a sitting with Mrs. Piper, RJ, 28 December 1893, H bMS Am 1095 (38).

11. AHGJ to WJ, [24 December 1893], *Correspondence*, 7:476–77.

12. WJ to AHGJ, 24 December [18]93, *Correspondence*, 7:475.

13. ALS, AHGJ to WJ, [25 December 1893], H bMS Am 1092.9 (305).

14. ALS, Sarah Hervey Porter to HJ II, 6 November 1911, H bMS Am 1092.10 (137).

15. WJ to AHGJ, [13 September 1894], *Correspondence*, 7:541.

16. ALS, WJ to AHGJ, 18 May 1894, H bMS Am 1092.9 (1860).

17. WJ to AHGJ, 23 May [18]94, *Correspondence*, 7:505.

18. Green and Perry, *The Light of the Home*, 119.

19. ALS, AHGJ to WJ [31 May 1894], H bMS Am 1092.9 (307).

20. Green and Perry, *The Light of the Home*, 132.

21. ALS, WJ to AHGJ, 18 May [18]94, H bMS Am 1092.9 (1860).

22. ALS, WJ to AHGJ, 18 July 1894, H bMS Am 1092.9 (1881).

23. WJ to Ellen Hunter, 18 November [18]94, *Correspondence*, 7:557. Ellen "Elly" Gertrude Temple Emmet Hunter (1850–1920) was Mary Temple's sister and first cousin to WJ and HJ. She first married Christopher Temple Emmet and then, after his death, Englishman George Hunter. She visited HJ at Lamb House often.

24. WJ to AHGJ, 16 May [18]94, *Correspondence*, 7:501.

25. ALS, WJ to AHGJ, 25 May [1894], H bMS Am 1092.9 (1865).

26. WJ to AHGJ, 27 May [18]94, *Correspondence*, 7:509.

27. ALS, WJ to AHGJ, 19 May [18]94, H bMS Am 1092.9 (1861).

28. WJ to Granville Stanley Hall, 27 May [1894], *Correspondence*, 7:508.

29. AHGJ to WJ, 16 September [1894], *Correspondence*, 7:544.

30. WJ to AHGJ, 6 January [18]95, *Correspondence*, 8:6.

31. WJ to AHGJ, 18 June [18]94, *Correspondence*, 7:518; WJ to AHGJ, 7 January [18]95, *Correspondence*, 8:7. Novick, in *Henry James: The Mature Master*, makes a strong case that Henry James actually made considerable artistic and personal gains from his forays into the theatrical world.

32. WJ to AHGJ, 10 April 1888, *Correspondence*, 6:371.

33. Famous American modernist writer Gertrude Stein (1874–1946) studied psychology with WJ while she was a Radcliffe student, graduating in 1897. A well-known anecdote claims that once during final exams she sent WJ a note saying, "I am so sorry but really I do not feel like an examination paper in philosophy today." He replied, "Dear Miss Stein, I understand perfectly how you feel. I often feel like that myself" (Allen, *William James*, 305). Stein did original experiments with Leon Solomons on the problems of consciousness, experiments in automatic motor action that included automatic writing, publishing their report, "Normal Motor Automatism," in the *Psychological Review* in 1896. Their work had import for WJ's psychic research in terms of finding the separation between the conscious and the unconscious mind, though their work did not solve this problem (Allen, *William James*, 373–75).

34. WJ to Ellen Emmet Hunter, 18 November [18]94, *Correspondence*, 7:557–58.

35. WJ to HJ, 12 December [18]94, *Correspondence*, 2:331.

36. WJ to HJ, 13 May [18]95, *Correspondence*, 2:360.

37. WJ to HJ, 8 April [18]95, *Correspondence*, 2:355–56.

38. HJ to WJ, 11 October 1898, *Correspondence*, 3:46.

39. ALS, WJ to AHGJ, 10 January [1895], H bMS Am 1092.9 (1902).

40. ALS, WJ to AHGJ, [11 January 1895], H bMS Am 1092.9 (1903).

41. ALS, AHGJ to WJ, 1 August [1895], H bMS Am 1092.9 (310).

42. ALS, AHGJ to WJ, 7 August [18]95, H bMS Am 1092.9 (311).

43. ALS, WJ to AHGJ, 29 August [1895], H bMS Am 1092.9 (1929).

44. WJ to AHGJ, 5 September 1895, *Correspondence*, 8:82.

45. WJ to AHGJ, 2 September [18]95, *Correspondence*, 8:80.

46. ALS, AHGJ to WJ, [9 September 1895], H bMS Am 1092.9 (312).

47. ALS, AHGJ to WJ, [9 September 1895], H bMS Am 1092.9 (312).

48. WJ to Sarah Wyman Whitman, 25 April [1896], *Correspondence*, 8:147–48.

49. WJ to AHGJ, 17 July [18]96, *Correspondence*, 8:167.

50. ALS, WJ to AHGJ, 14 August [18]96, H bMS Am 1092.9 (1965).

51. ALS, WJ to AHGJ, 15 August [18]96, H bMS Am 1092.9 (1966).

52. ALS, WJ to AHGJ, 27 August 1896, H bMS Am 1092.9 (1974).

53. WJ to Henry William Rankin, 1 February 1897, *Correspondence*, 8:228.

54. ALS, AHGJ to HJ, 23 April 1897, H bMS Am 1092.11 (36). Royce's "Infinite" refers to his philosophy of Idealism, which among other things postulated a greater, infinite consciousness that eventually would resolve evil in the world.

55. John Jay Chapman to WJ, 17 March 1897, *Correspondence*, 8:247. Chapman (1862–1933) was a writer and social activist, sometimes called a belated abolitionist. He knew WJ when he was an undergraduate and then a law student at Harvard.

56. HJ to AHGJ, 15 June 1897, Gunter, *Dear Munificent Friends*, 33–34.

57. WJ to HJ, 4 April 1897, *Correspondence*, 3:6.

58. "Alice Howe Gibbens, 1849–1922," 40. This quotation, reported by Harry many years after the occasion, does not refer to any one verse in the Bible, but its sense can be found in Revelation 21:16, 23, 24.

59. ALS, AHGJ to HJ, 23 April 1897, H bMS Am 1092.11 (36).

60. ALS, AHGJ to WJ, [21 April 1897], H bMS Am 1092.9 (314).

61. ALS, AHGJ to HJ, 23 April [18]97, H bMS Am 1092.11 (36).

62. ALS, AHGJ to HJ, 31 May [18]97, H bMS Am 1092.11 (37).

63. WJ to HJ, 5 June 1897, *Correspondence*, 3:8–9.

64. James wrote to Washington a few days after the ceremony, congratulating him on the dignity and simplicity of his speech and commending in particular its brevity (WJ to Booker T. Washington, 5 June 1897, *Correspondence*, 8:273). Booker T. Washington (1856–1915) was the son of a slave who became an important African American leader from 1890 to 1915. A conciliatory figure, he was called the "Great Accommodator" by WJ's student W. E. B. Du Bois.

65. ALS, AHGJ to HJ, 31 May [18]97, H bMS Am 1092.11 (37). This letter encloses a copy of the program.

66. WJ to HJ, 5 June 1897, *Correspondence*, 3:9.

67. ALS, AHGJ to HJ, 31 May 1897, H bMS Am 1092.11 (37).

68. HJ to AHGJ, 15 June 1897, Gunter, *Dear Munificent Friends*, 32.

69. AHGJ to WJ, 8 September 1897, quoted in "Alice Howe Gibbens, 1849–1922," 52–53.

70. See David A. Hollinger, "James, Clifford, and Scientific Conscience," in Ruth Anna Putnam, ed., *The Cambridge Companion to William James* (Cambridge: Cambridge University Press, 1997), 69–83, for James's essay as a reaction to Victorian positivism.

71. WJ to Amy Lothrop Coolidge, 22 April 1896, *Correspondence*, 8:143.

72. William James, "Reflex Action and Theism," in *The Will to Believe*, 106.

73. William James, preface to *The Will to Believe*, 9.

74. Francis Herbert Bradley to WJ, 21 September [18]97, *Correspondence*, 8:309. Bradley (1846–1924) was a leader of British Idealism and well respected during his lifetime.

75. WJ to AHGJ, 13 September 1897, *Correspondence*, 8:303.

76. Information on these episodes with Bob in the late 1890s comes from Maher, *Biography of Broken Fortunes*, chap. 7.

77. William James, *Manuscript Lectures* (Cambridge MA: Harvard University Press, 1988), 51n. Charles Godfrey Leland (1824–1903) was an American humorist writer and a folklorist.

78. William James, *Talks to Teachers on Psychology and to Students on Some of Life's Ideals* (Cambridge MA: Harvard University Press, 1983), 114.

79. Sutton, *Cambridge Reconsidered*, 82.

80. ALS, AHGJ to HJ, 13 January [18]98, H bMS Am 1092.11 (35).

81. AHGJ to HJ, 13 January [18]98, H bMS Am 1092.11 (35).

82. ALS, RJ to AHGJ, 12 February 1898, H MS Am 1095.2 (3).

83. ALS, AHGJ to HJ, 14 February 1898, H bMS Am 1092.11 (39).

84. ALS, AHGJ to HJ, 4 February 1898, H bMS Am 1092.11 (38).

85. Leigh Richmond Gregor (1860–1912) was professor of modern languages at McGill University in Montreal.

86. ALS, AHGJ to HJ, 13 January [18]98, H bMS Am 1092.11 (35).

87. ALS, AHGJ to WJ, 6 June 1899, H bMS Am 1092.9 (323).

88. HJ II, diary, 20 June 1898–27 September [1899?], H bMS Am 1094.5 (23), 13–14, 32, 17.

89. ALS, WJ to AHGJ, 23 June 1898, H bMS Am 1092.9 (2039). "Puella Aestivalis" is Latin for "summer girl."

90. WJ to AHGJ, 9 July 1898, *Correspondence*, 8:390.

91. AHGJ to WJ, [12 July 1898], *Correspondence*, 8:395.

92. WJ to AHGJ, 10 September 1898, *Correspondence*, 8:433.

93. ALS, AHGJ to HJ II, 4 September [18]98, H MS Am 2538. See chapter 10 for further information on the Dreyfus trial. "Alger" was Russell Alger, McKinley's secretary of war from March 1987 to July 1899. His conduct of the Spanish-American War was severely criticized. One of the charges against him involved making many of the soldiers sick from eating "embalmed beef." Khartoum refers to a battle in the South African Boer War, a victory won by General Gordon.

94. Donald McQuade, introduction to *Correspondence*, 9:xxvii.

95. WJ to George Holmes Howison, 27 November [18]98, *Correspondence*, 8:460.

96. ALS, AHGJ to HJ, 21 May [18]99, H bMS Am 1092.11 (40).

97. ALS, AHGJ to HJ, 18 June 1899, H bMS Am 1092.11 (41).

98. ALS, AHGJ to HJ II, 25 June [18]99, H MS Am 2538.

99. ALS, AHGJ to HJ II and WJ Jr., 15 July [18]99, H MS Am 2538. William and Mary Salter bought a farm at Chocorua around 1889. By 1892 they had sold it and bought Hill Top.

100. WJ to Elizabeth G. Evans, 13 July [1899], *Correspondence*, 9:7.

101. ALS, AHGJ to HJ, 18 June 1899, H bMS Am 1092.11 (41).

102. AHGJ to WJ [12 June 1899], *Correspondence*, 8:548.

103. ALS, AHGJ to HJ II and WJ Jr., 15 July [18]99, H MS Am 2538.

10. TO BAD NAUHEIM

1. ALS, AHGJ to HJ II and WJ Jr., 15 July [18]99, H MS Am 2538.

2. ALS, AHGJ to HJ II and WJ Jr., 15 July [18]99, H MS Am 2538.

3. WJ to EPG, 2 August 1899, *Correspondence*, 9:12.

4. WJ to EPG, 2 August 1899, *Correspondence*, 9:13.

5. ALS, AHGJ to HJ II and WJ Jr., 15 July 1899, H MS Am 2538.

6. Unpublished fragment, AHGJ to WJ Jr., c. 12 July 1900, H MS Am 2538.

7. WJ to ARJ, 2 September 1899, *Correspondence*, 9:35.

8. WJ to HJ, 8 August 1899, *Correspondence*, 3:77.

9. WJ to James Jackson Putnam, 19 September 1899, *Correspondence*, 9:48.

10. Leon Edel's notebook on William Baldwin, M, Edel Papers, container 27, 43–45.

11. Linda Simon, "The Empowered Physician: William Wilberforce Baldwin and Nineteenth Century Medical Therapeutics," http://mockingbird .creighton.edu/english/Simon.htm.

12. ALS, AHGJ to Boys, 6 August 1899, H MS Am 2538.

13. WJ to HJ II and WJ Jr., [14 September 1899], *Correspondence*, 9:42.

14. ALS, WJ to HJ II and WJ Jr., 6 August [18]99, H MS Am 2538.

15. WJ to HJ, 8 August 1899, *Correspondence*, 3:77; WJ to ARJ, 23 September 1899, *Correspondence*, 9:51.

16. WJ to MMJ, 10 August [18]99, *Correspondence*, 9:21.

17. ALS, AHGJ to HJ II and WJ Jr., 6 August [18]99, H MS Am 2538. Miss Cremlin's father had built a pontoon bridge over the Ganges in three days so that British troops could reach Lucknow.

18. ALS, AHGJ to HJ II and WJ Jr., 14 September 1899, H MS Am 2538.

19. ALS, AHGJ to HJ II and WJ Jr., 6 August [18]99, H MS Am 2538.

20. WJ to HJ II, 14 August 1899, *Correspondence*, 9:24.

21. ALS, AHGJ to HJ II and WJ Jr., 15 August [18]99, H MS Am 2538; WJ to HJ II, 14 August 1899, *Correspondence*, 9:24.

22. ALS, AHGJ to HJ II and WJ Jr., 15 August [18]99, H MS Am 2538.

23. ALS, AHGJ to HJ II, 22 August [1899], H MS Am 2538.

24. ALS, AHGJ to HJ II and WJ Jr., 15 August [18]99, H MS Am 2538.

25. WJ to HJ, 16 September [18]99, *Correspondence*, 3:86; WJ to HJ, 18 September [1899], *Correspondence*, 3:87.

26. WJ to EPG, 2 August 1899, *Correspondence*, 9:11.

27. ALS, AHGJ to HJ, 18 June [1899], H bMS Am 1092.11 (41).

28. HJ to WJ, 9 August [1899], *Correspondence*, 3:79–80.

29. WJ to HJ, 11 August 1899, *Correspondence*, 3:81.

30. HJ to AHGJ, 19 August 1899, Gunter, *Dear Munificent Friends*, 36.

31. ALS, MMJ to EPG, 4 October [1899], H *2002M-44(b), box 1, folder "Mary Margaret James."

32. ALS, MMJ to EPG, 4 October [1899], H *2002M-44(b), box 1, folder "Mary Margaret James."

33. See letters between WJ and HJ, *Correspondence*, 3:66–79.

34. AHGJ to HJ, 3 August [18]99, *Correspondence*, 3:70.

35. HJ to WJ, 5 August 1899, *Correspondence*, 3:72, 75.

36. ALS, AHGJ to HJ, 6 August [18]99, H bMS Am 1092.11 (42).

37. HJ to AHGJ, 1 December 1897, in Henry James, *Letters*, vol. 4, 1895–1916, ed. Leon Edel (Cambridge MA: Belknap Press, 1984), 64.

38. WJ to Ferdinand Schiller, 11 October 1899, *Correspondence*, 9:59.

39. ALS, AHGJ to WJ Jr., 24 October [1899], H MS Am 2538.

40. WJ to HJ, 11 October [18]99, *Correspondence*, 3:89.

41. Allen, *William James*, 402.

42. ALS, AHGJ to WJ Jr., 24 October [18]99, H MS Am 2538.

43. ALS, AHGJ to WJ Jr., 6 November [18]99, H MS Am 2538.

44. ALS, MMJ to AHGJ, Thursday [1899], box 3, folder 1, BANC MSS 72/35, Bruce Porter Papers: Additions, Bancroft Library, University of California at Berkeley.

45. ALS, MMJ to AHGJ, 5 November [1899], H *2002M-44(b), box 1, folder "Mary Margaret James."

46. ALS, MMJ to AHGJ, Thursday [1899], B BANC MSS 72/35, box 3, folder 1.

47. ALS, Sophie Weisse to AHGJ, [16 November 1899], H *2002M-44 (b), box 2, folder "Weisse, Sophie."

48. WJ to EPG, 29 October [18]99, *Correspondence*, 9:70.

49. ALS, AHGJ to WJ Jr., 24 October [18]99, H MS Am 2538.

50. WJ to William Baldwin, 2 November [18]99, *Correspondence*, 9:72.

51. ALS, AHGJ to Frances Rollins Morse, [25 December 1899], H bMS Am 1092.9 (4377).

52. ALS, AHGJ to WJ Jr., 6 November [18]99, H MS Am 2538.

53. WJ to Thomas Davidson, 2 November [18]99, *Correspondence*, 9:73.

54. WJ to MMJ, 10 November 1899, *Correspondence*, 9:79.

55. wj to hj, 31 October [1899], *Correspondence*, 3:92.

56. als, hj to ahgj, [14 November 1899], H bMS Am 1094 (1628).

57. als, ahgj to wj Jr., 11 November [18]99, H ms Am 2538.

58. als, ahgj to wj Jr., 11 November [18]99, H ms Am 2538.

59. hj to wj, 8 March 1870, Henry James, *Letters*, vol. 1, 1875–1883, ed. Leon Edel (Cambridge ma: Harvard University Press, 1974), 207.

60. als, hj to ahgj, [1 December 1899], H bMS Am 1094 (1631).

61. als, ahgj to Francis Boott, 9 December [18]99, H bMS Am 1092.9 (4373).

62. als, ahgj to wj Jr., 7 December [18]99, H ms Am 2538.

63. als, ahgj to Francis Boott, 20 December [18]99, H bMS Am 1092.9 (4372).

64. als, ahgj to Theodore Flournoy, 16 December [18]99, H bMS Am 1505 (82).

65. wj to Katharine Rodgers, 5 January 1900, *Correspondence*, 9:120. Katharine Outram Rodgers (born 1841) was wj and hj's cousin. Her paternal grandmother, Helen Robertson Rodgers, was the sister of their maternal grandmother.

66. als, ahgj to wj Jr., 26 December 1899, H ms Am 2538.

67. als, ahgj to wj Jr., 19 January 1900, H ms Am 2538.

68. als, ahgj to hj II, 18 February 1900, H ms Am 2538.

69. wj to President and Fellows of Harvard University, 20 December 1899, *Correspondence*, 9:99. The corporation granted him leave at half-pay.

70. wj to Francis Rollins Morse, 24 December 18[99], *Correspondence*, 9:104.

71. als, hj to mmj, 8 November 1906, H bMS Eng 1070 (29).

72. als, ahgj to wj Jr., 19 January 1900, H ms Am 2538.

73. Andrew Seth Pringle-Pattison to wj, 12 January 1900, *Correspondence*, 9:123.

74. wj to Frances Rollins Morse, 12 April 1900, *Correspondence*, 9:185–86.

75. als, ahgj to Elizabeth Glendower Evans, 17 January 1900, S, Evans Papers, Series II, Correspondence.

76. hj to wj, [15 January 1900], *Correspondence*, 3:97.

77. wj to Elizabeth Glendower Evans, [17 January 1900], *Correspondence*, 9:128.

78. als, ahgj to Elizabeth Glendower Evans, [17 January 1900], S, Evans Papers, Series II, Correspondence.

79. als, ahgj to Elizabeth Glendower Evans, [17 January 1900], S, Evans Papers, Series II, Correspondence.

80. wj to Joseph Thatcher Clarke, 20 January 1900, *Correspondence*, 9:131.

81. als, ahgj to wj Jr., 29 March [1900], H ms Am 2538.

82. wj to Francis Boott, 31 January 1900, *Correspondence*, 9:138.

83. Reproduction, watercolor by Mrs. Myers, H pfMS Am 1094, box 1 of 3.

84. J. Gordon Leishman, "The Bréguet-Richet Quad-Rotor Helicopter of 1907," www.enae.umd.edu/AGRC/Aero/Breguet.

85. als, ahgj to wj Jr., 19 January 1900, H ms Am 2538.

86. HJ to WJ, 20 August [1892], *Correspondence*, 2:225.

87. James, *Essays in Psychical Research*, 195.

88. AHGJ to WJ Jr., n.d. [c. February 1900], H MS Am 2538.

89. WJ to HJ, 25 February 1900, *Correspondence*, 3:103.

90. AHGJ to HJ, 25 February 1900, *Correspondence*, 3:103.

91. ALS, AHGJ to WJ Jr., n.d. [c. February 1900], H MS Am 2538.

92. ALS, AHGJ to WJ Jr., 20 March 1900, H MS Am 2538.

93. ALS, AHGJ to Frances Rollins Morse, 13 May 1900, H bMS Am 1092.9 (4378).

94. WJ to HJ II, 23 February 1900, *Correspondence*, 9:149.

95. ALS, AHGJ to WJ Jr., 29 March 1900, H MS Am 2538.

96. Paul Bourget (1852–1935) wrote plays, poetry, novels, and critical essays, his fiction mainly about the upper classes. He met HJ in 1884 and became his disciple, and while HJ disliked his fiction, he envied Bourget his financial success. The Bourgets gave HJ germs of ideas for several stories. His wife, Minnie (1867–1932), was a translator.

97. ALS, AHGJ to WJ Jr., 8 and 10 June 1900, H MS Am 2538. "St. Bartholomew's" refers to the 1572 massacre of French Protestant Huguenots. It was one of a series of bloody skirmishes in the sixteenth-century conflicts between French Catholics and Protestants.

98. ALS, AHGJ to HJ II, 4 April 1900, H MS Am 2538.

99. ALS, AHGJ to WJ Jr., 20 March 1900, H MS Am 2538.

100. ALS, AHGJ to HJ II, 4 April 1900, H MS Am 2538.

101. ALS, AHGJ to Elizabeth Glendower Evans, 15 April 1900, S, Evans Papers, Series II, Correspondence.

102. HJ to AHGJ, 14 February 1900, Gunter, *Dear Munificent Friends*, 37.

103. ALS, HJ to AHGJ, 21 February 1900, H bMS Am 1094 (1636).

104. ALS, HJ to AHGJ, 6 February 1900, H bMS Am 1094 (1634).

105. WJ to MMJ, 17 February 1900, *Correspondence*, 9:145–46.

106. ALS, AHGJ to WJ Jr., 20 March 1900, H MS Am 2538.

107. ALS, MMJ to parents, 3 March [1900], box 3, folder "Porter, Margaret (James) 22 letters 1898–1916," B BANC MSS 72/35.

108. WJ to MMJ, 11 February [1900], *Correspondence*, 9:143.

109. ALS, AHGJ to HJ II, 18 February 1900, H MS Am 2538.

110. ALS, AHGJ to WJ Jr., 19 January 1900, H MS Am 2538.

111. Allen, *William James*, 410.

112. ALS, HJ to MMJ, 1 April 1900, H bMS Eng 1070 (6).

113. ALS, AHGJ to WJ Jr., 29 March [1900], H MS Am 2538.

114. HJ to AHGJ and WJ, 26 April 1900, *Correspondence*, 3:116.

115. ALS, AHGJ to Frances Rollins Morse, 13 May 1900, H bMS Am 1092.9 (4378).

116. WJ to Hugo Munsterberg, 18 June 1900, *Correspondence*, 9:232.

117. WJ to HJ II, 23 June 1900, *Correspondence*, 9:235.

118. ALS, AHGJ to WJ Jr., 8 June 1900, H MS Am 2538.

119. ALS, AHGJ to HJ II, 10 August 1900, H MS Am 2538.

120. ALS, AHGJ to WJ Jr., 8 and 10 June 1900, H MS Am 2538.

121. ALS, AHGJ to WJ Jr., 26 December 1899, H MS Am 2538.

122. WJ to EPG, 6 June [1900], *Correspondence*, 9:219.

123. WJ to HJ, 7 August [1900], *Correspondence*, 3:125; WJ to George Bucknam Dorr, 22 July 1900, *Correspondence*, 9:256.

124. Swami Vivekananda (1863–1902) was a famous leader of Vedanta and Yoga and a major figure in Hindu history.

125. *The Complete Works of Swami Vivekananda* (Calcutta: Advaita Ashrama, 1956), 6:436–37.

126. WJ to HJ, 8 August [1900], *Correspondence*, 3:127.

127. WJ to HJ, 7 August [1900], *Correspondence*, 3:125–26.

128. ALS, AHGJ to EPG, 8 July [1900], H MS Am 2538.

129. WJ to AHGJ, 26 August 1900, *Correspondence*, 9:276.

130. WJ to AHGJ, 4 September [1900], *Correspondence*, 9:290.

131. ALS, WJ to AHGJ, 7 September [1900], H bMS Am 1092.9 (2152).

132. WJ to AHGJ, 8 September 1900, *Correspondence*, 9:296.

133. 8 September [1900], WJ, "Diary, 1901–1902," H MS Am 1092.9 (4552). These diary entries are in a handwritten diary dated 1902, but these events all took place during the fall of 1900, when William had returned alone to Bad Nauheim.

134. ALS, WJ to AHGJ, 12 September [1900], H bMS Am 1092.9 (2159).

135. 12 September [1900], WJ, "Diary, 1901–1902," H MS Am 1092.9 (4552).

136. WJ to AHGJ, 13 September 1900, *Correspondence*, 9:302.

137. 14 September [1900], WJ, "Diary, 1901–1902," H bMS Am 1092.9 (4552).

138. ALS, WJ to AHGJ, 10 September 1900, H bMS Am 1092.9 (2153).

139. ALS, WJ to AHGJ, 11 September 1900, H bMS Am 1092.9 (2157).

140. ALS, WJ to MMJ, 15 September 1900, H bMS Am 1092.9 (3014).

141. ALS, HJ to AHGJ [September 1900], H bMS Am 1094 (1632).

142. ALS, AHGJ to HJ II, 21 September [1900], H MS Am 2538.

143. ALS, AHGJ to HJ II, 21 September [1900], H MS Am 2538.

144. ALS, AHGJ to WJ Jr., 24 September 1900, H MS Am 2538.

145. ALS, HJ to MMJ, 25 September 1900, H bMS Eng 1070 (7).

146. ALS, AHGJ to WJ Jr., 24 September 1900, H MS Am 2538.

147. ALS, HJ to MMJ, 7 October 1900, H bMS Eng 1070 (8).

11. MENDINGS

1. 23 September [1900], WJ, "Diary, 1901–1902," H MS Am 1092.9 (4552).

2. HJ to AHGJ, 14 October 1900, Gunter, *Dear Munificent Friends*, 40.

3. ALS, AHGJ to HJ, 4 January 190[1], H bMS Am 1092.11 (44).

4. ALS, WJ to MMJ, 8 November [1900], H bMS Am 1092.9 (3017).

5. ALS, AHGJ to HJ II, 30 October 1900, H MS Am 2538.

6. Manuscript dictation to AHGJ, WJ to WJ Jr., 1 December 1900, H MS Am 2538.

7. ALS, AHGJ to WJ Jr., 2 November 1900, H MS Am 2538.

8. ALS, WJ to MMJ, 8 November [1900], H bMS Am 1092.9 (3017).

9. Simon, *Genuine Reality*, 295.

10. WJ to AHGJ, 8 September 1900, *Correspondence*, 9:297.

11. ALS, AHGJ to WJ Jr., 4 January 1901, H MS Am 2538.

12. ALS, AHGJ to HJ II, 29 December 1900, H MS Am 2538. Barrett Wendell (1855–1921) was a Harvard professor. He also wrote a book on Cotton Mather.

13. ALS, AHGJ to WJ Jr., 4 January 1901, H MS Am 2538. The book's full title was *Jesus Christ and the Social Question: An Examination of the Teaching of Jesus in Its Relation to Some of the Problems of Modern Social Life*. Francis Greenwood Peabody (1847–1936) was an ordained Unitarian minister and on the faculty of the Harvard Divinity School. WJ knew him and wrote to him in 1901, congratulating him on the book and its balance between individual ethical idealism and institutionalism (*Correspondence*, 9:418–19).

14. Manuscript dictation to AHGJ, WJ to WJ Jr., 1 December 1900, H MS Am 2538.

15. ALS, AHGJ to HJ II, 29 December 1900, H MS Am 2538.

16. ALS, AHGJ to HJ, 25 December 1900, H bMS Am 1092.11 (43).

17. ALS, HJ to AHGJ, 1 January 1901, H bMS Am 1094 (1647).

18. Hendrik Christian Andersen (1872–1940) was a Norwegian American sculptor. HJ met him in Rome in 1899, and they were close friends for years, entertaining strong feelings for one another, but they eventually drifted apart. HJ disliked Andersen's plans for large public statues, and Andersen did not appreciate James's complex fiction.

19. ALS, AHGJ to WJ Jr., 4 January 1901, H MS Am 2538.

20. HJ to AHGJ, 30 January 1901, Gunter, *Dear Munificent Friends*, 44.

21. ALS, AHGJ to HJ, 25 December 1900, H bMS Am 1092.11 (43).

22. ALS, WJ to MMJ, 8 November [1900], H bMS Am 1092.9 (3017).

23. See www.vroma.org. The Lapis Niger was uncovered in January 1899.

24. ALS, AHGJ to HJ II, 29 December 1900, H MS Am 2538.

25. WJ to HJ, 22 December 1900, *Correspondence*, 3:151.

26. ALS, AHGJ to HJ II, 23 December 1900, H MS Am 2538.

27. ALS, AHGJ to Elizabeth Glendower Evans, 10 November 1900, S, Evans Papers, Series II, Correspondence.

28. Manuscript dictation to AHGJ, WJ to WJ Jr., 1 December 1900, H MS Am 2538.

29. Ahlstrom, *Religious History*, 852.

30. ALS, AHGJ to WJ Jr., 4 January 190[1], H MS Am 2538.

31. AHGJ to HJ, 25 December 1900, H bMS Am 1092.11 (43).

32. ALS, AHGJ to Elizabeth Glendower Evans, 10 November 1900, S, Evans Papers, Series II, Correspondence.

33. ALS, HJ to MMJ, 12 November 1900, H bMS Eng 1070 (11).

34. ALS, HJ to MMJ, 17 December [1900], H bMS Eng 1070 (14).

35. ALS, HJ to AHGJ, 1 January 1901, H bMS Am 1094 (1647); ALS, HJ to MMJ, 9 December 1907, H bMS Eng 1070 (30).

36. ALS, WJ to AHGJ, 19 October 1898, H bMS Am 1092.9 (2090).

37. ALS, HJ to MMJ, 9 December 1907, H bMS Eng 1070 (30).

38. ALS, AHGJ to HJ II, 29 December 1900, H MS Am 2538.

39. HJ to AHGJ, 7 January 1901, Gunter, *Dear Munificent Friends*, 42.

40. ALS, MMJ to ARJ, 20 January 1901, box 3, folder 1, B BANC MSS 72/35. The Prince of Wales was Albert Edward (1841–1910), Queen Victoria's eldest son. He was heir apparent longer than anyone else in British history.

41. ALS, HJ to MMJ, [31 January 1901], H bMS Eng 1070 (16).

42. HJ to AHGJ, 30 January 1901, Gunter, *Dear Munificent Friends*, 44.

43. ALS, WJ to WJ Jr., 8 February 1901, H MS Am 2538.

44. HJ to AHGJ, [14 January 1901], Gunter, *Dear Munificent Friends*, 43.

45. ALS, AHGJ to WJ Jr., 4 January 190[1], H MS Am 2538.

46. ALS, AHGJ to Frances Rollins Morse, 5 February 1901, H bMS Am 1092.9 (4379).

47. William James, "Frederic Myers's Service to Psychology" (1901), in *Essays in Psychical Research*, 196.

48. AHGJ and WJ to HJ, 25 January 1901, *Correspondence*, 3:160.

49. ALS, AHGJ to HJ, 2 March 1901, H bMS Am 1092.11 (45).

50. ALS, AHGJ to EPG, 8 March 1901, box 1, folder "James, Alice Howe Gibbens," B BANC MSS 72/35.

51. Edith White Norton was the wife of Richard Norton (1872–1918), the son of Charles Eliot Norton.

52. ALS, AHGJ to EPG, 8 March 1901, box 1, folder "James, Alice Howe Gibbens," B BANC MSS 72/35.

53. ALS, AHGJ to HJ, 28 March 1901, H bMS Am 1092.11 (46).

54. ALS, HJ to AHGJ, [8 April 1901], H bMS Am 1094 (1651).

55. Transcript of ALS, MMJ to WJ Jr., 26 April [1901], M, Edel Papers, container 42, folder "Peggy James."

56. ALS, AHGJ to WJ Jr., 17 July 1901, H MS Am 2538.

57. Transcript of ALS, MMJ to WJ Jr., 26 April [1901], M, Edel Papers, container 42, folder "Peggy James."

58. HJ to AHGJ, [3 June 1901], Gunter, *Dear Munificent Friends*, 46.

59. James, *Varieties*, 299.

60. ALS, AHGJ to WJ Jr., 31 May 1901, H MS Am 2538.

61. ALS, MMJ to ARJ, 20 June [1901], box 3, folder 1, B BANC MSS 72/35.

62. ALS, AHGJ to WJ Jr., 17 July 1901, H MS Am 2538.

63. ALS, AHGJ to EPG, 28 June 1901, H MS Am 2538.

12. A FORM OF USE

1. ALS, AHGJ to WJ Jr., [late summer 1901], H bMS Am 1092.9 (4376).

2. WJ to Edwin Lawrence Godkin, 29 August 1901, *Correspondence*, 9:533.

3. ALS, AHGJ to EPG, 27 July 1902, H MS Am 2538.

4. I am grateful to Galena Eduardova, presidential scholar in Harvard's Ph.D. program in English, for her insights into Alice's life. She framed Alice through the lenses of Deleuze and Guattari, allowing me to conceptualize her life in ways other than through Freudian lenses.

5. Maj. Henry Lee Higginson (1843–1919) was a financier and patron of the arts. WJ to Henry Higginson, 4 September 1902, *Correspondence* 10:119.

6. WJ to Pauline Goldmark, 14 September 1901, *Correspondence*, 9:539.

7. HJ to AHGJ and WJ, 1 November 1901, *Correspondence*, 3:183.

8. WJ to AHGJ, 12 September 1901, *Correspondence*, 9:538.

9. WJ to Katharine Outram Rodgers, 30 September 1901, *Correspondence*, 9:548–49.

10. ALS, AHGJ to WJ Jr., 17 July 1901, H MS Am 2538.

11. WJ to Katharine Outram Rodgers, 30 September 1901, *Correspondence*, 9:548.

12. WJ to Joseph Thatcher Clarke, 19 August 1901, *Correspondence*, 9:532.

13. WJ to Katharine Outram Rodgers, 26 December 1901, *Correspondence*, 9:566–67.

14. WJ to EPG, 26 May [1902], *Correspondence*, 10:47.

15. Edwin Lawrence Godkin (1831–1902) was an American writer and editor of the *Nation* who published many of HJ's reviews. He also published WJ's review of Herman Grimm's novel *Invincible Powers* in November 1867. His wife was Katharine Buckley Sands Godkin (1846–1907).

16. Alice wrote to Henry before the lectures began, and he responded, "It breaks my heart to hear of Wm's bad state of nerves" (ALS, HJ to AHGJ, [26 May 1902], H bMS Am 1094 [1655]).

17. Allen, *William James*, 429–30.

18. David M. Katzman, *Seven Days a Week: Women and Domestic Service in Industrializing America* (New York: Oxford University Press, 1987), 65–67.

19. Faye E. Dudden, *Serving Women: Household Service in Nineteenth-Century America* (Middletown CT: Wesleyan University Press, 1983), 24–25.

20. Dudden, *Serving Women*, 178–79.

21. Katzman, *Seven Days a Week*, 138.

22. Conversations with Michael James; ALS, AHGJ to WJ Jr., 26 November 1904, H MS Am 2538.

23. ALS, AHGJ to WJ Jr., 28 September 1902, H MS Am 2538.

24. ALS, AHGJ to WJ Jr., 9 November 1902, H MS Am 2538.

25. ALS, AHGJ to WJ Jr., 26 November 1902, H MS Am 2538.

26. ALS, AHGJ to WJ Jr., 7 December 1902, H MS Am 2538.

27. ALS, AHGJ to WJ Jr., 21 December 1902, H MS Am 2538.

28. ALS, AHGJ to WJ Jr., 28 December 1902, H MS Am 2538; Katzman, *Seven Days a Week*, 307.

29. ALS, HJ II to MMJ, 20 November 1933, box 1, folder "James, Henry 1879–1947," B BANC MSS 72/35.

30. 23 August 1905, WJ, "Diary, 1905," H MS Am 1092.9 (4553).

31. ALS, WJ to MMJ, 27 April [c. 1907], H bMS Am 1092.9 (2980).

32. ALS, AHGJ to WJ, 28 August [18]98, H bMS Am 1092.9 (319).

33. ALS, AHGJ to WJ Jr., 26 November 1902, H MS Am 2538.

34. ALS, AHGJ to WJ Jr., 13 January 1903, H MS Am 2538.

35. ALS, HJ to AHGJ, 27 November 1902, H bMS Am 1094 (1657).

36. ALS, AHGJ to WJ Jr., 30 October 1902, H MS Am 2538. The paraphrase is from chapter 1 of Stevenson's *Lay Morals and Other Papers*, which discusses workplace ethics. He claims workers have a moral obligation to carry out their duties conscientiously and fully. He thought that his era was too materialistic and that people were blind to everything but money. Scottish writer Robert Louis Stevenson (1850–94) had been friends with HJ, who thought his early death was a tragedy.

37. ALS, AHGJ to WJ Jr., 26 November 1902, H MS Am 2538.

38. ALS, HJ to AHGJ, 27 November 1902, H bMS Am 1094 (1657).

39. ALS, AHGJ to WJ Jr., 26 November 1902, H MS Am 2538.

40. Edith Newbold Jones Wharton (1862–1937) was a major American writer and HJ's close friend. She was also a landscape architect and interior designer. After her marriage began to unravel around 1911 she moved permanently to France.

41. Karal Ann Marling, *Debutante: Rites and Regalia of American Debdom* (Lawrence: University of Kansas Press, 2004), 39–58.

42. ALS, AHGJ to WJ Jr., 7 December 1902, H MS Am 2538.

43. ALS, AHGJ to WJ Jr., 28 December 1902, H MS Am 2538.

44. ALS, HJ to AHGJ, 27 November 1902, H bMS Am 1094 (1657).

45. ALS, HJ to MMJ, 15 March 1903, H bMS Eng 1070 (24).

46. ALS, AHGJ to WJ Jr., 7 March 1903, H MS Am 2538.

47. ALS, MMJ to AHGJ, 8 May [1902 or 1903], B BANC MSS C-H 159, box 3, folder "Porter, Margaret (James) 22 letters 1898–1916."

48. ALS, AHGJ to WJ Jr., 28 September 1902, H MS Am 2538.

49. ALS, AHGJ to WJ Jr., 14 December [1902], H MS Am 2538.

50. ALS, AHGJ to WJ Jr., 18 December 1902, H MS Am 2538.

51. ALS, AHGJ to WJ Jr., 21 December 1902, H MS Am 2538.

52. ALS, AHGJ to WJ Jr., 4 January 1903, H MS Am 2538.

53. ALS, AHGJ to WJ Jr., 13 January 1903, H MS Am 2538.

54. ALS, ARJ to WJ Jr., 16 February 1903, H MS Am 2538.

55. ALS, AHGJ to WJ Jr., 18 January 1903, H MS Am 2538.

56. ALS, AHGJ to WJ Jr., 16 February 1903, H MS Am 2538.

57. ALS, AHGJ to WJ Jr., 13 January 1903, H MS Am 2538.

58. ALS, AHGJ to WJ Jr., 22 February 1903, H MS Am 2538.

59. ALS, AHGJ to WJ Jr., 22 March 1903, H MS Am 2538.

60. ALS, AHGJ to WJ Jr., 29 March 1903, H MS Am 2538.

61. ALS, AHGJ to WJ Jr., 10 April 1903, H MS Am 2538; ALS, AHGJ to WJ Jr., 10 May 1903, H MS Am 2538.

62. ALS, AHGJ to WJ Jr., 10 February 1903, H MS Am 2538.

63. James, *Talks to Teachers*, 14.

64. ALS, AHGJ to WJ Jr., 28 February 1903, H MS Am 2538.

65. ALS, AHGJ to WJ Jr., 28 June 1903, H MS Am 2538.

66. ALS, AHGJ to WJ Jr., 4 January 1903, H MS Am 2538.

67. ALS, AHGJ to WJ Jr., 18 January 1903, H MS Am 2538.

68. ALS, AHGJ to WJ Jr., 22 March 1903, H MS Am 2538.

69. ALS, AHGJ to WJ Jr., 29 March [1903], H MS Am 2538.

70. ALS, AHGJ to WJ Jr., 22 March 1903, H MS Am 2538.

71. ALS, AHGJ to WJ Jr., 10 February 1903, H MS Am 2538.

72. ALS, AHGJ to WJ Jr., 22 February 1903, H MS Am 2538.

73. ALS, AHGJ to WJ Jr., 7 March 1903, H MS Am 2538.

74. WJ to AHGJ, 24 January [1903], *Correspondence*, 10:182–83.

75. WJ to AHGJ, 24 January [1903], *Correspondence*, 10:182.

76. WJ to WJ Jr., 27 February 1903, *Correspondence*, 10:206. The Munsterbergs were of Jewish descent, though no longer practicing the religion.

77. ALS, AHGJ to WJ Jr., 29 March [1903], H MS Am 2538.

78. ALS, AHGJ to WJ Jr., 19 February 1907, H MS Am 2538.

79. Wincenty Lutoslawski (1863–1954) corresponded with WJ between 1893 and 1910. His main interest was Platonic philosophy, but he was also intrigued by spiritualism. He was the forerunner of Polish quantitative linguistics and the creator of stylometry.

80. ALS, WJ to MMJ, 22 October [1907], H bMS Am 1092.9 (3086).

81. Eliot, *A History of Cambridge*, 132, 136; Thomas Wentworth Higginson, *Old Cambridge* (New York: Macmillan, 1899), 18, 24.

82. ALS, HJ II to MMJ, 18 May 1930, B BANC MSS 72/35, box 1, folder "James, Henry 1879–1947."

83. W. E. B. Du Bois (1868–1963), sociologist, writer, editor, and historian, was an important early American civil rights leader who became a Pan-Africanist later in his life. In 1895 he became the first African American to earn a Harvard Ph.D.

84. William James, "The Social Value of the College-Bred: An Address Made at a Meeting of the Association of American Alumnae at Radcliffe College, November 7, 1907," in *William James: Writings* 1902–1910 (New York: Library of America, 1987), 1242–49.

85. ALS, AHGJ to WJ Jr., 30 November [c. 1903], H MS Am 2538.

86. ALS, AHGJ to WJ Jr., 22 March 1903, H MS Am 2538.

87. ALS, AHGJ to WJ Jr., 24 April 1903, H MS Am 2538.

88. ALS, AHGJ to WJ Jr., 28 June 1903, H MS Am 2538.

89. ALS, HJ to AHGJ, 16 July [1903], H bMS Am 1094 (1658).

90. ALS, AHGJ to WJ Jr., 7 June 1903, H MS Am 2538.

91. WJ to Katharine Outram Rodgers, 28 September 1902, *Correspondence*, 10:138; WJ to Joseph Thatcher Clarke, 30 September 1902, *Correspondence*, 10:140. Francis Tweedy began calling himself Alexander Robertson at about age seven, but the letters cited here have William saying that the name has now been "officially" changed.

92. ALS, AHGJ to WJ Jr., 22 March 1903, H MS Am 2538.

93. ALS, AHGJ to WJ Jr., 29 March [1903], H MS Am 2538.

94. ALS, AHGJ to WJ Jr., 10 April 1903, H MS Am 2538.

95. ALS, AHGJ to WJ Jr., 12 April 1903, H MS Am 2538.

96. ALS, AHGJ to WJ Jr., 5 June [1903], H MS Am 2538.

97. ALS, AHGJ to WJ Jr., 31 May 1903, H MS Am 2538.

98. Photocopy of typescript, HJ to WJ Jr., 8 July 1903, M, Edel Papers, container 72.

99. ALS, AHGJ to WJ Jr., 31 May 1903, H MS Am 2538.

100. ALS, Charles W. Eliot to AHGJ, 26 June 1902, H bMS Am 1092.9 (4301).

101. HJ II, card synopsis of HJ II to WJ, 27 June 1903, courtesy Michael James.

102. ALS, AHGJ to WJ Jr., 5 June [1903], H MS Am 2538.

103. ALS, postscript, HJ to AHGJ, 16 July [1903], H bMS Am 1094 (1658).

104. WJ to WJ Jr., 4 July 1903, *Correspondence*, 10:278.

105. ALS, AHGJ to WJ Jr., 31 May 1903, H MS Am 2538.

106. HJ to WJ and AHGJ, [31 August 1904], *Correspondence*, 3:278.

107. WJ to Ellen Hunter, 1 September [1904], *Correspondence*, 10:461.

108. Henry James, *The American Scene* (New York: Penguin, 1994), 16, 18, 20.

109. ALS, HJ to AHGJ, [27 January 1905], H bMS Am 1094 (1664).

110. ALS, HJ to AHGJ, 19 February 1905, H bMS Am 1094 (1666); ALS, HJ to AHGJ, [13 February 1905], H bMS Am 1094 (1665).

111. ALS, HJ to AHGJ, 19 March 1905, H bMS Am 1094 (1668).

112. HJ to AHGJ, 24 March 1905, Gunter, *Dear Munificent Friends*, 53; ALS, HJ to AHGJ, 30 March 1905, H bMS Am 1094 (1670); ALS, HJ to AHGJ, 13 April [1905], H bMS Am 1094 (1672).

113. 16 June 1905, WJ, "Diary, 1905," H MS Am 1092.9 (4553). Bruce Porter (1865–1953) was an architect and art lover. In 1917 he married HJ's niece Peggy.

114. HJ II's card synopsis of HJ II to HJ, 2 July 1905, courtesy of Michael James.

115. HJ to AHGJ, [12 July 1905], in James, *Letters*, 4:365–66.

116. WJ to HJ, 1 February 1906, *Correspondence*, 3:307.

117. 19 August 1905, WJ, "Diary, 1905," H MS Am 1092.9 (4553).

118. Encyclopaedia Britannica Online, s.v. "morphine," http://search.eb.com/eb/article-9053799.

119. 23 August 1905, WJ, "Diary, 1905," H MS Am 1092.9 (4553); WJ to HJ, 20 August 1905, *Correspondence*, 3:299–300.

120. N. Nicolodi, "Differential Sensitivity to Morphine Challenge in Migraine Sufferers and Headache-Exempt Subjects," *Cephalalgia* 16, no. 5 (1996): 297–307.

121. HJ to AHGJ, 8 September 1905, Gunter, *Dear Munificent Friends*, 57.

13. THE LULL BEFORE THE STORM

1. ALS, HJ to AHGJ, 4 February 1906, H bMS Am 1094 (1683).

2. WJ to AHGJ, 14 January [19]06, *Correspondence*, 11:144.

3. WJ to HJ, 1 February 1906, *Correspondence*, 3:307.

4. WJ to AHGJ, 3 January 1906, *Correspondence*, 11:137.

5. 29 July 1905, WJ, "Diary, 1905," H MS Am 1092.9 (4553).

6. ALS, HJ to AHGJ, 4 February 1906, H bMS Am 1094 (1683).

7. ALS, RJ to AHGJ, 22 January [1906], H bMS Am 1095 (44).

8. ALS, AHGJ to WJ Jr., 19 February 1907, H MS Am 2538.

9. WJ to AHGJ, 20 January 1906, *Correspondence*, 11:149.

10. February, March 1906, WJ, "Diary, 1906," H MS Am 1092.9 (4555).

11. HJ to AHGJ, 14 March 1906, Gunter, *Dear Munificent Friends*, 62.

12. 14 February 1906, WJ, "Diary, 1906," H MS Am 1092.9 (4555).

13. WJ to HJ, 1 February 1906, *Correspondence*, 3:307.

14. ALS, AHGJ to HJ II, 22 February 1906, H MS Am 2538.

15. Allen, *William James*, 452.

16. ALS, AHGJ to Elizabeth Glendower Evans, 25 March 1906, S, Evans Papers, Series II.

17. 17 February 1906, WJ, "Diary, 1906," H MS Am 1092.9 (4555); 21 February 1906, WJ, "Diary, 1906," H MS Am 1092.9 (4555).

18. William James, "The Moral Equivalent of War," in *Essays in Religion and Morality* (Cambridge MA: Harvard University Press, 1982), 171–72.

19. ALS, AHGJ to HJ II, 22 February 1906, H MS Am 2538.

20. 16 April 1906, WJ, "Diary, 1906," H MS Am 1092.9 (4555); ALS, AHGJ to HJ II, 22 February 1906, H MS Am 2538.

21. ALS, AHGJ to Elizabeth Glendower Evans, 14 March 1906, S, Evans Papers, Series II.

22. Allen, *William James*, 452.

23. 28 March 1906, WJ, "Diary, 1906," H MS Am 1092.9 (4555).

24. http://www.apa.si.edu/ongoldmountain/gallery2/gallery2.html.

25. Allen, *William James*, 455.

26. Some of this information comes from a letter, AHGJ to WJ Jr., 6 October 1906, H MS Am 2538.

27. ALS, AHGJ to Elizabeth Glendower Evans, 14 March 1906, S, Evans Papers, Series II; autographed typescript, AHGJ to Elizabeth Glendower Evans, 25 March 1906, S, Evans Papers, Series II.

28. Biographical sketch of Alfred Hodder, Princeton Library catalog, Princeton University.

29. TLS, AHGJ to Family, 18 April 1906, H MS Am 2538; AHGJ to WJ Jr., 26 April 1906, H MS Am 2538. Much of the account that follows comes from her letters.

30. William James, *Memories and Studies* (New York: Longmans, Green, 1912), 213.

31. WJ to HJ, 22 April [19]06, *Correspondence*, 3:312.

32. 18 April 1906, WJ, "Diary, 1906," H MS Am 1092.9 (4555).

33. Transcript and photocopy of ALS, HJ to WJ Jr., 11 May 1906, M, Edel Papers, container 72.

34. ALS, William Freeman Snow to HJ II, 1920, H bMS Am 1092.10 (162).

35. Another account says a crowd hanged a man who tried to rob a woman's body of her rings. See ALS, William Freeman Snow to HJ II, 1920, H bMS Am 1092.10 (162).

36. ALS, AHGJ to WJ Jr., 26 April 1906, H MS Am 2538.

37. Allen, *William James*, 455.

38. 27 April 1906, WJ, "Diary, 1906," H MS Am 1092.9 (4555).

39. ALS, AHGJ to WJ Jr., 26 April 1906, H MS Am 2538.

40. WJ to AHGJ, 7 June 1906, *Correspondence*, 11:232.

41. WJ to EPG, [20 June 1900], *Correspondence*, 9:234.

42. I thank Hunter Bear Gray, John Salter's son, for sharing information about

his father and the circumstances surrounding the adoption. Mr. Gray maintains a Web site at www.hunterbear.org with information about his father as well as information on his own extensive achievements as educator, social activist, and labor and civil rights organizer.

43. Francis Parkman (1823–93), American historian, wrote the history of the fall of Quebec, *Montcalm and Wolfe*, a book HJ praised. HJ wrote reviews of two of Parkman's other books, *The Jesuits in North America in the Seventeenth Century* and *The Old Regime in Canada*.

44. Email conversation with Hunter Bear Gray, 5 May 1904.

45. ALS, AHGJ to EPG, 8 July [1900], H MS Am 2538.

46. ALS, AHGJ to WJ Jr., 25 March 1901, H MS Am 2538.

47. WJ to AHGJ, 23 June [1902], *Correspondence*, 10:66.

48. ALS, AHGJ to WJ Jr., 10 June 1906, H MS Am 2538.

49. ALS, AHGJ to WJ Jr., 10 June 1906, H MS Am 2538.

50. Photocopy of typescript, HJ to WJ Jr., 18 June 1906, M, Edel Papers, container 72.

51. WJ to WJ Jr., 22 June 1906, *Correspondence*, 11:239–40.

52. ALS, AHGJ to WJ Jr., 24 June [1906], H MS Am 2538.

53. ALS, AHGJ to WJ Jr., 30 August 1906, H MS Am 2538.

54. ALS, AHGJ to WJ Jr., 9 July 1906, H MS Am 2538.

55. ALS, AHGJ to WJ Jr., 15 November 1906, H MS Am 2538.

56. ALS, AHGJ to WJ Jr., 31 July 1907, H MS Am 2538.

57. Hunter Bear Gray Web site, www.hunterbear.org.

58. ALS, AHGJ to WJ Jr., 17 January 1906, H MS Am 2538; ALS, AHGJ to WJ Jr., 29 November 1906, H MS Am 2538.

59. ALS, AHGJ to WJ Jr., 9 July 1906, H MS Am 2538. During the summers of 1905 and 1906 Aleck attended Camp Portanimicut on Cape Cod.

60. ALS, AHGJ to WJ Jr., 6 October 1906, H MS Am 2538.

61. ALS, AHGJ to WJ Jr., 3 February 1907, H MS Am 2538.

62. ALS, AHGJ to WJ Jr., 29 November 1906, H MS Am 2538.

63. ALS, AHGJ to WJ Jr., 5 March 1907, H MS Am 2538.

64. WJ to WJ Jr., 5 October 1907, *Correspondence*, 11:363.

65. ALS, AHGJ to WJ Jr., 16 December 1906, H MS Am 2538.

66. ALS, AHGJ to WJ Jr., 29 January 1907, H MS Am 2538.

67. Transcript and photocopy of ALS, HJ to WJ Jr., 29 January 1907, M, Edel Papers, container 72.

68. Transcript and photocopy of ALS, HJ to WJ Jr., 14 July 1906, M, Edel Papers, container 72.

69. Transcript and photocopy of ALS, HJ to WJ Jr., 12 November 1906, M, Edel Papers, container 72.

70. ALS, AHGJ to WJ Jr., 15 April 1907, H MS Am 2538.

71. ALS, AHGJ to WJ Jr., 21 April 1907, H MS Am 2538.

72. Transcript and photocopy of ALS, WJ Jr. to family, 26 February 1907, M, Edel Papers, container 72.

73. ALS, AHGJ to WJ Jr., 24 June 1907, H MS Am 2538.

74. 8 July 1907, WJ, "Diary, 1907," H MS Am 1092.9 (4556); ALS, AHGJ to WJ Jr., 30 June 1907, 8 July 1907, H MS Am 2538. This camp was at Long Lake Lodge, North Bridgton, Maine.

75. Transcript and photocopy of ALS, HJ to WJ Jr., 28 August 1906, M, Edel Papers, container 72.

76. Kitty M. Gage, "Bryn Mawr College for Women," *Education*, 7 September 1886, 25–33, http://clipt.sdsu.edu/tango/edtec572/womenedquest/Opening_Bryn_Mawr.html.

77. ALS, AHGJ to WJ Jr., 16 August 1906, H MS Am 2538.

78. ALS, AHGJ to WJ Jr., 6 October 1906, H MS Am 2538.

79. ALS, WJ to MMJ, 9 October 1906, H bMS Am 1092.9 (3060).

80. ALS, HJ to MMJ, 8 November 1906, H bMS Eng 1070 (29).

81. Quoted in Lewis, *The Jameses*, 615.

82. ALS, AHGJ to WJ Jr., 29 November 1906, H MS Am 2538.

83. ALS, AHGJ to WJ Jr., 4 January 1907, H MS Am 2538.

84. Lewis, *The Jameses*, 615.

85. ALS, AHGJ to WJ Jr., 4 January 1907, H MS Am 2538.

86. Lewis, *The Jameses*, 615; 27 March 1907, 3 April 1907, WJ, "Diary, 1907," H MS Am 1092.9 (4556). Lewis states that Peggy returned to Bryn Mawr in March, but diary entries have Peggy and Mary coming home on 27 March and returning on 3 April.

87. ALS, HJ II to MMJ, 4 May 1907, B BANC MSS 72/35, box 1, folder "James, Henry, 1879–1947 14 letters 1900–1919."

88. ALS, AHGJ to WJ Jr., 14 July 1907, H MS Am 2538.

89. ALS, AHGJ to WJ, 2 September 1907, H bMS Am 1092.9 (329).

90. ALS, AHGJ to WJ Jr., 4 August 1907, H MS Am 2538.

91. ALS, MMJ to AHGJ, 9 November 1907, B BANC MSS 72/35, box 3, folder "Porter, Margaret (James) 22 letters 1898–1908."

92. ALS, MMJ to AHGJ, 6 October [1907], B BANC MSS 72/35, box 3, folder 3.

93. Appendix B, in Lewis, *The Jameses*, 615–19.

94. Marianne Moore (1887–1972) served as editor of the literary journal the *Dial* from 1925 to 1929. Her 1951 *Collected Poems* won the Pulitzer Prize, the National Book Award, and the Bollingen Prize.

95. Lewis, *The Jameses*, 615–19.

96. 22 January 1907, WJ, "Diary, 1907," H MS Am 1092.9 (4556).

97. Samuel Eliot Morison, ed., *The Development of Harvard University since the Inauguration of President Eliot,* 1869–1929 (Cambridge MA: Harvard University Press, 1930), xxxiii.

98. Allen, *William James,* 456.

99. Allen, *William James,* 460.

100. ALS, AHGJ to WJ Jr., 3 March 1907, H MS Am 2538.

101. ALS, AHGJ to WJ Jr., 28 April 1907, H MS Am 2538.

102. ALS, AHGJ to WJ Jr., 30 June 1907, H MS Am 2538.

103. ALS, AHGJ to WJ Jr., 30 June 1907, H MS Am 2538.

104. Theodate Pope (1868–1946), American architect, designed Avon Farms at Farmington, a prep school for boys. She later married John Riddle, who served as ambassador to Russia and Argentina.

105. Richard Hodgson (1855–1905) died while playing handball in Boston in December 1905. HJ II and George Dorr were named executors of his estate, which proved to be in disarray. Barbara C. Mooney, "Author to Architect: Letters from Henry James to Theodate Pope," manuscript, M, Edel Papers, container 14, folder "[Pope, Theodate] Riddle," 7.

106. Mooney, "Author to Architect," 13–14.

107. ALS, AHGJ to WJ Jr., 4 August 1907, H MS Am 2538.

108. ALS, AHGJ to WJ, [21 January 1908], H bMS Am 1092.9 (331).

109. ALS, AHGJ to WJ, [21 January 1908], H bMS Am 1092.9 (331).

110. HJ to AHGJ, 1 February 1908, Gunter, *Dear Munificent Friends,* 69.

111. Frederick Canning Scott Schiller (1864–1937) admired WJ's work. They debated ideas on pragmatism, realism, and other ideas for nearly two decades.

112. ALS, RJ to WJ, [c. 1908], H MS Am 1095.2 (27).

113. William James, *Pragmatism* (Cambridge MA: Harvard University Press, 1975), 71.

114. ALS, AHGJ to WJ Jr., 30 June 1907, H MS Am 2538.

14. SUMMER'S END

1. Allen, *William James,* 461.

2. 7–27 January 1908, WJ, "Diary, 1908," H MS Am 1092.9 (4557).

3. 21 March 1908, WJ, "Diary, 1908," H MS Am 1092.9 (4557).

4. 30 April–3 May 1908, WJ, "Diary, 1908," H MS Am 1092.9 (4557).

5. German philosopher Georg Wilhelm Friedrich Hegel (1770–1831) developed the dialectical method, a radically new form of logic that mediated between oppositions without reducing them.

6. Gustav Theodore Fechner (1801–87) was a German experimental psychologist and the founder of psychophysics. He studied how the mind relates to the body.

7. Henri Bergson (1859–1941) was an important philosopher in the first half of the twentieth century. His three most important works were *Time and Free Will*, *Matter and Memory*, and *Creative Evolution*. His work on time and memory excited WJ.

8. Philosopher Bertrand Arthur William Russell, third Earl Russell (1872–1970), was a mathematician, logician, and social reform advocate. He is recognized as a founder of analytical philosophy. He was opposed to WJ's pragmatism and to his definitions of truth. WJ thought Russell misunderstood him. ALS, AHGJ to EPG, 26 May 1908, H MS Am 2538.

9. 8 May–6 June 1908, WJ, "Diary, 1908," H MS Am 1092.9 (4557).

10. ALS, AHGJ to WJ Jr., 12 June 1908, H MS Am 2538.

11. ALS, AHGJ to WJ Jr., 12 June 1908, H MS Am 2538.

12. ALS, AHGJ to WJ Jr., 17 June 1908, H MS Am 2538.

13. ALS, AHGJ to WJ Jr., 12 June 1908, H MS Am 2538. Ottoline Violet Anne Bentinck Morrell (1873–1938) was a renowned socialite who held a famous bohemian intellectual salon in Bloomsbury that HJ occasionally visited.

14. WJ to H. G. Wells, 11 September 1906, *Correspondence*, 11:267.

15. ALS, AHGJ to WJ Jr., 4 July 1908, H MS Am 2538; ALS, AHGJ to WJ Jr., 12 June 1908, H MS Am 2538.

16. ALS, AHGJ to WJ Jr., 4 July 1908, H MS Am 2538.

17. Thorstein Veblen, *The Theory of the Leisure Class* (1899; reprint, New York: August M. Kelley, 1975), 154–55.

18. Simon, *Genuine Reality*, 359–60.

19. ALS, AHGJ to WJ Jr., 4 July 1908, H MS Am 2538.

20. ALS, AHGJ to WJ, 1 July 1908, H bMS Am 1092.9 (333).

21. ALS, MMJ to AHGJ, 19 July 1908, H bMS Am 1092.9 (4316).

22. 31 July 1908, WJ, "Diary, 1908," H MS Am 1092.9 (4557).

23. ALS, HJ II to MMJ, 23 August 1908, B BANC MSS 72/35, box 1, folder "James, Henry, 1879–1947 14 letters 1900–1919."

24. ALS, AHGJ to WJ, 2 August 1908, H bMS Am 1092.9 (335).

25. ALS, AHGJ to WJ, 9 August 1908, H bMS Am 1092.9 (337).

26. ALS, AHGJ to WJ, 12 August 1908, H bMS Am 1092.9 (338).

27. 20–21 August 1908, WJ, "Diary, 1908," H MS Am 1092.9 (4557).

28. 22–26 August 1908, WJ, "Diary, 1908," H MS Am 1092.9 (4557).

29. 28–30 August 1908, WJ, "Diary, 1908," H MS Am 1092.9 (4557).

30. 2–5 September 1908, WJ, "Diary, 1908," H MS Am 1092.9 (4557).

31. 6 October 1908, WJ, "Diary, 1908," H MS Am 1092.9 (4557); ALS postcard, WJ to HJ, 7 October 1908, HM 66117, Huntington Library, San Marino, California. I am grateful to the Huntington Library for permission to use this material.

32. 16 October 1908, WJ, "Diary, 1908," H MS Am 1092.9 (4557).

33. Alan D. Weathers, "The Sensibility of Alexander James," master's thesis, 20 June 1986, 12. Courtesy of Michael James.

34. 30 May 1908, WJ, "Diary, 1908," H MS Am 1092.9 (4557).

35. James, *Talks to Teachers*, 87.

36. 18 August 1908, WJ, "Diary, 1908," H MS Am 1092.9 (4557).

37. ALS, AHGJ to HJ, 6 October 1908, HM 66107.

38. ALS, HJ to ARJ, 13 October 1908, H MS Am 2538.

39. ALS, HJ to MMJ, 30 December 1908, H bMS Eng 1070 (31).

40. Margaret Frances (Mrs. George) Prothero (1854–1934) was HJ's Rye neighbor part of the year. She helped HJ with household matters, particularly when he was ill. Sir George Walter Prothero (1848–1922) was a Cambridge professor who edited the *Quarterly Review* from 1899 to 1922. HJ to Margaret Frances Prothero, 12 January 1909, Gunter, *Dear Munificent Friends*, 205.

41. Typescript, "Memoirs," Elizabeth Glendower Evans, c. 1936, p. 9, S, Evans Papers, Series I, accession no. 54-2, 55–75.

42. ALS, AHGJ to HJ, 18 January 1909, H MS Am 2538. Roger Merriman, an historian, was the son of family friends Rev. Daniel and Helen Merriman.

43. WJ to HJ, 24 January [19]09, *Correspondence*, 3:375.

44. 11–13 March 1909, WJ, "Diary, 1909," H MS Am 1092.9 (4558).

45. ALS, HJ to ARJ, n.d. [1909], H MS Am 2538.

46. ALS, AHGJ to HJ, 18 January 1909, H MS Am 2538.

47. *The James Family*, 626.

48. WJ to HJ, 23 June [19]09, *Correspondence*, 3:390.

49. AHGJ to WJ, [13 June 1909], *Correspondence*, 12:265.

50. ALS, WJ to AHGJ, 14 June 1909, H bMS Am 1092.9 (2447).

51. WJ to HJ, 6 October [19]09, *Correspondence*, 3:398, 400n.

52. WJ to HJ, 2 August [19]09, *Correspondence*, 3:395.

53. ALS, HJ to AHGJ, 9 November 1909, H bMS Am 1094 (1693).

54. HJ to WJ, 17 August 1909, *Correspondence*, 3:398.

55. Lewis, *The Jameses*, 626.

56. Weathers, "The Sensibility of Alexander James," 15.

57. 15 November 1909, WJ, "Diary, 1909," H MS Am 1092.9 (4558).

58. 12–13 February 1909, WJ, "Diary, 1909," H MS Am 1092.9 (4558).

59. 13 February 1909, WJ, "Diary, 1909," H MS Am 1092.9 (4558).

60. 24 February 1909, WJ, "Diary, 1909," H MS Am 1092.9 (4558).

61. 28 April 1909, WJ, "Diary, 1909," H MS Am 1092.9 (4558).

62. 30 March 1909, WJ, "Diary, 1909," H MS Am 1092.9 (4558); 5 March 1909, WJ, "Diary, 1909," H MS Am 1092.9 (4558).

63. 25 June–6 July 1909, WJ, "Diary, 1909," H MS Am 1092.9 (4558).

64. 4 July 1909, WJ, "Diary, 1909," H MS Am 1092.9 (4558).

65. WJ to AHGJ, 11 June [19]09, *Correspondence*, 12:263.

66. WJ to HJ, 27 February 1910, *Correspondence*, 3:412.

67. ALS, WJ to AHGJ, 20 June 1909, H bMS Am 1092.9 (2451); AHGJ to WJ, [13 June 1909], *Correspondence*, 12:264.

68. WJ to AHGJ, 17 June [19]09, *Correspondence*, 12:268.

69. ALS, WJ to AHGJ, 14 June 1909, H bMS Am 1092.9 (2447).

70. Allen, *William James*, 469–70.

71. 9 November 1909, WJ, "Diary, 1909," H bMS Am 1092.9 (4558).

72. 12 December 1909, WJ, "Diary, 1909," H bMS Am 1092.9 (4558). See Maher, *Biography of Broken Fortunes*, 191, for a discussion of this episode.

73. 28 December 1909, WJ, "Diary, 1909," H bMS Am 1092.9 (4558).

74. 31 January 1910, WJ, "Diary, 1910," H bMS Am 1092.9 (4559).

75. WJ to HJ, 4 February 1910, *Correspondence*, 3:408.

76. ALS, AHGJ to HJ, 6 February 1910, H bMS Am 1092.11 (47).

77. 23 January 1910, WJ, "Diary, 1910," H bMS Am 1092.9 (4559).

78. See Gunter, *Dear Munificent Friends*, 189–93, for further information on Mrs. Prothero.

79. WJ to HJ, 18 February 1910, *Correspondence*, 3:411.

80. ALS, AHGJ to HJ, 16 February 1910, H bMS Am 1092.11 (49); ALS, WJ to MMJ, 13 February 1910, H bMS Am 1092.9 (3101).

81. Josiah Royce, "The Search for Truth," n.d., H bMS Am 1092.9 (4592).

82. James II, *The Letters*, 2:287.

83. Herman H. Spitz, "Contemporary Challenges to William James's White Crow," *Skeptical Inquirer* 28, no. 1 (2004): 53.

84. For further information on Mrs. Piper and her methods see Martin Gardner, "How Mrs. Piper Bamboozled William James," in *Are Universes Thicker than Blackberries?* (New York: W. W. Norton, 2003), 252–61.

85. Theodora Bosanquet (1880–1961) worked for HJ for years. She later wrote a book about him, *Henry James at Work* (1924), based on the diary entries she made during her time with him. She also published other texts. She was a member of the Society for Psychical Research, whose journal she edited.

86. Autographed typescript, Theodora Bosanquet to HJ II, 23 January 1910, H bMS Am 1094 (1373); 4 February 1910, WJ, "Diary, 1910," H bMS Am 1092.9 (4559).

87. 9 February 1910, WJ, "Diary, 1910," H bMS Am 1092.9 (4559).

88. WJ to HJ, 4 February 1910, *Correspondence*, 3:407.

89. ALS, AHGJ to HJ, 6 February 1910, H bMS Am 1092.11 (47).

90. ALS, WJ to AHGJ, 1 September [19]09, H bMS Am 1092.9 (2457).

91. Novick, *Henry James: The Mature Master*, 463. Novick's account of

Gammon's burning the papers offers another interpretation of earlier views that James burned correspondence and papers in the throes of his depression. Edel claimed that James burned papers to protect his privacy and possible future inquiries into his life. The truth may lie somewhere in between, as there is little doubt that HJ was depressed at the time.

92. ALS, HJ to AHGJ, 9 November 1909, H bMS Am 1094 (1693).

93. ALS, HJ to AHGJ, 9 December 1909, H bMS Am 1094 (1691).

94. ALS, HJ to AHGJ, 25 May 1909, H bMS Am 1094 (1692).

95. ALS, HJ to AHGJ, 15 February 1910, H bMS Am 1094 (1695).

96. ALS, WJ to MMJ, 13 February 1910, H bMS Am 1092.9 (3101).

97. WJ to HJ, 4 February 1910, *Correspondence*, 3:408.

98. ALS, [February 1910], WJ to MMJ, H bMS Am 1092.9 (3102).

99. WJ to HJ, 27 February 1910, *Correspondence*, 3:413n.

100. HJ to AHGJ & WJ, 4 March 1910, *Correspondence*, 3:413.

101. HJ to AHGJ and WJ, 4 March 1910, *Correspondence*, 3:414.

102. ALS, AHGJ to HJ, 13 March 1910, H bMS Am 1092.11 (50).

103. HJ to WJ, 15 March [1910], *Correspondence*, 3:417.

104. Henry James, "The Jolly Corner," in *The Altar of the Dead, The Beast in the Jungle, The Birthplace, and Other Tales* (London: Macmillan, 1922), 389.

15. LAST THINGS

1. WJ to HJ, 11 March 1910, *Correspondence*, 3:415.

2. ALS, AHGJ to HJ II, 17 March 1910, H MS Am 2538.

3. HJ to AHGJ & WJ, 15 March [1910], *Correspondence*, 3:418.

4. 22 March 1910, WJ, "Diary, 1910," H bMS Am 1092.9 (4559).

5. HJ to AHGJ & WJ, 15 March [1910], *Correspondence*, 3:417.

6. HJ to AHGJ & WJ, 15 March [1910], *Correspondence*, 3:418.

7. ALS, WJ to MMJ, 13 April [1910], H bMS Am 1092.9 (3105).

8. ALS, AHGJ to EPG, 19 April 1910, H bMS Am 1092.11 (14).

9. Emanuel Swedenborg, *Angelic Wisdom Concerning the Divine Love and the Divine Wisdom* (New York: Swedenborg Foundation, 1988).

10. ALS, 19 April 1910, WJ to MMJ [dictated to AHGJ], H bMS Am 1092.9 (3106).

11. ALS, AHGJ to EPG, 19 April 1910, H bMS Am 1092.11 (14).

12. ALS, AHGJ to WJ Jr., 22 April 1910, H MS Am 2538.

13. ALS, AHGJ to WJ Jr., 22 April 1910, H MS Am 2538.

14. ALS, AHGJ to WJ Jr., 22 April 1910, H MS Am 2538.

15. WJ to AHGJ, 7 May [1910], *Correspondence*, 12:498.

16. WJ to AHGJ, [6 May 1910], *Correspondence*, 12:496.

17. WJ to AHGJ, 9 May 1910, *Correspondence*, 12:502.

18. WJ to AHGJ, 12 May 1910, *Correspondence*, 12:513.

19. Émile Boutroux (1845–1921) was a professor at the Sorbonne and a spiritual philosopher who opposed scientific materialism.

20. ALS, AHGJ to HJ II, 5 June 1910, H MS Am 2538.

21. Mooney, "Author to Architect," 18.

22. HJ to WJ, 31 May 1910, *Correspondence*, 3:423. James spells Swinerton "Swynnerton" in a letter to AHGJ of 27 August 1911, H bMS Am 1094 (1720).

23. WJ to HJ, 28 May 1910, *Correspondence*, 3:422; WJ to AHGJ, 20 May [19]10, *Correspondence*, 12:519.

24. ALS, WJ to AHGJ, 24 May 1910, H bMS Am 1092.9 (2479).

25. WJ to AHGJ, 16 May [1910], *Correspondence*, 12:515.

26. Leon Edel, *Henry James: The Master* (Philadelphia: J. B. Lippincott, 1972), 443.

27. ALS, AHGJ to HJ II, 5 June 1910, H MS Am 2538.

28. AHGJ to HJ II, 10 June 1910, H MS Am 2538.

29. ALS, AHGJ to WJ Jr., 14 July 1910, H MS Am 2538.

30. WJ to HJ, 30 May 1910, *Correspondence*, 3:422–23.

31. 29 May 1910, WJ, "Diary, 1910," H bMS Am 1092.9 (4559).

32. WJ to AHGJ, 20 May [19]10, *Correspondence*, 12:519.

33. ALS, AHGJ to HJ II, 10 June 1910, H MS Am 2538.

34. Edel, *Henry James: The Master*, 442.

35. ALS, WJ to AHGJ, 21 May 1910, H bMS Am 1092.9 (2476).

36. WJ to AHGJ, 20 May 1910, *Correspondence*, 12:519; ALS, AHGJ to HJ II, 10 June 1910, H MS Am 2538.

37. WJ to Theodora Sedgwick, 20 June 1910, *Correspondence*, 12:559.

38. ALS, MMJ to AHGJ, c. 31 May 1910, B BANC MSS 72/35, box 3, folder 2 "Porter, Margaret (James) 27 letters 1910."

39. ALS, AHGJ to EPG, 14 June 1910, H bMS Am 1092.11 (15).

40. ALS, AHGJ to HJ II, 10 June 1910, H MS Am 2538.

41. ALS, AHGJ to WJ Jr., 14 June 1910, H MS Am 2538.

42. ALS, AHGJ to EPG, 14 June 1910, H bMS Am 1092.11 (15).

43. HJ to Edmund Gosse, 13 June 1910, James, *Letters*, 4:556.

44. Edel, *Henry James: The Master*, 444.

45. WJ to HJ II, 3 July [19]10, *Correspondence*, 12:568; Allen, *William James*, 487.

46. WJ to EPG, 2 July 1910, *Correspondence*, 12:567.

47. WJ to EPG, 1 July [19]10, *Correspondence*, 12:566.

48. ALS, AHGJ to Theodore Flournoy, 24 July 1910, H bMS Am 1505 (83).

49. Allen, *William James*, 487.

50. ALS, AHGJ to EPG, 15 July 1910, H bMS Am 1092.11 (16).

51. ALS, AHGJ to Theodore Flournoy, 24 July 1910, H bMS Am 1505 (83).

52. Allen, *William James*, 487.

53. ALS, MMJ to AHGJ, 9 July 1910, B BANC MSS 72/35, box 3, folder 2 "Porter, Margaret (James)."

54. Maher, *Biography of Broken Fortunes*, 193.

55. Edel, *Henry James: The Master*, 444.

56. ALS, AHGJ to HJ II, 14 July 1910, H MS Am 2538.

57. Edel, *Henry James: The Master*, 444.

58. ALS, AHGJ to HJ II, 14 July 1910, H MS Am 2538.

59. ALS, AHGJ to WJ Jr., 14 July 1910, H MS Am 2538.

60. ALS, AHGJ to Theodore Flournoy, 24 July 1910, H bMS Am 1505 (83).

61. ALS, AHGJ to WJ Jr., 14 July 1910, H MS Am 2538.

62. WJ to Theodore Flournoy, 9 July 1910, James II, *The Letters*, 2:349.

63. ALS, AHGJ to EPG, 15 July 1910, H bMS Am 1092.11 (16).

64. Mooney, "Author to Architect," 12.

65. HJ to AHGJ, 5 March 1913, Gunter, *Dear Munificent Friends*, 98.

66. ALS, AHGJ to EPG, 15 July 1910, H bMS Am 1092.11 (16). William Dean Howells (1837–1920) was a major figure in the literary world during his lifetime. He and HJ had been friends since 1866. His many books include *A Modern Instance* (1882), *The Rise of Silas Lapham* (1885), *A Hazard of New Fortune* (1890), and *A Traveler from Altruria* (1894).

67. ALS, AHGJ to Theodore Flournoy, 24 July 1910, H bMS Am 1505 (83).

68. ALS, HJ to MMJ, 26 July 1910, H bMS Eng 1070 (32).

69. Allen, *William James*, 488.

70. ALS, HJ to MMJ, 26 July 1910, H bMS Eng 1070 (32).

71. ALS, HJ to HJ II, 31 July 1910, H bMS Am 1094 (1376).

72. ALS, AHGJ to HJ II, 31 July 1910, H MS Am 2538.

73. ALS, AHGJ to Children, 31 July 1910, H MS Am 2538.

74. ALS, AHGJ to HJ II, 5 August 1910, H MS Am 2538. Howard Overing Sturgis (1855–1920) was a wealthy British socialite and writer. HJ critiqued *Belchamber*, his novel in progress, severely, but the two remained close friends.

75. Margaret Oliphant Wilson (Mrs. Frank) Oliphant (1828–97) was a prolific Scottish writer. HJ called her work loose and vivid.

76. ALS, AHGJ to EPG, 7 August 1910, H bMS Am 1092.11 (17).

77. 10 August 1910, WJ, "Diary, 1910," H bMS Am 1092.9 (4559).

78. ALS, AHGJ to Theodate Pope, 11 August 1910, Archives, Hill-Stead Museum, Farmington, Connecticut. I am grateful to the Hill-Stead for permission to use this material.

79. ALS, AHGJ to Theodate Pope, 7 August 1910, Archives, Hill-Stead Museum.

80. *The Complete Notebooks of Henry James*, 318.

81. Allen, *William James*, 490.

82. ALS, AHGJ to HJ II, 5 August 1910, H MS Am 2538; *The Complete Notebooks of Henry James*, 319.

83. ALS, AHGJ to Theodore Flournoy, 6 November 1910, H bMS Am 1505 (84).

84. Allen, *William James*, 490.

85. ALS, WJ Jr. to Leon Edel, 23 September 1933, M, Edel Papers, container 27, folder "James, William 3 [Billy] 1932–1953."

86. HJ to Grace Norton, 26 August 1910, James, *Letters*, 4:560.

87. Transcript of ALS, HJ to Mrs. Robertson James, 6 September 1910, M, Edel Papers, container 42, folder "Mrs. Robertson James."

88. Allen, *William James*, 491.

89. ALS, AHGJ to Frances Rollins Morse, 26 August 1910, H bMS Am 1092.11 (56).

90. Bjork, *William James*, 261.

91. Simon, *Genuine Reality*, 387.

92. Lewis, *The Jameses*, 583.

93. Sheldon M. Novick's *Honorable Justice: The Life of Oliver Wendell Holmes* (Boston: Little, Brown, 1989), 301, lists HJ and Holmes as pallbearers.

94. Allen, *William James*, 492.

95. ALS, AHGJ to Theodore Flournoy, 6 November 1910, H bMS Am 1505 (84).

16. THE PHILOSOPHER'S WIDOW

1. ALS, AHGJ to Barrett Wendell, 10 October 1910, H bMS Am 1907.1 (721). Barrett Wendell (1855–1921) was a prolific writer and cofounder of the Harvard *Lampoon*. He met HJ in London in 1895 and knew WJ as a colleague.

2. ALS, AHGJ to Theodore Flournoy, 6 November 1910, H bMS Am 1505 (84).

3. HJ to Mary Smyth Hunter, 1 October 1910, Lubbock, *The Letters*, 2:170.

4. ALS, HJ to Sydney Waterlow, 10 September 1910, M, Edel Papers, container 42, folder "Vaux Papers."

5. ALS, HJ to Mary (Mrs. Robertson) James, 7 September 1910, M, Edel Papers, container 42, folder "James, Mrs. Robertson."

6. ALS, AHGJ to Frances Rollins Morse, 20 September 1910, H bMS Am 1092.9 (4381).

7. HJ to Mary Smith Hunter, 1 October 1910, Lubbock, *The Letters*, 2:170.

8. "Alice Howe Gibbens, 1849–1922," 74.

9. Typescript, Elizabeth Glendower Evans, "Draft; Memoir," c. 1936, S, Evans Papers, Series I, accession no. 54-2, 55–76.

10. HJ to Jocelyn Persse, 27 October 1910, Susan E. Gunter and Steven H. Jobe, eds., *Dearly Beloved Friends: Henry James's Letters to Younger Men* (Ann Arbor: University of Michigan Press, 2001), 105.

11. Cited in Lewis, *The Jameses*, 583.

12. Mary Cadwalader Rawle (Mrs. Frederick) Jones (1850–1935) first met HJ in 1883, and they became good friends. She published two books, *European Travel for Women* (1900) and *Lantern Slides* (1937). See Gunter, *Dear Munificent Friends* for further information on her.

13. ALS, Benjamin Paul Blood to AHGJ, 9 November 1910, H bMS Am 1092.9 (4295).

14. ALS, Henry Adams to AHGJ, 27 January 1911, H bMS Am 1092.9 (4292).

15. HJ to AHGJ, 5 August 1913, Gunter, *Dear Munificent Friends*, 105.

16. William James, *Some Problems of Philosophy* (Cambridge MA: Harvard University Press, 1979), 113.

17. ALS, AHGJ to Theodore Flournoy, 2 April 1911, H bMS Am 1505 (85).

18. ALS, AHGJ to Frances Rollins Morse, 4 February 1911, H bMS Am 1092.11 (57).

19. ALS, HJ to HJ II, 18 May 1911, H bMS Am 1094 (1377).

20. HJ to AHGJ, [27 May 1911], Gunter, *Dear Munificent Friends*, 74.

21. ALS, HJ to AHGJ, 6 July 1911, H bMS Am 1094 (1716).

22. ALS, HJ to AHGJ, 18 October 1913, H bMS Am 1094 (1738).

23. ALS, AHGJ to HJ, 30 August 1911, H MS Am 2538.

24. ALS, AHGJ to WJ, 6 September [1887], H MS Am 2538.

25. ALS, HJ to MMJ, 13 September 1911, H bMS Eng 1070 (35).

26. ALS, AHGJ to HJ II, 17 March 1910, H MS Am 2538.

27. HJ to Margaret Frances Prothero, 9 September 1911, Gunter, *Dear Munificent Friends*, 213.

28. ALS, AHGJ to HJ, 30 August 1911, H MS Am 2538.

29. Transcript of ALS, HJ to Alice Runnells, 10 September 1911, M, Edel Papers, container 72; transcript of ALS, HJ to J. B. Warner, 29 September 1911, M, Edel Papers, container 72.

30. HJ to AHGJ, 13 November 1911, Gunter, *Dear Munificent Friends*, 81.

31. Unpublished report on William James as a candidate for admission to Harvard College, 24 June 1899, VA III 15.88.10, Faculty of Arts and Science, undergraduate folder "William James," 1903. Courtesy of the Harvard University Archives.

32. Family letters suggest his parents worried he might indulge in too much socializing while a Harvard undergraduate, and Michael James paints him as a weak, self-indulgent individual.

33. ALS, AHGJ to Alice Runnells James, [1912], H MS Am 2538.

34. ALS, HJ to MMJ, [31 July 1911], H bMS 1070 Eng (34).

35. ALS, HJ to WJ Jr., 8 January 1912, M, Edel Papers, container 72.

36. ALS, AHGJ to WJ Jr., 15 April 1912, H MS Am 2538.

37. HJ to Edmund Gosse, 30 January 1912, James, *Letters*, 4:600.

38. HJ to AHGJ, 23 July 1912, Gunter, *Dear Munificent Friends*, 89.

39. Searches for William's spirit went on literally for decades after his death. In 1978 a Marc Aronson of the Middle of Silence Gallery in New York tried to determine whether a book entitled *The Afterdeath Journal of an American*

Philosopher: The World View of William James, by Jane Roberts, was real or a hoax.

40. ALS, HJ to MMJ, 1 April 1912, H bMS Eng 1070 (39).

41. ALS, AHGJ to HJ, 27 April 1913, H bMS Am 1092.11 (52).

42. ALS, AHGJ to HJ, 27 April 1913, H bMS Am 1092.11 (52).

43. ALS, AHGJ to HJ, 17 May 1913, H bMS Am 1092.11 (53).

44. ALS, AHGJ to HJ II, 4 January 1913, H MS Am 2538.

45. HJ to AHGJ, 6 August 1912, Gunter, *Dear Munificent Friends*, 92.

46. ALS, HJ to AHGJ, 18 October 1913, H bMS Am 1094 (1738).

47. HJ to AHGJ, 23 July 1912, Gunter, *Dear Munificent Friends*, 88.

48. ALS, HJ to MMJ, [31 July 1911], H bMS Eng 1070 (34).

49. HJ to AHGJ, 5 March 1913, Gunter, *Dear Munificent Friends*, 100.

50. ALS, William Dean Howells to AHGJ, 29 April 1913, H bMS Am 1092.9 (4312).

51. ALS, AHGJ to HJ II, 4 January 1913, H MS Am 2538.

52. *The Complete Notebooks of Henry James*, 379.

53. Photocopy of ALS, MMJ to AHGJ, 10 August 1913, M, Edel Papers, container 42, folder "Mrs. William James."

54. HJ to AHGJ, 5 August 1913, Gunter, *Dear Munificent Friends*, 104.

55. ALS, MMJ to Alice Runnells and Billy James, 7 August 1913, B BANC MSS 72/35, box 3, folder 3.

56. Photocopy of ALS, MMJ to AHGJ, 5 August 1913, M, Edel Papers, container 42, folder "Mrs. William James."

57. ALS, MMJ to AHGJ, 15 August [1913], B BANC MSS 72/35, box 3, folder 3.

58. HJ to AHGJ, 5 August 1913, Gunter, *Dear Munificent Friends*, 104.

59. ALS, MMJ to AHGJ, 15 August [1913], B BANC MSS 72/35, box 3, folder 3.

60. HJ to AHGJ, 1 April 1913, James, *Letters*, 2:308–9.

61. ALS, HJ to MMJ, 28 October 1913, H bMS Eng 1070 (44).

62. HJ to AHGJ, 26 August 1912, Gunter, *Dear Munificent Friends*, 94.

63. ALS, HJ to HJ II, 23 September 1912, H bMS Am 1094 (1392).

64. ALS, AHGJ to HJ, 27 April 1913, H bMS Am 1092.11 (52).

65. ALS, AHGJ to HJ, 17 May 1913, H bMS Am 1092.11 (53). Sara Norton (1864–1922) was Charles Eliot Norton's elder daughter. Arthur George Sedgwick (1844–1915) was a lawyer, journalist, and assistant editor of the *Nation*. John Chipman Gray (1839–1915) cofounded the *American Law Review* and was a Harvard dean. ALS, AHGJ to HJ, 27 April 1913, H bMS Am 1092.11 (52).

66. ALS, HJ to MMJ, 5 November 1912, H bMS Eng 1070 (41).

67. ALS, AHGJ to HJ II, 25 December 1913, H MS Am 2538.

68. ALS, HJ to AHGJ, 18 March 1914, H bMS Am 1094 (1745).

69. ALS, HJ to AHGJ, 18 March 1914, H bMS Am 1094 (1745).

70. ALS, AHGJ to HJ, 17 May 1913, H bMS Am 1092.11 (53). Alice transcribed Minny's letters, keeping the copies, before she sent them to Henry. Since Henry destroyed the originals after using them, it is only thanks to Alice that copies of the letters survive at the Houghton. I am grateful to Pierre Walker for this note.

71. ALS, AHGJ to HJ, 14 March 1914, H bMS Am 1092.11 (54).

72. ALS, MMJ to AHGJ, 12 May [1914], B BANC MSS 72/35, box 3, folder 3.

73. ALS, AHGJ to EPG, 3 May 1914, H MS Am 1092.11 (18).

74. ALS, AHGJ to HJ II, [7 May 1914], H MS Am 2538.

75. ALS, AHGJ to MMJ, 12 July 1914, H MS Am 2538.

76. ALS, HJ to MMJ, 13 February 1914, H bMS Eng 1070 (46).

77. ALS, MMJ to AHGJ, 22 May [1914], B BANC MSS 72/35, box 3, folder 4.

78. ALS, MMJ to AHGJ, 5 May [1914], B BANC MSS 72/35, box 3, folder 4.

79. ALS, MMJ to AHGJ, 22 May [1914], B BANC MSS 72/35, box 3, folder 4.

80. ALS, MMJ to AHGJ, 8 May [1914], B BANC MSS 72/35, box 3, folder 4.

81. Susan E. Marshall, *Splintered Sisterhood: Gender and Class in the Campaign against Woman Suffrage* (Madison: University of Wisconsin Press, 1997), 5, 22–23.

82. Thomas J. Jablonsky, *The Home, Heaven, and Mother Party: Female Anti-Suffragists in the United States,* 1868–1920 (Boston: Carlson Publishing, 1994), xxiv–xxv, 40.

83. ALS, HJ to AHGJ, 29 August 1913, H bMS Am 1094 (1737).

84. ALS, HJ to AHGJ, 24 July 1914, H bMS Am 1094 (1747).

85. Appendix B, in Lewis, *The Jameses*, 621–22; H *2002M-44(b), James Family Scrapbook. Rupert Brooke (1887–1915) was a promising and handsome British poet of the pre-Romantic school. Though he wrote only five sonnets on World War I and saw only one day of military action near Antwerp, he became known as a war poet. On 23 April 1915, on his way to the battle of Gallipoli, he died of blood poisoning onboard ship. HJ wrote a long introduction to Brooke's posthumously published *Letters from America* (New York: Scribner's, 1916).

86. Appendix B, in Lewis, *The Jameses*, 621–22.

87. TLS, HJ to AHGJ, 13 October 1914, H bMS Am 1094 (1749).

88. HJ to AHGJ, 4 December 1914, Gunter, *Dear Munificent Friends*, 113. Brand Whitlock (1869–1934) was an American journalist, lawyer, municipal reformer, and diplomat. In 1913 President Woodrow Wilson appointed him minister to Belgium. He gained an international reputation for his commendable performance there.

89. HJ to AHGJ, 2 January 1915, Gunter, *Dear Munificent Friends*, 117–20.

90. It is possible that Pope was saved because of the mammalian dive reflex, wherein a person submerged in very cold water goes into a state of hibernation, slowing down all the body's systems. Interview with Hutch Foster, professional ski patroller, 24 May 2004.

91. HJ to AHGJ, 26 May 1915, Gunter, *Dear Munificent Friends*, 120–21.

92. ALS, AHGJ to HJ, 14 March 1914, H bMS Am 1092.11 (54).

93. TLS, HJ to MMJ, 12 October 1914, H bMS Eng 1070 (55).

94. Interview with Michael James, 20 June 2004, Cambridge, Massachusetts.

95. "Memories," by Frederika Paine James, n.d. Courtesy of Michael James.

96. ALS, ARJ to Leon Edel, 28 December 1987, M, Edel Papers, container 40, folder "Alexander R. James."

97. "Clay in His Hands," *Telegraph Sunday Magazine*, n.d. Courtesy of Michael James.

98. Michael James to Susan E. Gunter, 29 June 2004.

99. Michael James to Susan E. Gunter, 1 June 2004.

100. ALS, AHGJ to Theodate Pope, 6 January 1912, Archives, Hill-Stead Museum.

101. ALS, AHGJ to HJ II, 25 November 1914, H MS Am 2538.

102. "Alice Howe Gibbens, 1849–1922," 75.

103. ALS, AHGJ to HJ II, [14 April 1915], H MS Am 2538.

104. Sir George Otto Trevelyan (1838–1928) wrote a famous six-volume history of the American Revolution.

105. ALS, AHGJ to HJ II, 17 April 1915, H MS Am 2538.

106. ALS, AHGJ to Alice Runnells James, 29 June [1915], H MS Am 2538.

107. Frank Gellett Burgess (1866–1951) was a humorist and illustrator. He knew the Robert Louis Stevensons, and he visited HJ at Lamb House in 1898.

108. ALS, Bruce Porter to Katharine Hooker, 13 September [1908?], B BANC MSS 77/1, box 1, folder "Porter, Bruce 1901–1917"; manuscript, "Bruce Porter," 1917, B BANC MSS 77/1, box 1, folder "Porter, Bruce 1925–1941."

109. HJ to AHGJ, 15 March [1906], Gunter, *Dear Munificent Friends*, 66.

110. TLS, Bruce Porter to Katharine Hooker, 16 April 1905, B BANC MSS 77/1, box 1, folder "Porter, Bruce 1901–1917."

111. Transcript of ALS, HJ to Bruce Porter, August 1910, M, Edel Papers, container 41, folder "Porter, Bruce."

112. ALS, HJ to Bruce Porter, 15 May 1911, B BANC MSS 77/1.

113. HJ to MMJ, 15 July 1915, H *2002M-44(b), box 1.

114. Ahlstrom, *Religious History*, 488.

115. WJ to Henry William Rankin, 19 January 1896, *Correspondence*, 8:122. Rankin, a Massachusetts librarian, sent WJ material for *The Varieties of Religious Experience*.

116. ALS, AHGJ to HJ II, 21 July 1915, H MS Am 2538.

117. ALS, AHGJ to HJ II, 21 July 1915, H ms Am 2538.

118. ALS, AHGJ to HJ II, 21 July 1915, H ms Am 2538.

119. ALS, AHGJ to HJ II, 21 July 1915, H ms Am 2538.

120. ALS, HJ to MMJ, 1 December 1915, H bMS Eng 1070 (62).

121. "Alice Howe Gibbens, 1849–1922," 77.

122. ALS, HJ to MMJ, 1 December 1915, H bMS Eng 1070 (62).

123. Edel, *Henry James: The Master*, 542.

124. "Alice Howe Gibbens, 1849–1922," 77.

125. ALS, AHGJ to HJ II, 5 December 1915, H ms Am 2538.

126. ALS, AHGJ to EPG, 4 December 1915, H bMS Am 1092.11 (19).

17. PASSAGES

1. ALS, AHGJ to HJ II, 5 December 1915, H ms Am 2538.

2. ALS, AHGJ to EPG, 9 December 1915, H bMS Am 1092.11 (20). Lucy Christiana, Lady Duff-Gordon (1863–1945), was a leading fashion designer who was known as "Lucile." She had fashion houses in Paris, New York, and Chicago, designing costumes for high society ladies and for actresses. She was credited with training the first fashion models and putting on the first runway shows.

3. ALS, AHGJ to HJ II, 14 December 1915, H ms Am 2538.

4. ALS, AHGJ to HJ II, 14 December 1915, H ms Am 2538.

5. ALS, AHGJ to HJ II, 14 December 1915, H ms Am 2538.

6. ALS, AHGJ to HJ II, 19 December 1915, H ms Am 2538.

7. Theodora Bosanquet, "Diary Notes Made for Leon Edel; Dec. 1915 to Mar. 1916," H bMS Eng 1213.2.

8. ALS, AHGJ to HJ II, 28 December 1915, H ms Am 2538.

9. ALS, AHGJ to MMJ, 17 December 1915, H ms Am 2538.

10. ALS, Theodora Bosanquet to Leon Edel, 4 July 1952, M, Edel Papers, container 13, folder "Bosanquet, Theodora."

11. Bosanquet, "Diary Notes."

12. ALS, Theodora Bosanquet to Leon Edel, 4 July 1952.

13. ALS, Theodora Bosanquet to Eric S. Pinker, 6 July 1925, M, Edel Papers, container 13, folder "Bosanquet, Theodora."

14. ALS, AHGJ to HJ II, 14 December 1915, H ms Am 2538.

15. ALS, AHGJ to HJ II, 15 December 1915, H ms Am 2538.

16. ALS, AHGJ to HJ II, 17 December 1915, H ms Am 2538.

17. ALS, AHGJ to WJ Jr., 10 February 1916, H ms Am 2538.

18. ALS, MMJ to Leon Edel, 8 March [n.d.], M, Edel Papers, container 27, folder "James, Mary Margaret (1887–1952) and Porter, Bruce (1865–1953)."

19. ALS, AHGJ to MMJ, 17 December 1915, H ms Am 2538.

20. ALS, AHGJ to MMJ, 17 December 1915, H MS Am 2538.

21. ALS, AHGJ to HJ II, 19 December 1915, H MS Am 2538.

22. ALS, AHGJ to HJ II, 20 December 1915, H MS Am 2538.

23. ALS, AHGJ to HJ II, 21 December 1915, H MS Am 2538.

24. ALS, AHGJ to HJ II, 25 December 1915, H MS Am 2538.

25. ALS, AHGJ to HJ II, 28 December 1915, H MS Am 2538.

26. ALS, AHGJ to MMJ, 17 December 1915, H MS Am 2538.

27. The "Endless Turner" refers to the famous water scenes by British landscape watercolor painter Joseph William Turner. ALS, AHGJ to HJ II, 22 December 1915, H MS Am 2538.

28. Bosanquet, "Diary Notes."

29. ALS, AHGJ to WJ Jr., 10 January 1916, H MS Am 2538.

30. ALS, AHGJ to HJ II, 11 January 1916, H MS Am 2538.

31. ALS, AHGJ to HJ II, 22 December 1915, H MS Am 2538.

32. ALS, AHGJ to WJ Jr., 10 January 1916, H MS Am 2538.

33. ALS, AHGJ to HJ II, 28 December 1915, H MS Am 2538.

34. ALS, AHGJ to WJ Jr., 26 January 1916, H MS Am 2538.

35. ALS, AHGJ to WJ Jr., 6 February 1916, H MS Am 2538.

36. ALS, AHGJ to HJ II, 28 December 1915, H MS Am 2538.

37. ALS, AHGJ to EPG, 20 February 1916, H bMS Am 1092.11 (22).

38. ALS, AHGJ to WJ Jr., 10 February 1916, H MS Am 2538.

39. ALS, AHGJ to WJ Jr., 26 January 1916, H MS Am 2538.

40. ALS, AHGJ to WJ Jr., 10 February 1916, H MS Am 2538.

41. ALS, AHGJ to WJ Jr., 6 February 1916, H MS Am 2538.

42. ALS, AHGJ to WJ Jr., 10 February 1916, H MS Am 2538. Emily Sargent was the sister of artist John Singer Sargent, who had painted James's seventieth birthday portrait.

43. ALS, AHGJ to ARJ, 6 March 1916, H MS Am 2538.

44. ALS, AHGJ to WJ Jr., 10 February 1916, H MS Am 2538.

45. ALS, AHGJ to WJ Jr., 10 February 1916, H MS Am 2538.

46. ALS, AHGJ to HJ II, 1 March 1916, H MS Am 2538.

47. ALS, AHGJ to Barrett Wendell, 26 March 1916, H bMS Am 1907.1 (714).

48. ALS, AHGJ to HJ II, 1 March 1916, H MS Am 2538.

49. Bosanquet, "Diary Notes."

50. ALS, AHGJ to HJ II, 5 March [1916], H MS Am 2538.

51. ALS, AHGJ to WJ Jr., 14 March 1916, H MS Am 2538.

52. ALS, AHGJ to HJ II, 1 March 1916, H MS Am 2538. Violet Ormond was John Singer Sargent's married sister, and Bailey Saunders was a journalist and translator who had been an American childhood friend of HJ.

53. ALS, AHGJ to ARJ, 1916, H MS Am 2538.

54. ALS, AHGJ to HJ II, 5 March [1916], H MS Am 2538.

55. ALS, AHGJ to HJ II, 6 March 1916, H MS Am 2538.

56. ALS, AHGJ to WJ Jr., 14 March 1916, H MS Am 2538.

57. ALS, AHGJ to WJ Jr., 19 March 1916, H MS Am 2538.

58. Novick, *Henry James: The Mature Master*, 517; Edel, *Henry James: The Master*, 562.

59. Sophia Lucy Lane (Mrs. William Kingdon) Clifford (c. 1853–1929) was a popular English novelist and playwright. She and HJ had been friends for decades. WJ knew her husband, a mathematician and philosopher. Dudley Jocelyn Persse (1873–1943), nephew of Lady Augusta Gregory, was a British dilettante who frequently attended theatrical and musical performances with HJ. Sir Hugh Seymour Walpole (1884–1941) was a New Zealand–born writer and critic. HJ helped him launch his career, though he fiercely criticized Walpole's early fiction. His books include a series of historical novels on the Herries family.

60. ALS, AHGJ to MMJ, 17 December 1915, H MS Am 2538.

61. ALS, AHGJ to HJ II, 28 December 1915, H MS Am 2538.

62. ALS, AHGJ to WJ Jr., 13 April 1916, H MS Am 2538.

63. ALS, AHGJ to Alice Runnells James, 27 April 1916, H MS Am 2538.

64. ALS, AHGJ to WJ Jr., 24 April 1916, H MS Am 2538; ALS, AHGJ to Alice Runnells James, 27 April 1916, H MS Am 2538.

65. ALS, AHGJ to HJ II, 4 June 1916, H MS Am 2538.

66. ALS, AHGJ to WJ Jr., 28 May 1916, H MS Am 2538.

67. ALS, AHGJ to WJ Jr., 20 May 1916, H MS Am 2538.

68. Percy Lubbock (1879–1965) was an historian, biographer, and librarian. He met HJ at Lamb House in 1901. The two men had many mutual friends.

69. ALS, AHGJ to HJ II, 31 July 1916, H MS Am 2538.

70. ALS, AHGJ to WJ Jr., 9 November 1902, H MS Am 2538.

18. LIVING OPTION

1. Pragmatism still attracts important scholarly notice, as attested by the conference "Pragmatism and Idealism in Dialogue: William James and Josiah Royce a Century Later," hosted by the Harvard Divinity School under the direction of David Lamberth in May 2007.

2. ALS, AHGJ to Katharine Hooker, 27 December 1920, B BANC MSS 77/1, box 1, folder "Correspondence James, Alice H."

3. ALS, AHGJ to WJ Jr., 30 September 1918, H MS Am 2538.

4. ALS, AHGJ to WJ Jr., 14 March 1916, H MS Am 2538.

5. When Alexander James died, his wallet contained a picture of his mother. Michael James to Susan E. Gunter, 9 April 2003.

6. ALS, AHGJ to WJ Jr., 24 April 1916, H MS Am 2538.

7. Weathers, "The Sensibility of Alexander James."

8. ALS, AHGJ to WJ Jr., 28 May 1916, H MS Am 2538.

9. ALS, AHGJ to WJ Jr., 20 May 1916, H MS Am 2538. Beechnut was a character created by nineteenth-century writer Jacob Abbott (1803–79), who wrote the first book series designed for children. His tales contained moral, didactic sentiments but also contained lively narratives.

10. ALS, AHGJ to WJ Jr., 17 June 1916, H MS Am 2538.

11. ALS, AHGJ to WJ Jr., 25 June 1916, H MS Am 2538.

12. ALS, AHGJ to HJ II, 20 May 1917, H MS Am 2538.

13. ALS, AHGJ to WJ Jr., 18 July 1917, H MS Am 2538.

14. ALS, AHGJ to WJ Jr., 30 June 1918, H MS Am 2538.

15. Lewis, *The Jameses*, 596.

16. ALS, AHGJ to HJ II, Thanksgiving Day [1916], H MS Am 2538.

17. ALS, AHGJ to Horace Kallen, 11 January 1917, Horace Kallen Papers, Jacob Rader Marcus Center of the American Jewish Archives, Cincinnati Campus, Hebrew Union College, Jewish Institute of Religion. I am grateful for permission to cite this material.

18. ALS, AHGJ to HJ II, [16 April 1917], H MS Am 2538.

19. ALS, AHGJ to HJ II, 3 May [1917], H MS Am 2538.

20. ALS, AHGJ to Theodate Pope, 19 May 1920, Archives, Hill-Stead Museum.

21. ALS, AHGJ to Alice Runnells James, 30 August 1917, H *2002M-44(b), box 1, folder 4; ALS, AHGJ to WJ Jr., 29 [August] 1917, H *2002M-44 (b), folder "James, Alice H. G."

22. ALS, Bruce Porter to Katharine Hooker, Thursday night, c. 1917, B BANC MSS 77/1, box 1, folder "Porter, Bruce 1925–1941."

23. Marriage certificate, Margaret Mary James and Bruce Porter, box 1, folder "Miscellaneous," BANC MSS C-H 159, Bruce Porter Papers, Bancroft Library, University of California at Berkeley. Harold Witter Bynner (1881–1968) was an American poet and scholar. He met HJ in New York during his American tour.

24. ALS, AHGJ to WJ Jr., 17 June 1917, H MS Am 2538.

25. ALS, AHGJ to WJ Jr., 18 July 1917, H MS Am 2538.

26. ALS, AHGJ to HJ II, 29 September 1918, H MS Am 2538.

27. *Boston Herald* obituary of William James Jr., 28 September 1961, M, Edel Papers, container 27, folder "James, John."

28. HJ II's note card synopsis of HJ to Bruce Porter, 26 January 1918, courtesy of Michael James.

29. ALS, AHGJ to HJ II, 26 May 1918, H MS Am 2538.

30. R. McAllister Lloyd, "Henry James Our Third President," *TIAA CREF* in-

house publication, vol. 1, no. 5 (1968), M, Edel Papers, container 27, folder "James, Henry 3rd."

31. ALS, AHGJ to WJ Jr., 4 August 1918, H MS Am 2538.

32. ALS, AHGJ to HJ II, 4 August 1918, H MS Am 2538; ALS, AHGJ to WJ Jr., 4 August 1918, H MS Am 2538.

33. "Alice Howe Gibbens, 1849–1922," 82.

34. ALS, AHGJ to WJ Jr., 17 July 1918, H MS Am 2538.

35. "Alice Howe Gibbens, 1849–1922," 82.

36. ALS, Bruce Porter to MMJ, c. 3 March 1918, B BANC MSS 72/35, box 2, folder 1.

37. ALS, Bruce Porter to Katharine Hooker, 19 November [1925], B BANC MSS 77/1, box 1, folder "Porter, Bruce 1925–1941."

38. Sharon Wick, current owner of the 944 Chestnut Street house, graciously allowed me to see the house and garden, sharing with me historical information on the house.

39. ALS, AHGJ to WJ Jr., 17 July 1918, H MS Am 2538.

40. ALS, AHGJ to WJ Jr., 4 August 1918, H MS Am 2538.

41. ALS, AHGJ to WJ Jr., 18 August 1918, H MS Am 2538.

42. ALS, AHGJ to WJ Jr., 4 August 1918, H MS Am 2538.

43. ALS, AHGJ to WJ Jr., 6 August 1918, H MS Am 2538.

44. ALS, AHGJ to WJ Jr., 9 September 1918, H MS Am 2538.

45. ALS, AHGJ to WJ Jr., 17 November 1918, H MS Am 2538.

46. ALS, AHGJ to WJ Jr., 20 October 1918, H MS Am 2538.

47. ALS, AHGJ to WJ Jr., 27 October 1918, H MS Am 2538.

48. ALS, AHGJ to WJ Jr., 27 October 1918, H MS Am 2538. The phrase is from Hamlet's soliloquy: "And thus the native hue of resolution / Is sicklied o'er with the pale cast of thought" (Shakespeare, *Hamlet*, 3.1.92–93).

49. ALS, AHGJ to WJ Jr., 3 November 1918, H MS Am 2538.

50. ALS, AHGJ to WJ Jr., 29 September 1918, H MS Am 2538; ALS, AHGJ to WJ Jr., 28 January 1919, H MS Am 2538; ALS, AHGJ to WJ Jr., 3 November 1918, H MS Am 2538; and ALS, AHGJ to WJ Jr., 2 February 1919, H MS Am 2538. Mary Augusta Arnold (Mrs. Thomas Humphry) Ward (1851–1920) was a successful Victorian novelist and an antisuffragist. She and HJ were friends. Peter Alexeivich Kropotkin had been born into a wealthy noble family but had developed an interest in Russian peasants early in life. One of the most important leaders in the revolutionary intellectual tradition, he wanted to find a scientific basis for anarchism and also define a basis for anarchist ethics. While he disparaged individual acts of violence, he thought state governments would need to be abolished by force. Imprisoned in St. Petersburg in 1876, he escaped and finally settled in London but returned to Russia after the 1917 Revolution, eventually denouncing Lenin as a traitor to the cause.

51. ALS, HJ II to MMJ, 3 November [1918], B BANC MSS C-H 159, folder "James, Henry, 1879–1947 14 letters 1900–1919."

52. ALS, AHGJ to WJ Jr., 30 September 1918, H MS Am 2538.

53. ALS, AHGJ to WJ Jr., 14 January 1919, H MS Am 2538.

54. ALS, AHGJ to WJ Jr., 21 January 1919, H MS Am 2538.

55. John Dewey (1859–1952) was known as the father of functional psychology and a leader of the progressive movement in education. Influenced by Hegel, he developed a form of pragmatism that he called "instrumentalism," valuing science over any religion or metaphysics.

56. ALS, Mary Salter to AHGJ, 2 December 1918, H MS Am 2538.

57. ALS, AHGJ to WJ Jr., 8 December 1918, H MS Am 2538.

58. ALS, AHGJ to WJ Jr., 14 January 1919, H MS Am 2538.

59. ALS, AHGJ to WJ Jr., 22 March 1919, H MS Am 2538.

60. ALS, AHGJ to WJ Jr., 16 April 1919, H MS Am 2538.

61. ALS, AHGJ to WJ Jr., 22 March 1919, H MS Am 2538.

62. ALS, HJ II to MMJ, 21 July [1919], B BANC MSS 72/35, box 1, folder "James, Henry, 1879–1947 14 letters 1900–1919."

63. ALS, MMJ to AHGJ, 15 March 1920, B BANC MSS 72/35, box 4, folder "Porter, Margaret Mary 20 letters 1919–1920"; HJ II's note card synopsis of HJ II to MMJ, 15 November 1919 and 10 December 1919.

64. ALS, MMJ to AHGJ, 21 November [1920], B BANC MSS 72/35, box 4, folder "Porter, Margaret Mary 20 letters 1919–1920."

65. ALS, AHGJ to Katharine Hooker, 27 December 1920, B BANC MSS 77/1, box 1, folder "Correspondence James, Alice H."

66. Sir Henry Maximilian Beerbohm (1872–1956) was a writer, drama critic, and caricaturist. His cartoons satirizing HJ were well known. James Brand Pinker (1863–1922) was HJ's literary and dramatic agent; he visited Lamb House often. When HJ applied for citizenship in 1915, Pinker was a sponsor.

67. ALS, AHGJ to WJ Jr., 16 April 1916, H MS Am 2538.

68. Introduction to James, *Letters*, 1:xxii.

69. I thank Sheldon Novick for the information on Gosse advising omitting the salutations for some of the letters to young men.

70. James, *Letters*, 1:xxvii.

71. ALS, AHGJ to HJ II, c. 1920, H bMS Am 1092.10 (95).

72. ALS, AHGJ to HJ II, [27 May 1920], H MS Am 2538.

73. ALS, Sir George Walter Prothero to AHGJ, 10 April 1920, H bMS Am 1092.9 (4325).

74. ALS, MMJ to AHGJ, 22 May 1920, B BANC MSS 72/35, box 4, folder "Porter, Margaret Mary 20 letters 1919–1920."

75. ALS, John S. James to Leon Edel, 19 October 1962, M, Edel Papers, container

27, folder "James, John." This letter cites a letter from HJ II to Alice, advising her not to be upset about Lubbock's editing.

76. ALS, AHGJ to HJ II, 4 May 1921, H MS Am 2538.

77. "Alice Howe Gibbens, 1849–1922," 83.

78. TLS, HJ II, "Memorandum Concerning Letters Between my Father and Mother," 9 June 1936, H MS Am 1095.2 (66b).

79. ALS, AHGJ to HJ II, c. 1920, H bMS Am 1092.10 (95).

80. ALS, HJ II to AHGJ, c. 1920, H bMS Am 1092.10 (219).

81. ALS, HJ II to AHGJ, 7 May 1920, H bMS Am 1092.10 (219).

82. ALS, HJ II to AHGJ, 21 July 1920, H bMS Am 1092.10 (219).

83. ALS, HJ II to Ralph Perry, 25 February 1931, H MS Am 1095.2 (66).

84. ALS, AHGJ to Elizabeth Glendower Evans, 9 December 1920, S, Evans Papers, Series II, Correspondence. HJ II won a Pulitzer Prize for his two-volume biography of Charles William Eliot in 1931.

85. ALS, AHGJ to HJ II, 19 December 1920, H MS Am 2538.

86. ALS, John Jay Chapman to AHGJ, 31 December 1920, H bMS Am 1854.1 (17).

87. ALS, AHGJ to HJ II, [27 May 1920], H MS Am 2538.

88. ALS, AHGJ to Katharine Hooker, November 1924 [the dating on this is incorrect; internal dating suggests spring 1920], B BANC MSS 77/1, box 1, folder "Correspondence James, Alice H."

89. ALS, MMJ to Bruce Porter, 1 July 1920, B BANC MSS 72/35, box 4, folder "Porter, Margaret Mary 20 letters 1919–1920."

90. ALS, MMJ to AHGJ, 22 August 1920, B BANC MSS 72/35, box 4, folder "Porter, Margaret Mary 20 letters 1919–1920."

91. ALS, MMJ to AHGJ, November 1920, B BANC MSS 72/35, box 4, folder "Porter, Margaret Mary 20 letters 1919–1920."

92. ALS, AHGJ to HJ II, 14 May 1921, H MS Am 2538.

93. ALS, AHGJ to Bruce Porter, 13 November 1920, B BANC MSS 72/35, box 1, folder "James, Alice Howe Gibbens."

94. R. W. B. Lewis spells the name "Catharine," but Alice spells it in this way.

95. ALS, AHGJ to HJ II, 29 May 1921, H *2002M-44(b), box 1, folder "James, Alice H. G."

96. ALS, HJ II to MMJ, 10 December 1920, B BANC MSS 72/35, box 1, folder "James, Henry, 1879–1947 17 letters 1920–1929."

97. ALS, AHGJ to WJ Jr., 26 May 1921, H MS Am 2538. Philip King Brown (1869–1940) was a noted physician and medical researcher. He graduated from Harvard Medical School in 1893 and was medical director of a northern California sanatorium for many years. He had studied the treatments at Bad Nauheim, publishing a treatise on the effect of the baths on blood pressure in 1910.

98. Sir Wilfred Scawen Blunt (1840–1922) was a British poet and writer. His poetry was erotic and elegant. An anti-imperialist, he sympathized with the Muslim world.

99. Perhaps this remark concerned her dislike of those Jewish people who converted to Christianity.

100. ALS, AHGJ to HJ II, 4 May 1921, H MS Am 2538.

101. ALS, AHGJ to Horace Kallen, 12 January 1921, Kallen Papers.

102. McKinley's assassination was only one of the assassinations of heads of states by anarchists during the last two decades of the nineteenth century and the first two decades of the twentieth. By the 1910s leaders realized that the assassinations had not helped their movements, and they ended, for the most part.

103. Chronology, S, Evans Papers, 1856–1937.

104. WJ to Thomas Ward, January [7] [18]68, *Correspondence*, 4:250.

105. ALS, AHGJ to Elizabeth Glendower Evans, 27 May 1920, S, Evans Papers, 1859 (1882–1946), Series II, Correspondence.

106. ALS, Nicola Sacco to Elizabeth Glendower Evans, 23 November 1923, *Selected Letters of Nicola Sacco from the Dedham Jail*, www.law.umkc.edu/faculty/ projects/ftrials/Sacco V/sac-dedham.

107. ALS, AHGJ to Elizabeth Glendower Evans, 30 October 1921, S, Evans Papers, 1859 (1882–1944), Series II, Correspondence.

108. ALS, MMJ to Elizabeth Glendower Evans, 25 September [1930–31], S, Evans Papers, accession no. 54-2, 55–76, Series II, Correspondence.

109. Sacco and Vanzetti were pardoned by Massachusetts governor Michael Dukakis on 23 August 1977.

110. Barry Faulkner, "Alexander James 1890–1946," Memorial Exhibition Program, 5. Courtesy of Michael James.

111. ALS, AHGJ to HJ II, 1 December 1921, H MS Am 2538.

112. ALS, AHGJ to HJ II, c. 20 March 1922, H MS Am 2538.

113. Conversation with Michael James, 20 May 2005.

114. ALS, Eleanor Sidgwick to AHGJ, 4 May 1920, H bMS Am 1092.9 (4334).

115. ALS, AHGJ to Katharine Hooker, 27 December 1920, B BANC MSS 77/1, box 1, folder "James, Alice H."

116. ALS, AHGJ to Katharine Hooker, [November 1920], B BANC MSS 77/1, box 1, folder "James, Alice H."

117. ALS, MMJ to AHGJ, 15 May 1920, B BANC MSS 72/35, box 4, folder "Porter, Margaret Mary 20 letters 1919–1920."

118. ALS, MMJ to Bruce Porter, 6 July 1922, B BANC MSS 72/35, box 4, folder "Porter, Margaret Mary 26 letters, 1921–1947."

119. ALS, Bruce Porter to MMJ, 13 July 1922, B BANC MSS 72/35, box 2, folder "Porter, Bruce 10 letters 1918–1930."

120. I am indebted to Pierre Walker for this insight.

121. ALS, AHGJ to HJ II, 10 May 1922, H MS Am 2538.

122. ALS, AHGJ to HJ II, 17 May 1922, H MS Am 2538.

123. ALS, AHGJ to HJ II, c. July 1922, H MS Am 2538.

124. ALS, AHGJ to WJ Jr., 5 July 1922, H MS Am 2538.

125. ALS, ARJ to AHGJ, c. July 1922, H MS Am 2538.

126. ALS, AHGJ to WJ Jr., 15 July 1922, H MS Am 2538.

127. "Alice Howe Gibbens, 1849–1922," 85.

128. Conversation with Michael James, 28 May 2003.

129. ALS, AHGJ to HJ II, 23 July 1922, H MS Am 2538.

130. "Alice Howe Gibbens, 1849–1922," 79.

131. "Alice Howe Gibbens, 1849–1922," 83–84.

132. HJ II's note card, HJ II to MMJ, 27 August 1922, courtesy of Michael James.

133. HJ II's note card, HJ II to MMJ, 27 August 1922.

134. ALS, ARJ to HJ II, 3 September 1922, H MS Am 2538.

135. ALS, AHGJ to MMJ, 12 September 1922, H *2002M-44(b), box 1, folder "Mary Margaret James."

136. ALS, MMJ to Bruce Porter, 22 September 1922, B BANC MSS 72/35, box 4, folder "Porter, Margaret (James) 26 letters, 1921–1947."

137. The date on the mortuary stone is incorrect. Hermann died in 1885.

138. Edward H. Warren, Henry James's architect, was evidently living in Boston at the time at 224 Marlboro Street, the address listed in the will. Emily Sargent and Reine Ormond give London addresses.

139. Last will and testament, Alice H. James, Middlesex County Courthouse; Executor's Inventory No. 138542, Alice H. James, 12 March 1923, Middlesex County Courthouse.

140. ALS, John S. James to Leon Edel, 25 September 1962, M, Edel Papers, container 27, folder "James, John."

INDEX

Page references in *italics* refer to photographic inserts: the first number indicates the text page preceeding the insert; the second number is the photographic plate number.

scandal during, xvi, 13, 16–17;
events leading to, 10, 12; financial
cost of, 20; injuries/deaths related
to, 13, 155–56; Yankee occupation
of South, xvi
Claflin, Mary Bucklin, 28, 49
Claflin, William, 28
Clarke, Joseph Thatcher, 142, 173,
365n108
Clarke, Rebecca, 182, 198
Clifford, Lucy, 302, 399n59
Clifford, William, 60, 347n39
Cobb, Mrs. John C., *192–15*
Cogswell, Dr., 219
Colburn, Warren, 89
Comstock Act, 62
Confederacy/Confederate States, 13
Congregational Church, xv, 9
cotton fraud scandal, xvi, 13, 16–17
Crane, Stephen, 196
"Cure for Anarchy, The" (Salter), 104
Curtis, Ariana, 130
Curtis, Daniel, 130
Cushing, Miss, 58
Cutter, Jonas, 84
Cutting, Olivia, 308
Cutting, Olivia Murray, 308
Cutting, William Bayard, 308

Dana Hill, 111
Darwin, Charles, 35, 118
Data of Ethics, The (Spencer), 62
Davidson, Thomas, 28, 33, 65, 80, 145,
156, 174, 221, 340n4
Des Voeux, Dr., 278, 296
Deutschland, 21
Dewey, John, 314
Dew-Smith, Alice, 304
Dexter, T. C. A., 16
diphtheria, 83

Dix Mountain, 56
Dixwell's Folly Brook, 57
Donaldson, D. D.: *Research to Motor
Sensations on the Skin*, 318
Douglass, Frederick, 10
Dreyfus, Alfred, 169
Dreyfus case, xvi, 162, 169, 292
Driver, Dr., 210
Driver, Stephen, 163
Du Bois, W. E. B., 213
Duff-Gordon, Lady, 292
Dundas, Rebecca, 205
Duveneck, Frank, 136
Dyer, Louis, 141

Eckstein, Pastor, 21
Edel, Leon, 294
Edison, Madeleine, 277
Edison, Thomas Alva, 277
Edwards, Edward: *The Life of Raleigh*,
244
Edwards, Jonathan, 9
Eliot, Charles William, 41, 42, 55, 99,
111, 214, 217, 310, 356n48
Eliot, Dr., 208–9
Eliot, George: *Middlemarch*, 60–61
Eliot, Grace Hopkinson, 55, 149,
192–15
Ellis, Rufus, 8, 12, 17, 56
Emerson, Ralph Waldo, 11, 28, 34
Emerson, William Ralph, 113, 217
Emery, Joshua, 2, 4
Eminent Victorians (Strachey), 314
Emmet, Bay, 253
Emmet, Rosina Hubley, 151–52
empiricism, 240, 244, 305
Empress of Britain, 267
"Enoch Arden" (Tennyson), 211
Erb, Dr., 184
Erckmann, Émile, 135, 253

friendship with, 29–31, 45, 49, 56; wj's courtship of, 33, 45–53. *See also* James, Alice Howe Gibbens (AHGJ)

Gibbens, Daniel Lewis, Jr. (DLG), *192–2*; Civil War posts of, 12–14; correspondence with daughters, 8–9, 15; drinking habits of, 2, 4, 7, 16–17; estate of, 18, 20; father of AHGJ, 1, 331; life in Charlestown, 8; marriage to Eliza Putnam Webb, 2; as material witness in Mobile, 16–17; medical degree of, 2; ranching venture in California, 6–8; religious influences of, 8, 11; return to New England, 7–8; second return to Boston, 12; separation from Eliza, 4, 335n7; as ship's doctor, 10–12, 336n30; spiritual guidance of, 56; suicide death of, 17

Gibbens, Daniel Lewis, Sr., 2, 165, *192–3*, 280

Gibbens, Eliza Putnam Webb, *192–17*; on AHG's engagement to wj, 47; Daniel's separation from, 4, 335n7; death of, 308; diminished financial status of, 20–26; health of, 6, 84, 87; husband's suicide death, 17; life in Cambridge, 201; living with mother, 8; male friends of, 30; marriage to Daniel Gibbens, 2; mother of AHGJ, 1, 331; séances attended by, 92; travels to Europe, 89, 96; visits with grandchildren, 62

Gibbens, Frederick Hammond, 15

Gibbens, Margaret Merrill, *192–1*; birth of, 7; care of AHGJ's children, 84; marriage to Leigh Gregor, 160; travels to Europe, 51, 89, 96

Gibbens, Maria, 15

Gibbens, Mary, 56

Gibbens, Mary Sherwin, *192–1*; birth of, 4; childhood in California, 5; correspondence with father, 8; marriage to William MacKintire Salter, 88, 92; teaching career of, 25, 27–28; travels of, 51

Gibbens, Samuel Hammond, 15

Gifford, Lord, 197

Gilbert and Sullivan: *Iolanthe*, 73

Gilman, Daniel Coit, 65, 349n67

Gladstone, William, xv, 142

Godineau, Marguerite, 179, 204

Godkin, Edwin, 203

Golden Bough, The (Frazer), 191, 195, 207

Goldmark, Charles, 161, 248

Goldmark, Pauline, 152–53, 161, 201, 246, 248

Goldstein, J., 263

Gordon, George, 269

Gosse, Edmund, 140, 263, 300, 301, 315

Grand Army of the Republic, 12

Grand Union Hotel, 56

Grant, Fred, 233

Gray, Frank, 229, 231, 382–83n42

Gray, John, 280, 281

Gray, Mary "Mamie," 229

Great Awakening, 9

Great Earthquake, 226–27

Great Eastern, 36

Green, Nicholas St. John, 42

Gregor, Leigh, 160, 201, 211, 276

Gregor, Rosamund, 314

Grimm, Herman: *Unüberwindliche Mächte*, 36

Groedel, Theodor, 263

Gurney, Edmund, 81

Gurney, Ellen, 89, 97, 105

Gurney, Kate Sara Sibley, 106

Gwinn, Mary, 225–26

Hagen, Hermann August, 80

Hall, G. Stanley, 150, 254, 318; *Research to Motor Sensations on the Skin*, 318

Hanks, Sarah Humphrey Hale, 58

Hansa, 21

Harper's Ferry, 9

Harris, Thomas Lake, 289

Hartwell, Charley, 246

Harvey, George, 217

Havens, Catherine, 37, 44, 46, 47, 52

Haymarket Square Riot, xv, xvi, 104, 214

Hazel Blossoms (Whittier), 30

Hegel, Georg Wilhelm Friedrich, 244, 385n5

Heidelberg, Gibbens' visit to, 22–23

Henschel, George, 73

Higginson, Henry Lee, 201, 269

Hillard, Katharine, 50, 58

History of American Literature (Wendell), 189

Hodder, Alfred, 138, 225–26

Hodder, Jessie Donaldson, 138, 225–26

Hodder, Olive, 138

Hodges, Dr., 224

Hodgson, Richard, 239

Hodgson, Shadworth Hollway, 141, 365n103

Hoffman, Ralph, 216

Holmes, Oliver Wendell, 28, 42, 53, 269

Hooker, Katharine Putnam, as childhood friend of AHGJ, 55, 58, 114, 224, 288, 289, 305, 309, 311, 315

Hooker, Marian, 290

Hoppin, Lilly, *192–15*

Hotham, Charles, 249, 250

Howe, Julia Ward, 28, 29

Howe, Mark, 319

Howells, William Dean, 46, 166, 213, 265, 277, 344n71, 391n66

Howison, George Holmes, 28

humanism, 240–41

humanitarian movements, xv

Hunersdorf, Fräulein, 106

Hunter, Ellen Emmet, 148, 151, 217, 366n23

Hunter, Mary Smyth, 261, 270

Huxley, Thomas, 60, 347n39

hypnotism, 91–92

"Impressions of a Cousin, The" (Henry James), 76–77

Indian Rights Association, 229

intellectualism, 244

International Women's Congress, 323

Iolanthe (Gilbert and Sullivan), 73

Irish Home Rule, 142

Jackson, Nancy, 62

James, Aleck. *See* James, Francis Tweedy

James, Alexander Robertson (Aleck), *192–8, 192–20*, 286, 313; art studies of, 251, 285, 287; birth of, 119; education of, 184, 202, 208, 215, 216, 220, 232–34, 248–51; engagement to Frederika Paine, 285, 286, 306–7; health of, 208–10; learning problems of, 232–33; named Francis Robertson, 160, 215, 380n91; travels in Europe, 124, 125, 127, 130, 134

James, Alexander Robertson, Jr. (Sandy), *192–20*, 324, 327

James, Alice (AJ), *192–10*; animosity toward Aunt Kate, 71; coping with father's declining health, 66–70, 351n108; death of, 121; diary of, 99; estate/legacy of, 121; feminist views of, xiv; health of, 55, 98, 120; living in England, 98–99; relation-

James, Henry (HJ) (*cont.*)

192–11, 193, 195, 219, 246, 250, 275–76, 301, 303; on naming children, 80, 119; Order of Merit award, 297; relationship with AHGJ, 54, 66, 71–72, 75, 76–77, 99, 102, 116–17, 121, 130–31, 187, 218, 256–57; relationship with WJ, xiv, 182, 185; roles after WJ's death, 271; theatrical ventures, 150–51; travels in U.S., 218; as uncle, 130–31, 139, 183, 193–94, 208, 233, 234, 249, 250, 275–76, 278, 282; will and estate of, 301–2; works of: *The American,* 120, 140; *The American Scene,* 218; *The Better Sort,* 214–15; *The Bostonians,* 28, 77–78, 100; *Daisy Miller,* 150; *English Hours,* 255; *The Golden Bowl,* 191; *Guy Domville,* 151; *The High Bid,* 255; "The Impressions of a Cousin," 76–77; *Italian Hours,* 255; "The Jolly Corner," 257; "Lady Barbarina," 77; *Notes of a Son and Brother,* 281; "Pandora," 77; *A Passionate Pilgrim,* 34; *The Portrait of a Lady,* xiv; "A Question of Our Speech," 234; *Roderick Hudson,* 34; *A Small Boy and Others,* 280; *The Spoils of Poynton,* 156; "The Tone of Time," 190; *The Tragic Muse,* 116; *Transatlantic Sketches,* 34, 190; *Views and Reviews,* 255; *Watch and Ward,* 34; *The Wings of the Dove,* 25, 119, 187

James, Henry II (Harry), *192–15;* birth of, 61; as business manager of Rockefeller Institute, 277; care of ailing uncle HJ, 256–57; childhood of, 64; compiling WJ's letters, 315–19; diphtheria infection of, 83;

education of, 89, 127, 129, 130, 134, 137, 139, 140, 160–61, 362n33; law studies and career of, 201–2, 220; marriage to Olivia Cutting, 308; in 342nd Machine Battalion, 310; travels in Europe, 124, 125, 127, 284–85; visits with uncle Henry, 160–61, 256–57

James, Henry Sr., *192–4;* AHGJ's relationship with, xiv, 32, 65; death of, 70; declining health of, 66–70; financial security of, 34, 340n8; lecture on women and marriage, 32–33; patriarchal values of, xvi, 65; Swedenborg influences of, 11, 124; will and estate of, 71–72, 82, 350–51n107; works of: *Society, the Redeemed Form of Man,* 124

James, Hermann Hagen: birth of, 80; death of, 85–86; illness of, 84–85

James, John Runnells, 329

James, Margaret Mary "Peggy," *192–9, 192–11, 192–12;* birth of, 34, 98; depressive episodes of, 275, 277; education of, 134, 160, 170, 173–74, 177–78, 182–83, 187, 211, 219, 234–38; experience with mushrooms, 236–37; health of, 120, 173, 182, 193–94, 210–11, 273, 274; as Jimmy Psych, 235; marriage to Bruce Porter, 308–9; relationship with uncle HJ, 194, 196, 249; return to American life, 202–3; social activities in teens, 207–8, 219–20, 222; travels in Europe, 124, 125, 130, 160, 194, 246–47, 282

James, Mary Holton, as wife of Robertson James, 33, 34, 140

James, Mary Robertson Walsh: death of, 66–67; encouraging WJ and AHG's